The Middle English Bible

John Tapp

Dec. '21.

THE MIDDLE AGES SERIES
Ruth Mazo Karras, Series Editor
Edward Peters, Founding Editor

A complete list of books in the series is available from the publisher.

The Middle English Bible

A Reassessment

Henry Ansgar Kelly

PENN

University of Pennsylvania Press
Philadelphia

Publication of this volume was aided by gifts from the
UCLA Friends of English and the UCLA Division of Humanities.

Published by
University of Pennsylvania Press
Philadelphia, Pennsylvania 19104-4112
www.upenn.edu/pennpress

Printed in the United States of America on acid-free paper
10 9 8 7 6 5 4 3 2 1

A catalogue record for this book is available from the Library of Congress.
ISBN 978-0-8122-4834-0

For Barret and Caroline

No formal condemnation of [Wyclif's] English Bible
was ever issued, or, as far as we know, attempted.
—F. D. Matthew, "The Authorship of the Wycliffite Bible" (1895)

Wycliffe's chief bequest to posterity was the English Bible.
—James Gairdner, *Lollardy and the Reformation in England* (1908)

If the first English Bible was not produced by Wyclif and the Wycliffites, and was not censored by Arundel, the history of the late medieval English Church and of the liberation of the English people at the Reformation would need to be completely rewritten.
—Mary Dove, *The First English Bible* (2007)

By far the most important body of English prose since the Conquest.
—Robert Tombs, *The English and Their History* (2014)

Contents

Preface

I first entered the Bible-translation field when studying the Douai-Rheims Version, which was completed by the English priest Gregory Martin in 1580, but was revised by Bishop Richard Challoner in 1750. We medievalists usually tell our students to use this translation rather than the King James because it renders the Latin Vulgate, and not the Hebrew and Greek texts, but in fact Challoner's revision was largely in the direction of the King James language, which in turn was largely William Tyndale's text.[1] I decided that I should also examine the earlier complete translation of the Bible into English, produced at the end of the fourteenth century, now generally known as the Wycliffite Bible, and recognized as existing in two main forms, an original very literal rendering, call the Early Version, or EV, and a revision of it into a more idiomatic style, called the Later Version, or LV.

I soon found that the scholarship concerning this translation was affected by the same "wars of religion" that surrounded the history of the Protestant and Catholic Bibles of the sixteenth century and later. It seemed to me that there was need for a review of how it has been regarded over the years, and the points of controversy connected with it at each stage, especially concerning claims for and against its origin as a project of the religious dissident John Wyclif (d. 1384) and his followers.

Accordingly, in the first chapter below, I attempt to give a historiography of critical attention to the medieval translation, to which I give the neutral name of "Middle English Bible," or MEB.[2] I recount that, after seemingly being regarded as a straightforward rendering from Latin into English during the fifteenth and sixteenth centuries, notably in the report of Thomas More, it was first designated as Wyclif's by John Bale in the middle of the sixteenth century, an attribution that was repeated and elaborated subsequently. Its identity as Wycliffite was monumentalized in the elaborate edition of 1850 by the Reverend Josiah Forshall and Sir Frederic Madden, as by "John Wycliffe and his followers."[3] The most significant early challenge to this status came in 1894 from a figure almost forgotten today, the Benedictine historian Francis Aidan Gasquet. I conclude with an account of the most recent developments and trends.

In Chapter 2, I analyze the treatise *Five and Twenty Books*, which Forshall and Madden printed at the beginning of the Bible and referred to as the "General Prologue" to the translation, the author of which claims to be the main translator of the Middle English Bible. I conclude on the basis of linguistic and content analysis that the author most probably did participate in the final production of LV, perhaps supervising a few of the later books of the New Testament, and then joining the Old Testament LV team and producing a prologue to the major prophets, which was accepted by the leader or leaders of the translation "task force," before going on to compile *Five and Twenty Books*, which he submitted as a prologue to the Old Testament. I speculate that it was not accepted by the translators because of its stridently Lollard (Wycliffite) sentiments. Thereupon, I further conjecture, the author, characterizing himself as "a simple creature," supplemented his treatise with an account in which he took the chief credit for the entire translation enterprise.

Chapter 3 takes up the study of the Bible at Oxford and Wyclif's role in it and offers considerations on the production of EV and LV there, different from the account given in *Five and Twenty Books* (the latter shows the author, Simple Creature, not to be familiar with Oxford procedures). I will then consider some of the possible purposes for the two versions, especially EV, which may have been intended not primarily as a preliminary version but as an aid to the weakly Latinate clergy to understand the Vulgate text properly. Finally, I will offer a suggestion that EV and LV could each have been accomplished in a relatively short time with only a few participants.

In Chapter 4, I discuss controversies over the advisability of translating the Scriptures into English, from the point of view of three Oxford doctors of theology: the Dominican Thomas Palmer, the Franciscan William Butler, and the secular master Richard Ullerston, together with a report about Thomas Arundel when archbishop of York, and, finally, the views of the friar who wrote the dialogue *Dives and Pauper* and the *Longleat Sunday Gospels Commentary*.

Chapter 5 takes up the provincial constitutions formulated at Oxford in 1407, especially the seventh, *Periculosa*, which called for episcopal oversight of new biblical translations, and I discuss whether EV and LV were intended to be included in this supervision.

Chapter 6 attempts to trace the ways in which *Periculosa* was understood and enforced and examines alleged instances of persecution or the fear of persecution for the possession of EV and LV.

Finally, in Chapter 7, I take up Thomas More's assessment of the history of the vernacular Bible in England and his opinion of the trial of Richard Hunne, as compared with verifiable trial records, which demonstrate that Hunne was in fact accused of fostering English biblical translation and was convicted (posthumously) of approving of the Wycliffite sentiments in *Five and Twenty Books*, which was affixed as a prologue to his copy of the English Bible. More seems to have assumed that the rest of Hunne's Bible was Wycliffite as well, while he believed that the EV or LV Bibles that he had seen were orthodox translations produced before Wyclif's time.

In the Conclusion, I sum up the results of my investigations and speak of some of their implications.

The Middle English Bible was a highly significant project in its time, and it is surprising that the persons responsible for it left so few indications of how it was accomplished. Rita Copeland calls it "perhaps the greatest achievement of textual culture in medieval England."[4] I agree; but whether it was "the central and monumental achievement of the Wycliffite Lollard movement"[5] remains to be seen.

A Note on the Texts Cited in This Study

EV and LV are printed in parallel columns in Josiah Forshall and Frederic Madden, eds., *The Holy Bible, Containing the Old and New Testaments, with the Apocryphal Books, in the Earliest English Versions Made from the Latin Vulgate by John Wycliffe and His Followers* (FM); they are searchable in *The Bible in English (970–1970)* (*BIE*) online, without variants, however, and with the letter thorn transformed to *th*, and the letter yogh changed to *y* (which I change to *gh* where appropriate). I also regularize the allographs *i/j* and *u/v*, and also usually regularize *i* and *y*, which were normally interchangeable in Middle English, except where it is important to preserve the original forms for purposes of scribal identification or the like. See my "Uniformity and Sense in Editing and Citing Medieval Texts," *Medieval Academy News*,

Spring 2004, pp. 8–9; and "Letter," *Medieval Academy News*, Spring 2005, p. 6. In the main text, for the sake of clarity or ease of reading I often modernize the spelling of Middle English texts but sometimes quote the original spelling in the notes and examples. All translations are my own, unless otherwise specified.

Abbreviations

BIE	*The Bible in English (970–1970)*, Chadwyck-Healy online, http://collections.chadwyck.com/bie/htxview?template = basic.htx&content = frameset.htx
BL	British Library
CIC	*Corpus iuris canonici*, ed. Emil Friedberg, 2 vols. (Leipzig 1879–81, repr. Graz 1959)
CJC	*Corpus Juris Canonici*, 3 vols. (Rome 1582), http://digital.library.ucla.edu/canonlaw/index.html
CUL	Cambridge University Library
DMLBS	*Dictionary of Medieval Latin from British Sources* (Oxford 1975–2013)
DP	*Dives and Pauper*, ed. Priscilla Heath Barnum, EETS 275, 280, 323, 2 vols. in 3 (Oxford 1976–2004)
EEBO; ECCO	Early English Books Online; Eighteenth Century Collections Online
EETS	Early English Text Society
EEV	Early EV: forebear(s) of Oxford, MS Bodley 959, and Oxford, MS Christ Church 145 (OxCCC 145), ed. Lindberg, *The Earlier Version of the Wycliffite Bible*
Emden, *BRUC*	A. B. Emden, *A Biographical Register of the University of Cambridge to A.D. 1500* (Cambridge 1963)
Emden, *BRUO*	A. B. Emden, *A Biographical Register of the University of Oxford to A.D. 1500*, 3 vols. (Oxford 1957–59)
EV	Early Version of the MEB, ed. FM
FM	Josiah Forshall and Frederic Madden, eds., *The Holy Bible, Containing the Old and New Testaments, with the Apocryphal Books, in the Earliest English Versions Made from the Latin Vulgate by John Wycliffe and His Followers*, 4 vols. (Oxford 1850; repr. New York 1982)
FTB	*Five and Twenty Books*. See GP

GP	General Prologue, the name given by FM to the treatise *Five and Twenty Books* (*FTB*), which FM edit as the Prologue to LV (1:1–60).
HUO	*The History of the University of Oxford*, gen. ed. T. H. Aston, 8 vols. (Oxford 1984–2000)
LALME	*A Linguistic Atlas of Late Mediaeval English*, ed. Angus McIntosh, M. L. Samuels, and Michael Benskin, with Margaret Laing and Keith Williamson, 4 vols. (Aberdeen 1986)
LLV	Later LV: Oxford, MS Bodley 277, ed. Lindberg, *King Henry's Bible*.
LV	Later Version of the MEB, ed. FM
MEB	Middle English Bible (formerly known as Wycliffite Bible); the designation covers EEV, EV, LV, and LLV
MED	*Middle English Dictionary*, 17 vols. (Ann Arbor MI 1952–2001).
NT, OT	New Testament, Old Testament
OED	*Oxford English Dictionary*, 2nd ed., 20 vols. (Oxford 1989)
OxDNB	*Oxford Dictionary of National Biography*, 60 vols. (Oxford 2004); cited from the online edition, without volume or page numbers
PL	*Patrologia Latina*, ed. J.-P. Migne, 221 vols. (Paris 1844–64)
SC	Simple Creature, from the designation given to himself by the author of *Five and Twenty Books* (= GP) in chapter 15 (FM, 1:57, 59)

CHAPTER 1

A History of Judgments on the Middle English Bible

Nowadays the Middle English Bible (MEB) is almost always referred to as the Wycliffite Bible (WB), and it is usually assumed that it was always thought to be Wycliffite. The reality is quite different, as we will see in studying the reception of both forms of the translation (when they were differentiated) from age to age.

The Fifteenth to the Nineteenth Century: From Anonymous to Trevisa, Wyclif, Wycliffites

To begin with, let us see how the new English renderings of the Bible were regarded in the fifteenth century. Scholars who believe that it was a Wycliffite production take it for granted that it was recognized as such from the very beginning until the present day, but, as will be apparent in later chapters, it is very difficult to prove that this was the case. Sometimes, as we will see, there appears to have been no other concern about it than that it was in English. The only early attribution of authorship in the more than 250 surviving manuscripts of the MEB occurs in what might be termed a second-generation copy (Bodleian Douce 369.1), which attributes the greater part of the Early Version (EV) of the Old Testament to Dr. Nicholas Hereford, one of Wyclif's early followers, who was condemned in 1382 for supporting some of his master's doctrines. We will hear more about him later. The only name otherwise certainly attached to the MEB during the fifteenth century was that of John Trevisa, by William Caxton, in his edition of Trevisa's *Polychronicon*, where he listed the Bible as among Trevisa's other translations,[1] and this attribution was repeated subsequently, including even in the preface to the King James Bible of 1611: "Even in our King Richard the Second's days, John Trevisa translated them [the Gospels, or the Scriptures] into English, and many English Bibles in written hand are yet to be seen with divers [i.e., in the possession of various persons], translated, as it is very probable, in that age."[2]

When we come to the sixteenth century (Chapter 7 below) and can rely on the testimony of Thomas More, we see that the MEB was regarded not only as non-Wycliffite but as pre-Wycliffite; nevertheless, it was also considered by some to be forbidden. We will also see that the preface to the Rheims New Testament of 1582 considers the surviving renditions of the Bible to be non-Wycliffite and never prohibited.

However, the reformer John Bale, in his index of notes on the works of English authors, after saying that John Trevisa translated the whole Bible, says the same thing about John Wyclif.[3] But earlier in his treatment of Wyclif Bale has a more circumstantial entry concerning his translation of the whole Bible,[4] based on his inspection of a Later Version (LV), prefaced by the treatise *Five and Twenty Books* (*FTB*), which Josiah Forshall and Frederic Madden in their 1850 edition printed as the prologue to LV, and which they refer to as the "General Prologue" (GP).[5] The late Mary Dove, in her magisterial study of the Middle English Bible, identifies the manuscript that Bale saw as the one now at Princeton University.[6] She observes that the antiquarian John Leland, who provided Bale with many details about Wyclif's writings, did not come to a similar conclusion (that Wyclif translated the Bible).[7] In Bale's published *Catalogus*, he leaves out the detail of the incipit identifying *Five and Twenty Books*.[8] The only other person of Bale's era who made such a claim about Wyclif's translation of the Bible was the printer Robert Crowley, taking his cue from Bale's earlier *Summarium* (1548), in Crowley's edition of *Piers Plowman* in 1550. Crowley also printed *Five and Twenty Books* in 1550, under title of *The Pathway to Perfect Knowledge*, calling it "a prologue" by Wyclif.[9]

Bale adds interesting details in the *Catalogus* to his claim that John Trevisa translated the whole Bible. He did so at the request of Lord Berkeley, he says, and he gives an incipit to it: "Ego Joannes Trevisa, sacerdos."[10]

Attributions of authorship by later owners of MEB manuscripts are fairly rare. The person who inscribed an LV Bible to Edward VI in 1550 attributed the prologue (*Five and Twenty Books*), placed after the Old Testament, to Wyclif.[11] In 1615 an attribution to Wyclif was added to an LV copy of the New Testament Epistles and Apocalypse.[12] A later manuscript attribution was that of Baron Thomas Fairfax, who died in 1671; he noted that his LV

New Testament was Wyclif's translation.[13] An LV Bible at Emmanuel College in Cambridge was attributed to Wyclif and dated 1383 sometime after it was cataloged in 1600 by Thomas James and before it was seen by Henry Wharton in the 1680s.[14] But in an updated entry Wharton says that all of the many English Bibles that he has seen (all LV) are attributed to Wyclif, but that these attributions are recent conjectures.[15] An example is the seventeenth-century hand in the Fairfax complete Bible (LV), saying of its original date, 1408: "which is 25 years after Wickleff finished the translation"—that is, accepting 1383 as the date of Wyclif's version.[16] But it is noteworthy that an annotator of the seventeenth century surmises that the New Testament (EV) in Dublin Trinity College 75 is by John Purvey, based on John Foxe's description of him, and that he was also the author of the following prologue to the Old Testament (that is, *Five and Twenty Books*).[17]

It has been suggested by Dove that the earliest acknowledgment that there were two versions of the Middle English Bible was by Thomas James, the first librarian of the Bodleian, writing in 1612,[18] but I disagree. Dove thinks that James assigned EV to the thirteenth century and LV to Wyclif, but in fact James is quoting from the prologue (*Five and Twenty Books*) attached to an LV Bible. He says of the author-translator, "Of one thing I am sure, that he that translated the whole Bible into English (which Bible came forth, as I guess, some hundred years before Wyclif's) held these books [other than the twenty-five inspired books of the Old Testament] for Apocrypha." He adds a note: "The Bible hath been twice translated into English. The former edition is very ancient, whereof we have three copies (one in the Public Library, one in Christ Church Library, the other in Queen's College), the later translated by Wyclif."[19] The manuscript that he saw in the Public Library must have been Bodleian 277, the revised LV (I call it LLV), which has the first chapter of *Five and Twenty Books* (GP).[20]

However, we can hardly conclude that James knew the difference between EV and LV and accordingly attributed EV to Wyclif. The Bible that he saw at Christ Church was almost certainly EV (MS 145), and he considered it to be the same as the LV at Queen's;[21] and he seems to have known of no other English Bibles at Oxford. In his catalog of the libraries of Oxford and Cambridge, published in 1600, he names only three complete English Bibles at Oxford (Christ Church, Queen's, and one in New College, which perhaps was the same as the one he later cites as being at the Bodleian).[22] He identifies no Bible that he has seen as Wyclif's translation.

Archbishop James Ussher, who died in 1656, repeated James's statement in abbreviated form, which was exposed to public view when Henry Wharton brought out Ussher's *Historia dogmatica* in 1689 and again in 1690. Here Ussher specifies 1290 as the time of the earlier translation:

> *1290, Anglicanus Interpres.*
> Longe ante Wiclevi translationem (100 annis, ut conjicit Thomas Jamesius) prodiit universorum Bibliorum Anglicana Translatio: cujus tria in Oxoniensis Academiae Bibliothecis MSS extant exemplaria: unum in Bodleiana (publica), alterum in Aedis Christi, tertium in Reginalis Collegii Bibliotheca.
> (T. Jamesius, lib. vernaculo *De Corruptione Patrum*, part 2, loc. 24.)[23]

Ussher's entry on Wyclif is dated 1380. He cites Bale as saying that Wyclif translated the whole Bible. But he concludes from James's remarks and the listings in his catalog that various copies of old English Bibles exist that differ in translation—which is something that James does not say. Ussher ends by saying he has seen Wyclif's translation of the New Testament in Sir Robert Cotton's library.[24] The only Cotton MEB extant today is an LV complete Bible.[25]

If Thomas James was not aware of two extant versions of MEB, it seems that Thomas Fuller was. In his *History of the Worthies of England*, published in 1662, Fuller says that John Trevisa, who died around 1400, had the temerity to translate the Bible about fifty years after Wyclif, and he says that "[his] translation is as much better than Wyclif's as worse than Tyndale's."[26] Henry Wharton, in the commentary that he appended to his edition of Ussher, likewise showed himself to be aware of the difference between EV and LV, and he agreed with Fuller that Wyclif was the EV translator. He says that James and Ussher erred in dating the LV translation so early, since the prologue cites Nicholas of Lyre and Archbishop Richard Fitzralph. The author's impotent rage against Oxford academics proves that Wyclif was not the author, and the printers who published the prologue in 1550 were fantasizing ("hallucinatos esse") when they ascribed it to him. He admits that it is certain that Wyclif translated the Bible, since Bale said so, as did Jan Hus before him.[27] But he was clearly not the translator of the common version (LV), in spite of the fact that it is ascribed to him in all of the copies that he has seen. These ascriptions are recent, made by uncautious readers. He concludes that the prologue and translation (LV) must be by Trevisa. He says that he has not been able to find a complete Bible in Wyclif's version (that is, EV), but only of some books (the Epistles and Sunday readings).[28]

In Wharton's outdated entry on Wyclif, where he attributes LV to Wyclif, he speaks of a Lambeth New Testament with the Epistle to the Laodiceans, citing the prologue that says it was only recently translated into English. From this Wharton concludes either that there was an earlier translation of the Bible or that there was a double edition of Wyclif's translation.[29] This is the first acknowledgment I have seen that a translator (here, Wyclif) may have revised his own translation.

In the first part of the eighteenth century, as Dove shows, there was a movement among Protestant scholars to retrieve Wyclif's authorship of LV. John Russell in 1719 proposed an edition of Wyclif's whole Bible, in the LV text, and John Lewis in his *History* of Wyclif in 1721, annotating Bale, cites only LV manuscripts as copies of his translation and his prologue.[30] In 1731 he published an LV New Testament as Wyclif's, with a history giving a full account of Bible translation in England. In it, he says he was mistaken in ascribing the prologue to Wyclif, since it was written after his time. He takes notice of the ascription of the New Testament (EV) in the Dublin manuscript to John Purvey, and says that the prologue goes with it.[31]

In other words, in this first mention of Purvey in discussions of the MEB, Wyclif himself translated what we call the Later Version, and Purvey, later on, produced what we know as the Early Version and the General Prologue.

In 1728, Daniel Waterland of Cambridge University informed Lewis of his view that EV and LV were by the same person, namely, Wyclif, but later Waterland perceived that events described in the prologue (*Five and Twenty Books*) happened after Wyclif's time, and therefore it and LV must have been by a disciple of Wyclif's. He suggested as the likely candidate John Purvey, described by Bale as Wyclif's *librarius* and *glossator*. When Forshall and Madden started work on the MEB in 1829, they accepted Waterland's suggestion of Purvey as responsible for LV and the prologue, and by the time they published in 1850, they had embraced it as established fact.[32]

During all this time of the progressive "Wyclifying" of the Middle English Bible, Dove has found only one doubter, namely, Humfrey Wanley, who started to catalog the library of Robert Harley in 1708. When describing a copy of the treatise *Five and Twenty Books*, he cites passages from it that "seem to agree well enough with the person and opinions of Wyclif, who is also commonly said to have translated the Bible out of Latin into English, though I could never yet see such a book with his name written therein by the first hand—not to mention what Sir Thomas More wrote, that there were then divers translations of Scripture into English, allowed by Authority, and that the Wycliffites were only charged with keeping certain prefaces to biblical books of Wyclif's composure."[33] Even though More does not say this (rather he assumed that Wyclif did make translations, of which Richard Hunne possessed a copy, which, More hoped, had not been destroyed after his trial), it is significant that this is how Wanley reads him. He is saying, in effect, that there is nothing in the extant English Bibles that he has seen to connect them to Wyclif, unlike this clearly Wycliffite tract (which he assumes to be the same as the prologue printed in 1550 and ascribed to Wyclif and also found in certain English Bibles).

In the nineteenth century, the Latin works of John Wyclif were in high esteem, at least for their content if not for their style, and they were being systematically published.[34] But Wyclif had also achieved a high reputation as an English writer, so much so that Reginald Poole in 1895 called him "one of the founders of English prose-writing."[35] Four volumes of treatises attributed to him had recently been printed.[36] These followed upon the publication at midcentury of the Middle English translation of the entire Bible by Forshall and Madden, which they partially attributed to him, as can be seen from their title: *The Holy Bible . . . in the Earliest English Versions Made from the Latin Vulgate by John Wycliffe and His Followers*.[37] The editors suggested that only the New Testament portion of EV was by Wyclif himself, while the Old Testament and all of LV was by his followers.

By the end of the century, the entire English Bible, without distinguishing between versions or parts, was commonly said to be the work of Wyclif, "the Wyclif Bible." It was the example of the Egerton Bible, an EV copy, displayed in the British Museum as Wyclif's translation, that first inspired Cardinal Gasquet to embark on his revisionist history, as we shall see. But the first scholars who responded to Gasquet used a new term, "the Wycliffite Bible," which has found favor to this day.

Dom Aidan Gasquet's Objections to the Wycliffied Bible

The Wycliffite nature of the Middle English Bible as it solidified in the nineteenth century was challenged by only one person, the Benedictine historian Dom Aidan Gasquet, initially in an article published in the *Dublin Review* in 1894.[38] He held instead that the translations were not only orthodox productions, but also that they were approved of by the Church authorities. His theses were challenged on several fronts, but most trenchantly by Arthur Ogle, writing anonymously in 1900 and 1901,[39] and Ogle's arguments were taken up and relentlessly repeated by G. G. Coulton in various publications.[40]

Gasquet professes to identify a fallacious syllogism at work in the universal ascription of the early translations to Wyclif and his followers. It was presumed, begging the question, that the Catholic Church condemned translating the Scriptures into the vernacular. Therefore, only one possible conclusion could be drawn: the early translations must be by those who dissented from the Church. He asks: "May it not be possible that under the influence of a preconceived idea people have gone off on a wrong scent altogether?" And answers: "If we start with a foregone conclusion, we can have little hope that we shall read facts rightly, even though they be as plain as the proverbial pikestaff, and in this instance it appears to me that it has been assumed altogether too hastily that the English pre-Reformation Scriptures could not have been catholic, and must have been and were the outcome of the Wycliffite movement."[41]

Gasquet begins his original essay by documenting the widespread scholarly belief at the time, the last decade of the nineteenth century, that John Wyclif himself had had an active role in the English Bible project, starting with the label on the Egerton manuscript that stood as the premier exhibit in the King's Library in the British Museum: "The English Bible, Wycliffe's Translation."[42] He can easily show that the idea of translating the Bible into English and examples of English translations existed long before Wyclif's time and were not the outcome of his movement.[43] On the conclusion of Forshall and Madden that Wyclif translated the EV New Testament, he finds no evidence at all, and adds, "It is difficult to account for the silence of Wyclif himself, who in none of his undoubted writings, so far as I am aware, lays any stress on, or, indeed, in any way advocates having the Scriptures in the vernacular, except so far as is implied in the claim that the Bible is the sole guide in faith and practice for all."[44] It is admitted nowadays that Wyclif showed little interest in any kind of vernacular use until the end of his life.[45] Alastair Minnis puts it strongly: "The arch-heresiarch himself, John Wyclif, made no attempt to champion his 'vulgar' tongue (to the best of our knowledge). No justification of the translation of that most authoritative of all books, 'The Book of Life,' may be found anywhere in Wyclif's voluminous theological writings, though for centuries he has been lauded as the *fons et origo* of the First English Bible."[46] "Wyclif's dismissive, perhaps even insulting, remarks in *De veritate sacrae scripturae* (1378) about the skills needed for the making of material Bibles are very much his own—and evidently consistent with what Anne Hudson has termed his 'amazingly nonchalant' attitude to language transference."[47]

None of Wyclif's adversaries attribute any such enterprise to him, Gasquet says, except that Henry Knighton said that he translated the Gospel;

and John Hus reported that he translated the whole Bible, while Archbishop Arundel, writing to Pope John XXIII, at least implied the same.[48] Later scholars agree with Gasquet in dismissing the first two of these witnesses, and they *should* agree with him on his arguments against the third.[49] Finally, Gasquet observes, "From what we know of Wyclif's active, restless, and combative disposition, and of his particularly speculative turn of mind, we should hardly have been disposed to assign to him so tedious a task as that of mere translation."[50]

F. D. Matthew, in his 1895 response to Gasquet, cites a few pseudo-Wycliffian passages from his own *English Works of Wyclif* and from Thomas Arnold's *Select English Works of John Wyclif*, which, he says, certainly imply "the authorship of Wyclif or some associate of his,"[51] and Ogle rebukes Gasquet for not responding to this evidence.[52] But Gasquet had already written off the wholesale ascription of English works to Wyclif,[53] and most modern authorities agree in denying his authorship of everything previously assigned to him in English.[54]

What of the role of particular Wycliffites in the translation project? It was an easy deduction on Gasquet's part that the universal acceptance of Wyclif's secretary John Purvey as the translator of LV rested on no proof whatsoever: "I believe that practically the only direct evidence to connect Purvey with this translation is the fact that his name appears in a single copy of the revision as a former owner."[55] Ogle responds to this statement with indignant bluster, simply repeating what Forshall and Madden have to say—which indeed consists of no evidence at all.[56] The definitive dismissal of Purvey's participation in the project came only in 1981 in Anne Hudson's article in *Viator*.[57]

Gasquet was willing to admit the participation of the Wycliffite Nicholas Hereford in the EV Old Testament, if the big "if" of Forshall and Madden's assertion turns out to be true. Gasquet says, "If the note ascribing the version to Nicholas Hereford is, as Forshall and Madden testify, practically contemporary, it certainly furnishes us with strong evidence that Hereford had a main hand in the translation of the Old Testament."[58] Gasquet goes on to tell of Hereford's renunciation of Wycliffite doctrines, and Ogle can see no reason for his doing so "unless it be to suggest that the orthodoxy which Hereford may have resumed in 1391 possessed some kind of retroactive virtue."[59] Perhaps Gasquet was suggesting that he resumed work on the Bible, a possibility noted by Conrad Lindberg.[60]

In recent times, the authenticity of the ascription to Hereford has come into question, as Hudson points out. It appears in manuscript Douce 369.1 at Baruch 3.20. This is the manuscript that Forshall and Madden used as their base text of EV from 1 Esdras up to this point.[61] But this manuscript was written subsequently to another manuscript, Bodley 959, which preserves EEV, considered by Forshall and Madden to be "the original copy of the translator."[62] It breaks off at the same point, but has no attribution.[63] Hudson concludes: "The attempt to ascribe sections of the translation and its revisions to individual Wycliffites, or indeed to Wyclif himself, seems to me misguided, and furthermore, to show a singular failure to grasp the nature or magnitude of the undertaking."[64] I will, however, suggest reasons later for doubting that the project was as massive as is sometimes supposed.

That leaves us without Wyclif and without specific Wycliffites and only with the Wycliffite doctrine in the anonymous so-called General Prologue (GP). This is where Gasquet made his big mistake. He did not read this treatise on the Old Testament, which Gasquet calls *Five and Twenty Books* (*FTB*),[65] closely enough to take notice of its occasional antiestablishment statements. While he exposed the groundlessness of Forshall and Madden's assumptions about Purvey's authorship of *FTB* and LV, he accepted their position that the treatise and LV were by the same person, the position taken by Henry Wharton: "In some few copies there exists a lengthy prologue, which gives an account of the method employed by the translator. Whatever the author says of these methods is borne out in the actual version; and there is thus no room for doubting, as Henry Wharton long ago observed, that the prologues [*sic*] and the translation are by the same hand."[66] Gasquet goes on to cite the passage from chapter 15 of *Five and Twenty Books* that details the four steps outlined by the author in preparing his translation.[67] Gasquet concludes from this that he had no previous knowledge of EV.[68] (This would mean, of course, that LV was a fresh translation from the Bible, not a revision of EV.)[69] At least we can say that the author *reveals* no knowledge of EV and makes no reference to it.

Gasquet subsequently says, when speaking of the errors singled out for censure in the prologue of Richard Hunne's Bible, in Hunne's posthumous trial for heresy, that he can find no trace of such errors in the prologue to LV as edited by Forshall and Madden.[70] It is here that Ogle was able to convict him of a mistake that was thought by him and Coulton and many others to destroy his whole position.

From his statement in the preface to the reprinting of the *Old English Bible*, where he speaks of the challenges that he had received and his continued conviction as to the correctness of his views, it is evident that Gasquet thought that he had an adequate response to this objection. It should have been quite simple to guess what the general nature of such a response would be: if there had been no room for doubting that the author of the prologue was the same as the translator of the LV, now there is. In a lecture delivered in 1905 but printed only in 1912, Gasquet admits the Wycliffite nature of the prologue. In speaking of the Elizabethan period, he says: "Of Wiclif's works we have practically nothing. A print of the *Wiclif* at Nuremberg in 1546, another by Foxe at Strasburg in 1534; and, in England itself, the *Prologue of the Bible* in Henry's reign (if indeed the Prologue be by Wiclif at all), and nothing else, is all that we find in the way of influences."[71]

The only person who ever came close to suggesting such a probable response on Gasquet's behalf was Herbert Thurston, who brings up the possibility that prologue and text are by different authors. Here is what he says: "No doubt the existence of these errors in the Prologue is a serious blow to one of his arguments, if we admit, as Dom Gasquet himself seems to do, that the reviser of the translation was identical with the author of the Prologue. But, after all, the earlier version was not the work of the author of the Prologue, and it would still be possible to maintain without inconsistency that the earlier version was in its origin not Wycliffite but Catholic."[72] Thurston could have added that, even though a Wycliffite may have revised a non-Wycliffite EV, he did not inject any Wycliffite doctrines or sentiments into the resulting LV.

But Thurston's way out for Gasquet, that EV at least was Catholic in origin (a conclusion that Thurston himself thought was mistaken),[73] would not, I think, have satisfied Gasquet. I can see a different tack that may well have occurred to him, to judge from his original observation that the prologue appears in only "some few copies." Hudson has made this point more recently: "The important point to note is that the Prologue is not the regular concomitant of the LV translation, but an exceptional addition to it."[74] In explaining this state of affairs, Herbert Workman in 1926 in effect assumes that the prologue was originally present as an integral part of LV, but was eliminated in most copies because of its unorthodox contents.[75] But since the text of the Bible itself was so clearly orthodox, it does seem odd that the translator would prefix such a provocatively unorthodox prologue. In Chapter 2 we will consider the possibility that it was not an "official" prologue, but rather an attempt of an interloper with radical religious views to take the credit of the translation enterprise for himself and his cause. But even if it can be established that the author of the prologue was not a main force behind the Bible project, we will see that it remains undeniable that he was a participant in it. Gasquet, however, was willing to admit such Wycliffite participants, in the person of Hereford and even Purvey, and this, in effect, constituted another answer to Ogle's challenge, which comes in summary form in Gasquet's original article:

> Whether Hereford, or Purvey possibly (for at best we are, so far as this is concerned, dealing with possibilities), may have had any part in the translation does not, after all, so much concern us. Our chief interest is not with the translator, but with the work itself, and with the question whether it may fairly be claimed as the semi-official and certainly perfectly orthodox translation of the English Church; or whether, on the other hand, it must be regarded as a version secretly executed, clandestinely circulated, and still more stealthily studied, by the Lollard followers of Wyclif. This is the main point of interest.[76]

Ogle conceded Gasquet's first point, the orthodoxy of the English Scriptures. Later, in Chapter 5, we will look into the second point mentioned here: was it a "stealth" project, or was it out in the open and accepted by the authorities?

As we will see in Chapter 7, Thomas More assumed that EV and LV, whether or not he recognized the differences between them, were pre-Wycliffite and that there was also a later Wycliffite Bible, represented by Hunne's Bible with its clearly heterodox prologue. Gasquet's judgment about EV and LV was the same, if we read "non-Wycliffite" for "pre-Wycliffite" (and, of course, discount More's idea of a later translation that was indeed by Wyclif or Wycliffite).

Recent Developments

Later in the twentieth century, after Gasquet was forgotten, there were other efforts to modify or redefine the Wycliffite nature of the Middle English Bible. Anne Hudson has done much of this herself, in deflating exaggerated claims, some of which we have already seen, notably for the role of certain individuals like John Purvey and Nicholas Hereford.

First, there is David Fowler's suggestion in 1960 that both Wyclif and Trevisa took part in producing EV while living at Queen's College in the 1370s.[77] Sven Fristedt, however, believes that Trevisa and his colleagues had completed, or nearly completed, the first version of EV (what I call EEV) before Wyclif entered the picture. After Wyclif took up residence in Queen's in 1374, he assessed the project, and, in order to improve it, he set about furnishing a Latin Bible with English glosses, which were used by Hereford and others to produce the "first revision" of EV (basically the text of EV as Forshall and Madden present it).[78] Conrad Lindberg, who has been studying and editing manuscripts of the MEB since the 1950s, thinks, on the contrary, that Wyclif started preparing a critical text of the Latin Vulgate as soon as he came to Oxford, around 1354,[79] and that he himself translated the EV New Testament,[80] and also worked on LV before his death at the end of 1384.[81]

Let us look next at the proposal made by Michael Wilks in 1975.[82] Hudson purports to sum up his suggestion thus: "that there existed a pre- or non-Wycliffite vernacular bible which the lollards took over and modified."[83] However, Wilks does not put it this way; he only says that the EV New Testament had been produced by 1382, with no provable or likely connection to Wyclif (Wyclif's own view being that the Word of God should be delivered to the faithful not through providing translations to be read but through good preaching). Then, shortly afterward, Wilks suggests, Nicholas Hereford and other Wycliffites began work on translating the rest of the Bible, producing the EV Old Testament, and next John Purvey produced the whole LV Bible. Thus, he conjectures, there was "a takeover of an originally independent English bible project by the Wycliffite movement in the decade or so after Wyclif's death."[84]

Since Hereford and Purvey have been sidelined by Hudson, Wilks's hypothesis can be expanded to posit that the whole enterprise was originally nonpartisan. It may even have been anti-Wycliffite in sentiment. In a recent discussion of "ideological and political fissures" at Oxford, Patrick Hornbeck notes that "the reforming fellows of The Queen's College . . . distanced themselves from some of Wyclif's ideas whilst nevertheless sponsoring, in part, the English translation of the Bible" (Hornbeck takes it for granted that the latter was an idea of Wyclif's).[85] Ian Johnson puts it another way: if we acknowledge that the translation endeavor was a team effort, "we need not assume that the project was entirely driven by a single ideology of church reform, or that all the collaborators could even have been characterized as Wycliffite"; and although the so-called General Prologue was written by a member of the team, "it should perhaps be taken as a polemical interpretation of the project, not a definitive statement of its aims."[86]

More recently, David Lawton says it is possible "that 'Wycliffite Bible' is a misnomer and that the translation becomes so only when his followers take it up and it is irretrievably associated with them." He admits that we do not know whether it was Wycliffite in origin and says that "it may be time to abandon the ubiquitous modifier 'Wycliffite' for its earliest full versions." He believes, however, that the versions became associated with the Wycliffites very early on and that they were undoubtedly illegal in the fifteenth century.[87]

For my part, I think it likely that the enterprise was inspired by Wyclif, at least partially, because of his role in reviving Bible study at Oxford, and therefore could be called "Wycliffian" (see Chapter 3); but there is no indication was it was "Wycliffite," that is, undertaken to promote heterodox doctrines. The EV Gospels were used by the authors of the *Glossed Gospels*, an Oxford project that began, according to Hudson, probably "before 1390 or even 1385,"[88] but even though she calls them "Wycliffite," she can find little in them that is unorthodox.[89] And it is a project that was not successful, to judge by the small number of copies that have survived.[90] It may be that there was no effort to take over the Bible translation project until the LV process was nearly finished, and that the first attempt to appropriate it for Lollardy was by the "simple creature" who wrote the treatise *Five and Twenty Books*—a question to be discussed in Chapter 2.[91] But even so, it may be doubted that this was a widespread movement, since, as Fiona Somerset points out, few of the English Wycliffite writers made use of EV and LV.[92]

CHAPTER 2

Five and Twenty Books as "Official" Prologue, or Not

After having finished our survey of the various ways in which the MEB has been regarded over the centuries, it is fitting that our first order of business should be an analysis of the only writing of the time that deals with it, namely, the treatise beginning *Five and Twenty Books*, which Forshall and Madden printed as the prologue to the Later Version. Its Wycliffite sentiments are a main reason why the MEB itself is so firmly attributed to Wycliffites. Even scholars like Anne Hudson, who points out that the treatise is to be found in only a few copies of the Bible (and therefore it cannot be safely taken as an integral part of LV), believe that the author was, if not the sole or chief translator, as he claims, at least an important participant, and accept his account of the translation process as accurate.[1]

The General Prologue: A Latter-Day Prequel?

Let me start by giving a specific accounting of all ten manuscript copies of *Five and Twenty Books*/General Prologue:[2]

1. It survives in complete form as prologue to one complete LV Bible (Cambridge CCC 147).
2. Chapter 1 alone serves as prologue to two complete LV Bibles (Bodl. 277 and Royal 1.C.8 [added to the latter in the time of Henry VII]).[3]
3. It serves as prologue to one LV Old Testament; most of chapter 15 missing (Harley 1666).

4. It appears two times as prologue to the LV New Testament (CUL Kk and Princeton).
5. It comes one time between an LV Old Testament and LV New Testament (CUL Mm).
6. It comes one time after an EV New Testament (Dublin Trinity A.1.10).
7. Pertinent sections of chapters 1–11 are inserted piecemeal in the Old Testament of one complete LV Bible (Lincoln).
8. It survives one time as a separate pamphlet (OUC G3).

When the treatise was first printed, in 1540 by John Gough, it was given the title of *The Door of Holy Scripture*, and in a 1550 edition by Robert Crowley, it was called *The Pathway to Perfect Knowledge*, although Crowley identifies it as "a Prologue written about 200 years ago by John Wyclif."[4] Josiah Forshall and Frederic Madden in their parallel edition of EV and LV placed this Wycliffite work at the beginning, and they started the custom of referring to it as the "General Prologue," but taking it to be a prologue only to the Old Testament.[5] This is the way it is characterized in the Dublin Trinity manuscript: "A Prologue for All the Books of the Bible of the Old Testament."[6]

Today it is more commonly considered to be a prologue to the entire Bible, including the New Testament; so Mary Dove, who calls the treatise "The Prologue to the Wycliffite Bible."[7] Most neutral of all would be to follow Gasquet's lead and refer to it by its incipit, *Five and Twenty Books*.[8]

I should clarify that, even though the author refers to himself in the third person as "a simple creature," he uses this style only at one point, in the last chapter, elsewhere speaking in the first person (and that not very frequently).[9] Here is the whole third-person passage:

> For these resons and othere, with comune charite to save alle men in oure rewme whiche God wole have savid, **a simple creature** hath translatid the Bible out of Latin into English. First, **this simple creature** hadde miche travaile, with diverse felawis and helperis, to gedere manie elde Biblis, and othere doctouris, and comune glosis, and to make oo Latin Bible sumdel trewe; and thanne to studie it of the newe, the text with the glose, and othere doctouris, as **he mighte gete**, and speciali Lyre on the Elde Testament, that helpide ful miche in this werk; the thridde time to counseile with elde gramariens, and elde divinis, of harde wordis, and harde sentencis, hou tho mighten best be undurstonden and translatid; the fourth time to translate as cleerly as **he coude** to the sentence, and to have manie gode felawis and kunninge at the correcting of the translacioun.[10]

He romanticizes the actual process of translation, claiming that there is one master translator for the whole Bible, namely, himself.[11] Later, however, he does speak of translators in the plural, when he calls for the Church to approve the translation "of simple men."[12] (He refers to the intended audience of the translation as "simple men of wit.")[13]

Simple Creature (as we can call the author) implicitly includes the New Testament in his scope, since one of the examples he chooses to illustrate his technique is from Luke.[14] As we see from the cited passage, he presents himself as translating the Bible by a one-time process, with no middle stage (EV), and no glossing; with, however, much reading up on glosses and commentaries of authorities, especially Nicholas of Lyre for the Old Testament, and also lots of consultation with others, and with much correcting and improving as he proceeded.[15] There is nothing impossible, I admit, about a single person taking on the job of producing EV or of transforming EV into a more presentable form (LV), someone perhaps like John Trevisa—who from Caxton onward was credited with rendering the whole Bible into English. In the sixteenth century, the Douai-Rheims Bible was translated from the Vulgate by one man, Gregory Martin, at the planned rate of two chapters a day, and the whole was finished, having been corrected and annotated by no more than one or two of his colleagues at a time, and made ready for publication, in a very brief time, some months short of two years.[16] Trevisa himself is credited with translating Ranulf Higden's enormous *Polychronicon* in a similarly short period (ca. 1385–87).[17]

As we saw in the first chapter, David Fowler and Sven Fristedt think that Trevisa had a hand in EV. David Daniell sums up Fowler's case and leaves it an open question as to whether Trevisa was involved in the project.[18] On the face of it, Trevisa's participation might seem unlikely, in view of EV's "iconic" character (that is, its strict adherence to Latin grammatical constructions),[19] which is foreign to Trevisa's practice elsewhere. However, Fristedt has brought forth convincing evidence that Trevisa first produced a literal version of the *Polychronicon* similar to EV before giving it the sort of freer form that we find in LV.[20] Perhaps Trevisa's participation in LV, which Fowler considers but does not defend, deserves more consideration. A prosodic (*cursus*) analysis could possibly throw light on the question, but it is outside the scope of the present study.

We will discuss further implications of Simple Creature's alleged program, and Trevisa's possible role in the MEB, when taking up Scripture study at Oxford in Chapter 3.

Simple Creature's Wycliffite Sentiments and His Date of Writing

I have great doubt, on linguistic grounds and translation practices identifiable in the EV and LV texts, that the prologuist Simple Creature is himself the translator of LV, at least the greater part of it. But before I get into the peculiarities of his dialect, style, and principles, let me set out some of his views as we can deduce them from *Five and Twenty Books*. For the most part he avoids controversial topics, but he does manifest some Wycliffite teachings, although many are buried deep within the treatise. It would not be surprising if many users of the treatise in the Middle Ages, whether placed as a prologue to the Scriptures or as an independent work, would have missed the polemical elements, as Gasquet did.

The very first sentence of the treatise: "Five and twenty books of the Old Testament be books of faith, and fully books of Holy Writ,"[21] expresses a controversial position, but it is not recognizably Wycliffite; it follows St. Jerome in labeling the other books as "apocryphal" and not inspired, a view not widely accepted since patristic times, so far as I am aware, at least in the West. Wyclif himself was not dogmatic on the subject. In *De veritate Sacrae Scripturae*, he follows Jerome's count of 22 canonized books of the Old Testament, which correspond to the 22 letters of the Hebrew alphabet, whereas there were 24 books immediately accepted to the canon of the New Testament, corresponding to the 24 letters of the Latin alphabet (with three more soon added, namely, Mark, Luke, and Acts). But Wyclif says that many of the apocryphal books are inscribed in the Book of Life, and therefore they are to be accepted as constituting the same sort of truths as our canonical Scripture, and holds that it is foolish to debate excessively about it.[22]

The first near-Wycliffite passage is the assertion later in chapter 1 that Christian men and women, old and young, should study the New Testament assiduously, because it is open to the understanding of simple men, especially those who are properly meek and full of charity.[23] In chapter 2, the author becomes bolder in calling the pardons of the bishops of Rome lies ("leesingis") and associated with Antichrist.[24] Nothing else untoward occurs after that until chapter 10, when he takes occasion to use three stories from Kings and Paralipomena to chastise unworthy lords and prelates. "Alas, alas, alas!" he exclaims. In contrast to King Josaphat's promulgation of the law of God, some lords today order the preaching of indulgences, which are no more than bald-faced lies.[25] He denounces rulers who persecute those who preach the

Gospel[26] and criticizes making idols of saints and swearing by them.[27] He laments that those who abstain from needless oaths and reprove sin are called Lollards, heretics, and raisers of debate and treason against the king,[28] and he rebukes the giving of alms to dead images.[29] Less specifically Wycliffite, perhaps, are his denunciations in chapter 13 of the widespread practice of sodomy and simony at Oxford University (the "strong maintenaunce" of sodomy at Oxford was made known "at the laste parlement"), and his condemnation of the new proposal that would require spending nine or ten years in the arts (which deal with pagan traditions) before one is allowed to proceed to the study of God's word.[30] We will deal with the curricular complaint in the Chapter 3, where we will see that, far from being an accurate reference to events of 1387 and 1388, it shows him to be unfamiliar with the university and its rules and customs, and cannot be taken to indicate the date of his writing.

Beginning with John Lewis in 1731,[31] the sodomy complaint was connected to the denunciation of sodomy in the *Twelve Conclusions of the Lollards* posted during the parliament held in London in 1395, thereby dating the prologue subsequently, and many scholars have agreed with him; at the same time, of course, this would provide a date for the completion of LV, for those who believe that Simple Creature was responsible for both.[32] But Mary Dove has convincingly questioned the connection of sodomy at Oxford with that parliament. The accusation of sodomy against the clergy in *Twelve Conclusions of the Lollards* posted at the time does not concern Oxford; and the Oxford master reported as charged with sodomy then had in fact died years before.[33] But given Simple Creature's above-mentioned unfamiliarity with Oxford, a distorted report of one or other of these incidents may underlie his complaint of rampant sodomy at the university.

Seemingly the most seriously heterodox passage in GP is to be found in chapter 12, where Simple Creature appears to characterize the Eucharist as purely commemorative:

> If it seemith to comaunde cruelte either wickidnesse, either to forbede prophit either good doinge, it is a figuratiif speche. Crist seith, "If ye eten not the flesch of Mannis Sone and drinke not His blood, ye schulen not have liif in you." This speche semith to comaunde wickidnesse either cruelte, therfore it is a figuratif speche, and comaundith men to comune with Cristis passioun, and to kepe in mynde sweetly and profitably that Cristis flesch was woundid and crucified for us.[34]

As we will see, this passage was the basis of the most incriminating charges in the posthumous trial of Richard Hunne.[35] The fact is, however, that Simple Creature was not concerned here to introduce a controversial theological theory, since the statement comes in the midst of a large swatch of St. Augustine's discourse on ways of interpreting Scripture in his treatise *De doctrina Christiana*, and he translates it literally. Here is the original Latin:

> Si autem flagitium aut facinus videtur jubere, aut utilitatem aut beneficentiam vetare, figurata est. "Nisi manducaveritis," inquit, "carnem Filii Hominis et sanguinem biberitis, non habebitis vitam in vobis." Facinus vel flagitium videtur jubere; figura est ergo, praecipiens passioni dominicae communicandum, et suaviter atque utiliter recondendum in memoria quod pro nobis caro ejus crucifixa et vulnerata sit.[36]

It is a great irony that Augustine's sentiment was taken to accord with Wycliffite theology, though it would seem rather to contrast with Wyclif's usual statement of his view, which can be labeled "consubstantiation" as opposed to the transubstantiation of the orthodox Church; that is, Wyclif holds for the real presence of the body and blood of Christ along with the continuing presence of the substances of bread and wine.[37]

Simple Creature in my view reveals no awareness of EV. I think that Forshall and Madden and others are misreading the text when they say that the author in referring to the English Bible "late translated" is speaking of EV,[38] and that he is also saying that it needs correction. The expression comes after Simple Creature has set forth the principles he uses in his translation, and he concludes by saying, if anyone should find fault in the result, let him correct it, but first check to see if there is not some mistake in the Latin Bible used, for he has seen many Latin Bibles that have more need to be corrected "than hath the English Bible late translated."[39] The most natural way to take this, I think, is to say that he is referring to his own just completed Bible. If, however, he is taken to refer to EV, it would be his only such reference to EV in his treatise, or only one of two.[40] We will take this matter up again in the Chapter 3.

Finally, let us note that neither the just quoted passage nor any other part of the treatise necessarily reads like a prologue to the English Bible: there is no indication that the reader is to "look at the text following" or the like. It could just as easily be intended as a separate treatise.

The Conjunction *Either* Preferred to *Or* in GP and LV Old Testament

The most important differentiator between GP and most of EV/LV that I will put forward is a dialectal one, Simple Creature's overwhelming preference for *either* over *or*, as in: "The first is Proverbis, *either* Parablis."[41] He uses *either* 195 times in the sixty pages of his treatise, and *or* only two times (and *other* two times).[42] In Table 2.1 I give the incidences in FM's copy texts, which are followed by most of the other manuscripts.[43] I also give the related preference for *neither* over *ne*.[44]

Table 2.1. Dominance of *Either* in GP

GP (SC)	Chaps. 1–14 Harley 1666	Chap. 15 Cambridge Mm.2.15
	either 141, eithir 25, ether 1	either 22, eithir 6
	other 1, outher 1	
	or 0	or 2
	neither, neithir, nether 66	neither 6
	ne 1	ne 0

It is noteworthy that the two uses of *or* occur in a statement in which he hopes that wise men who know the Scriptures will judge that his translation renders the Bible as clear or even clearer than the original Latin:

> And where [i.e., whether] I have translatid as opinly *or* opinliere in English as in Latin, late wise men deme, that knowen wel bothe langagis and knowen wel the sentence of Holy Scripture; and wher [i.e., whether] I have do thus, *or* nay, ne doute, they that kunne wel the sentence of Holy Writ and English togidere, and wolen travaile with Goddis grace theraboute, moun make the Bible as trewe and as opin, yea, and opinliere in English than it is in Latin.[45]

The use of *either* for *or* is comparatively rare in England as a whole, to judge by the data provided by the *Linguistic Atlas of Late Mediaeval English* (*LALME*), especially when *either* is preferred so exclusively.[46]

When we look at a sampling of the Old Testament (Genesis at the beginning, 1 Samuel and Job in the middle, and 1 Maccabees at the end), we find that the EV prefers *or*, but LV Old Testament regularly transforms EV *or* into *either*.[47]

In the New Testament, looking only at the Gospels, we observe that EV Matthew, Mark, and John, like the Old Testament books, favor *or*, but Luke favors *either*, though there is much variation evident.[48] It turns out that EEV Luke prefers *or*, meaning that an *either*-speaking scholar like Simple Creature meddled with EEV to produce the EV mixed bag.[49] The striking thing is that all EEV Gospels use only *or*, and the same is true of all LV Gospels.[50]

Lindberg observes that all EV manuscripts show signs of revision.[51] But let us note Fristedt's view that some new readings are systematic changes to EEV made by the First Revision team (instructed by the postulated Latin Bible annotated by Wyclif), whereas other manuscripts "were tampered with by men of small learning who for reasons unknown sporadically and at random corrected texts from other manuscripts."[52] One typical First Revision characteristic is the introduction of glosses after *or* or *ether*.[53]

Let us now see what the rest of the New Testament shows us on *or* and *either*. First of all, we can say that there is a preference for *or* in the Pauline Epistles of both EV and LV.[54] Moreover, like the whole of EV, the rest of the LV is equally sparing in its use of *either*, with the notable exception of four books, namely, Acts, James, 1 Peter, and the Apocalypse.[55] Here at last, then, we may speculate that Simple Creature may have at least participated in a later phase of the Bible-translation project: but it is a far cry from his having done the whole thing.

There is another use of *either* in GP and the LV Old Testament that may indicate Simple Creature's participation in the LV Old Testament: namely, the phrase *ever-either* to mean "each of two."[56]

To summarize, we see that EV favors *or* in both the Old Testament and the New Testament. LV favors *either* in the Old Testament and *or* in the New Testament, except that four of the later books of LV (Acts, James, 1 Peter, and the Apocalypse) favor *either*. The phrase *ever-either* is also favored by GP and the LV Old Testament.

By the *either* criterion alone, therefore, we might conclude that Simple Creature, the author of GP, was the translator of the LV Old Testament and the four *either*-favoring books of the LV New Testament. But now we will look at some peculiarities that will tend to exclude the LV Old Testament from Simple Creature's handiwork.

Forsooth Shunned in GP and LV New Testament, but Not in LV Old Testament

At one point in his discussion of translation principles, Simple Creature takes up the frequent Vulgate use of the postpositive narrative particles *autem* and *vero* (which translate the still more frequent Greek postpositive *de*), saying that they can mean either "forsooth" or "but," and that he himself in his Bible translation commonly renders them as "but"; but he adds that the Latin particles can also mean "and," according to the grammarians.[57] In the sixty pages of *Five and Twenty Books* (GP), he never uses *forsooth* in these ways. Let us see what the practice is of our versions.

In the Old Testament, LV consistently continues the EV style of translating *autem* and *vero* as *forsooth* or, less frequently, *soothly*, in Genesis, 1 Samuel, Job, and 1 Maccabees. LV, however, invariably changes the postpositive position to initial.[58]

This usage would indicate that Simple Creature is not the translator of the LV Old Testament, in spite of LV's preference for *either*.

As for the New Testament, *forsooth* and *soothly* are favorite words for this context in the EV New Testament, but not in LV, where they were actively boycotted.[59]

Now let us look at a different stylistic use of *forsooth*. At the end of his treatise, as an afterthought, Simple Creature returns to translational style with three notes, all of which are relevant for our discussion. We will begin with the second, since it deals with *forsooth*. He says that the conjunction *enim* commonly means "forsooth," but, as Jerome warns, it can also signify cause, "forwhy."[60] It turns out, however, that out of the more than eight hundred uses of *enim* in the Vulgate New Testament, LV translates it as *forsooth* only once (Romans 9.28). LV does translate *enim* as *forwhy* twenty-six times, but this can hardly be interpreted as meaning that it was an important principle to the translator.[61] Rather, it is more likely that Simple Creature noticed this use in LV and turned it into a principle.

Simple Creature's Declarations on the Latin Prepositions *Ex* and *Secundum*

The other notes that Simple Creature adds at the end of his treatise deal with two prepositions.

Ex to Be Rendered as *Of* or *By* (According to SC)

First, he says that the Latin preposition *ex* can mean sometimes "of" and at other times "by," according to Jerome.[62] Jerome obviously knew nothing of English, of course, so Simple Creature is probably saying merely that *ex* often signifies agency, which he assumes would be rendered by *by*. In so saying, however, he shows how out of touch he is with the realities of EV and LV. It is obvious that *ex* is usually translated as *of*, but it is also translated in several other ways, among which *by* is very infrequent. LV never changes an alternative translation of *ex* in EV to *by*, except as part of a policy of changing every *after* to *by*.[63]

The fact that *by* is hardly used for *ex* in LV is all the more striking when we consider the explosion of uses of *by* elsewhere in LV. For instance, there are three times as many *by*s in LV Genesis as there are in EV Genesis.[64]

Secundum to Be Translated as *After*, or *By*, or *Up* (So Says SC)

The final note that Simple Creature makes at the end of his treatise concerns the Latin preposition *secundum*, which commonly means "after," but it may also mean "by" or "up," so either "*by* your word" or "*up* your word."[65] Actually, even though Simple Creature allows the use of *up* as a preposition, he himself does not use it in this way when the sense calls for it (which occurs only in chapter 15); for instance, he says: "*aftir* the sentence, and not onely *aftir* the wordis."[66] His translation note would seem to indicate that "after" is the usual meaning of *secundum*, but that on occasion *by* or *up* would better give the sense.

This opens up a very interesting set of questions. It turns out that *after* is by far the favored translation of *secundum* in EV, in both Old Testament and New Testament, but in the Old Testament LV it is replaced almost always with *by*.

But let us first deal with the unusual preposition *up*. First of all, we note that there is no use of *up* as a preposition in three of our four sample books of the Old Testament in EV, but EV 1 Maccabees has added some (Table 2.2).

Table 2.2. UP as Preposition in EV Old Testament

EV Gen.	EV 1 Sam.	EV Job	EV 1 Macc.
up 0	up 0	up 0	up 14

This calls for a closer look, since Forshall and Madden list what they consider the "very frequent" use of *up* for "after" as one of the characteristics of the translator who takes over EV after the middle of Baruch, continuing through the end of the Old Testament all the way to the end of the New Testament;[67] and Fristedt considers use of the preposition *up* to be a characteristic of Purvey (as author of GP and translator of LV), taking it as an innovation introduced into post-Baruch EV by later correctors.[68] Let me state right away that I find a few signs of a stylistic break in Baruch itself.[69]

I have surveyed the use of the preposition *secundum* from the Prophets to the end of the Old Testament, and also the preposition *juxta* when it means the same thing.[70] What we see is no change immediately after Baruch in the large book of Ezekiel, but then a sudden intrusion of *up*s into Daniel, complete dominance in the Minor Prophets, a half victory in First Maccabees, and complete retreat in Second Maccabees. It is clear that an *up* user came on the scene at this point in the translation, exerted his influence, and then departed.

The fortunes of *up* in the EV New Testament are very intriguing. In the Gospels of the EEV (Oxford, Christ Church College 145) there is no use of *up*, but in EV (Douce 369.2) there is an intrusion of *up*s into Luke and a few into John.[71] This may remind us of the intrusion of *either*s into EV Luke. The *either* user could have been Simple Creature, but not the *up* user (since he shows no use of *up* in GP). However, there is a marked use of prepositional *up* in the rest of the New Testament in EEV, which is entirely followed by EV.[72] It indicates a change of personnel in the translation of EEV after the Gospels.[73]

In the LV, there seems to be a complete lack of *up* as a preposition in the Old Testament, except for a flurry of uses in a single book, 2 Samuel.[74] It is also completely missing from the four Gospels and the rest of the LV New Testament.[75] This is a sobering thought for those who believe that Simple Creature is speaking for the LV translators.

The statement made by Simple Creature about the alternative translations of *secundum* reveals an unawareness on his part of what actually happened in the transition from the EV Old Testament to the LV: there was a massive rejection of *after* in favor of *by* in the translation not only of *secundum* but also of *juxta*, when it means the same thing. However, *after* remained in favor in the LV New Testament.[76]

Summary Judgment on Simple Creature

Let us make some interlocutory conclusions here on the basis of Simple Creature's translational practices and personal style in GP, which has been taken as written after the whole of LV was finished (except for Forshall and Madden, who believe that it may have been written before the LV New Testament was done):[77]

1. He says that the Latin preposition *ex* can be translated not only by *of* but also by *by*; but it is almost never translated by *by* in either EV or LV, even though LV greatly expands the use of *by* for other Latin prepositions.
2. He specifies that the Latin preposition *secundum* can be translated not only by *after*, but also by *by* and *up*. He does not realize that the LV Old Testament actively boycotted *after* and replaced it with *by*, while the LV New Testament kept *after*. Further, he does not know that, while the preposition *up* had found some favor in some parts of EV, especially in the New Testament Epistles, it had been entirely purged from LV.
3. It might seem that his recommendation to translate Latin *autem* otherwise than by *forsooth* was put into practice in the LV New Testament, but he seems oblivious of the continued use of *forsooth* throughout the LV Old Testament.
4. Furthermore, he shows no awareness that his recommendation of translating Latin *enim* by either *forsooth* or *forwhy*, which was the practice of the EV New Testament, was not followed in the LV New Testament (except minimally for *forwhy*).
5. Finally, while Simple Creature's personal style of favoring *either* over *or* was adopted for the LV Old Testament, it found favor only in LV Acts and Revelation and two minor Epistles (James and 1 Peter), and abortively in Luke (seen in EV's changes from EEV).

Thus, while one might be persuaded to see Simple Creature's hand in one or another section of EV or LV by resorting to one of these criteria, by taking all of them together we must conclude that his profile is not matched in the Middle English Bible and that his claim to be the sole or main translator is overstated, to say the least. If he did participate at any stage, he was not able to impose all of his preferences, except perhaps in a few later books of the New Testament.

Other Wycliffite Connections Disallowed

Forshall and Madden believe that in the EV phase the New Testament was translated first, assuming that the renderings of the Gospels found in the Wycliffite *Glossed Gospels*, which they take to be by Wyclif himself, were extracted and used in EV.[78] The assumption nowadays is the reverse: that the Wycliffites responsible for the glosses use the already-finished EV text.[79] However, the Swedish scholars Sven Fristedt and Conrad Lindberg continue to favor Wyclif's participation. Lindberg believes that Simple Creature is reporting Wyclif's translational principles in GP chapter 15.[80]

Forshall and Madden then identify the translator of the Old Testament as Nicholas Hereford, at least the first five-sixths of it, up to the middle of Baruch 3.20, where the fifth and last hand of MS Bodley 959 suddenly breaks off, because another manuscript, Douce 369.1, says at this point, though not in the hand of the scribe, "Explicit Nicholay de herford."[81] They argue that Douce was copied from 959 before the extensive corrections found in 959 were added.[82] Lindberg dates MS 959 to around 1400, and he thinks the ascription of this part of the Old Testament to Hereford to be likely, and probably the rest of the Old Testament as well. He estimates that the project would have taken Hereford around twenty years, beginning while he was still an adherent to Wyclif's doctrines, and continuing after his reconciliation to the Church authorities, which occurred by 1391.[83] Anne Hudson regards the interpretation placed on this ascription with skepticism, not necessarily doubting that Hereford might have been involved, but rejecting the notion that the work of translation was that of one man.[84]

Forshall and Madden are convinced that the translation of EV after Baruch 3.20 changes noticeably,[85] but Lindberg concludes that there is no material difference.[86] One example that Forshall and Madden give, that Hereford uniformly translates Latin *secundum* as *after*, whereas later it is frequently rendered as *up*, has been shown above to be true of only some books.

As noted earlier, John Purvey's role as the chief mover behind the LV translation was elaborated from earlier conjectures to a harder hypothesis by Forshall and Madden. It was brought to the peak of respectability and certainty by Margaret Deanesly, who holds, in her monograph of 1920, that Purvey was not only the author of LV and GP but of the *Glossed Gospels* and various other tracts.[87] Cardinal Gasquet's protest of 1894 went unheeded, but claims for Purvey were dismissed by most scholars after Hudson's article of 1981.[88] It would be tempting to keep Purvey available as the Wycliffite prologuist Simple Creature,[89] since his recanting of Lollard doctrine came only in

1401, whereas Hereford's was a decade earlier. Purvey came originally from northern Buckinghamshire (the village of Lathbury, by Newport Pagnell), which may have been a region of *either* speakers, and he does not seem to have been a scholar, since there is no record of him at Oxford[90]—which, of course, would fit with his ignorance of Oxford customs. In 1414, however, he was found to be in possession of a Bible (presumably Latin), a separate copy of the Gospels and a copy of the Pauline Epistles and other Latin works connected with the Bible, especially commentaries on the Epistles (by Lyre, "Bede," and "Parisiensis"); and he also possessed the two main collections of canon law, Gratian's *Decretum* and Gregory IX's *Decretals*.[91]

A Trial Scenario for Simple Creature

Let us first consider the possibility that Simple Creature, a native of *either* country (perhaps somewhere in Buckinghamshire away from the Oxford environs), came to his biblical scholarship late, well after EV was finished and when LV was just wrapping up. He managed to join the New Testament team in time to contribute to the revising of four books, namely, Acts, James, 1 Peter, and the Apocalypse.

It is possible that at some point Simple Creature turned his hand to work with fellow *either* speakers on the *Glossed Gospels*, even though EV was used throughout. These compilations are entirely derivative in content, and, except for some quasi-treatises on special topics, they show little or no Lollard bias.[92] The author of the Prologue to *Short Matthew* uses only *either*, at least in one of the two manuscripts that contain it (Mary Dove's editions do not take note of *either/or* variants), and calls himself Simple Creature.[93] The body of the work also uses only *either* in the excerpts given by Hudson.[94] The Prologue to *Short Luke* similarly uses only *either*.[95] Here the author calls himself "a poor caitiff," prevented from preaching for a while, for reasons known to God. Like Simple Creature in *Five and Twenty Books*, he uses both third-person and first-person pronouns to refer to himself.[96] *Short Luke* is based on *Long Luke*, and, in the selections given by Hudson, both use only *either*,[97] as do those from *Short Mark*[98] (Hudson considers Mark the last Gospel to be glossed).[99] *Long John* prefers *or*, though with a good sprinkling of *either*s,[100] whereas *Short John* uses *or* almost entirely,[101] and *Long Matthew* does so exclusively.[102]

The *Glossed Gospels* was undoubtedly a long-term project. It must have overlapped with the LV project, even though it continued to use basically EV texts throughout.[103] It is my guess that the LV undertaking was independent of the *Glossed Gospels* endeavor, and that Simple Creature, if he did indeed work on the *Glossed Gospels*, eventually sought out the LV Old Testament team, which had been outsourced to his home territory, in *either*-speaking country.[104]

Work on the LV Old Testament was nearing its end; specifically, I suggest, Isaiah had been finished: *or* was changed to *either*, and *up* mostly eliminated (as in other parts of the LV Old Testament), and, though *forsooth*s were drastically cut down, still a lot remained (Table 2.3).

Table. 2.3. *Or/Either, Up, Forsooth,* and *Forwhy* in Isaiah

Isaiah	EV	LV
Or/Either	or 22 or (gl) 24 ether 0	or 0 ether, ethir 21 ether, ethir (gl) 18
Up	(verb +) up 92 upon 227 up (prep.) 0	(verb +) up 18 upon 0 up (prep.) 0
Forsooth	forsoth(e) 157	forsoth(e) 37 (36 from EV) / sotheli 7 (6 from EV forsothe)
Forwhy	forwhi 0	forwhi 3

Note: "gl" refers to alternative translations of words preceded by *or* or *either*.

In EV, *forsooth* did service for *enim* in the Latin (which occurs ninety-seven instances in the Vulgate Isaiah) and other words; in LV, thirty-six of the instances that remain are carried over from EV (fourteen translating *enim*, seventeen translating *autem*). Only one new *forsooth* has been added (Isaiah 7.9, corresponding to no Latin term), and in two cases EV *forsooth* has been replaced by *forwhy* (Isaiah 10.22, translating *enim*, and 10.25, translating *autem*), and one time *forwhy* replaces *for* in EV (Isaiah 11.9, translating Latin *quia*). *Soothly* replaces *forsooth* six times in LV, and adds one (Isaiah 43.19, *utique*, EV *also*). It can hardly be thought that Simple Creature's influence has been at work here. But perhaps it was the use of *forwhy* twice in this book to translate *enim* that gave him the idea for his remark in GP (that *forwhy* is the rendering of *enim* when signifying cause).

Up to this point, the LV team had omitted all of the prefatory material found in EV, but Simple Creature now proposed to contribute a prologue to

Isaiah, which was accepted. The result fits his style, as we can see from a comparison with the EV Jerome prologue (Table 2.4).

Table 2.4. *Or/Either* and *Forsooth* in the Prologues to Isaiah

Isaiah	EV Prologue (Jerome)	LV Prologue (SC?)
Or/Either	or 3 or (gl) 2 ether 0	or 1 ether, ethir 11
Forsooth	forsothe 5	forsothe 0

We note that the new prologue has only one *or*, but this is doubtless a scribal stylistic improvement from *either* in the Royal manuscript, since the other collated manuscripts have *either*. Here is the sentence in which it occurs:

> Therfor men moten seke the treuthe of the text, and be war of goostli undurstonding *ether* moral fantasie, and 3ive not ful credence therto, no but it be groundid opinly in the text of Hooly Writ, in o place *or** other, *ethir* in opin resoun that may not be avoided; for ellis it wole as likingly be applied to falsnesse as to treuthe, and it hath disseived grete men in oure daies, by over greet trist to her fantasies.[105]
> **ether* FGKMNPQRSVUXY

In this statement, Simple Creature's Wycliffite leanings surface in a mild way, as Mary Dove points out.[106]

Dove calls this prologue a "Prologue to the Prophets," in keeping with some of the manuscripts, and with Simple Creature's own characterization of it in GP,[107] but more accurately it is only a "Prologue to Isaiah," as is recognized in other manuscripts.[108]

The treatise beginning with the words *The Holy Prophet David*,[109] advocating the translation of the Bible into English, fits Simple Creature's preference for *either* (seven times), but with a rather high incidence of *or* (two times). That the work is by the author of GP is suggested by Mary Dove, who says that the sentence "As Gregor and Grosted sein, to make unable curatis is the higheste wikkidnesse and tresun ayens God, and is lik sinne as to crucifie Crist" is a summary of part of GP chapter 10.[110] Or, in keeping with my scenario here, we may judge it to be Simple Creature's sketch of a sentiment that he will later expand in *Five and Twenty Books*. But in contrast to the larger treatise, his interest here is less on serious study of the Bible than in using it, as Dove says, "for comfort and consolation."[111]

In his Prologue to Isaiah, Simple Creature promised, impersonally, to write a discourse on the four levels of meaning in the Scriptures to be placed at the beginning of the Bible: "Of these foure undurstondingis schal be seid pleinlier, if God wole, on the biginning of Genesis."[112] This must have turned into a draft of GP, which in the final form begins with a very long summary of the Old Testament books and takes up the four senses of Scripture only in chapter 12.[113] He originally intended to draw on Nicholas of Lyre's commentary and other books, but at the time of his writing he did not have them to hand, and he was forced to rely instead on Augustine's *De doctrina Christiana* "as a default source," as Rita Copeland puts it, until a copy of Lyre arrived.[114] In other words, he was writing at a place significantly removed from Oxford, or from ready access to Oxford's libraries.[115] I should add here that Augustine's work was used for the same purpose by the author of a prologue to one of the *Glossed Gospels*, namely, the so-called *Intermediate Matthew*, an *or* speaker, whose biblical quotations resemble EV, whereas Simple Creature's quotations in *Five and Twenty Books* are akin to LV and sometimes are direct quotations of LV. It is judged that both the authors draw on some longer source using Augustine's work.[116]

In contrast to *Five and Twenty Books*, which, as we have seen, was attached to very few MEB manuscripts, the Prologue to Isaiah is included in all twenty-one of the LV manuscripts containing Isaiah.[117]

Since our analysis above indicates that Simple Creature's style is not matched anywhere in the LV Old or New Testament, except for four books in the latter, we should conclude that he was not a major force behind the project, and a claim on his part to be *the* translator would not sit well with the real translators. Accordingly, it may be that GP as first submitted by him ended with chapter 14, and after it was spurned by the LV administrators, Simple Creature hatched the idea of adding a final chapter, a new treatise that we can call after its opening words, "Forasmuch as Christ Saith," in which he takes credit for the whole enterprise. This is where he first identifies himself as our humble servant: "For these resons and othere, with comune charite to save alle men in oure rewme, whiche God wole have savid, a simple creature hath translatid the Bible out of Latin into English. First, this simple creature hadde myche travaile, with diverse felawis and helperis," and so on.[118] We can be sure that Simple Creatures's "divers fellows and helpers" did not take kindly to this description of their actual role in the production of EV and LV.[119]

CHAPTER 3

The Bible at Oxford

The MEB has been persistently connected with Oxford University, whether through its supposed origins in the circle of the Oxford professor John Wyclif or simply as a center for biblical studies. We shall now explore these connections and implications directly.

Loss of Interest in the Bible in the Mid-Fourteenth Century and Its Revival by Wyclif (and Others)

In a recent study of Wyclif, G. R. Evans refers to "the legend that Wyclif put Scripture back at the centre of theological studies, and sought to make its text available for ordinary people to read in their own language," and asks, concerning the first part of the legend, "Did Wyclif need to bring the study of the Bible back into a prominent position? Had it ever slipped from first place in theological studies?"[1] The answer to these questions is an undoubted "yes," and it seems that we must affirm the truth of Wyclif's important role in renewing academic interest in the Latin Bible. Furthermore, like his admired predecessor at Oxford, Robert Grosseteste (d. 1253), he sought to diminish the scholastic "track" by reducing all theology to the study of the Bible.[2] It may well be that we cannot avoid crediting to Wyclif the vernacular Bible as well, at least in the sense that his emphasis on the Bible was at least indirectly responsible for it. If so, we will have to decide whether the resulting project should be called simply "Wycliffian" rather than "Wycliffite" (the latter term, like "Lollard," carrying with it polemical and heterodox intentions and overtones).

From the beginnings of the universities in the twelfth century until well into the fourteenth, there were major faculties of theology only in three centers of Europe: Paris, Oxford, and Cambridge.[3] Originally at Oxford it seems that biblical exposition or exegesis was one of three "concentrations" for a theology degree, the others being the study of the *Sentences* of Peter Lombard and the study of the *Histories* of Peter Comestor. But by the mid-thirteenth century, Bible study had become an essential part of every theological education, along with the *Sentences*. However—and this is a sobering fact—even though the scholarly study of the Bible had flourished around the turn of the fourteenth century all over Europe, producing, notably, the commentaries of the Franciscan Nicholas of Lyre in France and the commentaries of the Dominican Nicholas Trevet in England, by the middle decades of the century interest in biblical exegesis had died out. According to William Courtenay, during the fourteenth century throughout the universities and other centers of study of Europe there was a "general separation of biblical exegesis and speculative theology," and after 1335, scriptural studies were "almost a silent topic for the next forty years."[4] Beryl Smalley refers to it as the midcentury slump.[5] Courtenay goes on to say that "the most important stage in the development of biblical studies in the late fourteenth century was the appearance of the treatises and commentaries of John Wyclif" written between 1371 and his death in 1384; and also, Courtenay adds, Wyclif's "English translation of portions of the Bible"[6]—which is another matter! He concludes that Wyclif's activity in this area should be seen "as part of the first wave of that reawakened interest" in Scripture study.[7] However, Wyclif's exact contemporary, the Franciscan William Woodford, who lectured on Lombard at the same time as Wyclif, was also chiefly interested in producing biblical commentaries.[8] Just before Wyclif's time, Richard Fitzralph (d. 1360) was vitally taken up with the text of Scripture, as shown in the dialogue on the subject in his *Summa*,[9] and another contemporary of Wyclif's, the Benedictine Adam Easton, taught himself Hebrew and made a new Latin translation, and he also collated readings from different versions of the Bible.[10]

The Oxford Theology Curriculum and Wyclif's Participation; Wyclif's Bad Latin

Whatever the practice was in the faculty of theology at Oxford in the 1300s, the statutes that continued in force favored the Bible over the *Sentences* and certainly over the *Histories*. In the earliest statute, passed in 1253, it is said that before one can incept (meaning "commence" in the academic sense of finishing all requirements and receiving a degree) as a master of theology (after fulfilling the requirements of a bachelor and being licensed), one must read (lecture on) a book of the Bible or one of the four books of the *Sentences*, or a book of the *Histories*.[11] A later statute requires lecturing on a book of the Bible or the *Sentences*,[12] but further on it says that one must have audited (taken courses on) the Bible for three years and lectured on a book of the Bible,[13] with no mention of the *Sentences*.

The requirements for proceeding from bachelor of theology to doctor of theology are obscurely stated: "After lecturing on a book of the *Sentences*, the one intending to incept must undertake study for at least two years or so before he ascends the magistral chair."[14] James Weisheipl tells us that this means that the new bachelor, called a "bachelor of the *Sentences*," is to first lecture on the *Sentences* before giving at least two years of "cursory lectures" on the Bible.[15] This procedure differed from that of the University of Paris, where the lectures on the *Sentences* followed those on the Bible. The Dominicans objected to the Oxford order, but the settlement of 1314 left the English custom in place.[16]

It is odd that Wyclif left no traces of a *Sentences* commentary or writing in the form of disputed questions or quodlibets, although he did leave behind *determinationes*, reflecting public academic disputes on controversial questions (but without using the term *questiones*). Given Wyclif's obsessive desire to write and publish constantly, and to rewrite and edit earlier writings, it is hard to believe that he would not have preserved such scholastic efforts if he took them seriously. We know from Woodford's testimony that Wyclif did lecture on the *Sentences*, but it may be that he merely summarized the material for the students without adding anything original of his own. Instead, he wrote treatises on a wide range of subjects; and those who argue that some of them were outgrowths of his *Sentences* work must deal with the point that none of them preserve the sentential mode of discourse.

It has been suggested that the sentential style of presentation was going out of fashion in England just at this time, which might account for Wyclif's failure to use it.[17] But perhaps there was another explanation for his dislike of the discourse. For some reason Wyclif had never learned to speak and write Latin properly; his academic style may have been the worst in medieval Christendom. Could he have realized that his linguistic skills were not equal to the question-oriented give-and-take of scholastic disputation? Blame for his poor Latin has been unjustly put on his scholastic studies.[18] Another spurious explanation is that by this time English scholars had stopped thinking in Latin and were instead thinking in English: "Wycliffe's Latin is base even as compared with that of such of his predecessors as Ockham; there is a gulf between it and that of Thomas Aquinas. Wycliffe in fact belongs to a time when scholars were ceasing to *think* in Latin. It is significant of his position that he is one of the founders of English prose-writing. To understand his Latin it is often necessary to translate it into English; certainly in obscure passages this is often the readiest way of getting at his meaning."[19] However, other writers of the time wrote good Latin, from his former scholastic colleague William Woodford to formulators of episcopal constitutions and registers to legal commentaries to chronicles to spiritual treatises and other kinds of composition. The idea that Wyclif's Latin is infected by English constructions is sound enough in his case, in contrast to other authors of the time. But the further notion that, even though he was linguistically inept in Latin, he was masterful in English needs reconsideration, since it is based on the assumption of his authorship of numerous English treatises. Perhaps, however, one might make a case that he served as an inspiration for the awkward Latin-based language of EV, though hardly for Fristedt's theory that Wyclif carefully doctored a Latin Bible with English glosses, which provided the basis for the First Revision (that is, from EEV to EV). The great mystery is that he went through the entire master of arts (MA) and bachelor of theology curricula with defective language skills and emerged at the level of theological master.

The above-stated possible reasons for Wyclif's neglect of sentential discourse, that it was going out of fashion and that his Latin was not up to it, lead me to consider another possibility: he elected to spend more time and effort on the Scripture track, coming up with an ambitious plan to produce postils on the entire Old and New Testaments. Though there seems to be nothing of his own in these commentaries, he must have preferred to produce a routine biblical commentary, unusual for his day, to creating yet another commonplace *Sentences* summary. His plan had the distinct advantage of giving him a supreme mastery of the Word of God, to prepare him for his lectures.

Bible Study at Oxford: Graduate Students and Extracurricular Auditors

We can only conjecture whether Wyclif's concentration upon the Bible during his theological studies and doctoral teaching had an immediate effect upon the way in which the Bible was taught at Oxford. It would not seem that his postils were a great success, since they survive, if at all, only in scattered copies,[20] and there is no indication that anyone after him attempted a similar feat, even in part.

It is assumed that Wyclif lectured from his postils between 1371 and 1376.[21] But every theology master must have lectured on the books of the Bible in his own way. And, contrary to what is often stated, I argue below that such lectures could be attended not only by arts masters who were proceeding to a degree in theology, but also by clerical auditors who came to the university with no intention of obtaining a degree.

Who were the clergy who went to Oxford to study the Bible? John Moorman, writing about the thirteenth century, says that rectors of parishes "were sent to the Universities for a few years not to read the usual 'arts' course but to study such subjects as would enable them to serve more efficiently in the parishes. Among the many licences which were granted to men who wished to leave their parishes for a time 'to frequent the schools' we find that some went to read theology, some Canon Law, while a few made the Bible the special object of their studies."[22] He finds the latter group of students specified under the designations "in Sacra Pagina" and "in Sacra Scriptura,"[23] but these phrases were simply different ways of designating theology: in other words, theology itself was thought of as primarily the study of the Bible.

In his recent book on study leaves for parish clergy, Donald Logan has found that well over a thousand curates (rectors) were given permissions in the first half of the fourteenth century from the diocese of Lincoln alone. They went to university (overwhelmingly to Oxford) for a few years to improve themselves.[24] Logan, however, believes that they would not have been allowed to study the Bible, because the MA was required for incepting in theology.[25] But, as we saw above, the curates he is speaking of, for the most part, like the majority of other students at Oxford, did not intend to get a degree,[26] and it would follow that they were under no constraint to follow degree programs.[27]

It is true that almost all of the licenses for study leave in the fourteenth and fifteenth centuries refer only to *studium litterarum*, but this should not make us think that the rectors studied only arts courses. The licenses are simply following the text of Boniface VIII's decretal *Cum ex eo* in the *Liber Sextus*, issued in 1298, allowing new appointees to rectorships to put off progression to the priesthood while in studies.[28] John Andrew in the Ordinary Gloss to the *Sext* (finished in 1304 or 1305) says at *litterarum* that because the pope does not make distinctions, he understands it as a general expression, to refer to grammar, canon or civil law, or theology.[29] The decretal allows dispensations for as long as seven years, and Andrew comments, "Note that a scholar should be proficient (*provectus*) in seven years," adding that a five-year period of proficiency is specified for a theology student in an earlier decretal, and the same period is set elsewhere for a student in civil law.[30] It is noteworthy that six of the priests studied by Logan who were given study leave were specifically allowed to study theology or canon law, even though they did not have the MA.[31]

We can get some notion of how such short-term concentrations operated from William Lyndwood, writing in the 1420s,[32] who himself received such a license and dispensation when he was a deacon (in his case to complete his doctorate in both laws).[33] Commenting on Archbishop John Peckham's 1281 constitution requiring those practicing as advocates in court to have studied canon and civil law for at least three years ("nisi prius ad minus per triennium audiverit jus canonicum et civile cum debita diligentia"), Lyndwood says that the stipulated time in Roman civil law for advocates is five years. He suggests that Peckham lessened the requirement only for those working in the smaller church courts, where three years of experience in cases and in studying practice and theory seems sufficient ("in talibus namque sufficere videtur quod aliquis sit exercitatus in causis et habeat practicam cum speculativo per triennium"). The would-be advocate must study as the disciple of a master or doctor ("ut discipulus sub magistro sive doctore"); the constitution seemingly allows the study to take place not only in a university ("studium generale") but elsewhere as well; Lyndwood, however, thinks otherwise: one should audit the laws under a doctor in a place where such laws are publicly taught ("quod debeat jura audire sub doctore in loco ubi jura hujusmodi publice docentur"). Afterward, the student can prove that he has fulfilled the forensic requirement by the testimony of the doctor under whom he studied ("per testimonium doctoris sub quo studuit"), or by a testimonial letter from the chancellor of the university where he studied ("litera testimonialis cancelarii universitatis in qua studuit").[34]

As for the curriculum to be followed by these three-year students, Lyndwood recommends that, even though the statute specifies both canon and civil law, they limit themselves to canon law, learning only such provisions of civil law as are cited in glosses to the canons; otherwise, they will be able to learn neither subject well.[35]

I take it that most of the rectors who went to Oxford to study theology spent their specified years of leave in a similar way, being able to set up their own individual programs of study.

We saw in Chapter 2 that Simple Creature condemned a supposedly new proposal that would put an end to the immediate access to Bible study that curates now enjoyed and force them to spend nine or ten years in the arts beforehand. It is important to look at his words on this point, because they have been mistakenly interpreted as a knowledgeable reference to a curricular squabble that occurred in Oxford in 1388, hence providing a sound date for his time of writing. He says:

> But alas! alas! alas! The most [greatest] abomination that ever was heard among Christian clerks is now purposed in England, by worldly clerks and feigned religious, and in the chief university of our realm, as many true men tell with great wailing. This horrible and Devil's cursedness is purposed of Christ's enemies and traitors of all Christian people, that no man shall learn divinity, neither Holy Writ, no but he that hath done his form in art, that is, that hath commenced in art, and hath been regent twain year after; this would be nine year either ten before that he learn Holy Writ.[36]

After proceeding to talk about the general degeneracy of morals at Oxford, and especially sodomy and simony, he returns to the subject of impeding the learning of Scripture:

> Yet on these three abominations God would graciously convert clerks, if they would do very [true] penance, and give them wholly to virtues; but on the fourth most abomination[37] purposed now to let [prevent] Christian men, yea, priests and curates, to learn freely God's Law, till they have spent nine year either ten at art (that comprehendeth many strong errors of heathen men against Christian belief), it seemeth well that God will not cease of vengeance till it and other be punished sore; for it seemeth that worldly clerks and feigned religious do this, that simple men of wit and of finding know not God's Law, to preach it generally against sins in the realm. But wit ye, worldly clerks and feigned religious, that God both can and may, if it liketh [pleases] Him, speed simple men out[side] of the university as much to ken Holy Writ as masters in the university; and therefore no great charge though never man of good will be poisoned with heathen men's errors nine year either ten, but ever live well and study Holy Writ by old doctors and new, and preach truly and freely against open sins, [un]to his death.[38]

We learn two things here: first, that Simple Creature is well aware that students at Oxford, specifically priests with the care of souls, at the present time can study the Bible without having to go through the arts curriculum;

and second, that he believes there is an effort underway to put an end to this easy access to Scripture instruction. He could hardly be wrong about the first point. Wyclif himself, writing in 1378, speaks of the practice of parish priests going on leave to universities to study the Bible. "It is permissible," he says, "for a rector to be away from his parish, for a time, to gather the seed of faith in theological schools, so that he may sow it 'in due season.'"[39] It is confirmed in a Wycliffite tract, *Why Poor Priests Have No Benefice*: "If such curates be stirred to go learn God's Law and teach their parishens the Gospel, commonly they shall get no leave of bishops but for gold; and when they shall most profit in their learning, then shall they be clept home at the prelate's will."[40]

But Simple Creature is clearly wrong about the second point, and it demonstrates that he and his immediate associates were not familiar with procedures at Oxford.

Simple Creature's remarks were seen by John Lewis[41] and others as being a reference to the proposal in 1387 or early 1388 to enforce the statute of 1253 stipulating that no one can incept in theology (qualify for theological regency, that is, teaching theology) without first finishing regency in arts.[42] According to Lewis, the proposal was "that hereafter no one should be an inceptor in divinity unless he had first completed his act in the liberal sciences, had read a book of the Canon and preached publicly in the university, which the Author [of the Prologue] represents as if it was purposed that 'no man should learn divinity nor Holy Writ till he had done his form, or commenced in art, and been regent two year after.'"[43] Lewis quite clearly tells us that the General Prologue author *mis*represented the proposal by interpreting it to refer to the *very beginning* of theology study rather than to its completion. He could also have told us that the GP author was mistaken in assuming that the policy was directed against all students at Oxford, whereas it was aimed only against friars, by the secular clergy. It had been customary to dispense friars from the requirement of inception (and formal study) in the faculty of arts, and now it was proposed to refuse to grant any such dispensations—which, however, were characterized as dispensations from the requirement of regency after incepting as masters of arts.

Simple Creature's garbled reference to the proposed Oxford reform has been taken as a sure date for the GP: it must have been written after the measure was proposed in 1387, and before it was inhibited by Richard II on March 17, 1387/8, and again on August 1, 1388 (the assumption being that Simple Creature could not have made his statement after the initiative was spiked and the crisis averted).[44] But Simple Creature has only heard the alarming news about the curricular proposal from "many true men," informants who would not necessarily have known about the king's actions against it; and doubtless the shock of the deadly proposal (as they understood it) was still reverberating in the land. Even if it was not, and Simple Creature was writing years later, he may have decided to present it as an ongoing threat, since it involved the enforcement of an existing requirement (he thinks). He need not have been writing as late as 1395 or 1396, since, as we saw in Chapter 2, Lewis's argument for associating the sodomy-at-Oxford complaint with the Lollard *Twelve Conclusions* has been called into question.

Simple Creature's Unrealistic/Inaccurate Ideas About the Production of the MEB

Before we ask whether the Middle English Bible could have been intended to play a role in the continuing education of priests at Oxford, let us try to draw some conclusions about how it was and was not undertaken and carried out.

Discussion of the so-called Wycliffite Bible has been dominated by the account given by Simple Creature in *Five and Twenty Books*. Let us look at it in detail:

1. "First, this simple creature had much travail, with diverse fellows and helpers, to gather many old Bibles, and other doctors, and common glosses, and to make one Latin Bible some-deal true."
2. "And then to study it of the new, the text with the gloss, and other doctors as he might get, and specially Lyre on the Old Testament, that helped full much in this work."
3. "The third time, to counsel with old grammarians and old divines of hard words and hard sentences, how those might best be understood and translated."

4a. "The fourth time to translate as clearly as he could to the sentence."
4b. "And to have many good fellows and cunning at the correcting of the translation."[45]

Therefore, Simple Creature's alleged steps are as follows: (1) establishing a sound Latin text, (2) studying it for the meaning of the Latin Bible, (3) consulting about how to render difficult Latin passages into English, (4a) producing a complete translation, and (4b) correcting it. There is no talk of producing glosses to any part of the Bible;[46] but elsewhere he says he has glossed Job and the prophets,[47] and provided marginal word glosses via Jerome, Lyre, and others to the whole Hebrew Bible, especially the Psalms.[48] And there is no sense of first executing a literal translation and then systematically transforming it into a more fluent version, though this is what Dove assumes he is talking about when speaking of his translation principles: "The writer of the prologue provided a fascinating account of ways in which the earlier version of the translation, which was never intended to be copied and circulated, was made syntactically and stylistically more comprehensible and accurate in the later version."[49] Hudson suggests that the *Glossed Gospels* project was part of the preparation outlined in number 2,[50] but this conflicts with the conclusion that the authors of the *Glossed Gospels* followed EV even after LV was available, because of its closeness to the Latin.[51] In other words, glossing the Gospels was not a step toward producing an accurate English translation or perfecting it. This is confirmed by the seeming lack of interest throughout these Gospel compilations in translation problems, for instance, Latin variants and grammatical ambiguities.

Hudson observes that Forshall and Madden and others after them thought that Simple Creature's entire program dealt only with LV, whereas she believes that it accurately describes the whole project from the beginning, including therefore EV, saying that "it is not to be expected that any contemporary writer would distinguish EV from LV in the clear-cut and over-simplified way done by Forshall and Madden."[52] For my part, I believe that a clear distinction would be recognized certainly by the producers of LV, because the revision was so systematic; for instance, all Latin absolute participles were translated literally into English in EV, but in LV all were removed. The cursory way in which Simple Creature speaks of the "correction" of his translation in this account (4b) would seem to preclude any such idea of a thoroughgoing revision. Later on, he tells of changing such absolute participles in the Latin text directly into English finite forms, not rendering them first into English participles and then eliminating them. Furthermore, the methods he suggests for resolving absolute constructions do not correspond to the actual practice of LV.[53] My suggestion, therefore, is that his account is largely imaginary, describing what he considers to be a reasonable way of progressing, from establishing the Latin text, to studying it, and translating it and correcting it.

Jeremy Catto finds manuscript evidence of all of the stages postulated (as he sees them), except for "the newly established Latin text."[54] There does seem to have been great interest in the Latin text of the Bible on the part of the translators, but not in producing a complete corrected Latin text. Rather, there was an effort to decide on the correct Latin reading in each passage of EV and LV as it was being worked on.[55] Fristedt concludes that there was no attempt to correct the Latin text until the whole of the original form of EV (that is, EEV) was completed,[56] and he places the search for old Latin Bibles by Simple Creature "and his numerous coadjutors" even later, when preparing to embark on LV.[57] There appears to have been little or no concern about the impossibility in certain cases of deciding which of two variant Latin readings is the correct one, and, accordingly, giving both as possibilities. What we have instead is an abundance of internal glosses, especially in EV, of alternative *translations* of the *same* Latin word.

Why EV Before LV? Unsatisfactory First Try, or Planned Preliminary Stage, or Study Help for the Clergy?

In analyzing *Five and Twenty Books* (GP) and its relationship to the MEB, we have already seen some differences between EV and LV. Let us remind ourselves that the biblical text that EV translates is the Latin Vulgate, and the LV revisers of EV seemingly had only the Vulgate before them as well, with no knowledge of the Hebrew or Greek texts or languages.[58] EV usually follows Latin grammatical constructions very closely, while LV systematically transforms some of them into more idiomatic forms. Albert Baugh pronounces LV "in every way superior to the early version."[59] But it all depends on what one means by "superior." When dealing with the Word of God, what is more important, accuracy or fluency?

Recently Lilo Moessner has given a more positive analysis of the EV and its "structural iconicity," that is, its fidelity to the Latin constructions, and finds that the grammatical structure of the LV "is not without flaw," and that LV does not always achieve the goal of being as clear, let alone clearer, than the original Latin.[60] Instead of an "iconic" or "mirror-image" metaphor, we can speak of "calques," that is, patterns, in the narrow sense of "loan translations," in which the donor language contributes a structure not entirely natural in the receiver language: it has a foreign or nonnative feel about it, and stands out as a "loaner."[61] Middle English examples are "again-buyer" for *redemptor* and "again-bite of inwit" for *remorsus conscientiae*.

Moessner finds that the usual designations of "literal" and "free" translations are inadequate and confusing, and notes with approval David Lawton's observation that the EV and LV present "a choice not between literal and free translation but between two understandings or types of literal translation."[62]

EV can be regarded in a number of ways. To begin with, we may think that it was a timid first try at Englishing the whole Bible, dominated by fear of distorting the meaning of the Latin original, and that its inadequacy was soon recognized and a redo was undertaken. Or we may think of it as a deliberate preliminary step taken to get the exact meaning of the Latin into English first, and then to adjust it in the interests of the vernacular idiom.[63] This second view is a common one, shared, for instance, by Conrad Lindberg: "When John Wyclif and his followers decided to take on the work of translating the Bible into English, they were faced with a twofold problem: how to be faithful to the Word and yet create a readable text. They solved it by making *two* translations, one more literal, the other more idiomatic."[64] As we have seen, Mary Dove assumes that EV was never intended for circulation.[65]

This second hypothesis, however, does not seem as plausible as the first. It is not easily credible that a systematic Latinate translation would be carried through to the end with the intention of then scrapping it for an idiomatic rendering, going though the whole Bible again. The envisaged process has been compared to Richard Rolle's twofold rendering of the Psalms, first word for word, and then less so.[66] But Rolle was dealing with a single book of the Bible, and he did the second version himself immediately after doing the first, whereas the adherents of a provisionary EV seem to think of it as handed over to a separate LV team for polishing.

It would seem much more likely that, after EV was produced, a change of translational philosophy occurred, which dictated the LV transformations. It might well be that John Trevisa underwent the same kind of conversion in translation theory when working on the *Polychronicon*. Sven Fristedt has identified a large relic of what looks like an original very literal translation; it occurs far along in the work, in chapters 15–26 of book 6. He compares it to the transformed rendering of the same chapters found in other manuscripts, with ablative absolutes and other participles removed, and so on—corresponding to the rest of the existing Englished work.[67]

It is possible to imagine Trevisa and Nicholas Hereford, who both arrived at Queen's College in 1369, working on EV, with Trevisa eventually turning aside, while still at Queen's, to produce a similarly literal version of the *Polychronicon*.[68] As Fristedt notes, David Fowler has "ascertained that Trevisa had his hand on the Latin *Polychronicon* as early as 1377,"[69] and therefore Trevisa may have been at work on Englishing it "for at least ten years"[70]—and possibly more. Then, when the decision was made to produce a more fluent version of the Bible, Trevisa perhaps participated in producing LV, before or while doing a like revision of his first rendering of Higden's work.[71]

However, there is a weighty argument against against such a hypothesis of Trevisa's participation in the MEB. Although we might admit that for Trevisa "the translation of the Bible is the most important precursor to the translation of the *Polychronicon*,"[72] it seems clear from the dialogue that serves as an introduction to the final version of his Englished *Polychronicon*,[73] that he is not aware of any significant effort to translate the whole Bible, a point made by Margaret Deanesly.[74] After mentioning some works translated out of Greek into Latin, the sensible lord of the exchange says, "[Also, Holy Writ was translated out of Hebrew into Greek and out of Greek into Latin, and then out of Latin into French.] Then what [= how] has English trespassed, that it might not be translated into English?"[75] He goes on to name some other translations, including King Alfred's rendering of a large part of the Psalter into English, and Bede's translation of St. John's Gospel into English. He continues: "Also the Gospel and prophecy and the right faith of Holy Church must be taught and preached to Englishmen that ken no Latin. Then the Gospel and prophecy and the right faith of Holy Church must be told them in English, and that is not done but by English translation, for such English preaching is very [= true] translation, and such English preaching is good and needful."[76]

We notice that lord of the dialogue fails to mention not only the MEB, but also Rolle's well-known translations of the Psalms. We will see that another fervent advocate of Bible translation from Queen's College, Richard Ullerston, will also fail to mention the MEB, though he does mention Rolle.

There is a third way of explaining EV, suggested by David Lawton and Lilo Moessner, and K. B. McFarlane before them: that translation was foreseen as having a permanent value in assisting persons with only elementary Latin, particularly run-of-the-mill clergy, to use as a guide to understanding the Latin text.[77] Lewis Brewer Hall also assumes that assisting the clergy with their understanding of Scripture was one of the purposes of EV, with the further assumption that they themselves could render the literal meaning in better English.[78] And, we should add, the unpromising minor clergy at Oxford and laymen (if there were any students not in minor orders) would also find such translations helpful, not to mention both clergy and laity everywhere throughout the realm.[79] Ullerston will make this argument for all biblical translations.[80]

We cannot, of course, prove that EV was designed to help the parish priests who went to Oxford to study the Bible, but, whatever its intended purpose, both masters and students would have been foolish not to welcome it, and LV as well, when it became available, as an aid not only to understanding the Latin Bible but also to preaching the Word of God (or "God's Law," if that is how they preferred to call it), especially the Gospel pericopes featured in Sunday masses.

The Transformation of EV to LV

From my analyses of EV and LV, especially in the Gospel of Luke, I confirm the long-standing view that LV systematically de-Latinizes EV. The translators responsible for LV employed a form of English that resonates better with Modern English than that of EV, for the most part. We need not assume, with McFarlane, that the reason for producing LV was that the presumed purpose of EV, "to enable a reader of weak Latinity to construe the Vulgate for himself," proved unsatisfactory.[81]

Most of the constructions endorsed by Simple Creature in the General Prologue turn out to be those used in transforming EV Luke to LV Luke, the book that I have analyzed most thoroughly, though it is not always true in other books. Anne Hudson shares with others the conclusion that, while more intermediate versions of EV are being discovered, the LV translation is remarkably uniform throughout, as well as being generally stable from copy to copy.[82] But I have found some interesting differences in various parts of the translation, and the stability of the text may help to establish that these differences are original rather than merely scribal.[83]

The obvious goals of all translators of the Bible are accuracy and clarity. Lindberg considers that these goals were aimed at in LLV, Bodley 277, Henry VI's Bible: it was "a conscious attempt to merge original features (at times more ancient than EV) with modernisms (not all the most recent) to form a text true to the double aim of this translation of the Bible: to be true to the Word, and to help the reader."[84] Modern-day scholars who have studied the EV and LV have usually judged them on the basis of literary style and fluency.[85] But, as Nicholas Watson notes, the Middle Ages had no word for "literary,"[86] though they did, of course, have criteria for judging what was awkward or not. Sometimes, nowadays, "literary" is contrasted with "literal," and "literalism" is often a bad word; but, properly understood, as fidelity to the original meaning, it is essential, particularly in the case of the Bible.[87] Even for Simple Creature in the GP, sticking to the letter is the best, and the LV often follows the EV word for word. But when clarity is sacrificed, the language should be modified, even at the expense of altering the original data. It is obvious that the supervisors of LV wished to resolve ambivalences and difficulties in the original Latin rather than to present the problems to the English readers and let them puzzle over them. This is sometimes taken to be a characteristic of the proto-Protestant reformist impulse behind this medieval Bible project.[88] Such a conclusion would make sense if, as has usually been assumed, the sentiments enunciated by the Wycliffite author of GP were, as he claimed, the driving force of the LV text. But if, as I think, he was a Johnny-come-lately to the enterprise, we need to arrive at other explanations. The rationale that first suggests itself is that for nonscholarly devotional reading it was assumed that plausible resolutions to textual problems were preferable to ambiguities or puzzles in the text.

The iconic method of translation followed in EV resembles that followed in various Vetus Latina translations of the Bible. In the Old Testament, these translations were replaced by fresh ones made by Jerome—still, however, following characteristics of the Hebrew (and Greek) and at the same time respecting the Latin versions he was replacing.[89] But in the New Testament, the iconicity was left more in place, since the old translations were only *edited* anew, the Gospels by Jerome, and the other books by unknown editors. It might not be too far from the truth to see the LV revision of the EV text of the Middle English Bible as a process somewhat in between these two methods of producing the Vulgate.

But whatever advantages could be perceived in the EV text in facilitating understanding of the Latin Bible, the peculiar virtues of more familiar kinds of speech found in LV proved preferable, as can be seen from the far greater survivals of LV manuscripts. This was the version that won the hearts of the English reading public of all persuasions.

LV Motivations as Inferred Versus GP Motivations as Stated

Let me single out one aspect of EV and LV and draw some conclusions from it, namely, the practice of EV to take over absolute constructions literally and the practice of LV to do away with such forms by resolving them finitely.[90] In doing so, LV was not rejecting a hidebound traditional way of writing, but resisting an innovation that was just appearing in the language. However, though LV was thereby conforming to earlier stylistic norms, there should have been a real objection to doing this on the level of accuracy; participial constructions are deliberately ambiguous, and "clarifying" them in one definite way or another, say, as causally or temporally related (using *because* or *when*), when the relationship might be the opposite, or simply circumstantial or appositional, destroys what might be considered a divinely inspired uncertainty.[91]

It has been concluded on the basis of the General Prologue that "the goal in the Wycliffite Bible is a translation that produces clear English while staying as close as possible to the Latin."[92] But it is apparent that Simple Creature's goals were much more ambitious; he wanted to outdo the Latin and make it *more* intelligible.

He hopes that he improves on the truth and clarity of the Latin text by taking these sorts of decisions, which might seem to imply a certain quality of arrogance in assuming the correctness of his judgments, making his version better than the original. Let us review what he (or an *or*-speaking interpolator) says at one point: "Whether I have translated as openly *or* openlier in English as in Latin, let wise men deem that know well both languages and know well the sentence of Holy Scripture; and whether I have done thus *or* nay, ne doubt, they that ken well the sentence of Holy Writ and English together and will travail with God's grace thereabout, may make the Bible as true and as open, yea, and openlier in English than it is in Latin."[93] He claims, of course, to rely on the context of each passage, but ultimately his main reliance is on divine inspiration and guidance. His final thoughts sum up his attitude: "Many such adverbs, conjunctions, and prepositions be set oft one for another, and at free choice of authors sometimes; and now those shall be taken as it accordeth best to the sentence. By this manner, with good living and great travail, men may come to true and clear translating and true understanding of Holy Writ, seem it never so hard at the beginning. God grant to us all grace to ken well and keep well Holy Writ, and suffer joyfully some pain for it at the last. Amen."[94] In this view, Simple Creature may have been influenced by one of his favorite works, Augustine's *De doctrina Christiana*, as well as Wyclif's *De veritate Sacre Scripture*. But both Augustine and Wyclif are speaking of seeking divine help in explicating, not translating Scripture.[95]

The fact remains that by disambiguating such ambiguities for the sake of fluency, a translation like LV forecloses meanings left open in translations like EV, which observe limits imposed by the original forms.

Other Factors In and About Oxford, and a Suggested Downsizing of the Translation and Revision Enterprises

Other scholars who may have participated in the translations have been suggested by Jeremy Catto, connecting supporters of the project with residents of Queen's College, Oxford, including Richard Ullerston, who will be treated below for his defense of Bible translation sometime in the decade 1400–1409, and also Philip Repingdon in his post-Wycliffite phase.[96] Repingdon, of course, may have begun his participation in his pre-Queen's period, and while he was still a Wycliffite.

Even though I have argued that Simple Creature himself was not an Oxford man, the general dialect of EV and LV has been associated with the university,[97] and one should not be surprised to find many other connections. Another locus at Oxford has recently been singled out by Anne Hudson as a probable center of translational activity, namely Greyfriars, the Franciscan house at the university: one of the reasons being the resources of its library.[98] Included in her suggestion is the supposition that the compilers of other works associated with the Wycliffites (associated with them *at least nowadays*, I would add) also took advantage of the house's facilities; she designates specifically the *Glossed Gospels*; the encyclopedia called *Floretum* in its full form and *Rosarium* in the abridged version; the revisions to Richard Rolle's English Psalms commentary;[99] and the large liturgical cycle of Wycliffite sermons.[100] She points out that "Wyclif and his disciples were not in the 1370s defined as enemies," and the intensive scholarly labor that went into at least the biblical and encyclopedic enterprises had nothing obviously Wycliffite about them, "even in the developed sense of that term let alone in that of the 1370s."[101] I agree and wish to push the argument further, specifically concerning the organization and production of EV and LV. I suggest that there was nothing hugger-mugger about this endeavor and no reason for secrecy. The question remains, however, whether it was, especially at its origins in the production of EV, a large-scale endeavor with such wide participation that it was too routine to be mentioned, or whether it was a small-scale enterprise on the level envisaged by Forshall and Madden, who saw Wyclif himself producing the EV New Testament and Nicholas Hereford most of the EV Old Testament, with John Purvey doing the whole LV Bible. If we dismiss Simple Creature's vision of painstaking preparation of an accurate Vulgate text and just think of getting down to work and doing it, it could have been accomplished in a short time with a minimum of fuss. There is the Douai-Rheims example to be remembered, and though that project was recognized as very important, there was hardly any mention of it left in writing, just notings of its beginning and end.

The production of the ur-EV text (that is, EEV) may have been the inspiration of a single master in the theology faculty at Oxford, perhaps even Wyclif himself, in his Wycliffian, pre-Wycliffite period (not very likely, I think, given his linguistic shortcomings). If Gregory Martin by himself translated the entire Vulgate in eighteen to twenty months, our hypothetical professor along with a half-dozen graduate students, with their MAs long behind them, could have completed the whole Bible in a matter of three or four months. The resulting text could then have been circulated as a whole or by books or groups of books, as a working text, not only for the use of other students and masters, but also with an eye to further refinement, perhaps with the familiar medieval request to readers to improve the text, as, for instance, when Simple Creature says, "I pray, for charity and for common profit of Christian souls, that if any wise man find any default of the truth of translation, let him set in the true sentence, and open, of Holy Writ."[102] Or perhaps a message like that of William Tyndale at the end of his 1526 New Testament:

> Count it as a thing not having his full shape, but as it were born afore his time, even as a thing begun rather than finished. In time to come, if God have appointed us thereunto, we will give it his full shape, and put out, if aught be added superfluously, and add to, if aught be overseen through negligence, and will enforce to bring to compendiousness that which is now translated at the length, and to give light where it is required, and to seek in certain places more proper English.[103]

At any rate, once the translation began to be reproduced, many changes were introduced into it by the copyists and users, some merely scribal, whether mistakes or dialectal features, some conscious corrections or intended improvements. We can only conjecture how many of the conscious improvements were "authorized" by the original translators or their supervisor. We must take very seriously Fristedt's demonstration that there was a consistent effort that transformed EEV into EV. But we can readily imagine that many changes were "sports," or mutations not naturally or deliberately selected to survive (to speak genetically). One example noted in the Chapter 2 is the intervention of an *either* speaker in the Gospel of Luke in Douce 369.2 (used by Forshall and Madden as their main EV text), predominantly not found in other EV copies, and not at all in LV.[104]

Then, after a few years, we can speculate, two other masters decided it would be a good idea to systematically revise the new translation in such a way that it would not adhere so closely to the Latin forms, to produce a text that would be more amenable to wider use, in sermons and in the liturgy in local parishes. One of these masters would take responsibility for the Old Testament; he and his students were predominantly *either* speakers and did not have a set objection to *forsooth*s (to mention a couple of features that we have noticed above). The other master gathered a group to handle the New Testament. They doubtless took to themselves whatever copies of EV happened to be at hand, doubtless in various states of correction or revision—whether or not acting in consultation with EV's original translators. Once again, the whole enterprise need not have taken a great deal of time.

The *terminus ante quem* for EV is 1397, because of the Egerton Bible found to have been in the possession of Thomas of Gloucester at his death.[105] What is the *terminus a quo*? Most of those who believe it to be "the Wycliffite Bible" date its beginnings to around 1380; but Conrad Lindberg, taking Simple Creature's schedule as authentic, traces its beginnings, as we have seen, to Wyclif's first arrival at Oxford in 1354, when he would have begun to prepare the Latin edition, with glossing beginning around 1360, with EV produced around 1370–80 and LV finishing around 1390.[106] If, on the other hand, we take EV to be a simple and quick translation, with no necessary involvement by Wyclif, our speculations can be wide-ranging, even *ante tempus dicti Johannis Wyclif.* As we will see below, "the time of John Wyclif" was defined as dating from when he began to disseminate his heresies.[107]

CHAPTER 4

Oxford Doctors, Archbishop Arundel, and *Dives and Pauper* on the Advisability of Scripture in English

Let us turn our attention now to various positions on the allowability or advisability of translating the Bible into the vernacular, specifically English. We will begin with works by three Oxford doctors of theology, namely, Thomas Palmer, a Dominican friar, William Butler, a Franciscan friar, and Richard Ullerston, a secular priest (like Wyclif and Hereford).

Thomas Palmer, OP: Partially for, Partially Against Translation

The prominent Dominican friar Thomas Palmer produced a treatise called *De translacione Sacre Scripture in linguam barbaricam*, which has usually been considered to be later than the others that we are considering here, but the recent researches of Cornelia Linde have called that judgment into question.[1] The work was edited by Margaret Deanesly in her *Lollard Bible* with some mistakes and with a misleading title, putting *Anglicanam* rather than *barbaricam*.[2] Linde establishes the correct title and finds no reason to doubt Palmer's authorship (which has been considered questionable in the past). Palmer mentions the Lollards adversely twice, but because of his mild treatment of them, Linde suggests that the exchange it details may have taken place comparatively early, perhaps in the 1380s.[3] The academic structure of the treatise might suggest that it was completed while he was still at Oxford, where he achieved his doctorate in theology by 1393, the year that he was appointed provincial of his order in England.[4] It was also in 1393 that he allegedly defended the recently reconciled Nicholas Hereford from a Lollard critic, but I judge that this response was written by Hereford himself.[5] However, when Palmer wrote in defense of images in 1398, he still cast his treatise in academic form, specifying that it was a determination made "in the schools of St. Paul, London."[6]

The treatise on translation begins, like most scholastic exercises, with a question favoring the "wrong side": "Utrum Sacra Scriptura in linguam anglicanam vel in aliam barbaricam sit transferenda," that is, "Whether Sacred Scripture should be translated into the English or any other barbarous tongue," and it opens with eighteen arguments for the affirmative, *Quod sic videtur* (we can call this part 1),[7] followed by another eighteen *Ad oppositum* (part 2),[8] corresponding to the *Sed contra* arguments that one finds in Thomas Aquinas's *Summa theologiae*. But then Palmer complicates the form by positing thirteen "other truths" (*aliae veritates*), of which the first is in favor of translation and the others against, or at least against translating all of Scripture (part 3).[9] Next comes a brief reply to some of the *veritates* (part 4),[10] followed by a *Responsio* on "not giving what is holy to dogs" (part 5).[11] Finally, there are answers to the original eighteen arguments in favor of translation (part 6).[12] Some parts are in rougher shape than others, and Linde suggests that it is to some extent a *reportatio* of an actual debate, which was not put into final form.

The bald distinctions "for" and "against" in this summary obscure Palmer's own point of view, which emerges throughout the treatise: he agrees that essential portions of the Bible should be translated, but believes that other portions should not be translated, and, in fact, he holds that some portions *cannot* be translated adequately into a barbaric vernacular like English, which lacks the necessary sophisticated elements of style and structure to accommodate the scriptural meaning. His position is summed up in the final argument of the treatise, where the expectation is that he will refute the eighteenth argument in favor of translation, which is this: "According to the rule of reason, we understand that all things are conceded that are not prohibited; but there is not found anywhere in Scripture that it is forbidden to be translated into a barbaric idiom."[13] But the response to argument 18, which constitutes the end of the treatise, addresses an argument against translating any part of Scripture, and refutes this argument:

> To the 18th, where it was argued thus: "The main reason why Scripture cannot be translated into a barbarous tongue seems to be that it is not ruled by grammatical rules and figures, with[out] which Sacred Scripture cannot be preserved from falsity and incongruity. But for this reason, no part of it should be translated, whether concerning things necessary for salvation or

> otherwise, because these rules, tropes, and figures are equally common in all parts of Sacred Scripture." To this the opposite should be said.[14]

His refutation is as follows:

> To this I respond by denying that these rules, tropes, and figures are equally common to all parts of Scripture, for some parts are seen to be true without them, and some are open and plain. "For my yoke is sweet and my burden light." And points of morality are, as it were, from natural law and are easy of belief, as the Psalmist says: "Your testimonies have become exceedingly believable." And therefore there is no need for them to be preserved from falsity and incongruity by means of figures and tropes or other means, as there is for other difficult things contained therein.[15]

Let us look at his references to the Lollards. The first of the eighteen arguments against translation is that many things in Scripture are *inutilia*, "because they would harm rather than profit" ("quia nocerent plusquam prodessent").[16] The second is that not every truth should be written in English, because many truths are not useful; but, according to the Lollards, "Every truth is contained in Sacred Scripture, because it contains the First Truth, which contains all other truths."[17] It has been suggested that he is hereby attributing to the Lollards a *sola Scriptura* doctrine, namely, that all necessary truths are in Scripture and none in tradition.[18] This, however, was not a usual Wycliffite view.[19] Rather, he must mean that, because the Lollards believe that all truths are somehow contained in Scripture,[20] they should all be made available to the general public.

The eighteenth argument against translation is that the Jews killed Jesus because they did not understand the spiritual meaning of his sayings. "How then," Palmer asks, "would simple uneducated persons not err, if they had it in the vernacular alone? Nowadays do not those who know only grammar, because of the bad understanding of Lollards and simple folk, persecute the disciples of Christ for expounding it spiritually? The answer is clearly yes."[21] We see that Palmer is accusing the Lollards, not of mistranslating Scripture, but of missing its true meaning in being overly literal.

William Butler, OFM: Completely Against

The Franciscan doctor of theology William Butler,[22] in his determination against translating Scripture delivered at Oxford in 1401 or early 1402,[23] starts out more cleanly, by simply arguing against the proposition that Scripture should be translated. In opposing such translation he gives a total of six reasons. Because the first part of his treatise is missing, we do not know the exact formulation of the assertion, but it is clear that the positive side was previously defended by others. We also know, however, that Butler was not present at this earlier defense, since at the beginning of his fifth argument he speaks against a point made by "the aforesaid assertors," which, he says, *was related* to him.[24]

Butler sums up his reasons against translation at the end: (1) the *allectiva conditio* (attractive nature) of Scripture (from which errors of interpretation easily arise); (2) the defective understanding of human nature (caused by original sin); (3) the analogy of the angelic hierarchy; (4) the singular conferral of the law of the Gospel (to be proclaimed rather than written); (5) the subtlety of Scripture's literal artifice; and (6) the mystical body of Christ (different functions for different members).[25] In the course of his third argument, he seems to be asserting that bishops were currently prohibiting their subjects from having the Scriptures in English.[26] But as Jeremy Catto observes, Butler makes no reference to Lollards, and, although the treatise by Palmer does mention Lollard interpretations of the Bible, it does not attribute any translation to them or accuse them of unorthodoxy.[27] Kantik Ghosh, however, argues that both Butler and Palmer do show awareness of Wycliffite issues, namely attacks against the prerogatives of the clergy, and he finds Ullerston's reticence about the Lollards deliberately or indeliberately naive.[28]

Richard Ullerston: Completely in Favor

Third, we address a Latin treatise preserved in the National Library in Vienna, advocating the translation of the Bible into English. Deanesly had attributed it to Purvey,[29] but Anne Hudson discovered from a copy of the end of the text in Gonville and Caius College, Cambridge, that it was by Richard Ullerston, a solidly orthodox and anti-Lollard doctor of theology from Queen's College, Oxford.[30] Ullerston's arguments were then used in an English tract titled *Against Them That Say That Holy Writ Should Not or May Not Be Drawn into English*, also attributed by Deanesly to Purvey, which reports Archbishop Thomas Arundel as having approved Queen Anne's English Gospels.[31] Only the third article of Ullerston's original three-article treatise on Bible translation has survived, having been preserved among the Hussites in Bohemia, and the title that comes at the end of the Caius text, *Tractatus de translacione Sacre Scripture in vulgare*, may refer only to this part. Hudson deciphers the date as 1401, but she admits that the final digit is not absolutely clear, concluding however that "from the shape of the stroke there seems no possible alternative."[32] To me, however, the last digit does not resemble the first digit at all, and it may well be a "7".[33]

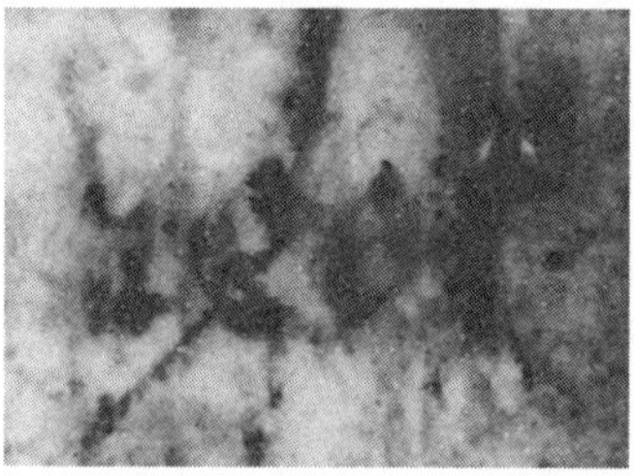

Last page of Ullerston's treatise on translation, Cambridge, Gonville and Caius College MS 803/807, fragment 36 verso detail.

Ullerston's first two articles (nonextant) dealt with the question of whether Jerome's translation is "true," and he concluded that it is. It is puzzling how he could write at great length on this subject without knowing the original languages from which Jerome was translating. The conclusion that he came to is clear from the third article, that it was allowable for Jerome to make his translation; and this remaining article deals with the question of whether it is allowable to translate Scripture into other languages as well, that is, tongues that are "less principal and famous" than Latin.[34]

He goes on to say that in the times of "our fathers"—it is not clear whether he means this literally, "in the previous generation," or is referring to earlier times, even the patristic era, or to all times up to now—there was never any question about this matter. He could have added that this was also seemingly still the case outside England, since it is only in England that we find a call for unrestricted access to the Scriptures. In other words, there was no need for such a demand in other countries, where vernacular translations were a matter of course.[35]

However, nowadays, Ullerston continues, there is great doubt, so much so that two valiant doctors in this *cathedra*, or seat of learning, spent the whole time of their lectures on much this point; one of them gave several arguments for the negative position, and the other offered scores (*vigenarii*) of arguments on the affirmative side. But neither of them was judged to have won his case.[36] Thus Ullerston resembles Butler, reacting to a debate that he did not personally participate in.

He then describes his plan of procedure: first he will recite some of the negative arguments of the first doctor, and then add some further negative arguments on his own, and finally he will respond to all of these arguments with positive arguments, by which responses his own position will be made clear.[37]

Ullerston's gently sarcastic tone in his introduction was missed by Deanesly, who mistranslates "nescio per quot argumentorum vigenarios" as "by I know not how many powerful arguments."[38] Hudson does not translate the passage, but she does identify the second doctor with Ullerston himself, and she thinks that all thirty of the negative arguments he gives are those of the first doctor.[39] Dove follows suit, saying that Ullerston's treatise "is set up as a debate between two doctors."[40] But in fact it is clear from what Ullerston says that he did not even attend the Oxford debate, and that the debate dealt with a somewhat different question from that of his article. Furthermore, only the first four of his negative arguments are those of the first doctor, which were supplied to him by a friend. When Ullerston begins to list the arguments against the proposition, he says: "The first doctor asks: 'Should Sacred Scripture be interpreted into all languages,' which *somewhat coincides* with my article" (that is, the positive position taken in his treatise).[41] Then, after giving the first four arguments, he says: "Now these arguments a certain man, a friend, set down, as written in the hand of the aforesaid first doctor."[42] He continues by giving twenty-six additional arguments against his own article (not against the question debated by the two doctors).[43] Later on, at the end of his response to the fourth argument, he says that this concludes his response to the arguments of "the reverend doctor."[44]

In proceeding as he does, Ullerston is not trying to give the appearance of being evenhanded,[45] but rather is following (or inventing) a modified form of scholastic argumentation. In the classic scholastic method, as demonstrated most familiarly by St. Thomas in his *Summa theologica*, a proposition is stated and arguments given in favor of it, and then the professor comes to the opposite conclusion, giving his reasons; finally, he responds to the original arguments one by one.[46] What Ullerston does is to start with a question, rather than a proposition; he gives arguments on the negative side and then he refutes the arguments, thereby affirming the positive side.

Let us examine Ullerston's treatise. It is divided into twenty-four chapters, and, whether this division was Ullerston's doing or not, it will be useful to follow it.[47] There is some hesitation on the part of the scribe as to where the divisions go, and some rubrics are crossed out. The chapters are as follows:

Chapter 1 (195ra): introduction; negative arguments 1–4 from the first doctor; negative arguments 5–10 from Ullerston.
Chapter 2 (195va): negative arguments 11–20.
Chapter 3 (196ra): negative arguments 21–30.
Chapter 4 (196rb): discourse on *translacio* and *interpretacio.*
Chapter 5 (196vb): discourse on what is licit and illicit.
Chapter 6 (197rb): discourse on translation; assurance of relying on Church teaching; preview of next three chapters.
Chapter 7 (197va): listing of Ullerston's motives for taking the affirmative side.
Chapter 8 (198rb): response to objections to his motives.
Chapter 9 (198vb): conjectured motives of those holding the negative side.
Chapter 10 (199rb): responses to arguments 1–2 of the doctor.
Chapter 11 (199vb): responses to arguments 3–4 of the doctor.
Chapter 12 (200rb): response to argument 5.
Chapter 13 (201ra): responses to arguments 6–8.
Chapter 14 (201rb): response to argument 9.
Chapter 15 (202ra): responses to arguments 10–12.
Chapter 16 (202va): responses to arguments 13–14.
Chapter 17 (202vb): responses to arguments 15–16.
Chapter 18 (203rb): responses to arguments 17–18.
Chapter 19 (203vb): responses to arguments 19–21.
Chapter 20 (204va): responses to arguments 22–23.
Chapter 21 (205ra): response to argument 24.
Chapter 22 (205va): responses to arguments 25–29.
Chapter 23 (206ra): response to argument 30.
Chapter 24 (207va): some extended arguments and nine brief arguments in favor of translation.

At the end of chapter 6, after stating his desire to conform to Church teaching,[48] he lays out what he will cover next: namely, some of the reasons that move him to take the affirmative side of the argument, followed by what he thinks might be reasons that others have for taking the opposite view.[49]

The last chapter is a puzzle. Ullerston has spent a huge amount of space in chapter 23 on the thirtieth objection, that the Gospel should not be preached to everyone, and he fails to come to a satisfying conclusion, moving instead in chapter 24 to support what he claims to have advocated somewhere above, that the law of Christ should be published with moderation in every idiom;[50] perhaps he is still responding to the thirtieth objection. He continues with an elaborate statement that prohibiting the translation of the Bible would be contrary to Christ's plan for his church, and that the work of translation is virtually inspired by the Spirit of God:

> Si enim Dominus Jhesus Christus peregre proficiscens ab hoc mundo tradidit servis suis bona sua, unicuique viz. secundum propriam virtutem, per quorum usum laudabilem possunt regnum ecclesie adipisci, quis prohibere potest fidelem servum ejus cui Dominus dedit talentum, interpretacionem viz. sermonum ejus in vulgare, ne sic transferat in vulgare, cum talis, Spiritu Dei actus, non minus posset aliud loqui quam [quod] Dominus in ore ejus posuerit, quam [quod] propheta gentilis Balaam, qui dixit, ut habetur Numeris 23, "Num aliud possum loqui nisi quod jusserit Dominus?" Et hoc idem senciendum est de illis qui habunt industriam aquisitam ad consilia peragenda, que et omnia alia ad sui laudem perficere nos concedat Jhesus Christus, qui sine fine vivit et regnat, amen.[51]

> For if the Lord Jesus Christ in passing from this world gave to His servants His goods, each according to his power, through the laudable use of which they can acquire the kingdom of the Church, who can prohibit His faithful servant to whom the Lord gave a talent, that is, the interpretation of His words into the vernacular, from thus translating into the vernacular, since such a one, driven by the Spirit of God, could speak nothing other than [what] the Lord had placed in his mouth, than [what] the gentile prophet Balaam [spoke], who said, as is read in Numbers 23.12, "Can I speak anything else but what the Lord commandeth?" And the same is to be thought about those who have acquired the skill to carry through with such tasks—which, and all things else, may Jesus Christ grant to us to perform to His praise, who lives and reigns without end, amen.

This statement and prayer have the look of a conclusion to the treatise. But there follows a list of nine succinct reasons for translating Scripture, in which Ullerston might seem to be including himself among the ranks of capable translators.[52] These reasons are clearly an afterthought, since they are not mentioned in the plan that Ullerston stated at the beginning. In the Caius fragment, where a later hand has numbered the reasons in the margin, the colophon follows, identifying Ullerston.

Perhaps a clue is to be found in the seventh of the nine propositions, which says that, just as preaching the Word of God and administering the sacraments is to be supervised by the wise counsel of prelates, the same is true of the use of translation.[53] This would seem to be a reference to the constitution dealing with Bible translation, *Periculosa*, proposed at the council of the province of Canterbury held at Oxford in November 1407. Ullerston was in residence at Queen's College at the time of the council, and may even have participated in it, as a member of the lower house or as an onlooker. Hudson and others have uniformly taken a more severe view of the purport and effect of the constitutions passed at this time, saying, for instance, that they forcibly closed down the debate on translation and formally forbade the vernacular translation of the Scriptures.[54] But in fact, as we will see in Chapter 5, all that the legislation required was episcopal or provincial supervision or license approving recent translations before being used for lectures.

The deference to bishops noted in the added proposition at the end of Ullerston's treatise is actually entirely in keeping with his response to the second argument of the first doctor, which said that Bible translation was properly a task for bishops to perform, but that the English bishops at that time were not adequate for the task.[55] Ullerston agrees that it would be fitting if bishops were sufficiently expert to accomplish the task, but says that it does not follow that if they are not able to do it on their own, all others would be insufficient. It only requires good men to be chosen who are adequately equipped for the enterprise. He gives the example of the translators who were chosen from each of the tribes of Israel and sent to Alexandria to render the Bible into Greek; none of them were said to be pontiffs.[56]

Ullerston in English: Reporting Archbishop Arundel's Approval of Queen Anne's English Gospels

The English treatise noted above, *Against Them That Say*, which draws on Ullerston's Latin treatise, has uniformly been judged to be Lollard in sentiment. Margaret Deanesly ascribes it to John Purvey;[57] Curt Bühler, who does not know Deanesly's work, terms it "a Lollard tract" in the title of his edition of 1938; while Hudson says, "In form it is a typical Lollard production: lists of authorities, biblical, patristic, canonistic and historical, cited in favor of a Lollard viewpoint and given a rough frame." She favors a date before 1407, because of "the absence of allusion to the prohibition of biblical translation."[58] If, however, we judge that biblical translation was *not* prohibited, we should revisit the subject, and the whole question of the treatise's Lollardy. As it stands, I can find only one passage in it that seems obviously

Wycliffite: after citing Fitzralph's statement that the Sacrament might well be made (that is, the Mass celebrated) in the vernacular of each country, the author says: "But we coveiten not that, but prey anticrist that we moten have oure bileve in Englishe."[59] The sentiment is very much out of tune with the rest of the treatise. Perhaps the text originally read "unto crist," which was distorted by an early copyist. Mary Dove says that the writer was probably a Wycliffite,[60] and that "by 'anticrist' the writer surely means the church authorities who are denying the people the Bible in English."[61] Like Hudson, she is writing under the assumption that the constitutions passed in 1407 and promulgated in 1409 banned biblical translations, but unlike Hudson she assumes that the author of this treatise knows of the ruling and is protesting against it.

Dove notes that the treatise appears "in most copies . . . in the context of identifiably Lollard material," but that, surprisingly, in the manuscript of the Pierpont Morgan Library (no. 648, ca. 1445–55), it comes between Nicholas Love's *Mirror of the Life of Jesus Christ* and Bridget of Sweden's *Revelationes*.[62] However, the only other medieval copy, besides Morgan, is the Trinity College Cambridge manuscript (B.14.50), which indeed includes this piece among Wycliffite treatises and excerpts.[63] The other four copies are in "collections of texts supposedly heralding the Reformation" produced in early modern times, as Dove tells us.[64] The Trinity manuscript, which Dove takes as her base text, has the reading as above, "prey anticrist"; but Morgan erases "prey," and three of the later copies omit "prey" entirely. Dove comments, "The notion of praying to Antichrist evidently daunted scribes."[65]

Immediately after making the above statement, the author identifies himself as someone who has had much personal experience in dealing with Jews: "We that have much communed with the Jews know well that all mighty men of them, in what[ever] land they be born, yet they have in Hebrew the Bible, and they be more active in the Old Law than any Latin man commonly, yea, as well the lewd men of the Jews as priests."[66] The most likely Englishmen of the time about whom this could be said were the keepers of the rolls, who also functioned as wardens of the Domus Conversorum. The warden from 1405 to 1415 was John Wakering, who shortly afterward became bishop of Norwich.[67] One of the residents of the Domus at this time was the daughter of Rabbi Moses, referred to as "bishop" of the Jews.[68] Of course, English clerics who traveled or resided abroad could also have had the opportunity to commune with Jews.

Dove demonstrates that *Against Them* draws almost entirely from various portions of Ullerston's treatise, far more extensively than cited by Hudson.[69]

Alastair Minnis says that the "anonymous Lollard" who compiled the work ignored "Ullerston's balancing arguments against translation,"[70] but, as we have seen, Ullerston included these arguments only in summary form and only for the purpose of refuting them.

Against Them's original material, apart from a few odds and ends, is mainly limited to three anecdotes at the end. The first is a very brief recollection of a sermon preached before the bishop of London by the Dominican friar John Tille in the hearing of a hundred people, saying that St. Jerome professed to have erred when he translated the Bible.[71]

This report of Tille's sermon is accepted as authentic by historians, like A. B. Emden. Tille achieved his doctorate in theology at Oxford by 1403; he was the prior of the London convent of Dominicans, that is, Blackfriars, from 1402 and again in 1408, after Thomas Palmer stepped down in 1407.[72] He may still have been at Blackfriars for the meeting of convocation in January 1409 at St. Paul's, when the Oxford constitutions were confirmed, and in April, when Archbishop Arundel sent the standard notice to the bishop of London to promulgate them throughout the province.[73] Dove in fact suggests that Tille was actually addressing the constitution dealing with the Bible, *Periculosa*, which starts out with the same quotation of Jerome about the dangers of translating the Bible.

The author of *Against Them* reacts to Tille by comparing him to the magician Elymas (Bar-Jesus), who tried to keep Sergius Paulus, proconsul of Paphos, from the faith by preventing him from hearing St. Paul preach the Word of God; whereupon Paul rebuked him and said he would go blind: "But Friar Tille, that said before the bishop of London, hearing a hundred men, that Jerome said he erred in translating of the Bible, is like to Elymas, the which would have letted a bishop or a judge to hear the belief, to whom Paul said, 'O thou, full of all treachery and of all fallacy, seeking to turn the bishop from the belief, thou shalt be blind to a time.' This is written in the Deeds of the Apostles, thirteenth chapter."[74] It is interesting that he interprets the *proconsul* of Acts 13 as a "judge or bishop," and then settles on "bishop." He goes on to cite Jerome much more fully than Ullerston does in his extant third article, but we must remember that Ullerston dealt entirely with Jerome's translation in his first two articles, and it may be that the English author had access to the whole treatise. Or, dare we suggest it, perhaps the author of the English treatise is Ullerston himself, or at least a rather disorganized intimate of his?

The second fresh anecdote that *Against Them* contributes goes back in time to a supposed bill in Parliament against current Bible translations:

> Also it is known to many men that in the time of King Richard, whose soul God assoil, into a Parliament was put a bill by assent of two archbishops and of the clergy, to annul the Bible that time translated into English, and also other books of the Gospel translated into English, which, when it was seen of Lords and Commons, the good duke of Lancaster, John, whose soul God assoil for His mercy, answered thereto sharply, saying this sentence: "We will not be the refuse of all men, for sithen other nations have God's Law, which is law of our belief, in their own mother language, we will have our in English, who that ever it begrudge." And this he affirmed with a great oath.[75]

It is usually thought that there is no historical basis to this story, but Ralph Hanna takes it at its face as a reference to a real clerical effort in Parliament to suppress "Lollard biblical translations" (he assumes that EV and LV were perceived as Lollard), perhaps in 1388 or in 1394.[76]

Against Dove's assertion that "it was not for parliament to legislate on such matters,"[77] we can point out that there was a statute against heretical preaching passed in the wake of the Blackfriars meeting of 1382, which invoked the archbishop of Canterbury and the bishops and other clergy of the realm.[78] And Parliament legislated against heretical books in the 1401 statute *Contra Lollardos*,[79] which followed the formulation sent forward by convocation.[80]

We must remember that the Church convocations were considered part of Parliament when they met together. In the Merciless Parliament of 1388 singled out by Hanna, the Monk of Westminster reports that there was a *magnus rumor*, or great discussion, in full Parliament on March 12 concerning the Lollards and their preachings and books in English ("de Lollardis et eorum predicacionibus et libris in Anglicis") whereby they were leading astray simple folk and even some substantial persons. Four of the implicated preachers were summoned for trial before a panel of bishops and scholars, and on reconvening on April 20, two of them were convicted and imprisoned and the other two reconciled.[81] As Emden clarifies, the panel was a committee appointed by the convocation of Canterbury, chaired by Thomas Southam, archdeacon of Oxford, a "civilian" lawyer.[82]

Another major chronicler of the time, "the Canon of Leicester," that is, Henry Knighton, also speaks of this Parliament's concerns about Lollard books. Earlier, at the time of the condemnation of Lollard errors in 1382, Knighton asserted that Wyclif himself, or the Lollards in general, had translated the Gospel into English, and he expressed his disapproval of exposing the laity to Scripture without the mediation of the clergy.[83] It is telling, then, that he does not refer to the English Scriptures in his account of Parliament in 1388, where he says that the king at the bidding of the whole Parliament ordered the archbishop of Canterbury (William Courtenay) and the other bishops to prosecute the Lollards and examine their English books more fully ("librosque eorum Anglicos plenius examinarent"). The king further appointed examiners of heretical books and their abettors in every county ("in quolibet comitatu certos inquisitores de hujusmodi libris et eorum fautoribus instituit"). Knighton records one of the commissions, to the dean of Newark (New Work, Novum Opus) College in Leicester, Thomas Brightwell, a former Wycliffite.[84] This commission, dated May 23, mentions by name writings of Wyclif, Hereford, and John Aston, and speaks of writings both in English and Latin, and the name of Purvey is added in other versions of the commission; but an earlier commission to the sheriff of Nottinghamshire, dated March 30, specifies only Wyclif and Hereford and does not mention the "English and Latin" qualification.[85]

H. G. Richardson admits that the letters patent cited by Knighton are genuine enough, but he says that "the other details of the chronicler's story have little basis."[86] There was, however, clearly some talk among the Lords and Commons about suspect writings at this time, but whether the subject of the Scriptures in English came up, we cannot tell. The tradition in circulation at the time of *Against Them* was that the clergy of the realm, led by both archbishops, Canterbury and York, attempted to suppress a current English translation of the entire Bible as well as other translations of the Gospels. Gasquet points out the Foxe reading of "Bible" for "bill" in his edition of *Against Them* and suggests that the incident referred to an attempt of the clergy to sanction an approved vernacular translation.[87] Perhaps John of Gaunt and his partisans were objecting to the phasing out of the already beloved EV by the new-fangled LV! A valid objection to LV would have been that it was less faithful to the literal meaning of the Vulgate. We know that Gaunt's brother Thomas of Woodstock, the Duke of Gloucester, possessed a lavish copy of EV. In fact, this was the Egerton Bible on display in the King's Library at the British Museum, labeled as "The English Bible, Wycliffe's Translation," which originally inspired Gasquet to question the Wycliffite connections with the Middle English Bible.[88] It is rubricated for public liturgical use and contains a lectionary, or table of liturgical readings, at the end.[89]

Gasquet considers Gloucester's ownership of this and other English Scriptures (a Psalter and two books of Gospels) to be evidence of their non-Wycliffite nature, since Gloucester was a firm supporter of Archbishop

Arundel.[90] Others, of course, argue the other way round, assuming the Wycliffite nature of the Bibles and taking Gloucester's possession of them as evidence of his connection with or interest in Lollardy.[91] There is, as Forshall and Madden noted,[92] a brief Wycliffite rant in the Egerton Bible lectionary, complaining about recent bishops, abbots, and others being honored as saints. This has been taken by Matti Peikola as evidence that Gloucester supported the Wycliffites' cause.[93] However, he points out that the common sanctoral that follows contains some of the objectionable saints, notably Thomas Becket and Swithun of Winchester;[94] and, even though the scribes were aware of the passage, neither of them seems to have composed it (or the lectionary itself),[95] and we cannot conclude that they, much less the duke, approved of it. Anne Hudson has recently given an example of a brief Lollard commentary, part of it quite strident, incorporated into Richard Rolle's Psalter commentary, and copied by several orthodox scribes with no sign of hesitation or unease.[96]

Let me add here some support to Gasquet's argument that the early and continued use of the English Bibles for the liturgy is one of the strongest indications for the widespread acceptance of the translations by the general populace.[97] Peikola reports that 40 percent of all surviving manuscripts of the Middle English Bible contain lectionaries,[98] and Gasquet's explanation is surely more plausible than Peikola's suggestion that these tables were placed in the Bibles by Wycliffites to persuade the ecclesiastical authorities of their orthodoxy,[99] and that the practice was continued by orthodox bookmakers once the Wycliffites lost control of English Bible reproduction.[100]

If a dispute over vernacular Scriptures did take place in 1388, it is certain that the current archbishop of York, Alexander Neville, did not participate in it, since he was not there; he was on the run from the Lords Appellant and was convicted of treason in absentia.[101] His replacement as archbishop was none other than the chancellor, Thomas Arundel, bishop of Ely; the papal provision was granted on April 3,[102] and it could hardly have reached England by June 4, when Parliament was dissolved.

The other parliament suggested by Hanna for the Bible debate, that of 1394, which was in session from January to March, conflicts with the final anecdote of *Against Them*, which is said to have taken place at the funeral of Queen Anne later that same year, at the end of July 1394.[103] In the former, the archbishops of Canterbury and York are said to have been opposed to Bible translation; in the latter, the archbishop of York at that time (1394), Thomas Arundel, identified as the current archbishop of Canterbury at the time of the writing of *Against Them*, is shown to be in favor of Bible translation. Here is the story:

> Also the bishop of Canterbury, Thomas Arundel, that now is, said a sermon in Westminster, there-as were many hundred people at the burying of Queen Anne, of whose soul God have mercy, and in his commendings of her he said it was more joy of her than of any woman that ever he knew, for notwithstanding that she was an alien born, she had on English all the four Gospelers, with the doctors upon them. And he said she had sent them unto him, and he said they were good and true, and commended her in that she was so great a lady and also an alien, and would so lowly study in so virtuous books. And he blamed in that sermon sharply the negligence of prelates and of other men, insomuch that some said he would on the morrow leave up his office of chancellor and forsake the world—and then it had been the last sermon that ever they heard.[104]

Note the word "last" in the final line. In Dove's base manuscript, the Wycliffite Trinity version, the text reads: "and þan it hadde be the lest sermoun þat euere þei herde." This makes sense: if Arundel forsook the world, this sermon would be his *last*, and he would never preach another sermon. Deanesly accepted this reading, but Bühler and Dove adopt the reading of the other, non-Wycliffite, medieval manuscript (Morgan), which has *best* instead of *lest*, producing a clause that does not make syntactic or semantic sense: "and then it had been the best sermon that ever they heard." It has been taken to mean: "it *would have been* the best sermon they had ever heard if Arundel had carried out his impulse to forsake the world and never preach again." This is how Mary Dove reads it: "It is difficult to gauge the tone of these words, but presumably those who thought Arundel would 'forsake the worlde' judged it 'the best sermoun that evere they herde' because he would no longer be in a position to prohibit the English Bible."[105] But this is just after they heard him praise Queen Anne to the skies for reading the Gospels in English! Rather, we must conclude that people thought it the best sermon they ever heard for two reasons: because he approved of the English Scriptures, and because he disapproved of unworthy clergy and laymen.[106]

Gasquet cites John Strype's acceptance of the historicity of this account, which shows, Strype says, that Archbishop Arundel "was for the translation of the Scriptures into the vulgar tongue, and for the laity's use thereof."[107] This certainly seems to be the purport of the story, as told by our author. His account of Arundel's sermon on this occasion was taken as historical by Herbert Workman in his exhaustive work on Wyclif,[108] and it is also accepted by Sven Fristedt,[109] and by Jonathan Hughes in his recent life of Arundel in the *Oxford Dictionary of National Biography*, reporting that the archbishop on this occasion expressed a desire to give up his chancellorship and to forsake the world.[110] It is also taken as historical by Katherine Walsh, who says that "it is unlikely that the remarks made by Archbishop Thomas Arundel in his sermon at Anne's funeral in 1396 [*sic*] were intended as a criticism of vernacular scriptures."[111] She adds: "Anne had grown up in a climate of easy availability of vernacular bibles, she possessed her own and she belonged in a tradition of patronage of this genre by the House of Luxembourg—the most spectacular example is the six-volume, exquisitely illuminated German bible made at Prague in the court *atelier* between 1387 and 1405 and commissioned by Anne's brother, the King of the Romans Wenceslaus of Bohemia."[112]

Anne's previous ownership of the Gospels in Czech, German, and Latin has been assumed from a passage in Wyclif's treatise *De triplici vinculo amoris*, in which he rails against the foolishness of those who damn writings as heretical because they are in English and deal sharply with the sins of their country. He then speaks of the possibility that Queen Anne had the Gospel set out in three languages, Bohemian, German, and Latin, and to hereticize her for this would be, implicitly, a Luciferian pride.[113] Johann Loserth criticizes those who take this possibility as a statement of fact,[114] and the same is true of Workman.[115] Loserth also points out that the whole passage in defense of the vernacular is obviously out of context, "so that it must be looked upon as a note, which by some hasty transcriber has been inserted in the wrong place" in the treatise.[116] What the passage says, in effect, is that criticizing the use of English in matters of religion would be like criticizing the new queen for having the Scriptures in her vernaculars of Czech and German—if she did.

We can sum up by saying that even though Richard Ullerston's treatise in favor of translating the Bible into English may have been associated with the debate on the subject that was taking place at the beginning of the century, he may have added further reasons after the bishops and other clergy passed the requirement, in 1407 and again in 1409, that new translations had to be approved by local bishops. This legislation likely sparked a new flurry of debate on the subject, of which Ullerston's hastily supplemented treatise was an early manifestation. The author of the English tract took advantage of it and freely drew on his arguments to make many of the same points, and then went off on his own to denounce a Dominican opposer of translation, John Tille, who tried to persuade the bishop of London and a hundred other listeners that St. Jerome himself was against biblical translation. Our author then recounted that the two archbishops and other clergy back in the time of Richard II were indeed against the Bible translations then in circulation, but that their efforts were opposed by John of Gaunt and the other laity, represented by the Lords and Commons of Parliament. And finally he recalled that a subsequent archbishop of York, who was now archbishop of Canterbury, expressed warm approval of the Gospels in English with commentaries that Queen Anne had submitted to him for his inspection. (This sounds like a complete set of *Glossed Gospels*; if so, it has not survived.) The author of *Against Them* would be affirming that these translations were already approved, and that any newer translations would simply have to be submitted to just the sort of episcopal inspection that Arundel performed for Queen Anne.

Dives and Pauper and the *Longleat Sunday Gospels*

The dialogue *Dives and Pauper*[117] was composed by a friar, perhaps a Franciscan, who reveals that he is writing in the year 1405.[118] He presents one of his interlocutors, the affluent layman Dives, as complaining that people are saying that the Bible should not be read by the unlearned laity, not even to teach it to their children (I modernize spelling and verb forms): "Reason giveth that men should teach their children God's Law and good thews [morals], and for to take heed to God that made us of nought and bought us so dear. But now men say that there should no lewd [uneducated] folk intermit them of [involve themselves in] God's Law, nor of the Gospel nor of Holy Writ, neither to ken it nor to teach it."[119] The other dialoguist, Pauper, who like his author seems very friarlike, responds that this is not right: "That is a foul error and well perilous to man's soul, for each man and woman is bound after his degree to do his business to know God's Law, that he is bound to keep. And fathers and mothers, godfathers and godmothers, are bound to teach their children God's Law, or else do [cause] them be taught."[120] Later on, Dives says that "God's Law is forgotten and defended [prohibited], that men shall not ken it, nor have it in their mother tongue,"[121] and this time Pauper lets the complaint pass by, without comment or correction. Dives's words have regularly been taken to refer to the provincial constitutions that were enacted at Oxford in 1407 and promulgated in 1409, and the dialogue consequently dated to 1410 or so.[122] However, there is good reason to think that Dives is not referring to any official restrictions against English Bibles. As I have stated before, and as we shall see in detail in Chapter 5, the constitutions did not forbid the translation of the Scriptures into English.

We should come to the same conclusion about a later work of the *Dives* author, which we can call the *Longleat Sunday Gospels*, that it too was written before the constitutions were issued.[123] The work consists of a new English translation of each of the Sunday Gospels and an explication of the text. The author says here that the teaching of the Gospel in English is prohibited, but only by *some* prelates ("thoghu it be these dayis defendit and inhibight be somme prelatis that men schulde techin the Gospel in Englich"),[124] which means that he is not referring to any legislation passed by *all* of the prelates of the southern province. He goes on to say, addressing the layman to whom he sends this compilation,

> Lief [dear] friend, sith it is leaveful to preach the Gospel in English, it is leaveful to write it in English, both to the teacher and to the hearer, if he ken [knows how to] write. For by writing is most secure examination of man's speech; and by writing, God's Law may best be couth [known] and best kept in mind. And therfore, lief friend, although some prelates have defended [forbidden] me to teach the Gospel and to write it in English, yet none of them hath defended you, nor may defend you, to ken the Gospel in English, that is your kindly [natural] language.[125]

This has been taken to mean that the reader had a "privileged position . . . apparently beyond the reach of episcopal enquiry even though the preacher himself might be persecuted."[126] The conclusion is based on the supposition that the constitution regulating Bible "reading" is already in force. But the author says at the beginning of his comment that reading the Bible in English is lawful to anyone who can read. He himself, unfortunately, has been specifically prohibited by certain bishops from teaching the Gospel and producing an English translation of the Gospel, but no bishop, he says, would be able or permitted to impose such a prohibition upon his reader.

He again contrasts his position with that of his reader, saying that though he himself is in danger for translating the Gospel, no bishop may forbid his friend from reading it: "Sith I have written the Gospel to you in well great dread and persecution, ye that be in such secureness that no prelate may let you nor disease you for kenning nor for keeping of the Gospel, ken it and keep it with good devotion, as ye will answer to Christ at the Day of Doom."[127] It is unlikely that he is speaking only of his friend, and suggesting that he is of such high standing that no bishop would dare to risk his displeasure. Rather, he would seem to be saying that there is no rule against laymen reading biblical translation and no grounds for lawfully imposing such a rule.

One thing we can be certain of: he has never heard of a general mandate from the archbishop and the other bishops of the province of Canterbury forbidding anyone from reading (whether lecturing upon or simply perusing) a new English translation of the Scriptures until it has been approved by his or her local bishop.

He goes on to speak of an attempt, undoubtedly again on the part of some bishops, to place unwonted restrictions upon preaching, and also, surprisingly, to venerate statues and pictures more than is proper:

> And as ye may hear, now preaching and teaching of the Gospel and of God's Law is arted [restricted] and letted more than it was wont to be, therefore take goodly the teaching that cometh to you freely. And though the persecution of Diocletian and Maximian be now newly begun to let teaching and preaching of God's word and God's Law and to compel men to worship graven images of stone and of tree, stand ye stiff in the faith, and worship ye yon God above all thing. And think that imagery and paint is but a book to the lewd people for to steer them to think on God and other saints and to worship God above all thing, and saints in their degree, as the Law showeth well, *De Cons.*, D. 3, c. *Perlatum.*[128]

It may be, however, that he is saying that the strictures against preaching and teaching are equivalent by counteracting the true purpose of religious art. The canon of Gratian that he cites, *Perlatum*, an excerpt from Pope Gregory the Great's letter to Bishop Serenus of Marseilles, can be read as authorizing literate persons to read the Bible:

> It is reported to us that, fired by inconsiderate zeal, you have destroyed images of saints under the alleged excuse that they should not be adored. We praise you for forbidding them to be adored, but we rebuke you for breaking them up. Tell me, brother, what priest has ever done or been heard of doing what you did? It is one thing to adore a picture and quite another to learn from the story the picture tells what is to be adored. For what writing [or: Scripture] does for those who read it, a picture does for uneducated people who look at it, for in it the ignorant see what they should follow, reading it even though they know not letters. Therefore, especially for the multitude of people, the picture takes the place of reading.[129]

The Longleat commentator ends by recommending that his friend not only read the Sunday Gospels in the following pages, but also the Gospels generally and the other books of the Bible:

> And sometime, when ye may, read of the Gospel and of God's Law, that ye may the more know your God and the more love Him and wit the better when ye do well and when amiss. Therefore read in books of God's Law, for not only they be blessed that hear God's Word and keep it, but also the teachers and the readers of God's Word be blessed of God. And therefore St. John saith in the Book of God's Privities, *Beatus qui legit et qui audit verba propheciae hujus et servat ea que in ea scripta sunt*, "Blessed be he that readeth and heareth the words of this prophecy and of God's Law and keepeth things that be writ therein" (Apoc. 1.3).[130]

The Longleat author tells us in one of his Sunday commentaries, on the Gospel of the Good Samaritan, that many bishops and other churchmen were opposed to the idea of allowing the laity to have easy access to the Scriptures, and he gives a reason for it: they themselves are so ignorant about fundamentals that they want to keep the people in deeper ignorance so that they might seem wise: "Many prelates and men of Holy Church be so lewd that they ken not answer, nor they ken well hear [the] Creed, and therefore they defend [prohibit] English books of God's Law, and suffer books of the Fiend's law. . . . They love no multiplication of God's Law, for they would not be asked nor opposed. And, for many of them be well lewd, therefore they would keep the people in overdone lewdness, that themselves in their lewdness might seem wise."[131] Once again, this is clearly not said in the context of a general provincial prohibition.

The upshot of this chapter is that there was no prohibition on translating the Scriptures into English at the turn of the fifteenth century, though some scholars and preachers and even bishops (to judge from the Longleat author) were beginning to think it advisable. Another testimony to this notion is found in *The Chastising of God's Children*, written around this time. The author, addressing a nun whom he is directing, says that some are against it, because of the inadequacy of English, but he allows it:

> Many men reprove it to have the Matins or the Psalter or the Gospels or the Bible in English, because they may not be translated into vulgar, word by word as it standeth, without great circumlocution, after the feeling of the first writer, the which translated that into Latin by teaching of the Holy Ghost. Nevertheless, I will not reprove such translation, nor I reprove not to have them on English, nor to read on them where they may stir you more

> to devotion and to the love of God. But utterly to use them in English and leave the Latin, I hold it not commendable, and namely in them that be bound to say their Psalter or their Matins of Our Lady.[132]

This antitranslation movement, however, was of recent vintage, and it inspired some strong opponents, notably Richard Ullerston and his vernacular inheritor in the treatise *Against Them*, who cited prominent lay supporters, led by John of Gaunt, and also Thomas Arundel, the current archbishop of Canterbury, when he was archbishop of York and chancellor of England.

CHAPTER 5

The Provincial Constitutions of 1407

The Constitution on Bible Translation (*Periculosa*) and the Middle English Bible

The Oxford constitutions were passed in November 1407, and then, two further convocations later, were confirmed at the meeting in London in January 1409, after being discussed "by repeated promulgation" (*repetita promulgatione*) but left unchanged; in the following April, they were ordered by Archbishop Arundel to be put into effect throughout the province.[1] They have often been regarded as the sole work of Arundel himself; and *Periculosa*, the meaning of which should be very simple, has been interpreted as forbidding English translations altogether, "prohibiting scriptural translation on the authority of Jerome."[2] We are told by one historian that in virtue of this legislation, "the Wycliffite translations of the Bible were outlawed," and "for the next 125 years, it was illegal to make or own any Wycliffite Bible in England without special license, and anyone caught in possession of a copy could in theory be tried for heresy and burnt to death."[3] Others assure us that the legislation "banned the Lollard Bible,"[4] or that "possession of the Lollard Bible was prohibited after 1409,"[5] or that all English Bible translation and reading was forbidden,[6] that the mere possession of an English Bible "was an offence punishable by death"[7] or "sent people to the flames."[8] Advocacy of translating the Bible was "labeled outright heresy."[9] The constitution "categorically prohibited all disputation on this issue."[10] Even before this, we are told, "making a translation of the Bible from the official Latin Vulgate of Jerome was an act that challenged the authority of the church and initiated linguistic separation from the wider Latin-speaking church in Europe."[11]

Let us examine these claims in light of the actual text of the legislation, aided by Gasquet's analysis, and then examine how the EV and LV should have fared, or actually did fare, if or when the mandate was enforced. Let me begin by quoting what Sir Thomas More said about the "constitution provincial" on Bible translation: "Many men talk of it, but no man knoweth it."[12]

Periculosa reads as follows:

> Periculosa quoque res est, testante beato Hjeronymo, textum Sacre Scripture de uno in aliud idioma transferre, eo quod in ipsis translationibus non de facili idem sensus in omnibus retinetur, prout idem beatus Hjeronymus, etsi inspiratus fuisset, se in hoc sepius fatetur errasse. Statuimus igitur et ordinamus ut nemo deinceps textum aliquem Sacre Scripture auctoritate sua in linguam Anglicanam vel aliam transferat per viam libri, vel libelli, aut tractatus, nec legatur aliquis hujusmodi liber, libellus, aut tractatus jam noviter tempore dicti Johannis Wicliffe sive citra compositus, aut in posterum componendus, in parte vel in toto, publice vel occulte, sub pena majoris excommunicationis majoris, quousque per loci diocesanum, seu, si res exegerit, per concilium provinciale, ipsa translatio fuerit approbata. Qui vero contra hoc fecerit, ut fautor hereseos et erroris similiter puniatur.[13]

Here is Gasquet's translation (I supply in brackets the parts that he omits; the italics are his):

> It is dangerous, as St. Jerome declares, to translate the text of Holy Scripture out of one idiom into another, since it is not easy in translations to preserve exactly the same meaning in all things [and Jerome himself, even though he was inspired, admits that he has often been in error in this matter]. We therefore command and ordain that henceforth no one translate any text of Holy Scripture into English or any other language in a book (*per viam libri*), booklet, or tract, and that no one read any book, booklet, or tract of this kind lately made in the time of the said John Wyclif or since, or that hereafter may be made either in part or wholly, either publicly or privately, under pain of [major] excommunication until *such translation shall have been approved and allowed by the diocesan of the place, or* (if need be) *by the Provincial Council.* He who shall act otherwise let him be punished [similarly] as an abettor of heresy and error.[14]

In reprinting the 1894 article in the *Old English Bible*, Gasquet adds the Latin, and italicizes the adverb emphasizing the newness of the designated compositions: "jam *noviter* . . . compositus" ("now *newly* composed"). His comment on the mandate is:

> Now it is obvious from the words of the decree that in this there is no such absolute prohibition as is generally represented. All that the fathers of the Council of Oxford forbade was unauthorized translations. The fact that no mention is made of any Wycliffite translation of the entire Bible is not without its significance, and in view of the Lollard errors then prevalent, and of the ease with which the text of Holy Scripture could be modified in the translation in any and every manuscript, so as apparently to be made to support those views, the ordinance appears not only prudent and just, but necessary.[15]

We note that it is the *reading*, not the possession, of a recent unlicensed translation that is prohibited.[16] The literal translation of this clause is "nor is any such book to be read." Moreover, the reading intended is not private perusal but formal reading, that is, lecturing or expounding, as in the Oxford statute, "unless he has read a book of the canon of the Bible or a book of the *Sentences* or of the *Histories*" ("nisi legerit aliquem librum de canone Biblie vel librum *Sentenciarum* vel *Historiarum*"),[17] and as it was explained in the previous constitution, *Quia insuper*: no treatise from Wyclif's time onward "is to be read in schools, halls, hospices, or any other places" in the province, "or taught from it" ("legatur in scholis, aulis, hospitiis, sive aliis locis quibuscumque . . . sive secundum ipsum doceatur") until approved for publication by university committee.[18] This will be made clearer when we look at William Lyndwood's explanation of the constitution.

We note too that a translation need be approved only once for each diocese (or for the whole province, by a council), meaning that copies of it would be thenceforward allowed; and there is no requirement to give licenses to individual readers. Perhaps the clergy, speaking in the archbishop's name, had in mind a license in the book itself, like the modern nihil obstat and imprimatur, or the *Censure and Approbation* in the 1582 Rheims New Testament. We should also observe that conviction under this edict would not be of heresy, but, at most, of favoring heresy (as will be explained below). Hudson has characterized the effect of the legislation as forcibly closing down "debate about the legitimacy of biblical translation into the vernacular,"[19] but, taken at its face value, it would seem to be rather an invitation to enter into such debate.

It might strike us nowadays that this mandate was very impractical and difficult to enforce. There would be difficulty first of all in trying to ascertain the date of any given translation in any given manuscript, and then determining whether another manuscript contains the same translation or whether the translation has been altered, since each copy would have different foliations (but of course the same capitulations). All very true, but these problems did not seem to occur to the legislators who formulated the process, or, if they did, they did not worry them. Gasquet in his comment cited above seems to assume that every copy of every translation would have to be inspected. But the constitution does not say so and implies otherwise.

We should also note that the fifth constitution, *Similiter quia*, approved of the traditional method used in elementary schools of explicating Scripture: "Ordinamus quod magistri . . . se nullatenus intromittant . . . de expositione Sacre Scripture nisi in exponendo textum prout antiquitus fieri consuevit" ("We ordain that teachers . . . not be involved in the explanation of Holy Scripture except in explaining the text as has been the custom from of old"). The authoritative canonist William Lyndwood in his *Provinciale*, which he released for publication in 1434, takes this to mean that they should stick to the grammatical level and not go into mystical or moral levels, since this is beyond the capacity of their students.[20] It also means that there was no prohibition against explaining the Bible in one's native tongue.

Since modern scholars have grouped the two versions of the Middle English Bible, EV and LV, under the title of "Wycliffite Bible," it has seemed obvious to them that the Oxford and London councils were taking aim at them in their constitution. This could only be true, however, if the members of the convocations were not familiar with these translations and did not bother to inspect them—for doing so would have revealed that they were entirely without fault and therefore admissible for general use. This is the force of Gasquet's observation that the constitution does not refer to complete translations of the Bible, or name them as Wycliffite.

We must realize that these constitutions would have been discussed by both of the houses of convocation, the upper house of bishops, and the lower house of clergy proctors. If the clergy did examine these versions and found them to be straightforward renderings of the Latin text, they may also have concluded that they had been produced before Wyclif's time and were therefore outside the framework of the mandate. Or, if they were recognized as being recent enough to be contemporary with Wyclif in his controversial phase or finished after Wyclif's death, they would need to be given a stamp of approval, say, by having them examined or vouched for by a knowledgeable participant at the councils, like Bishop Philip Repingdon, whom I will discuss below. Let me say here that Repingdon is one of the persons most likely to have been involved in drawing up the constitutions, and he also may well have been one of the translators who worked on one or both of the two versions of MEB.

It may have been the treatise *Five and Twenty Books* that raised the alarm about Bible translations among the Canterbury clergy. This would be especially plausible if the treatise were read unattached to a copy of some form or part of an English Bible. But even if it had been encountered so attached, and even if the EV or LV text had been recognized and acknowledged as completely orthodox, there still might be suspicion that the translation was altered or glossed to match some of the heterodox and subversive opinions expressed by Simple Creature. If so, however, this suspicion did not dominate the formulation of the constitution, which does not call for the inspection of every work containing Scripture in English.

An example of the sort of book or treatise that the bishops were to be on the lookout for is the *Longleat Sunday Gospels*, discussed in Chapter 4, which contained a new translation of the Gospel passages read on the Sundays of the liturgical year, written after the same author composed *Dives and Pauper* in 1405. Presumably they would have found nothing objectionable about these translations, but the fact that the author admitted that some bishops had forbidden him to make translations would undoubtedly have given them pause.

Arundel's 1410 Endorsement of Nicholas Love, Who Recommends the English Bible for the Laity

What about a book like Nicholas Love's *Mirror of the Life of Jesus Christ*, which, while assuming that the laity should read the Bible in English (which I will explain below), contained only summaries of Scripture passages? Would it fall under the scope of *Periculosa*? In the view of Arundel himself, it obviously did not. Far from assuming that each local bishop should approve it for his own diocese, he recommended it for the entire province of Canterbury.

In a Latin note prefixed to many copies of Love's work (seventeen out of the surviving fifty-seven manuscripts), it is stated that, around the year 1410, the original copy of this work was presented by its compiler to Archbishop Thomas Arundel for inspection and due examination before it would be freely disseminated. After he inspected it for a few days, he returned it to the said author and commended and approved it in every particular, and, by his metropolitan authority, he decreed and mandated that it should be publicly disseminated as a Catholic work for the edification of the faithful and the confuting of heretics, or Lollards.[21]

It has been assumed by many scholars that Love was complying with the Oxford-London constitutions in getting a license for his book, but in fact his action fitted neither the requirement for theological tracts, which were to be submitted to a panel of university censors (see below), or for Bible translations, which were to be submitted to the local ordinary. Love was prior of Mount Grace in North Yorkshire, hence out of the province of Canterbury altogether; and the ordinary at London was not the archbishop of Canterbury but the bishop of London.

Love's book has been seen as an implicit or explicit attack on the "Wycliffite Bible," that is, the EV and LV editions of the Middle English Bible.[22] An alternative suggestion is that "Love makes the Bible irrelevant to lay devotion."[23]

The plain fact is, however, that on the first page of his treatise he commends the reading of the Bible in English by the laity (I modernize):

> There is no sin or wickedness but that he shall want it and be kept from it, the-which [= Every sin and wickedness will be lacking and kept away from the one who] beholdeth inwardly and loveth and followeth the words and the deeds of that Man in whom God's Son gave Himself to us into example of good living. Wherefore now both men and women and every age and every dignity of this world is stirred to hope of everlasting life. And for this hope and to this intent, **with Holy Writ**, also be written divers books and treatises of devout men, not only to clerics in Latin, but also in English to lewd men and women and them that be of simple understanding. Among the which be written devout meditations of Christ's life more plain in certain parts than is expressed in the Gospel of the four Evangelists.[24]

The words that I have boldfaced, "with Holy Writ," mean that "in addition to Holy Writ" there are other books written in English that the laity can read. If it does not mean that the Bible is available to be read in English, there would be no sense in mentioning the Bible in this context. And it is quite obvious that reading the Bible is thought to be a good thing.

The upshot is that, once again, Arundel is to be seen as a *supporter* of the English Bible rather than an opponent.

Condemnation of Wyclif's Nonbiblical Propositions on St. Patrick's Day, 1411

The claim is made by some students of these matters that Archbishop Arundel sent a copy of the Oxford constitutions to the Pisan pope John XXIII in 1412 and reiterated his condemnation of the Wycliffite Bible.[25] But in fact what Arundel sent to the pope, in 1411 and not 1412, was a collection of heterodox passages taken from the works of Wyclif. Arundel and his fellow bishops do mention the Bible, however, at the end of an account of Wyclif's activities, before discussing the method by which the errors were extracted, and I will analyze their comment in the next section.

We should remember that even works by Wyclif himself were not condemned in the provincial council at Oxford in 1407; rather, the sixth constitution, *Quia insuper*, required only that his works and the works of others from his time forward be first inspected by a board of twelve censors *before being allowed to be copied and lectured upon*. Such a committee was to be set up at Oxford or at Cambridge, or one at each university, as the archbishop would deem best.[26]

The next convocation took place in London in July 1408, and the one following, also in London, in January 1409, at which time, as we have seen, the Oxford constitutions were reaffirmed, and then, in April of 1409, ordered to be promulgated throughout the province. H. E. Salter believes that Arundel immediately in 1407 ordered an Oxford panel of twelve to be set up, and, after having learned at the July 1408 convocation that nothing had been done, wrote a letter of rebuke to Oxford, to which the university replied in a letter that Salter dates around August of 1408, preserved in a Cotton Library manuscript (Faustina C 7).[27]

It is my conclusion, however, that the kind of committee called for in *Quia insuper*, to screen works of Wyclif and others for publication, was never established. Rather, in the first convocation held after promulgation of the constitutions in 1409, namely the convocation that met in London in February and March of 1410, it was decided to set up the Oxford "Committee of Twelve" to search Wyclif's works for heresies and errors.[28] Also at this 1410 convocation, there occurred, among other things, the trials of John Whitehead and John Badby, and a new set of constitutions on the conduct of the clergy was passed, including one stating that heresy trials were not to be committed to simpletons and incompetents ("idiotis aut personis non competentibus").[29]

When the Committee of Twelve was concentrating on the task that Arundel set for them, that is, singling out Wyclif's errors, they wrote to him to explain that their progress was slow because of the large number of books, lectures, treatises, and *opuscula* that Wyclif had produced.[30] By the early part of 1411 they produced a collection of 267 censured excerpts from Wyclif's Latin works.[31] It is noteworthy that none of the denounced articles were taken from Wyclif's scriptural commentaries or concerned textual questions or matters of translation.[32]

The propositions were transmitted to Arundel and other bishops of the province of Canterbury, who had assembled in the chapter house of St. Paul's for the defense of the faith.[33] We know from a later letter of Arundel's, *Quia nos certas conclusiones*, June 23, 1411, that the final meeting of the bishops took place on March 17, 1411.[34] This gathering has been considered a convocation,[35] or, more recently, seen as part of the February 1410 convocation (with the date changed from March 1411 to March 1410).[36] It was, however, a *sui generis* meeting, best referred to as a committee. Another such special committee had been convoked by Archbishop Courtenay and held at Blackfriars on May 17–21, 1382, later referred to as the "Earthquake Council," in which twenty-four Wycliffite propositions were condemned. It consisted of a selection of bishops, theologians, and experts in canon and civil law.[37]

Arundel informs his addressees in *Quia nos*, five members of the University of Oxford, that the conclusions singled out by the twelve Oxford censors, who were appointed on the authority of the provincial council, were, by decree of the archbishop and his suffragans there present with him, given to Bishops Repingdon of Lincoln and Hallum of Salisbury to review, and then, at the St. Patrick's Day bishops' meeting, the transmitted articles were condemned by them and the other bishops present, among whom were Clifford of London, Beaufort of Winchester, Mascall of Hereford, Bubwith of Bath and Wells, and Chichele of St. David's. They and the books in which they appeared were condemned "on the authority of Holy Mother Church and the said provincial council"—that is, the council of February–March 1410, which had commissioned the excerpting of the errors.[38]

The New Wycliffite Bible Stratagem Announced, End of March 1411

However, before Arundel sent his letter of June 23, 1411, to Oxford requiring everyone to take an oath to avoid these propositions and the works containing them, and probably not long after the St. Patrick's Day meeting, perhaps before the end of March, he wrote a letter, *Miserator et misericors Dominus*, to John XXIII, in his name and the name of the other bishops of the province, sending him the condemned articles.[39]

In this letter, before describing the process by which the excerpts were made, Arundel gives a hard-hitting account of Wyclif's campaign against orthodoxy, ending thus: "Ipsam ecclesie sacrasancte fidem et doctrinam sanctissimam totis conatibus impugnare studuit, nove ad sue malitie complementum Scripturarum in linguam maternam translationis practica adinventa."[40] That is, to translate it "iconically," as much as possible, in the EV style: "The very faith and holy doctrine of the sacrosanct Church he strove with all his efforts to impugn—the stratagem of a new translation of the Scriptures into the mother tongue [having been] devised as a complement to his malice." Arundel makes no further reference to Bible translation, and none of the condemned theses refer to the subject.

The final ablative absolute in this sentence is a strangely weak and seemingly anticlimactic way of ending the summary of Wyclif's activities. As we saw in Chapter 3, such absolute constructions are ambiguous by nature and not looked upon with much favor in English; they are systematically disambiguated in LV. Here is the recommendation of Simple Creature: "In translating into English, manie resolucions moun make the sentence open, as an ablatif case absolute may be resolvid into these thre wordis, with covenable verbe, 'the while,' 'for,' 'if,' as gramariens seyn."[41] Modern scholars follow suit in this case; for instance, Margaret Deanesly translates it thus: "To fill up the measure of his malice, he devised the expedient of a new translation of the scriptures into the mother tongue."[42] That is, she specifies Wyclif as the agent—a definite possibility, but not clear in the text. Let me do a glossing of the sort used in interlinear Bibles, to be read in the order of the numbers:

2	**9**	**11**	**12**	**10**	**4**	**5**	**7**
of a new	***for***	***of his***	***malice***	***a complement***	***of the Scriptures***	***into***	***tongue***
nove	**ad**	**sue**	**malitie**	**complementum**	**Scripturarum**	**in**	**linguam**

6	**3**	**1**	**8**
the maternal	***translation***	***a stratagem***	***having been devised***
maternam	**translationis**	**practica**	**adinventa**

It should be clear that the main stress in this clause is on the *newness* of the translation, *nove* being unexpectedly placed at the beginning, far away from the substantive with which it goes, *translationis*. I suggest that Arundel and his colleagues were familiar with both EV and LV, and, recognizing their orthodoxy, believed them to antedate, at least in their inception if not completion, the Wycliffite stratagem of making a new translation, and therefore to fall outside the mandate to be vetted by bishops. The bishops and clergy were to be on the alert for any translations that, unlike EV and LV, distorted the text in ways that would promote Wyclif's malignant teachings.[43]

Deanesly interprets Arundel here to be attributing the *adinventio*, or devising, of the *practica*, or expedient, of a new Bible translation to Wyclif himself, while leaving open the question of who actually did the translating—that is, allowing for the possibility that his followers may have carried out or finished the project. In her view, this is what happened: Wyclif devised and promoted the idea, but "his secretary, John Purvey, did the bulk of the work."[44]

I am suggesting instead that the archbishop was allowing for the possibility that the actual devising as well as the carrying out of the project may have been the work of Wyclif's disciples. And, if he and his fellow bishops, notably Repingdon of Lincoln, were familiar with, as is likely, the treatise *Five and Twenty Books* (GP), Arundel was leaving open the question of whether its author was Wyclif himself or a similarly malicious spokesman for Wyclif. His mention of a Wycliffite Bible project at the end of his account of Wyclif in his letter to the pope also reflects the fear, expressed in *Periculosa*, that the work of mistranslating the text of Scripture is still ongoing, since the constitution first speaks of future translations before referring to recent translations.

With this understanding of the archbishop's statement, we can conclude that he left the *old* translations, the Early Version and the Later Version, safely in place to be read by the faithful, as entirely true to the inspired Word of God.

In arriving at this conclusion, I am simply following in the footsteps of Cardinal Gasquet. When he addresses *Periculosa*, Gasquet rightly points to the clergy's emphasis upon the newness of the censured translation enterprise. In reprinting his *Dublin Review* article in 1897, Gasquet provides part of the Latin text of *Periculosa*: "jam *noviter* tempore dicti Johannis Wycliff sive citra compositus, sive in posterum componendus," italicizing *noviter*. He could also have italicized *deinceps* ("from now on") at the beginning of *Periculosa*. In addition, he gives the heading of the constitution from Arundel's register, *Ne quis texta S. Scripture transferat in linguam Anglicanam*, which he renders, "that no one translate into English *passages* of Holy Scripture," as well as the Lambeth manuscript heading, *Ne textus aliquis S. Scrip. in linguam A. de cetero transferatur per viam libri aut tractatus* ("That no text of Sacred Scripture from henceforth be translated into the English tongue by way of book or tract"),[45] which he uses in his supplementary article as part of his argument that the constitution was not referring to complete translations of the Bible.[46]

Gasquet takes up the bishops' 1411 letter, *Miserator*, in his second article, in response to allegations of its meaning and importance from both F. D. Matthew and Frederic Kenyon. He begins by speaking of the 267 condemned passages: "It is at least remarkable that in the whole of this long list there is no mention whatever of the supposed translation."[47] He made the same point earlier about the Lollard interrogatories formulated after the Council of Constance.[48] He then addresses the passage cited above, on which "Kenyon relies to prove that Wyclif made *a* translation." Kenyon translates the passage thus: "filling up the measure of his malice by devising the expedient of a *new* translation of Scripture in the mother-tongue." It is Gasquet who italicizes "new," and he observes that Matthew omits it in his translation: "devising a plan of translation of the Holy Scriptures into the mother-tongue."[49] Gasquet says that the passage indicates that Arundel knew of some recognized translation that Wyclif tried to supersede by his own rendering, "suiting his translations to his heresies."[50] In other words, he is not referring to EV and LV here, but is worried about some new tendentious translations. Arundel had personally approved of the English translations current in the days of King Richard, and the Canterbury Councils of 1407 and 1409 (well into the reign of Henry IV, who himself owned an English Bible) gave a pass to whatever translations were in circulation before Wyclif's time; he and the other bishops of the province were only concerned to make sure the newer translations remained faithful to the Word of God.

Kenyon agrees with Gasquet that "the Lollards were persecuted, but not their Bible," and goes on to say: "Such hostility as was shown to this was only temporary, and was confined to a few persons, such as Archbishop Arundel."[51] However, Gasquet does not agree that the English Bible was Lollard, and he does not agree that Arundel was hostile to it. He says: "The very documents relied on as evidence of Archbishop Arundel's 'hostility' proceed not from him alone but from all the bishops of the province of Canterbury."[52] And, of course, they do not say what they have been made to say by the proponents of the thesis that the Church authorities condemned the Early Version and Later Version of the Middle English Bible.

CHAPTER 6

Treatment of the English Bible in the Fifteenth Century

The Proliferation of MEB Copies

Earlier I cited a dozen or so modern scholars who are convinced that the Canterbury Council of Oxford in 1407 legislated against the Middle English Bible. As one of them, Ralph Hanna, puts it, the constitutions formulated there "banned the Lollard Bible." But Hanna, like others, also holds that the ban was ineffectual: "The translation, in fact, turned out to be so good an idea that, whatever official pronouncements said, it could be re-appropriated to orthodoxy and used, without particular anxiety, as a convenient consultation text."[1] Mary Dove expresses a similar view in her chapter on censorship in *The First English Bible*.[2] Michael Sargent makes a telling comment: "What I find interesting is that Dove does not treat the expanding transmission of the text as a case of expansion and transmission (as would be done, for example, in the case of a text by Chaucer, or Hilton, or *Piers Plowman*), but as a case of the failure of censorship to achieve its goals—that is, not as a positive thing, but as the negative of a negative: the absence of the absence of the Wycliffite Bible."[3] Yet Sargent himself asserts that the constitutions of 1407–9 "were so spectacularly unsuccessful in accomplishing their primary aim of curtailing the circulation of the Wycliffite Bible."[4]

Kathleen Kennedy in her recent book *The Courtly and Commercial Art of the Wycliffite Bible* has given the same sort of assessment of the 1407–9 constitutions: the Wycliffite Bible was "illegal after 1409," and "thereafter translating the bible or reading a translation were heretical and criminal acts."[5] But she goes on to give a great deal of evidence that copies of the English Bible continued to be made in great abundance throughout the fifteenth century (in contrast to very little copying of the Latin Bible), both in London and in outlying districts, with no indication that it was a contraband writing that endangered its makers and users. For this discrepancy between actual illegality and seeming legality, she finds none of the current explanations, such as those of Hanna and Sargent and Anne Hudson,[6] or various rationalizations that have been put forward, to be satisfactory.[7]

An obvious solution to the problem, of course, is to deny the premise that the MEB, whether EV or LV, was illegal. This was Gasquet's position, which seems reasonable, as discussed above: since it is admitted by all today that there is nothing erroneous in EV or LV, the same assessment would have been made at the beginning of the fifteenth century, if the clergy of Canterbury considered the translations in their convocations at Oxford in 1407, when *Periculosa* was formulated, and at London in 1408 and 1409, when it was reviewed; and it must have passed muster as acceptable for general insruction, whether or not it was thought to have any Wycliffite connections in its production. Therefore, once we remove the "given" of condemnation, the proliferation of the MEB looks like the normal process of the usual "expansion and transmission of texts."

Misinterpretations of *Periculosa*, Now and Then

But we must face another question. If modern readers of *Periculosa* have misconstrued its meaning so badly, is it not possible that people of the Middle Ages came up with the same faulty understandings? That is the judgment of Eric Colledge: once the constitutions were passed, they were "thereafter interpreted by the ultra-cautious or the ultra-conservative as an out-and-out prohibition of the use of existing English Bibles."[8] He gives a tentative *terminus ante quem* of 1408 to *The Chastising of God's Children* because of its sentiment, cited at the end of Chapter 4 above, approving of English translations of the Scriptures as long as they do not detract from the recitation of the Latin liturgy. That is, he assumes that such overinterpretations of the ultra-cautious would have taken effect immediately.

Let us look at the evidence and judge each event or text by its merits. But we must be on the alert. Since most scholars from the nineteenth century to the present have so badly misunderstood the purport of *Periculosa*, it is altogether likely that they have similarly misinterpreted subsequent data to fit with their faulty assessment of the constitution. Specifically, most writers have inherited the assumption that EV and LV were Wycliffite in origin and were known as "the Wycliffite Bible," and that for that very reason were condemned by Archbishop Arundel. Accordingly they also assume that copies were sought out and suppressed and their owners punished, even condemned as heretics. Let us clear our minds of such assumptions and take another look, and see if and when we can conclude to overcautious condemnations of texts of the Early Version or the Later Version of the Middle English Bible.

Implementing *Periculosa*: Bishop Repingdon

The procedure assumed in the mandate of April 13, 1409, sent by Archbishop Arundel to the bishop of London, was that each of the bishops was to direct his archdeacons and all other jurisdictional superiors to explain the council's constitutions to all of the curates of the diocese, that is, all parish priests (rectors and perpetual vicars) and other priests having the care of souls. The usual way for this to happen would be for the archdeacon to call a chapter in each of the rural deaneries within his jurisdiction, at which every parish priest was to attend. A report from each of the bishops on the fulfillment of this obligation was due back by the feast of St. John the Baptist, June 24.

Arthur Ogle in his *Church Quarterly* review of 1900–1901 charges Gasquet with neglecting bishops' registers, and Mary Dove in 2007 says basically the same thing, that he ignored the records of heresy trials.[9] Let us begin by examining one register, that of Philip Repingdon, bishop of Lincoln from 1405 to 1419, asking, first of all, how the mandate was carried out. Lincoln was by far the largest diocese in the province, being divided into eight archdeaconries, extending from the Thames to the Humber estuary. Repingdon was a reformed Wycliffite and an earnest opponent of heresy. A month after he took office as bishop he directed the archdeacon of Huntingdon to search out and prosecute unlicensed preachers who were spreading heretical doctrines.[10] But it was one thing to issue an order like this and another to have it successfully executed, a very difficult matter with any kind of orders from above. The editor of Repingdon's register, Margaret Archer, tells of his vigorous efforts to remedy all sorts of abuses, and concludes: "At the end of his episcopate these abuses were still prevalent, and the problem of how to enforce the bishop's mandates, monitions, and injunctions was no nearer to a solution."[11]

Repingdon was one of the bishops who had formulated and approved the constitutions of 1407–9. He may also have been one of the supporters or even translators of the Bible project. Repingdon has already been singled out as a likely participant on the commonly accepted theory that the MEB was a Wycliffite enterprise, but Jeremy Catto suggests that he would have favored it even after his rejection of Wyclif's doctrines. As noted above, he sees a favorable attitude to Bible translation among other orthodox residents of Queen's College, Oxford, where Repingdon resided in 1386–87.[12]

Repingdon's episcopal register records the summons of the clergy of Canterbury to the Oxford council on November 28, 1407, to counter Satan's heretical activities.[13] In contrast, the summons to the London convocation on January 14, 1409, mentions only the matter of the papal schism and Council of Pisa.[14] The copy of the constitutions sent by the bishop of London to Lincoln was dated May 20, 1409, and it was not until June 28, four days after the deadline, that Repingdon ordered his archdeacons to "celebrate" the constitutions in the synods and chapters in their jurisdictions (that is, in each of the rural deaneries in the archidiaconate), at the same time reporting his action to the archbishop. The archdeacons were in turn to make a report by November 1.[15] One reason for the time lag, of course, was that multiple copies of the text of the constitutions would have had to have been made for distribution throughout the diocese.

There is no record of any of the required reports from the field in the register, let alone mention of any copy of an English Bible turned in by a cleric or parishioner from any of the more than 1,900 parishes in Repingdon's vast diocese (about 20 percent of all the parishes of England)[16] for him to peruse and approve (or not), in accord with the requirements of *Periculosa*.

It has been said that Repingdon's fairly frequent licensing of preachers in his diocese was in response to one of the constitutions that required such licensing,[17] which may be true even though the first such license was given in 1405, before the constitutions were first passed, and the second in 1408, before the constitutions were ordered to be implemented.[18] Furthermore, in the first surviving commission he set up for licensing preachers, in March 1413, he does refer to and paraphrase the first of the Oxford constitutions, *Quod nullus*, but he does so in a vague and rather distant way, as "a certain provincial constitution," as nothing in the forefront of current attention, and seems to quote it from memory.[19] But in the second such commission, ordered in November 1416, he refers to the form required by "the provincial constitution recently issued against evangelical detractors,"[20] which may be to a later mandate.

Repingdon's visitation records from May to June 1413 have survived, in which some charges of heresy were made.[21] Later that year Archbishop Arundel summoned a convocation to discuss the spread of heresy and other problems,[22] and afterward Repingdon ordered his archdeacons to conduct investigations on the six articles of inquiry determined at the convocation: searching for (1) heretics or heresy suspects or supporters; (2) apostates from religion (religious who have abandoned their order) or curates not in their proper locations; (3) sufficient chaplains in hospitals; (4) concubinary clerics and their concubines; (5) married men exercising ecclesiastical jurisdiction; and (6) other beneficed clergy who neglect residency requirements.[23]

Shortly after this, in January 1414, the Lollard rising led by John Oldcastle occurred in the Lincoln diocese, and in February Repingdon called for a council of cathedral clergy to investigate the heresy that was rampant in the city and diocese, though in fact the council may not have taken place.[24] A month later, he conducted an investigation into heresy in Oxford,[25] by which time Wycliffism was all but extinct at the university.[26] At the convocation held in London in 1416, the new archbishop, Henry Chichele, issued on July 1 a constitution against heresy, *Cum inter ceteras*, requiring every bishop and archdeacon to make inquiries at least twice a year in each rural deanery concerning persons suspected of heresy, including those possessing suspect books written in English ("libros suspectos in lingua vulgari anglicana conscriptos habentes"),[27] which was immediately put into effect by Repingdon.[28]

The formulary of the new constitution would be sufficient to cover the terms of *Periculosa*, but, of course, would not single out English Bibles for attention. The constitution was specifically invoked, along with its wording ("libros suspectos in lingua vulgari conscriptos"), in the inquisition ordered in the case of a perpetual vicar named John Bagworth, because he had several suspect books written both in the vernacular and in Latin ("eo quod ipse quamplures libros suspectos in vulgari et latino sermone conscriptos").[29]

I go into details about Repingdon because E. F. Jacob, in introducing his edition of Archbishop Chichele's register, says that "in 1413 Bishop Repingdon of Lincoln directed his archdeacons to confiscate all unauthorized translations of the bible and other suspected English works," citing folio 83 of Repingdon's register.[30] But all that is contained on that page is part of lengthy paperwork about the setting up of a chantry.[31] He undoubtedly means "folio 38," which contains the text of the constitutions of 1409;

and the business about the confiscation of English Bibles is simply Jacob's overreading of *Periculosa*. Jacob is equally faulty in saying that "in 1416 he had to forbid the citizens of Lincoln to attend sermons in English under pain of excommunication," citing folios 176v–177r of the register.[32] But what the register contains there is a commission to the archdeacon of Northampton to carry out the provisions of *Cum inter ceteras* (Chichele's constitution of 1416).[33]

The upshot is that there is no indication that Bishop Repingdon had any opinion about English Bibles or took any action concerning them. But since he was such a conscientious enforcer of the provincial constitutions, he may well have followed the requirement of *Periculosa* and examined copies of the EV or LV translation to make sure that they had not been tampered with and were still the same orthodox renderings with which he had been long familiar. If so, they would need no further approval. Other bishops of the province may have given their approval as well, or confirmed that they needed no approval. As we will see, Thomas More says that bishops in his day were approving *readers* of English Bibles, rather than the Bibles themselves (which obviously needed no approval). This sort of action is not likely to have made it into bishops' registers,[34] which in any case have only been sporadically preserved and not all of those edited. For instance, of the bishops of the eighteen sees of the province who were in office in 1409, only twelve registers have survived, and of these only six have been edited.[35] And roughly the same rates of survival and editing hold for the rest of the fifteenth century. Specifically, there are no extant registers for William Lyndwood's tenure of the episcopacy of St. David's (1442–46) or for Reginald Pecock in the dioceses of St. Asaph (1444–50) and Chichester (1450–57). We will hear about both Lyndwood and Pecock below.

What do we find in the other printed or calendared registers of Repingdon's time? The register of Robert Mascall of Hereford has only the summons to the convocation at Oxford in November 1407 to deal with heresy.[36] Bishop Hallum of Salisbury's register records that the 1409 constitutions were fully published in the cathedral and in the archdeaconries of the diocese,[37] but no follow-up (that is, the required response to the archbishop by June 24) is recorded.[38] Bishop Robert Rede of Chichester reported to the archbishop on June 5 that the constitutions were duly published and that the required actions and reports would be accomplished as soon as possible.[39] No action seems to have been recorded in the register of Bishop Edmund Stafford of Exeter,[40] and there is nothing in the register of Bishop Nicholas Bubwith of Bath and Wells.[41]

The Convocation of 1428 and the Role of William Lyndwood

The chief opponent of Wycliffite ideas after Repingdon's time was the Carmelite friar Thomas Netter of Walden, who in his *Doctrinale antiquitatum fidei catholice ecclesie*, written in the second and third decades of the fifteenth century, deals with the 267 condemned articles of Wyclif and the 45 articles condemned at the Council of Constance in 1415, as well as with various trials of Wycliffites, most recently the trial of William White in 1428.[42] It has been noted with some surprise that he never refers to "the Wycliffite Bible" in this massive work, which fills 1,500 large double-columned pages in its eighteenth-century edition.[43] He does not show the slightest interest in the text of the Bible, whether in Latin or English, or its possible distortion.[44] What he cares about is misinterpretations of the text. At one point he apostrophizes Wyclif: "In my judgment, therefore, O Wyclif mine, by corrupting the sense of Scripture thou deniest the Scriptures, all the more injuriously as thou hast pledged them a false kiss through hypocrisy, the which Manichaeus had not done. Many perhaps believe not that thou art a falsary. In how many places above have I already shown the corruptions of the Scriptures put forth by thyself, and the very laws of God foully vitiated by thy presumptions?"[45] He proceeds to give five examples of such falsifications, all taken from Wyclif's treatises.[46]

There is very little evidence in these early days that anyone was ever formally suspected of heresy from the fact of possessing an English Bible. Two cases are often cited by scholars from the convocation of 1428–29, those of John Galle and Ralph Mungin,[47] but only the first is relevant, namely, that of the London chaplain John Galle, or Gale, who is not otherwise known (I will treat Mungin below).

Galle was brought before convocation as already suspect (*notatus*) of heresy and error. When interrogated, he confessed to nothing wrong, maintaining that his belief was that of a good Catholic in accord with the teaching of Holy Mother Church. But the fact that he was found to be in possession of the Gospels in English obviously aroused the interest of the synod, especially with the title given to it, *Book of the New Law*, which may have been a Lollard way of referring to the New Testament.[48]

How would the examination of Galle be conducted in convocation? We have seen an array of overreadings of the constitution *Periculosa* on the part of modern scholars, some so extreme as to seem ludicrous. Would such misinterpretations be possible on the part of the assembled clergy some two decades after the mandate was passed? We have noted Colledge's judgment that once the Oxford constitutions were passed, they were sometimes overinterpreted as prohibiting all existing English Bibles.[49] We will see some indications later on that he is at least partially right on this point: some people did think there was an absolute ban on English Scriptures. But we can be morally certain that no one would have been able to get away with such a mangling of the sense of the constitutions at this convocation, since the proceedings were conducted under the watchful eye of the chief arbiter of law for the province, William Lyndwood, official of the court of Canterbury (that is, chief judge of the appeals court of the province of Canterbury).[50] We will see his views of *Periculosa* at length below. He may in fact have been the formulator of the mandate, or at least involved in its composition.

Born around 1375, Lyndwood was already rector of a parish in Lincolnshire when Repingdon became bishop, and one of the latter's first actions in 1405 was to renew Lyndwood's study leave (discussed above).[51] He finished his double doctorate, in canon and civil law, within two years, probably at Oxford, in time for the provincial council held there in November 1407. In September 1408, Lyndwood was appointed to be official (judge) of the consistory court of the diocese of Salisbury, by the bishop, Robert Hallum.[52] Lyndwood was immediately put to use by Arundel's successor as archbishop of Canterbury, Henry Chichele, a former associate of his at Oxford,[53] first as his chancellor and simultaneously auditor of causes in his court of audience (1414) and then as official of Canterbury (1417).

Let us try to imagine some of the comments that might have been made when Galle's Gospel book was examined, perhaps by a joint session of the upper and lower houses of convocation, on July 21, 1428:

Master Lyndwood. Sir John, bring hither thy testament.

Archbishop Chichele.[54] We must determine if it contains a translation not approved by his bishop, my lord of London, or not previously approved by an earlier council. Who can tell us?

John Southam, Archdeacon of Oxford.[55] Leave it to me; I have examined many volumes of English Scriptures over the years, being archdeacon when *Periculosa* was put into effect, and also as official of Lincoln, and I have never seen but two different renderings of the Gospel, the old Oxford version that was, and still is, used to help rectors learn their Vulgate, and a revised version, that also seems to have been made at Oxford. Ah, yes, 'tis the original rendering; one can easily tell from the two-score *forsooth*s in the first chapter of Matthew: it reads, for instance, "Isaac forsooth begat Jacob; Jacob forsooth begat Judas and his brethren; Judas forsooth begat Phares and Zaram of Thamar; Phares forsooth begat Esrom," and so on. In contrast, there are no *forsooth*s in the revised version. Some believe that removing the *forsooth*s betrayeth the Word of God, by leaving all the *autem*s unaccounted for. As you recall, the Latin reads: "Isaac *autem* genuit Jacob, Jacob *autem* genuit Judam et fratres eius, Judas *autem* genuit Phares et Zara de Thamar, Phares *autem* genuit Esrom," and on and on. But most of us judge such matters to be merely a question of style.

RICHARD FLEMING, BISHOP OF LINCOLN.[56] Clearly Sir John falleth not under the constitution, since both of these versions have long been approved. Verily, forsooth, we have had to instruct our pastors to cease bringing them in for inspection.

ARCHDEACON SOUTHAM. As memory serveth, we determined this very point when the constitution was first formulated, in the month of November, MCCCCVII, at the Oxford council.

MASTER LYNDWOOD. Yes, that is definitely true.

ARCHBISHOP CHICHELE. I was not present at the Oxford meeting, but I recall hearing this manner of discussion during the subsequent year, and also at the convocation at Paul's in January when the Oxford constitutions were confirmed.[57]

BISHOP FLEMING. How so, was it adjudged that these translations were in use before the time of the heretic John Wyclif?

ARCHDEACON SOUTHAM. The modified version was found to be substantially the same as the original version, except for grammatical forms, *et cetera similia*. No one could remember when the original came into use. I recollect speaking to my uncle Thomas about it, who was archdeacon before me. He had been at Oxford since shortly after the first visitation of the plague, and it seemed to him that the old translation had always been available for copying. There was, however, some talk that it was inspired by Master Wyclif or carried out by some of his disciples. But whether this was so or not is a question for the chronicles, making no difference to our new law. Many of us at the Oxford council were already well familiar with the rendering, and we agreed that it was a true and sound version of the Holy Scriptures throughout, perfectly designed to explain the Vulgate text to inexpert Latinists. Moreover, by that time, this rendering and the modified version were already in use in various parish churches throughout the realm. Therefore, both versions stood approved, and this approval was renewed at a convocation in London in the following year, MCCCCVIII,[58] when the constitutions were confirmed.

Archbishop Chichele I see that we are agreed on this point. We should therefore return the book to Sir John.

Master Lyndwood. In order to be certain in this case, however, I suggest that we examine, *ad cautelam*, some passages likely to be tampered with by Lollards. The chief heresy of the *Wycliffistae* is the denial of transubstantiation. What of the chapters on the Last Supper? Sir Archdeacon, I pray thee, consult the Gospel of Matthew, in the sixth and twentieth chapter: sayeth it "This is my body"? Or is there something to suggest continued substance of bread? Or a merely symbolic presence of Our Lord?

Archdeacon Southam. No, it is straightforward, "This is my body." I find that the same is true of Mark, *capitulo quattuordecimo*, and Luke, *capitulo vicesimo secundo*. In Luke, *Hoc facite in meam commemorationem* is rendered as "Do ye this thing into my commemoration," with an added gloss, "or into mind of me," which seemeth to me a reasonable alternative.

Master Lyndwood. Well, then, let him keep it. Come, Sir John, take it back. Let me remind all here present that *Periculosa* does not censure the mere possession of a new and unauthorized rendering of Scripture but the formal *reading* thereof, that is, using it to instruct others about the Scriptures. I make this clear in the commentary on these constitutions in my *Provinciale*, which I hope to publish soon. You may, if you see fit, enact at this council or in the future a more stringent statute, decreeing that ownership alone or private use of unexamined translations be declared an offense; or you may require that all such translations be called in for inspection, to search for possible Lollard interventions; but for the present there is no obligation or authority, by law, to do so.

The above exchange is my own fantasy. What we do know is that at the end of the discussion of Galle's case, the convocation voted to have him transferred for further examination to the custody of his own ordinary, the bishop of London.[59] The meeting was then adjourned until the following November, the day after the feast of St. Martin *in hieme*.

One piece of business that the convocation took care of at this time was to approve the *Modus et forma procedendi et processus faciendi contra hereticos*, after it had been vetted by Lyndwood.[60] Another was the trial of the London priest Ralph Mungin; this is the other case that modern scholars cite from this convocation to demonstrate the operation of *Periculosa*. Mungin had been tried earlier under the bishop of London without resolution, and he was now to be tried before convocation.

In convocation trials, the sole judge was the archbishop acting as metropolitan; the suffragan bishops of the province and the other members of the gathering from the lower house served as his assessors.[61] Chichele began to preside over the Mungin case when it began on November 26, when the charges that had been leveled against him earlier were rehearsed: for the past twenty years (*per viginti annos elapsos*) he was defamed in Oxford University and elsewhere in the province concerning heresy and Lollardy. When asked whether he wished to abjure the articles, he replied that he did not think it right to do so.[62] On December 2, Chichele brought forward the earlier articles against Mungin (that Mungin did not think it lawful to bear arms against heretics in Bohemia, or to own private property); Mungin denied the truth of both charges, and the archbishop asked the bishop of London's vicar-general to produce testimony to the court proving the charges.[63]

On the next day, December 3, in front of a large assembly, Bishop Fleming stood in for Chichele, and Lyndwood, serving as promoter of the judge's office,[64] leveled seventeen additional articles against Mungin, the fourth of which stated that when he was in London he possessed and distributed books by Wyclif (presumably in Latin) and other books in English containing errors of Wyclif and of Peter Clerk (a heresy suspect whom Mungin admitted knowing, but without having been influenced by him). Mungin denied the contents of this article. But he did admit that twelve years earlier, or for the last twelve years (*per duodecim annos elapsos*), he possessed a book called *Trialogus* and also the *Evangelia* of Wyclif, which he sold to a chaplain named John Botte.[65]

The fifth charge was that in the said books (*in dictis libris*) there were heretical doctrines and opinions condemned by the Roman Church, which Mungin said was true—presumably limiting his admission to the books he admitted having (whereas Lyndwood's preformulated charge referred as well to the vernacular books of the previous article, which Mungin denied possessing). The sixth article charged Mungin with communicating such teaching, opinions, and books to various people, which he absolutely denied.[66]

On the day following, December 4, Chichele resumed the bench and admitted testimony supporting the two old charges, and then, without calling for further testimony proceeded to sentence. He found Mungin, both through a canonical inquistion and his judicial confession, vehemently suspect of opinions savoring of heresies and errors. In addition, he found two points proved against him, namely, the articles on Bohemia and private property; and finally he also found (without saying how) that Mungin knowingly possessed various books containing heresies and errors and had not revealed them to the local bishop or handed them over or destroyed them, as the law required.[67] For his pertinacious refusal to abjure in the face of all this, Mungin was convicted of more than vehement suspicion of heresy, and less than actual heresy: namely, of being reputed and pronounced as a heretic ("pro heretico, ut hereticum reputandum et pronunciandum"). However, even though convicted only as an "as-if heretic" and not as a "real heretic," he would still be liable to the penalties of a convicted heretic.[68] Such a conviction without repentance and abjuration could conceivably have brought with it the death penalty. But instead Mungin was sentenced to life imprisonment and penance in the prison of the bishop of London.[69]

The important point for our discussion here is that Mungin was not charged with having the Bible in English, nor did he admit it. He admitted having only two works, *Trialogus*, which was known to be by Wyclif, and Wyclif's *Evangelia*, after having admitted that he had passed on books by Wyclif and others containing heretical teachings; and since he was not convicted upon the testimony of witnesses, it must have been these admissions that were taken to prove the charge. Modern writers who insist on speaking of "the Wycliffite Bible" have assumed that the reference was to the Gospels of the EV or LV text of the Middle English Bible. But the first work, the *Trialogus*, was in Latin, and the *Evangelia* was also doubtless in Latin, referring either to one of his series of sermons on the liturgical Gospels, *Super Evangelia dominicalia* or *Super Evangelia de sanctis*,[70] or, perhaps, his last work, the unfinished *Opus evangelicum*,[71] or even the *Glossed Gospels*, which, however, are not identified as by Wyclif in any of the surviving manuscripts. He may also have been referring to Wyclif's commentary on the Gospels, *Postilla super Evangelia*,[72] which, however, did not contain the sort of errors alluded to in his general admission.

We recall that none of Wyclif's treatises were condemned in the constitutions of 1407/9, it only being commanded that they be examined before being allowed to be copied and used for lectures. Nothing came of this, but the committee that was set up at another convocation, in 1410, met and condemned various propositions of Wyclif's, including some from the *Trialogus* and *Opus evangelicum*; one of the committee members was none other than Richard Fleming, the bishop of Lincoln who presided over Mungin's trial when he responded to the charges read by Lyndwood.[73] The 267 propositions passed on by the committee were condemned by the bishops, along with the books containing them, which included the *Trialogus* and *Opus evangelicum*. They were sent to Pope John XXIII, who convened a council in Rome the next year, 1412, which condemned some of his books, including *Trialogus*, and, subsequently, on February 2, 1413, he gave order that all of his works be burned.[74] Even more decisive, at the ecumenical council of Constance in 1415, after Wyclif's propositions were condemned, he himself was posthumously convicted of heresy, his writings again ordered to be burned, and his bones removed from consecrated ground.[75] No action was taken on this latter command until the spring of 1428, when, on the insistence of the pope, Martin V, Wyclif's body was exhumed and burned, and his ashes scattered, by the current bishop of Lincoln, Richard Fleming.

It is not surprising, therefore, that later in the same year, 1428, when a heresy suspect confessed to having owned works of Wyclif's containing errors against the faith, he was blamed for not having turned them in to his bishop or destroyed them.

The New Provincial Constitutions of 1431 (All English Scripture to Be Examined) and Bishop Stafford's Enforcement

On January 10, 1431, Archbishop Chichele summoned a new convocation of the clergy, which met at St. Paul's in London on February 19, and the extant records show sessions lasting through March 21.[76] These records, however, do not preserve the set of new constitutions that were passed dealing with various concerns in the province, including the question of English translations of the Bible. For that we must go to the register of John Stafford, bishop of Bath and Wells.[77] Stafford, by the way, had served as a rector in the Lincoln diocese, and Bishop Repingdon early on in his episcopate gave him a study leave.[78] Stafford received his doctorate in civil law at Oxford in 1413, and the next year he was called on to assist Repingdon in his heresy inquiry there.[79] When Chichele became archbishop, Stafford was appointed an advocate in the Court of Arches, and was still there when Lyndwood became head of the court in 1417. In 1419, Stafford took over Lyndwood's old jobs of the archbishop's chancellor and auditor of causes. He participated in the trial of the heretic William Taylor in 1420, and, in 1428, having become bishop of Bath and Wells in 1424, he served on the convocation committee charged with coming up with more effective responses to heresy. He would later succeed Chichele as archbishop of Canterbury (1443–52).

On August 24, 1431, during the period that Lyndwood was preparing the index to his *Provinciale*, Bishop Stafford issued a mandate under date of August 24 supposedly directed "against sorcerers, false swearers or perjurers, and Lollards, or books of Lollardy or other books written in English,"[80] but, as we will see, the section dealing with books actually concerns only English translations of Scripture. In the section on perjury, he refers to the "deliberation of the general council last celebrated at London" ("ex deliberacione consilii generalis Londonii ultimo celebrati"),[81] and, as can be observed in the section on the Bible, he speaks of the constitutions passed there. The text reads, in the original:

> Premissis insuper adjiciendo, vobis auctoritate premissa mandamus quatinus, omnibus et singulis jurisdiccionum premissarum expresse monendo, inhibentes sub excommunicacionis pena ne quisquam sua temeritate sacram Scripturam seu aliquam ejus partem [in] li[n]guam Anglicanam, que nostra vulgaris esse dinoscitur, ullo modo transferat, neque libros Scripture in idioma Anglicum translate, per octo dies a tempore monicionis et inhibicionis hujusmodi continue numerandos, penes se retinere vel occultare presumat, sed nobis vel commissario nostro in hac parte infra tempus predictum eos deferat actualiter ad examen; contravenientes vel non parentes in hac parte, monicione vestra, immo dicti consilii atque nostra hujusmodi culpa sua precedentibus, mandamus dicta auctoritate fore excommunicacionis majoris sentencia sanctorum patrum constitucionibus in hac parte proinde lata actualiter involtos et excommunicatos nuncietis seu faciatis publice nunciari donec in premissis paruer[i]nt cum effectu; quorum absolucionem . . . nobismet ex causa specialiter reservamus.[82]

Here is a translation:

> Moreover, adding to the above, by the foregoing authority we order you to admonish everyone in the aforesaid jurisdictions that it is prohibited under pain of excommunication for anyone by his own temerity to translate Sacred Scripture or any part of it into the English tongue, which is counted our vernacular, or to keep or hide books of Scripture translated into English, during the eight days counted continuously from the time of this admonition and prohibition; rather, one must actually bring them during the said time to us or our deputy appointed for this matter, for examination. Those who contravene or fail to obey, by their own fault, after your admonition and that of the said council, and ours, have gone before, we order you to declare, or have declared publicly, by the said authority, as actually bound by the sentence of

> greater excommunication passed in the constitutions of the holy fathers, and to be excommunicated in fact, until they shall effectively obey; and the absolution of such persons . . . we specially reserve to ourselves for cause.

In other words, he orders the dean of the cathedral chapter, the three archdeacons of the diocese, and the abbot of Glastonbury, in their respective jurisdictions, to forbid anyone under pain of excommunication to translate Scripture into English on their own or to keep or hide books of Scripture in English, but to bring them to the bishop for examination (*ad examen*), during the week after hearing this admonition and that of the "said council," that is, the previously mentioned latest council held in London. Failure to obey will result in automatic excommunication, as legislated in the "constitutions of the holy fathers," which most naturally would refer to the recent London convocation.

This new constitution on the Bible is doubtless referring to *Periculosa* in the first part, when saying it is prohibited to make new translations without authorization. But in the second part it goes beyond the requirements of *Periculosa*, calling for not just recent translations to be inspected but all books containing Scripture translated into English; and the excommunication threatened is automatic, not provisional upon conviction. But it is a serious mistake to hold that Stafford's implementation constitutes "a general mandate that no part of the Scriptures in English was permitted in his diocese."[83] Such a view confuses inspection with confiscation.

No other reference to this mandate has come to light. Perhaps it was designed not as permanent law, but as calling for a one-time roundup and examination. It would seem to have been even more impractical than *Periculosa*, and the wording, at least as transmitted by Stafford, does not strike one as the sort of thing that Lyndwood would have approved of. However, Lyndwood was doubtless present at the convocation, since on March 20, the day before gathering ended, the Privy Council appointed him as a councillor and assigned him to attend on Henry VI in France[84]—unless, of course, he was already in France.

Lyndwood on *Periculosa* (1434); Excommunication Policy (1434)

As we will see below, when Bishop Stafford again concerned himself with the question of Bible translations, in 1441, he did not cite the 1431 constitution but reverted to the 1407 Oxford constitution *Periculosa*. The reason may be that in the meantime Lyndwood had published his *Provinciale*, a collection of important provincial constitutions with his commentary on them, and it is *Periculosa* that is treated therein as the definitive legislation on the subject.

At Archbishop Chichele's urging, Lyndwood began to gather together and edit the previously issued constitutions of the Canterbury Province, including those of 1407/1409, in preparation for writing a commentary on them, which he started in 1423, finishing in 1430 or so. He did not publish the result until 1434, after he had compiled an elaborate index for it. Let us see what he had to say about *Periculosa*, which he places in the title *De magistris*, "On teachers."[85]

In his summary rubric, Lyndwood characterizes the legislation thus: "Scriptura Sacra non transferatur in linguam vulgarem, nec translata interpretetur, donec rite fuerit examinata, sub pena excommunicationis et nota hereseos." That is, "Sacred Scripture is not to be translated into the common tongue, nor expounded after being translated, until it is properly examined, under pain of excommunication and suspicion of heresy."[86]

He spells out the import more fully in the *divisio textus*. The constitution, he says, contains four parts. In the first part, Archbishop Arundel gives the motivating cause of his statute. In the second, beginning with the word *Statuimus*, he prohibits Sacred Scripture from being translated into English or another language by the translator's own authority ("prohibet Scripturam Sacram transferri in linguam Anglicanum vel aliam, auctoritate propria ipsius transferentis"). In the third part, at *Nec legatur*, he prohibits the use of, or lecturing on, certain translated books ("prohibet usum sive lecturam certorum librorum translatorum"). In the fourth and last part, he adds the penalty for contravention.[87]

The term *lectura* used in this summary was a new word in medieval Latin, which had no private connotation.[88] Lyndwood does not explicate *legatur* here, but he does so in the previous constitution, *Quia insuper*, where the word is used in a similar context about treatises not to be "read" until approved. The word means reading "by way of teaching or examination."[89] Or, he continues, "you can understand it to mean simple lecturing" (*de simplici lectura*), as in the decretal *Cum ex injuncto*, where, in the excised section at the beginning, it tells of a large multitude of laymen and women in the city and diocese of Metz who had the Gospels translated into French, and also Paul's Epistles, the Psalter, Gregory's *Moralia on Job*, and many other books, "and they took up these translations so that men and women in secret gatherings could presume to utter such things to each other, and preach to one another."[90] Note that as the decretal stands in the *Liber Extra*, it begins by commending the desire to understand Scripture, and only frowns on holding secret conventicles, usurping the office of preaching, and ridiculing unlearned priests.[91]

The word *textus* used in *Periculosa* means, as James of Genoa's *Catholicon* says, the mere words of a treatise, without glossing of letter or meaning.[92] *Liber* here means a newly compiled book. It does not refer, Lyndwood observes, to the giving of a public sermon, where the biblical text is expounded in the vernacular.[93] And when the constitution says *per viam libri*, "you can understand it thus, making a book containing the whole Bible. For the word 'book,' simply taken, means a whole and complete book, not referring to numbered parts, as when a volume is often divided into many books (the Bible being an obvious case)."[94] Or, he continues, "you can take it thus: translating a single book of the biblical text. But such a limited translation could be called a *libellus*, the word that follows."[95] The word *tractatus* refers to a treatise of one's own sayings or the sayings of other doctors, while making use of the text of Scripture, translated for the occasion.[96]

Lyndwood says that the words *noviter . . . compositus* mean that it is not prohibited to lecture on any works with the text of Holy Scripture translated into English before Wyclif's time,[97] which he defined in the previous constitution as dating "from the time he began to disseminate his heresies until his death."[98] Archbishop Ussher comments that we are hereby assured that there were such pre-Wyclif translations.[99]

Since Lyndwood was writing some twenty years and more after the EV and LV texts of the Middle English Bible were produced, and the copies containing them (as described in the editions of Forshall and Madden and Lindberg) are almost never dated, how could Lyndwood or anyone else be expected to know if they were produced before Wyclif turned heretical? (EEV and EV may, in fact, have been finished before then.) This is especially true if, as suggested above in my imagined dialogue on the Galle case, these translations were already well known and cleared at the time of the Oxford constitutions; and also true if there was nothing in these copies to indicate the identity of the translators or any connection with Wycliffite doctrine, as must almost always have been the case, especially since the translations themselves could not have been assessed by an objective reader as anything but straightforward efforts to render the meaning of the Latin Vulgate into English.

On the need for approval of recent translations, Lyndwood says: "The reason is that, although it is the bare text of Scripture that is being translated, the translator can err in his translation; or, if he compiles a book, booklet, or treatise, he can mix what is false and erroneous with what is true, as frequently happens."[100] There seems to be no suggestion on Lyndwood's part of such mixing being done maliciously. Where the constitution states that the approval might have to come from the provincial council (which, Lyndwood says, should be held at least once a year),[101] the reason could be that the matters require a deeper examination and the investigation of several experts ("quia materie . . . requirunt altiorem indaginem et plurium sapientum investigationem"), or because it concerns the faith or the universal Church and its administration ("vel quia concernunt fidem vel Ecclesiam universalem et ipsius regimen"), or the like.[102]

Lyndwood specifies that the penalty named in *Periculosa* for failure to comply is liability to prosecution as a favorer of heresy, which upon due proof would result in conviction of the crime of vehement suspicion of heresy (rather than a conviction of heresy itself), with the threatened penalty of excommunication, *ferenda sententia*, to be issued at that time (after being found guilty), as opposed to *lata sententia*, already issued (automatic excommunication).[103] He adds that a charge of "favorer of error" would come from giving occasion to others to err from hearing a lecture on such books or treatises.[104]

As we have seen, the constitution on Bible translations passed in 1431 called for automatic excommunication of those who failed to observe it by not turning in their books containing English rendering of Scripture for inspection. Lyndwood signed off on the index to his *Provinciale* on January 25, 1434. Later that year, Archbishop Chichele called a council (but named convocation in the records), which met on October 7, and issued a constitution on October 23 mandating the announcement three times a year of persons automatically excommunicated. The list as presented at that time makes no reference to heretics.[105] But this 1434 constitution on excommunication as reported in Bishop Stafford's register, specifying "the cases and articles in which, by the provincial constitutions, sentences of the greater excommunication are incurred by delinquents *ipso facto*" includes "heretikes, lollardes, and fautours of hem," but no reference to persons who refused in 1431 to turn in their books containing English Scriptures. Moreover, the formula issued by Chichele on February 23, 1435, as given in the 1679 edition of Lyndwood's *Provinciale*, though considerably shorter, has a similar phrase.[106] Here is the complete 1434 provincial mandate in Stafford's register (I modernize the spelling and verbs):

1. First, all they be accursed that presume to take away or (de)prive any church of the right that (be)longeth thereto or else, against right, strive

to break or trouble the liberties of the church; and also they that purchase any manner letters from any temporal court to let [hinder] any process of spiritual judges in such causes as (be)long unto spiritual court, and all they that with thuple [disturbance] and noise come to spiritual courts and put the judges or the parties that there plead in-fere [together], or else, forasmuch as the parties sue in spiritual court such causes as (be)long to spiritual court, make or procure any of the said parties, their advocates, procurators, or other ministers of spiritual court to be indicted, arrested, or any other wise to be vexed.

2. Also all they that presume to disturb or trouble the peace and tranquillity of the king and his realm of England, and they that wrongfully withhold any right that (be)longeth to the king.
3. Also all they that wittingly bear false witness or procure false witness to be borne, or else wittingly bring forth in judgment false witness, to let rightful matrimony or procure disheriting of any person.
4. Also all they that of malice put any crime or slander to any man or woman which was not slandered before among good men and worthy, so that he or she so dis-slandered be called to judgment and purgation assigned them on the same crime or ground in any other wise.
5. Also all they that receive the king's writs or mandments to take such as be accused, and for meed or favor or any other willful cause do not due execution thereof and they let such execution or procure wrongful deliverance of such as be accused.
6. Also all they that take away, waste, or withdraw anything out of houses, manors, granges, or other places of archbishops and bishops, or any person of Holy Church against their will or against the will of such persons as be ordained and deputed keepers therof.
7. Also all they that draw out of sanctuary any man or woman that fleeth to the church or churchyard or cloister for frith [protection] or immunity of Holy Church, or let or forbid necessary livelihood to be given to such persons being within sanctuary. And they that put violent hands on priest or cleric.
8. Also all that use any witchcraft or give thereto faith or credence. And all false jurors and others that be sworn on book or any other holy thing; willful burners of houses; usurers; all they that do simony or sacrilege; **heretics, Lollards, and fautors of them**; famous thieves, robbers, and ravishers; falsaries of the pope's letters, the king's letters, or letters of any ordinary of Holy Church; and all counterfeiters of testaments or last wills, and they that let execution of true testaments or last wills. And

they that let or procure to be letted tithes to be taken and led away by them that the tithes be due unto, or else arrest, plead, or vex in any other wise such leaders-away of tithes or procure them to be arrested, pleaded, or in any other wise vexed for that cause. Also felons, maintainers of felonies, conspirators, and maintainers of false quarrels wittingly, and cherishers of them.

9. Also all they that use false weights or false measures, and in especial all they that use a weight that is called "ancel," "shaft," or "pounder," or hold or keep that weight, privily or openly.[107]

It is noteworthy, however, that in the copy of the articles printed by Gerald Bray in the *Records of Convocation* the telling phrase about heretics and Lollards, along with the previous designation of doers of simony and sacrilege, is missing.[108]

A case that occurred in the diocese of Chichester in 1438 throws an interesting light on the question of vernacular Scriptures. Shortly after Richard Praty took over as bishop in July, it was reported to him that a parish priest named John Boreham had been preaching Wycliffite errors for twenty years, and "that he had had, and still possessed, tracts and books in the vernacular containing condemned material." Boreham admitted some non-Wycliffite charges against him (connected with the practice of magic), but denied all of the Wycliffite articles except for one, that he possessed books by Wyclif that he had not reported to his ordinary (one of Praty's predecessors). But he *had* admitted that he possessed the four Gospels in English.[109] Whether or not the bishop inspected these Gospels cannot be known, but the priest was undoubtedly allowed to keep them. There was, of course, no policy of seizing and destroying books of Scripture, whether in Latin or the vernacular.

Bishop Stafford's Enforcement of *Periculosa* (1441)

As I noted at the beginning of the last section, when Bishop Stafford returned to the question of Bible translation in 1441, he specifically cites *Periculosa*, which he identifies as from the Council of Oxford, as does Lyndwood in the *Provinciale*, and perhaps Stafford is now drawing upon Lyndwood; but he adapts its text to his own diocese, formulating an admonition, *Periculum animarum*, forbidding anyone to read, keep, or possess ("legere, retinere, vel possidere") books of Scripture in English written in or after the time of John Wyclif until they are approved by him or a provincial council, with any contravener to be punished as a favorer of heresy and error and suspect of heresy. And since (the admonition continues) an investigation has turned up some such books, not only with Scripture in English but also others, publicly containing heresies and errors, he orders them to be broken up and burned in the sight of the present congregation.[110] We note that it is not specific translations that are to be approved, but the actual books containing recent translations.

Whatever these books were that Stafford swept in, we can be sure that they were not copies of the EV or LV texts of the Middle English Bible, or, if they were, that he and his clerics did not read them carefully, since no such heresies or errors could have been found in them, unless *Five and Twenty Books* or some other partisan addendum were attached to them.

Bishop Stafford's admonition was read in the marketplace (presumably at Wells) on the Thursday before Palm Sunday in 1441, and the bishop subsequently ordered the dean and the archdeacons to repeat it in English in all churches and other venues of their jurisdictions.[111]

It is noteworthy, by the way, that Bishop Stafford was a champion of English instruction of the faithful. On March 20, 1435, he sent out a letter to his archdeacons containing an English translation of the instructional part of Archbishop Peckham's *Ignorantia sacerdotum* of 1281 and ordered them to see to it that a copy be made for every parish church, to be purchased by the curate of each church for sixteen pence and carefully preserved and expounded to the parishioners four times a year under penalty of a heavy fine.[112]

Periculosa and Syon Abbey in the 1440s (?)

In *The Mirror of Our Lady*, we find two provisions of *Periculosa* referred to. This work was written for the Brigittine sisters of Syon Abbey sometime between their founding in 1415 and around 1450,[113] with scholars nowadays favoring a date later rather than earlier in this range.[114] The first provision treated is *Periculosa*'s requirement to get episcopal permission to make a new translation. The author says: "Forasmuch as it is forbidden under pain of cursing that no man should have nor draw any text of Holy Scripture into English without license of the bishop diocesan, and in diverse places of your service are such texts of Holy Scripture, therefore I asked and have license of our bishop to draw such things into English to your ghostly comfort and profit, so that both our conscience in the drawing and yours in the having may be the more sure and clear."[115] The bishop in question would presumably be the bishop of London, in which diocese Syon was located. From what the author says here, the permission that he obtained would be sufficient for the sisters to read his translations without further ado.

However, in the first of his two prologues, which he seems to have added after he wrote the body of the text, he says that he has translated only a few of the psalms, "for ye may have them of Richarde Hampoule's drawinge, and out of Englisshe Bibles, if ye have license therto."[116] He assumes that the Richard Rolle translations need no permission to be read. As for complete English Bibles, it is not clear whether he thinks that they need to be approved. It is clear, though, that he believes that the nuns themselves need to be approved before they are allowed to read them. This is an idea that is completely foreign to *Periculosa*, but we will meet with it again later on, notably in bishops at the turn of the sixteenth century, as witnessed by Thomas More: according to them, the reader needed to be licensed, not the Bible.

Bishop Reginald Pecock and the English Bible

Above I raised the question of whether Reginald Pecock approved the Middle English Bible in either of his dioceses (St. Asaph, 1444–50, and Chichester, 1450–57). If he did not explicitly approve it in the terms called for in *Periculosa* (supposing that the constitution was construed to apply to EV and LV), he definitely approved of it in itself, which comes to the same thing; for he consistently used the LV in his own vernacular writings, as the editor of his *Repressor*, Churchill Babington, has established.[117] In this work Pecock twits the Lollards for claiming that they do nothing that is not expressly mentioned in the Bible, and he lists a number of things that they do that are not mentioned or allowed in Scripture, like shaving their beards or playing games, or using translations of the Scriptures. On the last-named point the text reads: "Also thou shalt not find expressly in Holy Scripture that the New Testament should be writ in English tongue to laymen, or in Latin tongue to clerks; neither that the Old Testament should be writ in English tongue to laymen or in Latin tongue to clerks; and yet each of these governances thou wilt hold to be leaveful and to be a meritory, virtuous, moral deed for to thereby deserve grace and glory, and to be the service of

God, and therefore to be the law of God."[118] We note that Latin is acknowledged to be as much a translation as English. Pecock himself, of course, agreed with the principles stated here, specifically the morality or acceptability of the laity's use of English Bible translations;[119] and, in employing the LV texts in the treatises that he wrote for the laity, and pointedly for the lay Lollards he wished to persuade, he was giving the stamp of orthodoxy to this translation.

But in an earlier passage in the *Repressor*, which Gasquet quotes, Pecock indicates that laymen should not read the Bible except with the permission of their bishop: "This what I have now said of and to Bible-men, I have not said under this intent and meaning, as that I should feel to be unleaveful [to] laymen for to read in the Bible and for to study and learn therein, with help and counsel of wise and well learned clerks and with license of their governor the bishop."[120] Strictly speaking, of course, this would include as well the reading of Latin Bibles—though presumably most persons who could read Latin would at least be in minor orders, hence clerics. And the lawfulness would require not only the bishop's permission but also consultation with learned clerics, which would go far beyond the requirements of *Periculosa*.

But it all comes down to being a practical matter. It is clear that the English Scriptures that the Lollards are reading have no inaccuracies or tendentious phrasings, but nevertheless they are being wrongly used or subjected to false interpretations. In another surviving work, the *Rule of Christian Religion*, Pecock says that he is addressing two kinds of people. One sort relies only on the English Bible: "One is of them which hold themselves so stiffly and so singularly, foolishly, and only to the use of the Bible in their mother's language, and namely [especially] to thereof the New Testament, that they trow, say, and hold both privily and as far openly as they dare, all other books, written or [either] in Latin or in the common people's language, to be written into waste."[121] The other sort relies not only on the English Bible but also other books in English, some of which are misleading or pernicious:

> Another sort is of them which, over, and besides, and with the reading and studying in the Bible, and namely in the New Testament, translated into their mother's language, they admit, receive, and allow the reading, studying, and use of other books had in their mother's language. But they apprize so much those unsavory books which they have in their mother's language among them in use, with the use of the Bible in their mother's language, that they trow and hold and say, as far as they dare for dread of their prelates, that those now-said books had [possessed] among them in their

> mother's language, besides the Bible, be noble and worthy and profitable books to all Christian men's learning and ruling, and be as rich jewels to be dearworthily beclipped [embraced], loved, and multiplied abroad of [by] all Christian people, notwithstanding in very truth some of them be treating and teaching unsavorily, unseemly, unformally, rudely, boistrously, unsufficiently, suspectly; and some of them be teaching and treating untruly and perilously the matters which they take on hand to treat, teach, and declare.[122]

It is interesting to see that, even though elsewhere Pecock used the LV English translation to make his teaching points, in the *Rule* itself he regularly cites the Latin text of the Bible. It has been suggested that he does this in order to downplay the text in favor of his own rational explanation of the point at hand.[123] But I think it more likely that he is emphasizing that, while the English versions are an acceptable aid to understanding the Bible, the original Latin that they translate should not be lost sight of.

It is important to remember that the opposition that Pecock engendered from other members of the clergy, which culminated in his being charged with heresy, which he confessed and abjured in December 1457,[124] was never in any way connected with the question of translations of the Bible into English.

Archbishop Bourchier's Extreme Call-In of English Scripture (1458)

John Stafford succeeded Henry Chichele as archbishop of Canterbury in 1443, serving until his death in 1452, but no further indication of his interest in regulating English Bibles, either in his own diocese of Canterbury or in the whole province, has come to light.[125] But the archbishop under whom Pecock was prosecuted, Thomas Bourchier, who served from 1454 to 1486, on his own motion (that is, without benefit of proposal and passage in a convocation) sent a mandate, *Inter solicitudines*, to the whole province, probably in March 1458 (so, just months after Pecock's abjuration), telling of reports of persons engaged in studying not only Reginald Pecock's condemned English books, but also of books taken from Sacred Scripture translated from Latin into English ("e Latino in Anglicum ex Sacra Scriptura traductos sive translatos"). The bishops are to demand that all such books be turned in to them within twenty days under pain of excommunication, or, if delaying for fifteen days more, under pain of being condemned as favoring heresy; or, after another fifteen days' refusal, being condemned as equivalent to heretics (*tamquam heretici*).[126] The archbishop does not say what is to be done with the books containing Scripture in English; but since he associates them with books by Pecock, which were under order to be burned, he may well have intended the same fate for the vernacular Scripture volumes.

It is definitely the case, on paper, at least, that the possessors of such English works of Scripture would be eligible to be burned at the stake if they were apprehended more than sixty days after the announcement and showed themselves to be unrepentant. Here at last, then, we find the possession of an English Bible declared to be a burnable crime. But it is unthinkable that conviction could or would follow on so paltry an offense. It is also improbable that there was a widespread turn-in of Bibles. We see in the next section that Thomas Eborall, Pecock's successor as master of Whittington College and one his opponents, a few years after Bourchier's decree, gave his approval to an LV New Testament. Are we to suppose that it was collected in 1458 and then returned? Or that it was never turned in at all and that Eborall was not scandalized by the fact? It would make more sense if the decree were interpreted to mean, or actually meant, that only such English scriptural works were to be confiscated that were being used in conjunction with Pecock's works (though Pecock wrote far more books in Latin than he did in English).

Some MEB Approvals

In a case noticed by Forshall and Madden and Gasquet,[127] treated also by more recent scholars, an expensive LV New Testament that a woman bought in London, probably in the 1460s, was first vetted by two experts with doctorates in theology from Oxford, Thomas Eborall and William Ive. An inscription reads: "This booke . . . was overseyn and redd by doctor Thomas Ebbrall and Doctor Yve or that my moder bought it" (that is, "before my mother bought it"), and the amount paid is given as thirty-one marks.[128] If *Periculosa* was in view during this process, we might conclude either that the judgment of these two authorities was being sought to see whether the Bible in question came under the mandate (that is, whether or not it was a bona fide pre-Wyclif production), or else that Eborall and Ive were delegated by the bishop of London to act as censors for him. Gasquet's assessment is as follows: "We have here then a mere chance record of the fact that this particular copy of the New Testament had been 'overseen and read' by two learned doctors, deputed, it is hardly too much to conclude, by rightful authority for the purpose. This, by the way, is of course a copy of the later of the two versions now known as Wyclifite Scriptures."[129] No such examination would have been required if the suggestion in the text of *Periculosa* as passed at the Oxford council in 1407—that it might be thought necessary to approve a specific translation by a provincial council—had been followed through either in 1407 or when the constitution was renewed and reaffirmed at the London convocation in 1409. Both the EV and the LV texts of the Middle English Bible could have been examined and approved once and for all (I argue above that they must have been approved, one way or another).

It has been thought significant that Eborall and Ive were successively masters of Whittington College in London, the former from 1444 to 1464, and the latter from 1464 to 1470.[130] But Caroline Barron suggests that it may be more significant that their position as master also entailed that they were rectors of the associated parish of St. Michael Paternoster Royal, and that it was in this capacity that they were consulted by one of their parishioners.[131] If so, the consultation likely occurred before Eborall left the college and passed on to his new duties as rector of All Hallows in Honey Lane.[132] If this scenario is the true one, then it may simply have been a matter of a wealthy lady making sure that she was making a wise purchase. It is, however, presuming too much to conclude definitely, with Sheila Lindenbaum, that they "licensed" the Bible "for a wealthy female owner to read."[133]

The Eborall-Ive inspection is associated by Richard Rex with a later incident in which another doctor of theology from Oxford, James Preston, serving as a parish priest in Coventry (perpetual vicar of St. Michael's from 1488 until his death around 1507), has biblical dealings with a woman of his parish.[134] Alice Rowley, married to the mayor William Rowley until he died in 1506, testified in heresy proceedings in 1511 that the vicar "had a book of the New Law from her and gave it back to her afterwards. And, as she asserts, he favored it and others." Shannon McSheffrey and Norman Tanner think it more likely that the last remark means that she was claiming the vicar's favor for herself and her friends.[135] I judge that Rex is right in interpreting it to refer to the book, and in assuming that it was an English New Testament that he inspected and approved of; but his idea that "the power to approve the possession of the English Bible was probably in practice devolved to qualified theologians"[136] remains speculative.

Finally, let us recall that in 1482 William Caxton listed the Bible as among John Trevisa's translations, thus indicating his belief, and obviously that of others, that the LV text of the Middle English Bible was by an author of undoubted orthodoxy. Other witnesses to this belief have been cited, including the preface to the King James Bible. It is quite clear that Caxton does not consider the English Bible to be a contraband production. It does raise the question, however, why Caxton did not print the Bible; it would surely have sold very well.

Other Evidences of Use, Possession, and Bequeathal

A further argument that Gasquet offers to show the acceptability of the English Bible is its possession by persons or institutions of unimpeachable fidelity, such as religious houses and members of such houses. As he puts it: "Another point which must not be overlooked is the good catholic company in which this version of the Scriptures, or parts of it, are occasionally found."[137]

One example of use that has recently come to light is a large Sunday sermon cycle compiled late in the fifteenth century for the secular clergy and probably by the secular clergy, in which over half of the Gospel translations given use LV.[138] The editor, Stephen Morrison, finds it puzzling. First of all, since LV was "viewed, one is led to believe, with deep suspicion after Archbishop Arundel's 1407 *Constitutiones*," why was it owned by "the humbler members of the clergy"? Second, he asks how one is to explain that the "robustly orthodox" compilers of the sermon cycle "were energetically pursuing a policy (that of making the Englished Scriptures—or parts of them —available to the unlettered laity) which their opponents had long advocated?"[139] An obvious answer, of course, is that we have been misled in our beliefs on these subjects.

Particularly noteworthy cases of possession are those in which books of Scriptures are passed on after death in wills. Gasquet says:

> It is, of course, obvious that this could never have been done had the volume so left been the work of Wyclif or of his followers, for it would then indeed have been, as a modern writer describes the Wyclifite books, "a perilous piece of property." Thus, before the close of the fourteenth century, namely, in 1394, a copy of the Gospels in English was bequeathed to the chantry of St. Nicholas, in the Church of Holy Trinity, York, by John Hopton, Chaplain there. Fancy what this means on the theory that the English Scriptures were the work of Wyclifite hands! It means nothing less than that a catholic priest publicly bequeaths, in a will proved in his Bishop's court, the proscribed work of some member of an heretical sect.[140]

One way of countering the reasoning that Gasquet here presents against the Wycliffite consensus can be seen expressed by Diarmaid MacCulloch:

> Wyclif's Oxford admirers had followed his teaching on the unchallengeable authority of the Bible by producing the first complete translation of the Vulgate into English, so that all might have a chance to read it and understand it for themselves. In 1407 all existing versions of the Bible in English were officially banned by the English Church hierarchy, and no replacement was sanctioned until Henry VIII's Reformation in the 1530s. In the intervening period, only the most obviously ultra-respectable could get away with open possession of a vernacular Bible, and indeed, their respectability seems itself to have made their copy of the text respectable.[141]

MacCulloch adds an example of this process by reporting the will of John Clopton, "a wealthy and highly respectable East Anglian gentleman," who bequeathed an English Bible to the archdeacon of Suffolk in his will of 1496.[142] This case is particularly significant, since archdeacons were responsible for enforcing provincial and diocesan laws in their districts. We can doubtless assume that the archdeacon in this instance would have found the bequest a welcome one, and not a banned object to be destroyed.

Heresy Suspects and English Bibles

Let us now look further at allegations of "the persecution of the lollards for possessing copies of the vernacular scriptures," as Herbert Workman puts it. Workman lists only passages from Foxe.[143] The first example that he gives is Foxe's account of the convocation trial of Ralph Mungin in 1428,[144] which I treated above. He next lists the suspects arrested in Norfolk and Suffolk between 1428 and 1431, apparently referring to a witness's testimony against Margery Backster, that she invited her to come and "hear her husband read the Law of Christ unto them, which Law was written in a book that her husband was wont to read to her by night."[145] The next reference is to the testimony given in 1430 by one William Wright about neighbors belonging to the sect of Lollards in and around the village of Martham in Norfolk. Prominent among them is "Sir Hugh Pie," presumably a priest; he once owned "a book of the New Law in English," now used by one Richard Fletcher, "a most perfect doctor in that sect," who "can very well and perfectly expound the Holy Scriptures." One of Pie's frequent conversants was William

White, and Pie bequeathed to White's servant Alice "a New Testament, which they then called the Book of the New Law," which "was in the custody of one Oswald Godfrey of Colchester." Another member of the group was Nicholas Belward of Southelem, who had "a New Testament which he bought at London for four marks and forty pence," and he taught others, "and studied diligently upon the said New Testament."[146] But there is no word of any prosecution that followed. The final reference in Foxe's third volume (in the Pratt edition) is to the testimony given by William Christopher, in his own name and the name of other witnesses, against Nicholas Canon of Eye in Norfolk in 1431, but none of the charges have to do with the Bible.[147]

All of Workman's other references are to Foxe's fourth volume, beginning with accusations brought in 1486 against nine persons in Coventry. It was charged as a heresy against one for holding that everyone is bound to know the Lord's Prayer and the Creed in English; and another was charged for relying upon his prayers in English and also upon a book he had with the Epistles and Gospels in English, and also for saying that no priest speaks better from that pulpit than that "priest." Both were convicted, along with the seven others, and all recanted.[148] However, it is not known what weight was put upon the vernacular charges, since both suspects had more serious things laid against them, like denying the power of priests to absolve sin. Workman's next reference is to a charge against Richard Butler in the period 1509–18, that he had certain chapters of the evangelists in a great book of heresy, containing divers errors and heresies.[149] The next references concern charges brought against Richard Hunne in 1514,[150] which I will deal with in Chapter 7; and the final instances concern delations recorded in the register of John Longland in his first year as bishop of Lincoln, 1521, which include many statements of ownership and use of English versions of Scripture.[151]

I will not pursue here the later Foxe references, but let me cite a more recent account, that of Christopher de Hamel. He says:

> There is no shortage of tales of committed Lollards who were arrested for heresy and who were found to be in possession of Wycliffite Bibles. Many confessed to reading the text aloud in secret meetings. The most detailed records of heresy trials survive from the very end of the fifteenth century and the beginning of the sixteenth. Five Lollards were burned at the stake in London in 1496 with their manuscripts tied around their necks. Very many others were charged with Lollard heresy, including Thomas Watts,

> Christopher Shoemaker, James Brewster, William Sweeting, John Southwick, Nicholas Durdant, John and Joan Barret, John Butler, Thomas Geffrey, Richard Hunne, and so on, among countless others, all of whom owned Wycliffite Bibles. . . . Most died as martyrs, usually by being burned alive.[152]

However, not all of these persons owned English Bibles, and none were charged with it as an offense, except for Brewster and Hunne. To begin with, de Hamel's account of the 1496 incident does not accurately reflect the reports found in two London chronicles. One, in modern spelling, reads thus: "Also, the Sunday next before [the twelfth day of October, 1496], at Paul's Cross stood four Lollards with the books of their lore hanging about them, which books were, at the time of the sermon, there burned with the fagots that the said Lollards bore. And, among their erroneous opinions, one was that the sacrament of the altar was but material bread; and another was that it was leaveful for a man and woman to be joined in marriage all the times of the year, and no season except."[153] The other report is simpler: "And on the Sunday next ensuing four heretics did their open penance at Paul's, in manner and form as before in this book is often rehearsed; and, in the sermon-while, many of their books were burned before them."[154] In both reports, it is the books that were burned, not the heretics (who were four in number, not five). The Lollards were simply doing penance after having abjured their errors;[155] and there is no suggestion that "the books of their lore" included English Bibles.

Thomas Watts, of Dogmersfield in Hampshire in the diocese of Winchester, was charged in 1514 and found guilty of various Lollard doctrines, none of which involved his possession of the New Testament in English, which he used to read to his family and others, or another book containing the Lord's Prayer, the Hail Mary, the Creed, the Ten Commandments, and a treatise on baptism in English.[156] Christopher Shoemaker, who was executed in 1518 in Newbury, was said to have read "out of a little book the words which Christ spake to his disciples," but presumably he was condemned not for that but for his heterodox views on the Eucharist and pilgrimage.[157]

Brewster and Sweeting were executed together at Smithfield in 1511. Sweeting is not said to have anything to do with a Bible, but his friend Brewster, an illiterate carpenter from Colchester in Essex, was, according to Foxe, charged with "having a certain little book of Scripture in English, of an old writing almost worn for age, whose name is not there expressed," which, along with all the other accusations against him, he confessed as true.[158] This was in the diocese of London, and, as we will see from the Hunne case in Chapter 7, possession of an English Bible was indeed considered to be prohibited there.

John Southwick is reported by Foxe as having abjured his opinion about the Eucharist in 1520, with no mention of the Bible.[159] Nicholas Durdant and Joan Barret were at the wedding of Robert Durdant's daughter, where a certain epistle of St. Paul was read and much commended by "Durdant" (either Robert or Nicholas).[160] Thomas Geffrey was detected by John Butler for various things, including having a Scripture book in English, "which book the said Geffrey gave to the bishop of London when he was accused." Geffrey is also reported as having read to and taught Butler "in the Acts and preachings of the Apostles."[161] Similarly, John Barret, Joan's husband, goldsmith of London, was reported to have memorized and recited the Epistle of St. James to his wife and maid; and Joan is said to have lent the Gospels of Matthew and Mark to the detector, John Scrivener, who turned them over to the bishop.[162] Among other persons detected for possessing or reading the English Scriptures are Richard Bennet (reading the Epistle of James in English),[163] and Joan Gun, of Chesham, said by John Hill to have "instructed and taught the said Hill, before his abjuration, in the Epistle of St. James, and other opinions,"[164]—oddly referring to a book of the Bible as an opinion.

One report, from the Lincoln diocese, indicates that confessed offenders and other witnesses were asked by the authorities about their possession of English Scriptures:

> John Grosar, being put to his oath, detected Thomas Tikill, Thomas Spencer, and his wife; and John Knight. This John Grosar was examined whether he had a book of the Gospels in English; who confessed that he received such a book of Thomas Tikill, morrow-mass priest in Milk Street, and afterwards lent the same book to Thomas Spencer, which Thomas Spencer with his wife used to read upon the same. After that it was lent to John Knight, who at length delivered the book to the vicar of Rickmansworth.[165]

John Butler seems to have been more detector than detectee; however, one of the things he was detected for was having from Roger Bennet "a certain book in English, containing *A Dialogue Between a Jew and a Christian*." He was one of many persons who abjured in 1521.[166] One of his other detections was that he was brought to "Durdant's house," where "a certain English book" was read; "at which time Durdant desired them not to tell that he had any such English book in his house, lest he should be burned for the same."[167]

We can agree that there was a current belief among some dissidents that possessing any work in English, not just the Scriptures, was a serious offense, and admittedly, as John Thomson says, most of the books reported as owned by Lollards are portions of the Bible in the vernacular. Thomson also says, however, that "any ownership of books was liable to give rise to suspicion."[168] That would hold for Latin books as well as English. Of course, it only stands to reason that the dissidents would have found justification for their beliefs from the Bible, and that the authorities would be legitimately concerned about it. We see an example of such tendentious reading of Scripture in the Kentish proceedings of 1511–12: a group consisting of John Bampton and others who read the English Gospel of Matthew together and "were well contented and pleased, saying that it was pity that it might not be known openly, the which reading in the said book, as they understood it, was against the sacraments of the altar, baptism, matrimony, and priesthood."[169]

De Hamel acknowledges that "most Lollards were prosecuted for practising heresy, of which owning a Wycliffite Bible would have simply been one further piece of corroborative evidence. Where Bibles are mentioned in trials, this is usually in the context of giving public readings. Lollards who seemed to be aping priests were sentenced without mercy, but simple possession alone would probably not bring a conviction."[170] A more accurate statement of the situation, to my mind, is Mary Dove's assessment that owning English Bibles implicated only those who were suspected of heterodoxy in the first place. In fact, she thinks that individual English Bibles were given the stamp of approval not by any episcopal licensing but simply by the fact of being owned by persons of good reputation: "Rather than leading to the enforcement of legislation for the approval of individual volumes containing scripture, or scriptural passages, in English, Arundel's *Constitutions* seem to have resulted in a situation whereby the perceived orthodoxy of the owner was made to vouch for the orthodoxy of the translation owned."[171] But we must remember that one reason for failing to seek permission for such volumes was the idea that the translations they contained were pre-Wyclif and so in need of no approval.

In sum, we may point out that if a person were suspected of heresy, every aspect of that person's life would be potential grounds for suspicion. If he or she possessed a book of the Scriptures, whether in Latin or in English, it would be thought likely that it was being used for heterodox purposes.

CHAPTER 7

The End of the Story
Richard Hunne and Thomas More

Thomas More on EV/LV and *Periculosa*

We come now to the account that Thomas More gives of the English Bible in his *Dialogue Concerning Heresies*. I have been arguing above, following in the footsteps of Cardinal Gasquet, that EV and LV were produced in Wyclif's time and later, but mainly independently of him and free from his heterodoxies, though I have raised the possibility that EV could have been produced before Wyclif manifested any of his troublesome views. More, on the contrary, believed that both versions (insofar as he distinguished between them) were written long before Wyclif's time, and that Wyclif himself produced objectionable translations that were successfully prohibited and suppressed. As More tells the Messenger of his dialogue, "Ye shall understand that the great arch-heretic Wyclif, whereas the whole Bible was long before his days by virtuous and well learned men translated into the English tongue, and by good and godly people with devotion and soberness well and reverently read, took upon him of a malicious purpose to translate it of new, in which translation he purposely corrupted that holy text, maliciously planting therein such words as might in the readers' ears serve to the proof of such heresies as he went about to sow, which he not only set forth with his own translation of the Bible but also with certain prologues and glosses which he made thereupon."[1] It was for this reason, More continues, that the constitution was passed at Oxford—and here he gives a fair translation of *Periculosa*, and shows it to his interlocutor, as it is reproduced in Lyndwood's *Provinciale*.[2] He comments, "I trow that in this law ye see nothing unreasonable. For it neither forbiddeth the translations to be read that were already well done of old before Wyclif's days; nor damneth his because it was new, but because it was nought; nor prohibiteth new to be made, but provideth that they shall not be read if they be mis-made, till they be by good examination amended, except they be such translations as Wyclif made and Tyndale, that the malicious mind of the translator had in such wise handled it, as it were labor lost to go about to mend them."[3] We see that More adds the idea that the bishop would *correct* any errors before approving it.

The Messenger says that sometimes English Bibles have been burned along with convicted heretics, whether the translation is old or new or good or bad. More thinks that this is not true, and he appeals to his own experience: "Myself have seen and can show you Bibles fair and old written in English which have been known and seen by the bishop of the diocese and left in lay men's hands and women's, to such as he knew for good and Catholic folk that used it with devotion and soberness."[4] It would be natural to take More to mean the "bishop of the respective diocese" in which the prospective reader resided. Such Bibles can only be one or other of the two versions of the MEB, EV or LV, which More believed to antedate Wyclif, and therefore to be in need of no vetting; and he tells us that in fact there were bishops of his own day who assumed, or assured themselves of, the orthodoxy of the translation. These bishops therefore approved these Bibles without further ado, but allowed them only for individual persons who would profit by them and not abuse them. Margaret Deanesly notes two English Bibles in religious houses that More probably saw, one at the Sheen Charterhouse, which was none other than the LLV formerly owned by Henry VI which, of course, was not prefaced by *Five and Twenty Books*, and the other at Syon Abbey, that is, the EV New Testament owned by Lady Danvers and given to the abbey by her in 1517,[5] which Gasquet describes at length.[6]

More on Hunne's Trial

The Messenger says that there was a recent case in London of Bibles being burned, and also the dead body of the man who owned them, even though no fault was found in the Bibles except that they were in English. "Who told you this tale?" More asks. "Divers honest men," the Messenger replies, and goes on to recount his version of the fate of Richard Hunne in 1514. They proved his heresy after his death "by nothing else but by the possession of a good English Bible." More responds that he knows the case "from top to toe," having participated in it. He was "at the judgment given in Paul's, whereupon his books and his body were burned."[7] During the trial, the documentary evidence against Hunne was exhibited: "At such time as he was denounced for an heretic," More says,

> there lay his English Bible open, and some other English books of his, that every man might see the places noted with his own hand such words and in such wise that there would no wise man, that good were, have any great doubt after the sight thereof what naughty minds the men had, both he that so noted them and he that so made them. I remember not now the specialties of the matter nor the formal words as they were written. But this I remember well, that besides other things framed for the favor of divers other heresies, there were in the Prologue of that Bible such words touching the Blessed Sacrament as good Christian men did much abhor to hear, and which gave the readers undoubted occasion to think that the book was written after Wyclif's copy and by him translated into our tongue. And yet, whether the book be burned or secretly kept, I cannot surely say. But truly, were the clergy of my mind, it should be somewhere reserved for the perpetual proof of the matter, there hath gone so much suspicious rumor thereof. Which, as I believe, were all well answered and the mind fully satisfied of any man that wise were, and good therewith, that once had overlooked, read, and advisedly considered that book.[8]

More assumes that the translation that followed after the prologue was also that of Wyclif, whereas it could only have been the same translation that he spoke of earlier as pre-Wycliffite and episcopally approved. But having such a preface in itself fulfilled More's definition of a Wycliffite Bible, and reading from it would be an offense against *Periculosa*. However, this would be a comparatively minor offense, unless it could be shown that the prologue contained heresies and that Hunne approved of them. As we have just seen, More says that is what happened: his English Bible and other books of his were displayed at the trial showing his annotations in his own hand approving of "naughty" things, specifically in the prologue to his Bible, against the sacrament of the Eucharist.

If More had examined Hunne's alleged Bible for himself, he would undoubtedly have had to revise his recollection to agree with the Messenger's assessment. He hoped that it survived the flames, and it is thought by some nowadays that his hope was realized, since an LV Bible with prologue that seems definitely to have been used in the trial is currently in the Archbishop Parker collection at Cambridge, Corpus Christi College (CCCC) MS 147.[9]

It was first identified as Hunne's Bible to Montague Rhodes James by Arthur Ogle, when Ogle spoke to James after publishing his review of Gasquet in 1900–1901, and James referred to the suggested connection in his catalog of Corpus Christi College manuscripts.[10] But the identification was called into question by E. Jeffries Davis in 1915, on the grounds that the passages annotated or marked for censure in the prologue did not match well with passages on which the thirteen posthumous charges against Hunne were based.[11] A similar mismatch was reported by Mary Dove in 2007,[12] but she did not see the response that Ogle had made in 1949, pointing to discreet dot signs in the margins (three dots forming inverted triangles).[13] The upshot is that CCCC 147 was definitely used to formulate the charges against Hunne. However, that does not mean that it was Hunne's Bible, as we shall see.

Hunne's Trial Reconstructed

Let us review the case.[14] Hunne had been arrested and confined in the Lollards' Tower of Lambeth Palace at the instigation of Dr. William Horsey, chancellor of Bishop FitzJames of London.[15] The six articles objected to Hunne on December 2, 1514, before his death, which were "collected against him by the said Horsey and his accomplices," as John Foxe says, were for offenses that should mainly have been classified not as heresies but at most as errors, consisting mainly of anticlerical gibes. Here are the first five, as given by Foxe from the bishop of London's register: (1) saying that it was not God but the covetousness of priests that required tithes; (2) insulting bishops and priests, saying that they were the scribes and Pharisees that crucified Christ; (3) saying that bishops and priests taught but did not fulfill the word of God; (4) defending the heresies of Joan Baker, recently abjured; (5) saying that the bishop of London was more of a heretic than Joan Baker. Here is the sixth article entire: "That the said Richard Hunne hath in his keeping divers English books prohibited and damned by the law: as the Apocalypse in English, Epistles and Gospels in English, Wyclif's damnable works, and other books containing infinite errors, in which he hath been a long time accustomed to read, teach, and study daily."[16]

Perhaps the sixth charge was intended to apply only to Bibles that contained such errors. But it looks very much as if there was thought to be a ban against all English Bibles, including pre-Wyclif ones or ones that may have been cleared by a bishop. The charge does not refer to Hunne's Old Testament with its damning Wycliffite prologue, but only to books of the New Testament.

Hunne's written reply to all of the charges, recorded in the register, was one of submission: "As touching these articles, I have not spoken them as they be here laid; howbeit unadvisedly I have spoken words somewhat sounding to the same, for which I am sorry, and ask God mercy, and submit me to my lord's charitable and favorable correction."[17]

A day later, Hunne died under suspicious circumstances, his body being found on the morning of December 4. On the next day, December 5, the coroner's jury met, and on the day following declared the death to be a murder committed by none other than the chancellor, Dr. Horsey, together with the bishop's summoner, Charles Joseph, and John Spalding, the bell ringer of St. Paul's Cathedral.[18] All three of the accused would have been ordered to prison, and when Bishop FitzJames continued the heresy proceedings a few days later, on December 10, after calling a diocesan convocation, Horsey's role of formulating charges was taken over by "Dr. Hed,"[19] that is, Thomas Head, who is identified by Foxe as FitzJames's vicar-general and chancellor when he performed a similar function in 1518 in the trials of John Stilman and Thomas Man.[20] Perhaps Head was vicar-general only at this later time, while Horsey resumed his position of chancellor when released from prison in 1516. Or he may have been the bishop's commissary, who is referred to in Spalding's deposition.[21]

The process began on December 10 with the preacher at Paul's Cross reading out the articles upon which Hunne had already been examined (without referring to his response), and he added thirteen new articles (compiled by Dr. Head) "contained in some of his books," and he invited anyone who wished to do so to come to the bishop of London and see "this book" for himself.[22]

The thirteen extra charges are excerpts or paraphrases from GP, most of them not rising to the level of heresy. I list them all here as Foxe translates them from the subsequently lost register of Bishop FitzJames, and at the end of each I append the corresponding passage from GP identified by Ogle.[23]

1. The said book damneth all holy canons, calling them ceremonies and statutes of sinful men and uncunning, and calleth the pope Satan and Antichrist.

   GP, chap. 2, p. 3: "It semith opin heresie to seye that the Gospel with his treuthe and fredom suffisith not to salvacioun of Cristen men without keping of ceremonies and statutis of sinful men and unkunninge, that ben maad in the time of Sathanas and of Antecrist."

2. It damneth the pope's pardons, saying they be but leasings [lies].

   GP, chap. 10, p. 30: "Summe Cristene lordis senden general lettris to alle her ministris and leegemen eithir tenauntis, that the pardouns of the bisschopis of Rome, that ben opin leesingis, for they graunten many hundrid yeeris of pardoun aftir domes day, be prechid generaly in her rewmes and lordschipis."

3. The said book of Hunne saith that kings and lords, called Christian in name, and heathen in conditions, defile the sanctuary of God, bringing clerks full of covetousness, heresy, and malice to stop God's Law, that it cannot be known, kept, and freely preached.

   GP, chap. 10, p. 30: "Summe Cristene lordis in name, and hethene in condiscouns, defoulen the sentuarie of God, and bringin in symonient clerkis, ful of coveitise, eresie, and ypocrisie, and malice, to stoppe Goddis Lawe, that it be not knowen and kept, and frely prechid."

4. The said book saith that lords and prelates pursue full cruelly them that would teach truly and freely the Law of God, and cherish them that preach sinful men's traditions and statutes, by which he meaneth the holy canons of Christ's Church.

   GP, chap. 10, p. 30: "Summe Cristen lordis in name not in dede preisen and magnifien freris lettris, ful of disceit and leesingis, and make hire tenauntis and meine to swere by herte, boonis, nailes, and sides, and other membris of Crist, and pursuen ful cruely hem that wolden teche treuly and freely the Lawe of God, and preisen, maintenen, and cherischen hem that prechen fablis, lesingis, and sinful mennis tradiciouns either statutis."

5. That poor men and idiots have the truth of the Holy Scriptures more than a thousand prelates and religious men and clerks of the school.

   GP, chap. 10, p. 30: "So now a fewe pore men and idiotis, in comparisoun of clerkis of scole, mown have the treuthe of Holy Scripture ayens many thousinde prelatis and religiouse that ben yoven to worldly pride and coveitise."

6. That Christian kings and lords set up idols in God's house and excite the people to idolatry.

   GP, chap. 10, p. 30: "But it is for to drede ful sore lest kingis and lordis ben now in the formere sinnes of Manasses; God graunte that they repenten verily and make amendis to God and men, as he dide, in the ende; for they setten idolis in Goddis hous, and exciten men to idolatrie, and scheden innocent blood in many maners, as Manasses dide."

7. That princes, lords, and prelates so doing be worse than Herod that pursued Christ, and worse than Jews and heathen men that crucified Christ.

   GP, chap. 10, p. 32: "Grostede seith . . . 'He that yeveth thus the cure of soulis to unable men is werse than Eroude, that pursuede Crist, and worse thanne Jewis and hethene men, that crucifieden Crist.'"

8. That every man swearing by Our Lady or another saint or creature giveth more honor to the saints than to the Holy Trinity; and so he saith they be idolaters.

   GP, chap. 10, p. 33: "Comunly they sweren by Oure Lady of Walsingham, Seint Joon Baptist, Seint Edward, Seint Thomas of Caunterbury, and such othere seintis, and chargen more this ooth than though they sweren by the Hooly Trinite; and in al this they onoren more these seintis than they onouren the Hooly Trinite. Though it were leeveful to swere by seintis, this is idolatrie, to charge more an ooth maad by suche seintis than by God Almighty either by the Hooly Trinite."

9. He saith that saints ought not to be honored.

   GP, chap. 10, p. 33: "Lordis and prelatis moun see how they don opin idolatrie, whanne they gessen to onoure seintis."

10. He damneth adoration, prayer, kneeling, and offering to images, which he calleth stocks and stones.

    GP, chap. 10, p. 34: "But of scheding of blood and sleeing of pore men by withdrawing of almes, and in yevinge it to dede stockis either stoonis, either to riche clerkis and feyned religiouse, were to speke now, if a man hadde the spirit of goostly strengthe. Now men knelyn, and preyen, and offren faste to dede imagis, that han neither hungir neither coold."

11. He saith that the very Body of the Lord is not contained in the sacrament of the altar, but that men receiving it shall thereby keep in mind that Christ's flesh was wounded and crucified for us.

    GP, chap. 12, p. 43: "Crist seith, 'If ye eten not the flesch of Mannis Sone and drinke not his blood, ye schulen not have liif in you." This speche semith to comaunde wickidnesse either cruelte; therfore it is a figuratif speche, and comaundith men to comune with Cristis Passioun, and to kepe in minde sweetly and profitably that Cristis flesch was woundid and crucified for us."[24]

12. He damneth the University of Oxford with all degrees and faculties in it, as art, civil, canon, and divinity, saying that they hinder the true way to come to the knowledge of the Laws of God and Holy Scripture.

    GP, chap. 13, p. 51: "But alas! alas! alas! The moost abominacioun that ever was herd among Cristen clerkis is now purposid in Ingelond, by worldly clerkis and feined religiouse, and in the cheef Universitee of oure reume, as manye trewe men tellen with greet weiling. This orrible and Develis cursednesse is purposid of Cristis enemies and traitouris of alle Cristen puple, that no man schal lerne divinite, neither Hooly Writ, no but he that hath doon his fourme in art."

13. He defendeth the translation of the Bible and the Holy Scripture into the English tongue, which is prohibited by the laws of our Mother, Holy Church.

    GP, chap. 15, p. 59: "Yit worldly clerkis axen gretly what spirit makith idiotis hardy to translate now the Bible into English, sithen the foure greete doctouris dursten nevere do this?" (Note: Ogle adduces the whole of chapter 15 to verify this charge.)

Nine of the thirteen charges (nos. 2–10) come from chapter 10, with no. 1 from chapter 2, no. 11 from chapter 12, no. 12 from chapter 13, and no. 13 from chapter 15. Foxe's translation, given here, in the first four charges attributes the sentiment to "the said book," while charges 5–8 begin simply "That." The final charges, nos. 9–13, attribute the sentiments directly to Hunne, but this would probably not be evident in the original Latin, where a pronoun like *ipse* would naturally be taken to refer to the book (*liber*) rather than to Hunne.

The one charge that might seem to amount to heresy is no. 11, on the Eucharist, which is based on the statement in GP that the words of Christ about eating His flesh are to be taken merely figuratively. We saw above in Chapter 2 that this is simply a translation of Augustine's *De doctrina Christiana*. Ogle believes that it was made to stand as a downright denial of transubstantiation only "by a piece of bold garbling" on the part of Hunne's prosecutor, Dr. Head.[25]

For our purposes, of course, the last article is the most important, since it declares that translation of the Bible is prohibited by the Church. This indicates that the last article (no. 6) of the earlier set should be interpreted to mean that the bishop of London and his officers did indeed believe that all English translations of the Bible were forbidden.

The English Bible shown by Ogle to be the one used to formulate the charges against Hunne, CCCC 147, far from having marginal comments approving the incriminated passages in GP, has notations denouncing some of them. These comments, according to a note written in the margin by the Elizabethan archbishop of Canterbury, Matthew Parker (1559–75), are in the hand of Geoffrey Blyth, bishop of Coventry and Lichfield from 1503 to 1530. In 1511–12, Blyth or his deputies had presided over the trials of sixty-seven heresy suspects during a period of five months, resulting mainly in abjurations but one execution.[26] One hypothesis is that Blyth was called on to help formulate charges against Hunne.[27] Ogle supposes instead that the bishop's chancellor, Dr. Head, somehow acquired the Bible with Blyth's marginalia already present in it and proceeded to single out some of the passages that Blyth had marked and to mark other passages with a three-dot sign, and then posthumously charged Hunne with having owned the Bible and having approved and held thirteen of the marked passages.[28]

However, even though we can agree with Ogle that CCCC 147 was used to find objectionable passages in the GP and that thirteen of these passages formed the basis of the posthumous charges against Hunne, CCCC 147 could not have been the Bible claimed to have been Hunne's, which, according to More, was displayed at Paul's Cross, since it contains Blyth's antiheretical comments and not pro-heretical notes in Hunne's hand, as More stated. No other surviving copy of the GP has such notes at the designated passages, except for the main manuscript that Forshall and Madden use for chapter 15, Harley 1666, where there is this annotation next to the statement about the Eucharist: "Hou men schulden ete Cristes flesch and his blood."[29]

Ogle postulates that the whole case against Hunne was fraudulent: the Bible was not Hunne's at all, but was claimed to be his, with no proof offered. But since his time, we have found out more about the trial, and, as we will soon see, there was testimony that Hunne possessed a Bible with prologue. So a more likely explanation is that there were two Bibles involved, one being Hunne's, and the other the one with Blyth's annotations, which was used to point to objectionable passages in the prologue.

It appears that depositions were obtained from only six witnesses, and these, More says, were read publicly. They are preserved only in a copy made by Archbishop James Ussher (d. 1656) from Bishop FitzJames's register.[30] Their testimony is as follows:

1. Hunne's servant Thomas Brooke deposes that at Hunne's command he brought four books to him in his prison, namely, the Bible in English, a book of the four Gospels, the *Prick of Conscience*, and a book of the Ten Commandments, all of which Hunne kept locked up.
2. Thomas Higdon deposes that one Roger, parish clerk of St. Botolph's, told him that Hunne's Bible belonged to one Thomas Downe, and that it used to lie on display in St. Margaret's Church in Bridge Street (Hunne's parish), sometimes for a month at a time, when he (Roger?) was clerk there.[31] If the "he" here refers to Roger, it would mean that Roger was clerk at St. Margaret's before becoming clerk at St. Botolph's. Or the reference could be to Hunne, saying that Hunne functioned as parish clerk at St. Margaret's, and so he would have been responsible for putting the Bible on display there.
3. John Cawood (the parish priest of St. Margaret's) deposes, in response to the 6th article [of the original charges], that Hunne had a book called the Apocalypse, and other books, for instance, a large Bible in the mother tongue, which was shown to him at the time of his examination; and he says also that Hunne used to read this and other books at the door of his home.
4. Hugh Saunders deposes that Hunne said to him that he had a beautiful Bible in English (with a prologue prefixed).
5. John Davis deposes that Hunne read to him from the end of the said prologue the good reasons why the Bible could be translated into English.[32]
6. John Young, bishop of Gallipoli (FitzJames's suffragan), who was also archdeacon of London[33] (and who was also serving as one of FitzJames's assessors or consultants at the trial), testified to the same thing in the same stilted terms, which, of course, shows collusion.[34]

The upshot is that, by a generous assessment of the value of this testimony, only two of the charges levied against Hunne could be considered to be proved by the requisite two witnesses. The first is the sixth and last of the antemortem charges, or at least a part of it: it could be concluded that among the prohibited books that Hunne possessed and used to read from were "Epistles and Gospels in English," if these could be construed to be contained in Hunne's great Bible, and that they were among the parts of the Bible that he read from. The second charge that might seem to have been proved against Hunne is the thirteenth and last of the postmortem charges, which I repeat here in its entirety: "He defendeth the translation of the Bible and the Holy Scripture into the English tongue, which is prohibited by the laws of our Mother, Holy Church."

It turns out, then, that the Messenger was absolutely right in his report of the trial, and More was absolutely wrong: Hunne *was* convicted for possessing an English Bible.[35] Here is a case, finally, in which the use of an English Bible, and the defending of translation of Bibles, was enough to bring about a condemnation of heresy by English bishops. Bishop FitzJames in his sentence mentions, as approving the condemnation, Bishop Ruthall of Durham, the newly consecrated bishop of Lincoln, William Atwater,[36] and the bishop of Gallipoli, along with the theologians, canonists, and other clergy present, and, finally, the mayor, aldermen, and sheriffs of London. He does not, however, specify in the sentence that the possession and use of English Scriptures is a crime, but says instead that Hunne was found guilty of making many heretical assertions to others and of using condemned books containing heresies, and also that he was proved by witnesses to have died impenitent in his heresy and in fear of the coming sentence against him.[37] These conclusions, however, are wildly at variance with the actual testimony received against him. We observe that there is no reference in the testimony to marginalia in his Bible and other books, let alone testimony that any such notation was in his own hand.

We may also underline the obvious fact that no action was taken against the clergy and parishioners of Hunne's parish church or against Thomas Downe for using the same Bible that brought Hunne to his conviction as a heretic.[38]

More on Bishops and the English Bible

Let us resume More's conversation with the Messenger. The latter responds, why then do the bishops keep English Bibles out of people's hands? They don't, More replies, except for censured ones, like Wyclif's and Tyndale's; older versions from before Wyclif's time "remain lawful and be in some folks' hands had and read." More could hardly be speaking for all of the bishops, who may have had divided views on the subject. The man who would become bishop of London the next year, 1530, namely, John Stokesley, would show himself to be adamantly opposed to having his subjects read the

Scriptures, for it did nothing else but lead them into heresy.[39] The Messenger may be more right than More when he responds to suggest that the bishops, in spite of what they might say, do not really want English Bibles readily available. Surely, he says, it is "not for naught that the English Bible is in so few men's hands, when so many would so fain have it." More agrees: "That is very truth." He addresses the question of why an English translation of the Bible has never been printed. "I think there will no printer lightly be so hot to put any Bible in print at his own charge, whereof the loss should lie whole in his own neck, and then hang upon a doubtful trial whether the first copy of his translation was made before Wyclif's days or since. For if it were made since, it must be approved before the printing."[40] More admits here that it would be tricky to try to determine whether a given translation goes back before Wyclif's time, but it does not seem to occur to him that the printer's wiser course would be to determine this question beforehand by going to his bishop with the translation in hand. And if it could not be safely determined that it was pre-Wyclif in composition, it would be simple to pass on to the next question: is it a good translation? We have seen from More's own testimony that this was already being done. Why then could not this translation (whether the EV or LV text of the MEB, and perhaps revised or updated as needed) have been handed over to a printer with full episcopal approval? An answer, of course, is that the bishops More speaks of approved these Bibles only for approved persons, who, in the bishops' opinion, would use them properly.

More goes on instead to marvel that no one has made a new translation and obtained episcopal approval for it: "And surely, how it hath happed that in all this while, God hath either not suffered or not provided that any good virtuous man hath had the mind in faithful wise to translate it, and thereupon either the clergy or at the least wise some one bishop to approve it, this can I nothing tell." However, he proceeds to conjecture that in fact a given bishop would be likely to hesitate to take such a step on his own, without the approval of his fellow bishops:

> But howsoever it be, I have heard, and hear, so much spoken in the matter and so much doubt made therein, that peradventure it would let and withdraw any one bishop from the admitting thereof, without the assent of the remnant. And whereas many things be laid against it, yet is there in my mind not one thing that more putteth good men of the clergy in doubt to suffer it than that, that they see sometime much of the worse sort more fervent in the calling for it than them whom we find far better—which

> maketh them to fear lest such men desire it for no good, and lest, if it were in every man's hand, there would great peril arise, and that seditious people should do more harm therewith, than good and honest folk should take fruit thereby.[41]

More says that this is not his own point of view:

> Which fear, I promise you, nothing feareth me, but that whosoever would of their malice or folly take harm of that thing that is of itself ordained to do all men good, I would never for the avoiding of their harm take from other the profit which they might take and nothing deserve to lose. For else if the abuse of a good thing should cause the taking away therefore from other that would use it well, Christ should Himself never have been born, nor brought His faith into the world, nor God should never have made it, neither, if He should for the loss of those that would be damned wretches have kept away the occasion of reward from them that would with help of His grace endeavor them to deserve it.[42]

He repeats the same thing over again many times. Not translating the Bible because it might be misused is like a surgeon who cuts off a leg to prevent gout in the toe, or cutting off a man's head to prevent toothache.[43]

He returns to the episcopal legislation:

> Finally, methinketh that the constitution provincial of which we spake right now hath determined this question already. For when the clergy therein agreed that the English Bibles should remain which were translated afore Wyclif's days, they consequently did agree that to have the Bible in English was none hurt. And, in that they forbade any new translation to be read till it were approved by the bishops, it appeareth well thereby that their intent was that the bishop should approve it if he found it faultless, and also of reason amend it where it were faulty.[44]

He puts forth in effect a program for a new translation:

> It might be with diligence well and truly translated by some good Catholic and well-learned man, or by divers dividing the labor among them, and after conferring their several parts together each with other. And after that might the work be allowed and approved by the ordinaries, and by their authorities so put unto print, as all the copies should come whole unto the

> bishop's hand—which he may after his discretion and wisdom deliver to such as he perceiveth honest, sad, and virtuous.[45]

After the decease of such persons, he says, the copies should be returned. And the bishop might well wish to provide such Bibles free of charge.[46]

Good Catholic Men Step Forward: The Douai-Rheims Translation

The old medieval translations, though recognized as orthodox, seemed to lapse out of view after More's time as the new Protestant translations proliferated. No "good Catholic and well-learned man" came to the fore to undertake a fresh translation until a full half-century later in the person of the exiled Oxford scholar Gregory Martin, of the University of Douai.[47] I have remarked above on the amazing speed with which he and his colleagues brought their work to conclusion. The New Testament was printed in 1582, some months before Martin's death, with the approval of the vicar-general of the archdiocese of Rheims and other curial officials.[48] The printing of the Old Testament was put off for lack of funds until 1610, just a year before the King James Version appeared.

In the preface to the Rheims New Testament, Martin (or whoever wrote it),[49] summarizes the 1407 Oxford constitution *Periculosa* thus:

> Strait provision was made that no heretical version set forth by Wyclif or his adherents should be suffered, nor any other[s], in or after his time, be published or permitted to be read, being not approved and allowed by the Diocesan before; alleging St. Jerome for the difficulty and danger of interpreting the Holy Scripture out of one tongue into another, though by learned and Catholic men. So also it is there insinuated that neither the translations set forth before that heretic's time, nor other[s] afterward, being approved by the lawful Ordinaries, were ever in our country wholly forbidden, though they were not, to say the truth, in quiet and better time, much less when the people were prone to alteratio[n], heresy, or novelty, either hastily admitted or ordinarily read of [= by] the vulgar, but used only, or specially, of [by] some devout religious and contemplative persons, in reverence, secrecy, and silence, for their spiritual comfort.[50]

Neither More nor Martin go so far as to say that *Periculosa* required episcopal approval of the persons who could read the approved translations, though by

More's own account the bishops of his day seemed to think that to be the case: that laypersons should not read the Scriptures in English without their license. Martin suggests that this was in fact the practice of the authorities, and he goes on to say that it was a wished-for restriction that was finally made a requirement at the Council of Trent:

> The order which many a wise man wished for before was taken by the deputies of the late famous Council of Trent in this behalf, and confirmed by supreme authority, that the Holy Scriptures, though truly and Catholically translated into vulgar tongues, yet may not be indifferently read of [by] all men, nor of any other[s] than such as have express license thereunto of their lawful Ordinaries, with good testimony from their curates or confessors, that they be humble, discreet, and devout persons and like to take much good, and no harm, thereby.[51]

In fact, the two decrees of Trent on the Bible do not refer to translations, except very indirectly, and only require approval of editions of the Scriptures, especially the Vulgate, and books on sacred subjects, and not of those who may read them.[52] In this matter, the decrees resemble *Periculosa*. But, while More was theoretically in favor of allowing the vernacular Scriptures to be available to all, so that good persons could profit by them, in spite of harm that might be brought to others, in his proposed program the bishops would limit distribution of copies to suitable persons.

I conclude that More was more right than wrong in his views about the English Bible. He was wrong to think that EV and LV antedated Wyclif, at least Wyclif's arrival at Oxford, but right in recognizing them as orthodox. He was right in seeing *Periculosa* as not prohibiting EV and LV or any other good translation of the Bible. He was right in saying that there was widespread acceptance of these versions among the faithful, an acceptance that continued on the part of bishops into his own time, but blind to the fact that this view was not shared by his own bishop, Richard FitzJames, and wrong in thinking that Richard Hunne was not convicted for possessing and defending English Bibles. The message that English Bibles were actually prohibited by the authorities of his diocese was well learned by some people, represented by the Messenger of More's dialogue, but More did not learn it, and presumably he spoke for many others, whether they were intellectuals like him or not.

Conclusion

The complete Latin Vulgate Bible was first translated into English in a very literal rendering, which I call the Early Early Version (EEV). This version was then systematically but conservatively revised into the Early Version proper (EV), and it in turn was revised more radically into a more fluent and less Latinate English, known as the Later Version (LV). Together the three versions constitute the Middle English Bible (MEB). EV must have been in existence by 1395 or so, since an elaborate copy of it, the Egerton manuscript, was found in the library of Thomas, Duke of Gloucester, at his death in 1397, and the earliest provable LV copy is the Fairfax Bible, dated 1408, but the manuscript that preserves the Old Testament portion of EEV, namely, Bodley 959, dated "ca. 1380–90," or "certainly before 1390," or "ca. 1400," seems to have corrections from LV. We have no idea about the *termini post quem* of the three versions.

The only clue as to the identity of any of the versionists comes in a manuscript slightly later than Bodley 959, namely, Douce 369.1, containing most of the EV Old Testament: an added line says that the translation was done by Nicholas Hereford; he was an adherent of doctrines of John Wyclif. Near the end of the fifteenth century, William Caxton attributed a Bible translation to John Trevisa, and in the sixteenth century John Bale credited both Trevisa and Wyclif himself with Bible translations. By the twentieth century, the consensus was that EV and LV were both done by "Wycliffites."

The most striking thing about the whole translation project is that it was referred to by only one writer of the time, namely the Wycliffite author of the treatise *Five and Twenty Books*, an account of the books of the Old Testament. In an addendum describing the process that was supposedly used in translating the Bible, this writer, styling himself as "a simple creature," claims to have been the mastermind behind the whole undertaking and the sole or chief translator. In the eighteenth and nineteenth centuries, he was identified as John Purvey, supposedly Wyclif's secretary, and, in the 1850 edition of the MEB by Josiah Forshall and Frederic Madden, the treatise was considered to be the "General Prologue" to LV, or at least to the LV Old Testament, and Purvey to be the translator of LV. By the end of the twentieth century, however, it was concluded that there was nothing to connect Purvey to the MEB. But the author of *Five and Twenty Books* ("Simple Creature") has remained in place as a main player in the translation project.

In Chapters 2 and 3 above, I tried to cast doubt upon Simple Creature's centrality: his claim of an elaborate pre-translation preparation of the Latin text was imaginary; his description of an immediate translation from the Latin to a participle-free English rendering belied the actual process, that EV was produced before it was converted to LV; and his advocacy of some other translation preferences are not borne out in LV. Furthermore, his unfamiliarity with academic procedure at Oxford University showed him to be an outsider to the main undertaking. Ironically, however, the only person whom I can conjecture to be a candidate for Simple Creature is John Purvey. He was a nonuniversity scholar who possessed Latin books of the Bible and biblical commentaries and may have shared the treatise author's dialectal preference for "either" over "or."

In considering the translation and revision projects in the context of the study of the Bible at Oxford University, study that was unquestionably stimulated by John Wyclif's emphasis on biblical rather than "sentential" theology, I have suggested that EEV may have been a relatively simple undertaking, quickly achieved, designed to assist the clergy of the realm in understanding the Latin Bible. Converting EEV to EV need not have taken long, and LV too may have been accomplished in a relatively short period of time by virtue of teamwork. I have indicated some of the ways in which we may be able to distinguish individuals or teams by studying various linguistic features, for instance, the systematic substitution of one preposition for another.

Even though the two versions of the Middle English Bible survive, in whole and mainly in part, in over 250 manuscripts, there are almost no external references to it or its manuscripts before the seventeenth century. This is not surprising, since the same lack of reference will be found for most other medieval works, for instance, the mid-fourteenth-century *Prick of Conscience*, which exists in nearly 130 manuscripts in two rescensions.[1] Around 40 percent of the MEB manuscripts, including Egerton and Fairfax, are fitted out for liturgical use, indicating a general acceptance of the translations by the faithful at large.

But there were signs of worry on several fronts: one was that the English language could not adequately render the meaning of the Scriptures; another was that followers of Wyclif might produce distorted or heterodox translations; and a third, seen in Thomas Palmer's treatise, was that access to the vernacular Scriptures would provide occasion for untrained readers to make erroneous interpretations of the Word of God. These worries resulted in the Canterbury legislation of 1407, the constitution *Periculosa*: because it is difficult to translate without error, any rendering of the Bible made from the time of Wyclif onward must be first approved and allowed by the local bishop or a provincial council.

It is the almost universal judgment of scholars today that the Middle English Bible in both its major forms was considered to be Wycliffite, and they bestow upon it the designation "Wycliffite Bible," a term that came to life only at the end of the nineteenth century; and they assume that the provincial legislation constituted a strict prohibition of it. This interpretation is affirmed even though it is admitted on all hands that there is nothing erroneous or tendentious about it, in either version: meaning, therefore, that there would be no reason to prohibit it. More literal and accurate interpretations of *Periculosa* were produced throughout the ages, by William Lyndwood in 1434, Thomas More in the sixteenth century, Archbishop Ussher in the seventeenth century, and, most forcefully, Cardinal Gasquet at the turn of the twentieth century, but without noticeable effect on scholarly opinion.

Since EV and LV had already been in circulation by 1407 and were undoubtedly familiar to many of the clergy, especially to someone like Philip Repingdon, who may have had a hand in the translation, and who was probably involved in formulating the constitutions, it is not likely that they were being targeted by the mandate. Another likely participant in the Oxford council was Dr. Richard Ullerston, a known proponent of translating the Scriptures. One of the addenda that he made to his treatise on the subject was that all such translating should be subjected to the counsel of prelates, which corresponds to the mandate.

All of the constitutions of 1407 (including the one on Bible translation, *Periculosa*) were reaffirmed two councils later, in 1409, and ordered to be put into effect by every bishop of the eighteen dioceses of the province. We have seen some records of the promulgation of the legislation into local jurisdictions, but so far no survival of the required follow-up reports. But if the word was out that possessors of the older translations, that is, the EV and LV texts, were exempt from turning in their books, then there would have been few or no results at all, since, as far as we know, no new translations were made in recent years, except for works like the *Longleat Sunday Gospels* (by the author of *Dives and Pauper*), and it is probable that this is the sort of smaller work of translation that *Periculosa* was aimed at. But doubtless some owners of EV and LV texts would have wanted to make sure that they were in the clear and have them checked, and, if the authorities were doing their duty properly, their Bibles would have been returned to them.

If the EV and LV texts were recognized as good renderings, then it would not matter whether the Bibles that Lollard suspects were found in possession of were in Latin or English; but, of course, the authorities would have to be on the alert for heretical glossings or interpolations. It could well be that when one heresy suspect, the priest John Galle, was brought before convocation in 1428 and was found to be in possession of the Gospels in English, it may have added to the suspicion in the minds of some of the clergy, but hardly in the mind of William Lyndwood, who acted as the promoter in the trial held during the convocation of another priest, Ralph Mungin. Lyndwood understood the purport of *Periculosa* accurately, as set down in his *Provinciale* (already nearly finished at this time, but not released until he completed his index to it, in 1434). I tried to convey a likely exchange of views at this time in my invented dialogue in Chapter 6.

The bishops and other clergy of convocation did, however, proceed in 1431 to pass another constitution requiring *all* English Scripture to be turned in for inspection, under penalty of automatic excommunication. We see that mandate being enforced by Bishop Stafford of Bath and Wells, but later on, in 1441, he reverted to the terms of *Periculosa*. And surely, when Lyndwood became a bishop himself (of St. David's, in 1442), he would not have misenforced *Periculosa*, and he would have felt comfortable in citing LV himself, as did another slightly later bishop in a Welsh see, Reginald Pecock.

Stafford went on to become archbishop of Canterbury, without returning to the subject of English Bibles, as far as we know. But his successor, Thomas Bourchier, in an order sent to the whole province, went further than the 1431 constitution and ordered all works of English Scripture brought in (with no suggestion that they would be returned), accompanied by a warning that those who delayed in turning them in for over sixty days would be held as equivalently guilty of heresy. However, this search was mandated in conjunction with the ordered confiscation of Bishop Pecock's works.

As I have noted, EV and LV were widely used in the province of Canterbury, notably in connection with the liturgy. There are no certain examples on record of EV and LV texts being handed in to bishops for approval. In Thomas More's time, bishops were not being asked to approve English Bibles, which were accepted as orthodox, but rather they were asked to approve particular persons as readers of such Bibles. More stoutly maintains that *Periculosa* did not mandate a ban on English Bibles, but his own bishop, Richard FitzJames of London, who had received his doctorate in theology at Oxford as early as 1481, prosecuted the merchant-tailor Richard Hunne for heresy, based largely or entirely on the assertion of such a ban, which was allegedly violated by Hunne's possession and use of a Bible with Wycliffite prologue attached. Hunne was charged with holding the prologue's errors, one of which was declared to be that translation of the Bible into English was prohibited by the Church. This was the only article that was proved by witnesses, and yet he was found guilty of numerous unnamed heresies. More himself was present at the proceedings and was deceived into thinking that they had made their case.

More's interpretation of *Periculosa* was accurate; but, as his discussion with the Messenger makes clear, it was often misinterpreted to be more stringent than it actually was, and even More did not realize that the faulty understanding of the statute reached to Church authorities like Bishop FitzJames and his subordinates. It has been misinterpreted in similar ways in modern times, as I noted in Chapter 5—and the instances cited could be multiplied.

The issue of religious heterodoxy in connection with the Middle English biblical translations turns out to be something of a red herring in need of sidelining, so that we can get down to the important work of analyzing the astounding achievement of systematically rendering into English the entire Old Testament and New Testament, first in a way that preserves the Latin structures so as to leave ambiguities intact and the grammatical forms obvious; and then to subject the whole to a complete overhaul, interpreting away ambiguities and substituting expressions more familiar and suitable to the idioms of the day.

This enterprise of first producing a literal translation from the Vulgate and then a stylistic revision seems to have been centered at Oxford, but it is noteworthy that no record of its planning, inception, and execution has been preserved. Many scholars have assumed that this was due to its being a hush-hush operation, a samizdat affair carried on in fear and trembling. But we must realize that this project was about as far as imaginable from the clandestine assemblage of political pamphlets. There was no prohibition against doing it, and it had been done before, in recent memory, by Richard Rolle, at least for the Psalms.

Earlier on, especially from the time of Forshall and Madden through that of Margaret Deanesly, it was all thought to have been a rather simple affair, with two or three persons producing EV and one person doing the LV revision. But of late, it has been objected that it would have had to be a vast undertaking, entailing a great deal of scholarship and labor by many persons. It is true that a good deal of time and searching through libraries was required for producing the *Glossed Gospels*, which came after EV was produced; but this enterprise went its own way, and ignited no sparks, falling into almost total oblivion. A good deal of time and library work would also have been necessary if the program claimed to have been followed by Simple Creature, the author of *Five and Twenty Books* (GP), had actually been put into play, by first producing a meticulous edition of the Latin Bible. But once we dismiss this notion, we can see our way to imagining a more streamlined process, similar to that undertaken by Gregory Martin and his colleagues in producing the Douai-Rheims Bible in under two years' time, with almost no fanfare. Much work is still to be done in estimating the number of persons actually involved in first achieving EV and then transforming it into LV. Clues can be had from different linguistic usages in the manuscripts, so long as they can be separated from the vagaries of mere copyists. I have offered a few methods of attempting this task, which will no doubt need refining, if there is any validity to them.

Why is it important to study these translations? I would like modern students of those times to expand their interest from questions of religious orthodoxy to include other important subjects, including the uses that were made of the texts by persons of all levels and persuasions, as determinable from the surviving copies, from decorative elements, or devotional indications, or explanatory additions, polemical or not. Much good work has been done in studying liturgical markings, illuminations, and glosses, but much more remains.

There is even more opportunity for linguistic research. We have here an unparalleled situation in the history of the English language: to see academics of the latter part of the fourteenth century putting their minds to work on deciding the best ways to render meaning in English from Latin, and the best ways of making it sound like acceptable English. The discourse of the author of *Five and Twenty Books*, when he emerges as "a simple creature" in the last chapter, gives a good insight into the sort of topics that must have been discussed. In Chapters 2 and 3, we saw that his observations were on target for some of the favored usages of LV, and sometimes not. Furthermore, we saw that he betrays no awareness of the actual method that was used, of a two-step process, first taking care for literal accuracy, and then making it more acceptable "to pious English ears."

In Chapter 2 we were able to see many of the varying choices made by translators in the various parts of the Old Testament and New Testament in both EV and LV, in connection with the practices of claims of Simple Creature, with further such choices outlined in the Appendices. It is my hope that these examples will stimulate others to analyze these understudied texts and to formulate some conclusions about their influence in the formation of the English language.

It is time to clear the books of the long-entrenched misunderstandings that have stood in the way of our appreciation of the most popular and successful of all Middle English writings. In so doing, I suggest that we give a belated salute to the Benedictine historian Dom Francis Aidan Gasquet, who attempted to show the way over a century ago, when the world was not ready to follow. Gasquet as an English Benedictine was destined to spend his life in humble pastoral work rather than monastic intellectual labor, but he managed to escape from this devolution of their tradition and to prepare the way for the sort of work manifested by Dom David Knowles in a later generation. As Knowles demonstrates, Gasquet was self-trained as a historian, not having had the advantage of going to university, and I conjecture that this unconventional career path may have contributed not only to the many minor flaws in his work but also to his numerous novel and important insights into the religious culture of the Middle Ages.

I would like to nominate Gasquet as a patron saint of revisionism, specifically of a "fresh look" into religious and literary history; and he can also stand as a patron of linguistic studies, because of his work as head of the papal commission that produced the magisterial eighteen-volume edition of the Vulgate Old Testament, which he continued even after becoming cardinal librarian of the Vatican. Gasquet had a guardian angel of sorts in each of these enterprises. Knowles reminds us that Gasquet's housemate during much of the time that he produced his work on the pre-Reformation Church in England was the accomplished medievalist Edmund Bishop, who served as his scholarly adviser and guide. When Gasquet was appointed to head the Vulgate commission in 1907, he called to Rome to assist him the brilliant monk from the abbey of Solesmes in Paris Dom Henri Quentin, who assured the scholarly basis of the ensuing production. Cardinal Gasquet deserves to live in honor (and not in some manufactured scandal), not least for his clear vision of the nature of the Middle English Bible.

Appendices

APPENDIX A

A Note on the Manuscripts, Versions, and Dates of the Middle English Bible

Suggestions of dates for the beginning and ending of the Early Version (EV) and Later Version (LV) of the Middle English Bible (MEB) are much tied up with theories of authorship. For instance, if Wyclif himself translated the EV New Testament, he must have done it before his death on the last day of 1384. If Nicholas Hereford abruptly left off translating the EV Old Testament, it must have happened in 1382, when he fled England for Rome. We know that the whole EV was finished by the time of the earliest datable manuscript, namely, British Library Egerton 617–18, which was among the Duke of Gloucester's forfeited possessions in 1397.[1] It is generally assumed that both versions took many years to complete, but this may not have been so.

The manuscripts considered and used by Forshall and Madden are numbered and described in their edition (FM), pages xxxix–lxiv of volume 1, and the manuscripts actually used are summarized on pages xxxiv–xxxvii. Mary Dove in *The First English Bible* has descriptions of the most important manuscripts in appendix 4 (pp. 235–66), and she has an index of all the known manuscripts (pp. 281–306; keyed to the FM numeration), coming to a total of around 253. Another list is given by Kathleen Kennedy in *The Courtly and Commercial Art of the Wyclliffite Bible* (2014),[2] with a total of 259, but she omits some of Dove's fragmentary copies and includes seventeen English Books of Hours, not all of which are relevant.[3]

The text of EV printed by Forshall and Madden in the left-hand columns of their edition is a revision of the presumed original version, preserved in the text edited by Conrad Lindberg, which I designate as EEV (Early Early

Version).[4] However, some of the readings of the two manuscripts of this text may have been altered to conform to LV.[5] Sven Fristedt calls EV as edited by Forshall and Madden the "First Recension" and gives a list of typical changes made.[6]

Lindberg has recently edited another, later, version of LV—which I call LLV—a Bible once owned by King Henry VI, but certainly not by Henry IV before him.[7] Lindberg, whose knowledge of these texts is incomparable, having spent six decades editing them, holds that John Wyclif himself was a full participant in their production. He believes that he must have started his work on the Latin text soon after his arrival at Oxford in 1354. He conjectures that the formal preparation of the Latin text, as described in the so-called General Prologue would have taken around a decade, say from 1360 to 1370, the production of EV another decade, to 1380 or so, and LV to around 1390, with Wyclif participating until the end of his life (his death occurred on the eve of New Year's Day 1385).[8] LLV would then be placed in the decade 1390–1400.[9] At the end of Chapter 3 above I suggest that, on the contrary, EEV, EV, and LV could each have been produced in a much shorter time, even a period of several months (with perfect teamwork), especially since there is no evidence at all, whether textual or otherwise, for any kind of effort to edit the Latin Bible in fourteenth-century England, except on the part of the Benedictine scholar Adam Easton and the piecemeal work of the translators as they moved through their translations.[10]

APPENDIX B

Cardinal Gasquet and His Critics

Francis Gasquet (b. 1846), the son of a French naval officer and a Yorkshire mother, early on joined the Benedictine order. As a historian he was mainly self-taught, not being allowed as a Catholic to attend Oxford or Cambridge. At the time that he first published his conclusions on the early English Bible in 1894,[1] he was referred to as "Dom Francis Aidan Gasquet" or "Father Gasquet" or "Dr. Gasquet" (his earlier writings had earned him a papal doctorate of divinity). When he reprinted his biblical essays in 1908, he was "Abbot Gasquet," and from 1914 on he was "Cardinal Gasquet," and he has commonly been referred to as such ever since. In 1907, he had been appointed head of the Vatican commission for the reform of the text of the Vulgate Bible, and he became librarian of the Holy Roman Church in 1921.[2]

The controversy started by Gasquet is assessed by Mary Dove in her *First English Bible* (2007), in which she notes that "the bitterness of the debate Gasquet inaugurated reminds us how much was at stake: if the first English Bible was not produced by Wyclif and the Wycliffites, and was not censored by Arundel, the history of the late medieval English Church and of the liberation of the English people at the Reformation would need to be completely rewritten."[3] Dove asserts that Margaret Deanesly in her *Lollard Bible* of 1920 "re-established the medieval English Bible as the Wycliffite Bible, prohibited by Arundel."[4] Dove sums up the case against Gasquet by saying that "he ignored the evidence provided by records of heresy trials," and that "his claim that the Wycliffites had no particular interest in the scriptures in English was patently unsustainable." Furthermore, "evidently he had not read the Prologue" to the Wycliffite Bible, and his inaccuracies, she concludes, are castigated by David Knowles.[5]

We may look first at Knowles's review of his fellow monk's scholarly career, in his Creighton lecture of 1956, *Cardinal Gasquet as an Historian*.[6] Knowles starts out by rejecting G. R. Elton's assessment that Gasquet's work "is best ignored." Although admittedly Gasquet made many mistakes, Knowles says, "it is foolish utterly to neglect or despise him."[7] We must remember that he had the frequent counsel of a scholar of the highest repute, Edmund Bishop, especially until 1901, when they ceased residing together, after which "Gasquet's work never again reached its earlier standard."[8] Knowles considers "the affair of *The Old English Bible*" to be "the palmary instance" of Gasquet's practice of ignoring "even the most cogent evidence against anything he had written." The facts of this case were repeated again and again by G. G. Coulton, "and accepted, at least tacitly, by all subsequent writers on the subject."[9] Even Knowles seems to give the impression here that there is nothing to be said in favor of Gasquet's treatment of this topic.

Much of Gasquet's scholarly endeavor, in such works as *The Eve of the Reformation* (1900) and *England Under the Old Religion* (1912), was dedicated to demonstrating that the dark picture of religion in England before the Reformation, as largely venal and corrupt, was a distortion typical of what Peter Marshall calls "a strong strain of Protestant triumphalism" characteristic of religious historiography in the reign of Queen Victoria.[10] Gasquet's theme has been renewed with great success by more recent historians, notably by Eamon Duffy in his 1992 study *The Stripping of the Altars*, subtitled *Traditional Religion in England, 1400–1580*.[11] Of Gasquet's major publications, Marshall sums up: "There are plenty of familiar echoes here for readers familiar with more recent historical debates, and Gasquet's claim to be a progenitor of modern revisionist interpretations, both of late medieval parish religion and of the Reformation, probably deserves to be more widely recognized."[12] His studies on the medieval English Bible are of a piece with these themes. Marshall notes that other early revisionists, James Gairdner and Henry Maynard Smith, joined Gasquet in stressing the orthodox acceptance and use of the English Bible.[13]

Duffy also touches on the Gasquet-Coulton matter. He concludes that while Coulton "is almost always right, and Gasquet almost always wrong" on the points of contention, "a modern reader of their works cannot avoid the sense that Gasquet, for all his criminal carelessness and breathtaking disregard for evidence, had a surer sense of what medieval religion had actually been about than did his formidable opponent."[14] It will become clear, however, that Duffy's summation of Gasquet's failings is hyperbolic. He made only one major error: not recognizing the Wycliffite nature of *Five and Twenty Books*.

Gasquet's study "The Pre-Reformation English Bible" first appeared in the *Dublin Review* in 1894, where he sums up his revisionist view thus: "Startling as the assertion may seem to many, I have come to the conclusion that the versions, now known as the Wycliffite Scriptures, are, in reality, only authorized catholic translations of the Bible."[15] He was immediately challenged by F. D. Matthew in the *English Historical Review* in 1895[16] and by Frederic Kenyon, writing in 1895 or 1896, in his book *Our Bible*.[17] Matthew especially could be expected to be a formidable opponent, since he was thoroughly familiar with Wyclif's Latin works, supplying as he did the marginal English summaries in the editions as they were published. He was also an expert on what we must now call Pseudo-Wyclif, having brought out in 1880 a fourth volume of English works supposedly by Wyclif, *The English Works of Wyclif, Hitherto Unpublished*, which he would reedit in 1902, and he appeals to these English treatises to prove that he did indeed have an interest in translating the Bible. Matthew, by the way, titles his review "The Authorship of the Wycliffite Bible," and Kenyon also uses the expression "Wycliffite Bible" to refer to the Middle English Bible, and it has remained the standard designation, along with the "Lollard Bible."

Gasquet responded by reprinting his article with substantial additions and a supplementary article in his volume *The Old English Bible and Other Essays*.[18] Furthermore, in the essay "The Printed English Bible" in his book *The Eve of the Reformation*, which first came out in 1899, he says: "There is absolute evidence of the possession of vernacular Bibles by Catholics of undoubted orthodoxy with, at the very least, the tacit consent of the ecclesiastical authorities."[19]

His treatment in the *Old English Bible* was politely received, though thought unlikely, by J. H. Lupton in an entry in Hastings's *Dictionary of the Bible*, in a volume that did not appear until 1904,[20] but it was severely opposed in Arthur Ogle's long anonymous review in 1900–1901.[21] Knowles says that Ogle's review was the "first telling shot" against Gasquet's work.[22]

Gasquet reprinted his collection in 1908, with texts unchanged, except for the addition of a large footnote to the second essay on the Bible, in which he responds further to Kenyon, and a new preface, "To the Reader," in which he says,

> At one time I had entertained the design of adding a third Essay to the two on *The Pre-Reformation Bible*, which were much discussed at the time they

> first appeared, and the conclusions embodied in them were challenged in various quarters. Other occupations have prevented my carrying out this intention, and thus making use of material which, since the original papers were published, has been growing under my hand—material which, to me at least, seems to strengthen my contention as to the Catholic origin of the version which it has hitherto been the fashion without much justification to attribute to Wyclif himself.[23]

G. G. Coulton gleaned most of his criticisms of Gasquet's position on the English Bible from Ogle's review. In 1915, in his "Rough List of Misstatements and Blunders in Cardinal Gasquet's Writings," he opens with *The Old English Bible*. He says, "It will be best to begin with this book, since this was the first in which Cardinal Gasquet's methods were pilloried, not by the present writer, but by a well-known Anglican clergyman, in the *Church Quarterly*."[24]

Of the twelve errors culled from Ogle, only one is important, the first, establishing the Wycliffite character of the so-called General Prologue, which Coulton believed was fatal to Gasquet's whole case, and he was indignant that the abbot would republish his essays without addressing the subject. Coulton continued to attack Gasquet on this point for the rest of his long life. On the occasion of the meeting of the Catholic Biblical Congress at Cambridge in 1921, Coulton published a pamphlet, *The Roman Catholic Church and the Bible*, and a second edition was called for within a few weeks, as Coulton himself tells us in the "Preface to the Second Edition."[25] He repeats his earlier complaints about Gasquet's Bible theses,[26] in the course of what Herbert Thurston calls his "outrageous attack" on the cardinal.[27]

Coulton renewed his attack in two pamphlets in 1937, *Sectarian History* (mainly a defense of H. C. Lea),[28] and *The Scandal of Cardinal Gasquet: A Sequel to "Sectarian History,"*[29] which Thurston responded to,[30] and in two others of 1938 and 1939: *Details of the Gasquet Case* and *A Premium upon Falsehood: A Postscript to "The Scandal of Cardinal Gasquet."*[31] He returns to it again in his autobiography, *Fourscore Years* (1944).[32]

Coulton did not himself do research on the subject of the Middle English Bible, but he suggested it "as a subject needing investigation" to Margaret Deanesly.[33] Deanesly, surprisingly, attributes to Gasquet something that he did not hold, namely, that EV and LV were "the authorized versions of orthodox Catholics, made before Wyclif's time,"[34] a conclusion about Gasquet that, even more surprisingly, James Gairdner had come to earlier, in 1908.[35] On the contrary, while Gasquet maintained that the versions were orthodox, he accepted that Wyclif's partisan Nicholas Hereford had worked on EV, and he admitted at least the possibility that Wyclif's secretary John Purvey had also contributed to the project, although he said that there was no proof at all to connect him to the enterprise, except that he happened to own a copy later on.[36] Deanesly put Purvey into the picture far more extensively than Forshall and Madden had done, as the author of even more vernacular works than previously attributed to him.

Alfred Pollard in his review of Deanesly responds to her "little note especially devoted to my destruction," that is, countering Pollard's favorable view of Caxton's attribution of the English Bible to John Trevisa, and his suggestion that Trevisa may have completed Hereford's translation of EV. Deanesly speaks of it as Caxton's "guess," but Pollard says that the real guesswork in this matter concerns Purvey's supposed role: "The attribution of the second Wyclifite version to John Purvey, first made by Waterton [*sic*, for Waterland] in 1729, was really a guess, possibly a happy one." Of the whole translation project, Pollard says, "Miss Deanesly is more inclined to regard the smoldering embers of the last heresy as the predisposing cause of an appetite for vernacular Bibles than to contemplate this appetite as due to the natural desire of an educated burgher class to have the best of good literature made accessible to them in their own tongue, as long as they did not thereby imperil their salvation."[37] This, of course, puts Pollard on Gasquet's side of the argument.

In 1926, Herbert Workman in his life of Wyclif dedicates a chapter to the question of "Wyclif and the Bible," in which he accepts all of the Deanesly assertions about the role of Purvey and other Wycliffites in the making of the EV and LV, observing only deep in a footnote that Pollard considers the attribution of LV to Purvey to be weak.[38] He notes that the doubts about the Wycliffite nature of the translations raised by Cardinal Gasquet have circulated so widely that, even though they have been answered by Kenyon, Matthew, the *Church Quarterly* reviewer (whom we know to be Ogle), and "above all by Deanesly," it is advisable "to add the positive proofs of Wyclif's authorship," that is, to show that his was "the conception of the plan and the organization of the work for his followers."[39] Workman speaks of "the claim of Cardinal Gasquet that Hereford's and Purvey's Bible"—as Workman calls EV and LV—"was in reality a sort of authorized version made by some unknown orthodox writers, the reading of which was encouraged by the Roman Church"; but he sides with Gasquet against Protestant writers who say that the medieval Church prohibited the circulation of vernacular Scriptures.[40] He says that Forshall and Madden were wrong to say that powerful measures were undertaken to suppress the Wyclif Bible, and he approves of what Matthew admitted in his 1895 article, that "no formal condemnation of his English Bible was ever issued, or, as far as we know attempted."[41] He admits further that "Purvey's translation, in fact, was orthodox, as Dr. Gasquet claims, apart from an occasional gloss and from the *General Prologue*—which last, in consequence, many manuscripts omit." He cites as an example of an unorthodox gloss Luke 17.19, which he says, was "overlooked by Gasquet." But this gloss is not from LV but from one of the *Glossed Gospels*.[42] We note that Workman does not twit Cardinal Gasquet, who was still alive and, since 1919, librarian of the Holy Roman Church at the Vatican, with having overlooked the Wycliffite nature of the prologue.

Arthur Ogle rehearses his case against Gasquet in the book he published in 1949 on the case of Richard Hunne,[43] referring for details to Coulton's *Medieval Studies* of 1915 and his *Sectarian History* of 1937. He simplifies the matter by saying:

> There are two facts connected with this first English Bible for both of which there is sufficient evidence: first, that it was the work of Wyclif and his colleagues, second, that copies of it, or parts of it, were owned and used, under episcopal license, by devout and orthodox persons during the century or so before the Reformation. Dr. Gasquet uses the latter fact to throw doubt upon, or deny, the former: a line of argument open to anyone sufficiently ignorant of, or indifferent to, the abundance of known facts.[44]

Since Ogle concedes the second fact, that EV and LV were officially approved during the fifteenth century, and since he had already, in his earlier review, conceded another of Gasquet's contentions, that both EV and LV were entirely free from error,[45] it only remains to assess Gasquet's arguments against the factualness of the first fact that Ogle so confidently asserts, that the versions were "the work of Wyclif and his colleagues."

APPENDIX C

Present Participles in *-inge* and *-ende* in EV

Lilo Moessner, in her study of Psalms 1–50 of the MEB, notes that in Middle English "the present participle is usually formed with the ending -*ing*, which gradually replaced the earlier endings *-ende/-ande*," and therefore is surprised at the *-ende* forms in EV, and attempts to give a technical reason for it.[1] She is not aware, however, that these forms are to be found only in the portion of the printed EV that uses Douce 369.1 as the copy text, namely, the section of the Old Testament from 1 Esdras to Baruch 3.20.[2] Since Forshall and Madden do not give the variants for participles, it will be necessary to study the other surviving manuscripts individually to see if the forms are repeated elsewhere. The editors call participial *-ende* "peculiar" in the case of Douce 369.1[3] and "remarkable" in the case of Oxford Christ Church College 145, which has the same feature.[4] This latter manuscript, OxCCC 145, contains the entire Old Testament and New Testament. It is the text that preserves EEV, from the point at which Bodley 959 ends in Baruch to the end of the Old Testament and for the entire New Testament. Forshall and Madden collate OxCCC 145 only for the New Testament, but, as noted, normally they do not include *-ende* participles in their lists of variants.[5]

The manuscript that preserves the first part of EEV, from Genesis to Baruch 3.20, namely, Bodley 959, uses *-inge* (*-ynge*) regularly, with the exception of the fifth and last scribe, who gradually changes to *-ende* (see Table C.1).[6] Why would Scribe 5 make himself undergo such a conversion, adopting a dialect that must have been unnatural to him? Does it reflect a recent change of residence from, say, Northamptonshire, where *LALME* puts him,[7] to an *ende*-ending neighborhood? Such areas were comparatively rare by the beginning of the fifteenth century.

The most frequent incidence of the form, according to *LALME*, was in East Anglia.[8] But John Gower, most likely a Londoner with Kentish connections, used it,[9] which proves that it was not considered outlandish or provincial at the time.

Table C.1. Present Participles in EEV Bodley 959 Scribe 5

	-inge	-ende
Eccles.		
48	3	0
49	0	0
50	10	0
51	8	0
Isaiah		
1	4	0
2	1	0
3	2	0
4	3	0
5	3	0
6	4	1
7	4	0
8	7	0
9	8	1
10	6	0
11	1	0
12	1	0
13	7	0
14	8	0
15	2	0
16	8	0
17	3	0
18	3	0
19	9	0
20	2	0
21	9	0
22	2	0
23	4	0
24	4	0
25	2	0
26	5	0
27	3	0
28	9	0
29	9	0
30	19	0
31	9	0
32	9	0
33	3	0
34	2	0
35	2	0
36	4	0
37	10	0
38	4	0
39	0	0
40	2	1

	-inge	-ende
Isaiah		
41	10	0
42	7	0
43	5	0
44	15	0
45	13	0
46	6	0
47	2	0
48	2	0
49	6	0
50	3	0
51	2	0
52	1	4
53	2	0
54	5	0
55	4	0
56	10	0
57	4	0
58	2	0
59	1	0
60	5	0
61	6	0
62	0	0
63	6	0
64	3	0
65	3	0
66	5	0
Jeremiah		
1	3	0
2	10	0
3	7	0
4	8	3
5	5	2
6	6	0
7	9	0
8	8	0
9	6	1
10	2	0
11	7	1
12	2	0
13	2	5
14	2	1
15	0	1
16	1	0
17	8	0
18	7	3

	-inge	-ende
Jeremiah		
19	1	0
20	2	6
21	0	2
22	4	2
23	2	9
24	0	1
25	1	8
26	0	11
27	0	4
28	0	3
29	0	11
30	1	4
31	1	9
32	0	1
33	1	6
34	0	6
35	0	9
36	0	17
37	0	7
38	0	7
39	0	4
40	1	3
41	2	2
42	0	5
43	1	6
44	0	18
45	0	1
46	0	9
47	0	0
48	0	11
49	0	9
50	2	6
51	1	8
52	0	5
Lament.		
1	0	12
2	0	3
3	0	11
4	0	3
5	0	1
Baruch		
1	0	6
2	0	6
3	0	1

It may be that Scribe 5 was grooming himself for his next job, which, according to Forshall and Madden, may have been to finish Douce 369.1, for they assure us that his was the third and last hand of this manuscript, that is Scribe C (or Scribe 3). This, of course, is the manuscript that they use for the main text of the middle part of the EV Old Testament, as stated above. All three Douce scribes use *-ende* throughout, with our Scribe 5 /Scribe 3 starting at Esther 2.4 and finishing off at the same abrupt place as he did in Bodley 959, namely, Baruch 3.20.[10]

APPENDIX D

EITHER/OR Preferences in the MEB

A. EV Old Testament Preference for OR, LV Old Testament Preference for EITHER

When we look at a sampling of the Old Testament (Genesis at the beginning, 1 Samuel and Job in the middle, and 1 Maccabees at the end), we find that the EV prefers OR to EITHER (I distinguish instances where the EITHER or OR introduces internal glosses or alternative translations, shown by "gl").

Table D.1. Dominance of OR in EV Old Testament

EV OT	Gen. OxCCC 4	1 Sam. (1 Kings) OxCCC 4	Job Douce 369.1	1 Macc. Douce 369.2
	ether 0 oither 1 or 20 or (gl) 2	ether 0 othere 6 or 25	ether 0 other 0 or 48	ether 0 other 2 or 11 or (gl) 84

But the LV Old Testament regularly transforms EV OR into EITHER.[1]

Table D.2. LV Preference for EITHER in the Old Testament

LV OT	Genesis BL Royal 1.C.8	1 Samuel (1 Kings) BL Royal 1.C.8	Job BL Royal 1.C.8	1 Maccabees BL Royal 1.C.8
	ether 11, ethir 5 ether (gl) 4 or 0	ether 22, ethir 5 ether (gl) 11, ethir (gl) 2 or 0	ether 11, ethir 26 ether (gl) 2, ethir (gl) 8 or 0	ether 9 ether (gl) 29 or 2 or (gl) 2

B. OR Preference in EV Gospels—Except Luke

In the New Testament, looking only at the Gospels, we see that EV Matthew, Mark, and John, like the Old Testament books, favor OR, but Luke favors EITHER.[2]

Table D.3. EV Gospels Favor OR, Except for Luke

EV Gospels	Matthew Douce 369.2	Mark Douce 369.2	Luke Douce 369.2	John Douce 369.2
	ether 2	ether 0	ether 22, ethir 3 ether (gl) 14, ethir (gl) 5	ether 1
	other 5, othir 1	other 0	other 5, othir 1 other (gl) 1, othir (gl) 2	other 0
	or 46 or (gl) 157	or 16 or (gl) 44	or 1 or (gl) 10	or 6 or (gl) 115

There are thirty-two cases of conjunctive OR in the Latin of Luke, either *aut* or *an* (never *vel*). The translation in EV is by OR only once, namely, for the first *aut*, in Luke 2.24, specifying that the Temple offering can be turtledoves or culvers.

Table D.4. Only One OR in EV Luke

Vulgate Luke 2.24: par turturum aut duos pullos columbarum	EV: a peire of turtris, *or* twey culvere briddis	LV: a peire of turturis, *or* twei culver briddis

For all of the others, EV Luke translates with EITHER or OTHER: EITHER twenty-five times (in the form of *ether* or *ethir*), and six times as OTHER. Here are the first three EITHERs:

Table D.5. The First EITHERs of EV Luke

Vulgate	EV	LV
Luke 5.23: Quid est facilius dicere, "Dimittuntur tibi peccata," *an* dicere, "Surge et ambula"?	5.23: What is lightere to seye, "Sinnes ben forgovun to thee," *ethir* to seie, "Rise up and walke?"	5.23: What is lighter to seie, "Sinnes ben forgovun to thee," *or* to seie, "Rise up and walke"?
Luke 6.9: Interrogo vos si licet Sabbato bene facere, *an* male? Animam salvam facere *an* perdere?	6.9: I axe you, if it is leefful to do wel in the Sabot, *ether* ivele? For to make a soule saf, *ether* for to leese?	6.9: I axe you, if it is leveful to do wel in the Sabat, *or* ivel? To make a soule saaf, *or* to leese?

An OTHER translates the *aut* at the beginning of EV Luke 6.42 (signifying "or let me put it another way").[3]

Table D.6. Example of OTHER in EV Luke

Vulgate Luke 6.42: *Aut* [Gutenberg et al.] quomodo potes dicere fratri tuo, "Frater, sine, ejiciam festucam de oculo tuo"?	EV: *Othir* hou maist thou seye to thy brother, "Brother, suffre, I schal caste out a festu of thin ighe"?	LV: *Or* hou maist thou seye to thy brother, "Brothir, suffre, I schal caste out the moot of thin ighe"?

There are also thirty-two internal glosses in EV Luke, and only ten of them use OR, starting at 1.19, "evangelise *or* telle."[4] One of the three OTHER glosses comes in Luke 6.41 (see Table D.7), right before the verse quoted in Table D.6.

Table D.7. An OTHER Gloss in EV Luke

Vulgate Luke 6.41: Quid autem vides festucam in oculo fratris tui ?	EV: Sothly what seest thou in thy brotheris ighe a festu, *othir* a mot?	LV: And what seest thou in thy brotheris ighe a moot?

C. OR Preference in EEV Luke, as Opposed to EV Luke

We must remember that these data hold only for the manuscripts chosen by Forshall and Madden as base (Douce 369, part 2, for the EV Gospels and Royal 1.C.8 for LV), but, as their apparatus shows, there are sometimes other manuscripts that regularly read OR for each EITHER in their texts, especially in the glosses; and EEV, that is, Oxford Christ Church College 145, is lacking most of the glosses altogether. In other words, the Douce text has undergone revision in a way not followed up in LV.[5] EEV Luke is lacking all of the EITHERs and OTHERs.

Table D.8. Absence of EITHER and OTHER in EEV Luke

EEV Luke OxCCC 145
ether 0 other 0 or 32 or (gl) 13

What we see here is that all thirty-two of the OR words in the Latin Vulgate, that is, *aut* and *an*, in the text of Luke were translated into English in the EEV as OR. In addition, the EEV translator added thirteen internal glosses or alternative translations introduced by OR. But these OR glosses are mostly not the same as the OR glosses of EV (Table D.3).

What happened to the Douce manuscript (Table D.3 above) or its exemplar is that Simple Creature or another EITHER-saying scholar came along and changed twenty-five of the internal ORs to EITHER, and then an OTHER-speaking colleague changed five more to OTHER.[6] They left only the first OR in place, in 2.24 (Table D.4). Then the two meddlers looked at the thirteen OR glosses of the original EEV translator (Table D.9), and accepted or modified only three of them, and added nineteen more, all introduced by EITHER or OTHER. In addition, an OR speaker came along and added another ten glosses, introduced by OR (Table D.3).[7]

D. OR Preference in All EEV and LV Gospels

LV Luke uses only OR, with the exception of one EITHER.

Table D.9. LV Luke Follows EEV Use of OR

EEV Luke OxCCC 145	EV Luke Douce 369.2	LV Luke BL Royal 1.C.8
	ether 22, ethir 3 ether (gl) 14, ethir (gl) 5 other 6 other (gl) 3	ethir 1
or 32 or (gl) 13	or 1 or (gl) 10	or 31

This means that the LV translator either eliminated all of the EITHERs from an EV-type copy, or, more likely, was using an EEV-type exemplar.

The one exception of EITHER in LV Luke appears in 16.13, the second member of an EITHER + OR construction, making it EITHER + EITHER (the only such construction in Luke).[8]

Table D.10. The Lone EITHER + EITHER Construction in LV Luke

Luke 16.13 Vulgate: Nemo servus potest duobus dominis servire: *aut* enim unum odiet et alterum diliget, *aut* uni adherebit et alterum contemnet.	EEV (OxCCC): No man servaunt mai serve to two lordis; forsothe, *outher* he shal hate the one and loven the other; *or* cleve to the oen and dispisen the other.	EV (Douce): No man servaunt may serve twey lordis; forsothe, *ether* he schal hate oon, and love the tothir; *ether* he schal cleve to oon, and dispise the tohir.	LV: No servaunt may serve to twei lordis; for *ether* he schal hate the toon and love the tothir, *ethir* he schal drawe to the toon, and schal dispise the tothir.

We see that all of the LV Gospels favor OR.

Table D.11. OR Preference in All LV Gospels

LV Gospels	Matthew BL Royal 1.C.8	Mark BL Royal 1.C.8	Luke BL Royal 1.C.8	John BL Royal 1.C.8
	ether 3, ethir 5 or 42 or (gl) 1	ether 2, ethir 1 or 22	ethir 1 or 31	ether 1 or 6

Note that all of the glosses in the LV Gospels have also been eliminated, except for Matthew 10.18, where, however, the glossing is reversed (EV "presidentis, or meyris," LV "meyris, or presidentis").

These data clearly call for a correction of the *LALME* report that the Royal 1.C.8 scribe uses only *ether* or *ethir*, and not *or*; and also, I would say, a reconsideration of the classification of this scribe as coming from Buckinghamshire,[9] since it is obvious that he is only following his exemplars throughout.[10] Perhaps it is the supervisor of the LV Old Testament translation team (which transforms EV OR to EITHER) that comes from Buckinghamshire.

E. OR Preference in EV and LV Pauline Epistles

Let us now see what the rest of the New Testament shows us on OR and EITHER. First we will look at St. Paul's long Epistles. For these I will count the first member in EITHER + OR constructions, for reasons that I explain below.

Table D.12. Dominance of OR in EV Pauline Epistles

EV Epistles	Romans Douce 369.2	1 Corinthians Douce 369.2	2 Corinthians Douce 369.2
	either 1, ether 4 other 1 or 21 or (gl) 137	either 8, eithir 4, ether 8, ethir 1 or 35 or (gl) 122	ether 2, ethir 6 or 13 or (gl) 86

Table D.13. Continued Preference for OR in LV Pauline Epistles

LV Epistles	Romans BL Royal 1.C.8	1 Corinthians BL Royal 1.C.8	2 Corinthians BL Royal 1.C.8
	ether 5 other 2 or 21	ether 16, ethir 10 or 30	ether 3, ethir 6 or 12 or (gl) 1

Once again, it is clear that the Royal 1.C.8 scribe is not a habitual EITHER speaker, though he does put EITHER in four places where EV has OR (namely, 1 Cor. 2.1, 14.23, 14.27, and 2 Cor. 1.17). The other EITHERs are organic to EV and also EEV, and come mainly in constructions answering to the Latin *sive* + *sive* + *sive* and so on. Look, for instance, at 1 Cor. 3.21–22.

Table D.14. Example of EITHER + EITHER + EITHER + + Construction

Vulgate 1 Cor. 3.21–22: Omnia enim vestra sunt, *sive* Paulus, *sive* Apollo, *sive* Cephas, *sive* mundus, *sive* vita, *sive* mors, *sive* presentia, *sive* futura.	EEV (OxCCC 145): Forsothe alle thingis ben youre, *outher* Powil, *outher* Apollo, *outher* Cefas, *outher* the world, *outher* lif, *outhir* deth, *either* thingis present, *either* thingis to come.	EV (Douce 369.2): Forsoth alle thingis ben youre, *either* Poul, *either* Apollo, *eithir* Cephas, *that is, Petre, eithir* the world, *either* lif, *eithir* deeth, *either* thingis present, *eithir* thingis to cominge.	LV (Royal 1.C.8): For alle thingis ben youre, *ethir* Poul, *ether* Apollo, *ether* Cefas, *ether* the world, *ether* liif, *ether* deth, *ether* thingis present, *ethir* thingis to cominge.

F. OR Preference in Later EV and LV New Testament—Except for Four LV Books

The rest of the LV New Testament is equally sparing of EITHERs, like the whole of EV.

Table D.15a. Sparse EITHERs in Last Half of EV New Testament

EV Epist.	Gal. Douce 369.2	Eph. Douce 369.2	Phil. Douce 369.2	Col. Douce 369.2	1 Thess. Douce 369.2
	or 6 or (gl) 30	ether 1 or 8 or (gl) 26	ether 5 or 0 or (gl) 21	ether 5 ethir 1 or 5 or (gl) 21	or 2 or (gl) 21

EV Epist.	2 Thess. Douce 369.2	1 Tim. Douce 369.2	2 Tim. Douce 369.2	Titus Douce 369.2
	ethir 2 or 1 or (gl) 23	ether 1 ethir 2 or 2 or (gl) 37	or 0 or (gl) 24	or 2 or (gl) 21

Table D.15b. Sparse EITHERs, Continued

Philem. Douce 369.2	Heb. Douce 369.2	Acts Douce 369.2	James Royal 1.B.6	1 Pet. Royal 1.B.6	2 Pet. Royal 1.B.6
or 1 or (gl) 3	ether 1 or 3 or (gl) 73	ethir 1 or 22 or (gl) 146	or 6 or (gl) 32	other 2 or 7 or (gl) 27	or (gl) 29

Philem. Douce 369.2	1 John Royal 1.B.6	2–3 John Royal 1.B.6	Jude Royal 1.B.6	Apoc. Royal 1.B.6
or 1 or (gl)3	or (gl) 8	or (gl) 2	or (gl) 6	or 7 or (gl) 42

Now let us look at the same books in the LV text. Here is what the Royal 1.C.8 scribe produces:

Table D.16a. Sparse EITHERs in Most LV Epistles

LV Epistles.	Gal. Royal 1.C.8	Eph. Royal 1.C.8	Phil. Royal 1.C.8	Col. Royal 1.C.8	1 Thess. Royal 1.C.8	2 Thess. Royal 1.C.8	1 Tim. Royal 1.C.8	2 Tim. Royal 1.C.8	Titus Royal 1.C.8
	or 8	ether 1 or 7	ether 2 ethir 2 or 2	ether 4 ethir 1 or 5	or 2	ethir 2 or 1	ethir 3 or 1		or 2

Table D.16b. Sparse EITHERs Continued in LV, Except in 4 Books

Philem. Royal 1.C.8	Heb. Royal 1.C.8	Acts Royal 1.C.8	James Royal 1.C.8	1 Pet. Royal 1.C.8	2 Pet. Royal 1.C.8	1 John Royal 1.C.8	2–3 John Royal 1.C.8	Jude Royal 1.C.8	Apoc. Royal 1.C.8
ethir 1	ether 1	ether 20 ethir 6 ethir (gl) 1	ether 1 ethir 5 ethir (gl) 1	ether 2 ethir 6					ether 3 ethir 4 ether (gl) 1
or 1	or 2				or 1				

We notice that it is only in a cluster of books near the end of the LV New Testament that EITHERs are used for OR, namely, Acts, James, 1 Peter, and the Apocalypse.

G. EVER-EITHER Usage in GP and LV Old Testament

There is another use of EITHER in GP that may have some importance in arguing that SC was involved in the LV Old Testament. The phrase EVER EITHER is used five times to mean "each of two." The same usage is found in the EV Old Testament only four times (4 Kings 4.11 and Job 20.12, 22.2, 24.12). LV repeats these instances and contributes fifty-nine more, in places where EV has only EITHER, an idiom preserved into modern times, as in "Place it on *either* side." EVER EITHER is not used at all in the New Testament in either version, except once in the FM Douce EV text (Luke 7.42),[11] but not in EEV or other manuscripts, except Egerton. To show it graphically:

Table D.17. EVER EITHER in GP and MEB Versions

	ever either
GP	5
EV OT	4
LV OT	63
EEV NT	0
EV (Douce, Egerton) NT	1
LV NT	0

This is a rare usage that has been found elsewhere, in Reginald Pecock, who also uses the negative form NEVER NEITHER.[12]

H. EITHER/OR Test on *Thirty-Seven Conclusions* and *Wyclif's Wicket*

Using this one criterion alone, we can challenge Forshall and Madden's claim that the author of GP (*Five and Twenty Books*) was also the author of the *Thirty-Seven Conclusions of the Lollards*, on the basis of "the style, language, arguments, manner of quotation, and authorities quoted."[13] Here are my rough counts in the 180 small pages of Forshall's edition of *Thirty-Seven* (so, perhaps, nearly the size of GP), from which it is conclusive that the author is not an EITHER favorer, and therefore clearly not the same person as the author of *Five and Twenty*:

Table D.18. Dominance of OTHER and OR in *Thirty-Seven Conclusions*

Thirty-Seven Conclusions Cotton Titus D.1	EITHER	OTHER	OR
	either 20, eyther 17	other 4, othir 84	119

The author often varies *othir* and *or*, and only occasionally *eithir*. The *eyther* forms come all at once, in conclusion no. 35, pp. 127–30 (one per page) and 131–32 (thirteen instances, or fourteen, counting the first member of an *either* + *or* construction, *eyther* + *eyther*).[14]

I add here the recent allegation by Richard Rex that the author of *Wyclif's Wicket*, which exists only in a 1546 printing, claims to have participated in the translation of Genesis, "from which it can be inferred that he was one of Wyclif's Oxford disciples who produced the Lollard Bible."[15] I disagree with this interpretation; I take the *Wicket* author to be referring rather to the words of Genesis that he has just quoted, "Be it do." This is a translation not found in either EV or LV. And while the author does use EITHER, he prefers OR three to one.[16]

APPENDIX E

The Uses of FORSOOTH

A. FORSOOTH for *Autem/Vero* in Both EV and LV Old Testament

EV Old Testament consistently uses FORSOOTH or, less frequently, SOOTHLY, for Latin *autem* and *vero* in our four sample books, Genesis, 1 Samuel, Job, and 1 Maccabees, and LV follows suit, except that LV makes FORSOOTH and SOOTHLY initial rather than postpositive.

Of these four sample books, Job shows the most variation in LV.

Table E.1. FORSOOTH and SOOTHLY in EV and LV Job

Vulgate Job	EV	LV
autem 51, vero 5	FORSOOTH 51 AND 1 (nil) 1	FORSOOTH 27 SOOTHLY 14 BUT 9 FOR 1

Simple Creature himself is not in the habit of using FORSOOTH or SOOTHLY. Each word occurs only once, in neither case as a narrative particle.[1]

B. FORSOOTH for *Autem/Vero* in EV New Testament, Not in LV New Testament

FORSOOTH and SOOTHLY, present in EV New Testament, are mainly absent in LV. Here are the figures for Luke. The five instances in LV Luke are simply repeats from EV.

Table E.2. LV Removal of FORSOOTH and SOOTHLY in Luke

EV Luke	LV Luke
FORSOOTH 246	FORSOOTH 1 16.17 *forsothe* (EV) it is lighter hevene and erthe to passe (Vulgate *autem*)
SOOTHLY 187	SOOTHLY 4 1) 4.23: *sothely* (EV) ye schulen seye to me this liknesse (Vulgate *utique*) 2) 5.10: *sothely* (EV) in liik maner James and Joon (Vulgate *autem*) 3) 12.39: *sothely* (EV) he schulde wake (Vulgate *autem*) 4) 18.8: *sothely* (EV) I seye to you (Vulgate 0)

The standard practice in the EV Gospels is the same as the LV 1 Maccabees, using both FORSOOTH and SOOTHLY for *autem*, but not in LV. Here again are the figures for Luke. Note that LV Luke uses FORSOOTH only once, in Luke 16.17,[2] and SOOTHLY twice, in Luke 5.10 and 12.39.[3]

Table E.3. Translations of *Autem* in EV and LV Luke

Vulgate Luke	EV Luke	LV Luke
autem 360	**FORSOOTH 188** **SOOTHLY 146** BUT 16 AND 3 TRULY 1 THEREFORE 2 (nil) 4	FORSOOTH 1 SOOTHLY 2 **BUT 96** **AND 239** TRULY 1 THERFORE 2 FOR 7 (nil) 12

As is clear, LV's favorite translation is AND. Here is an example:

Table E.4. *Autem* to FORSOOTH in EV and to AND in LV

Vulgate Luke 23.3: Pilatus *autem* interrogavit eum.	EV: *Forsothe* Pilat axide him.	LV: *And* Pilat axide hym.

Similarly, FORSOOTH is omnipresent in EV Matthew, but occurs only five times in LV Matthew, twice to translate *autem* (27.20 and 27.50), twice to render *amen quippe* (5.18 and 13.17) and once for *quidem* (26.24). FORSOOTH shows up only six times more in the rest of the New Testament (Mark 13.37, John 14.28, Rom. 9.28, 2 Tim. 4.12, Acts 4.36, and 2 Pet. 1.13).

Vero, as in the Old Testament, so too in the New Testament, is less plentiful than *autem*. It appears in the whole of the New Testament 157 times, 25 of them in Matthew. In EV Matthew BUT is the favored translation, as in LV.

Table E.5. *Vero* in EV and LV Matthew

Vulgate Matthew	EV Matthew	LV Matthew
vero 25	**FORSOOTH 5** SOOTHLY 2 **BUT 16** TRULY 2	FORSOOTH 0 SOOTHLY 0 **BUT 16** **AND 5** FOR 3 (nil) 1

But FORSOOTH and SOOTHLY are used more frequently in EV Luke for the seventeen instances of *vero*:

Table E.6. *Vero* Loses FORSOOTH and SOOTHLY in LV Luke

Vulgate Luke	EV Luke	LV Luke
vero 17	**FORSOOTH 7** **SOOTHLY 6** BUT 4	FORSOOTH 0 SOOTHLY 0 **BUT 8** **AND 9**

C. FORSOOTH and FORWHY as Translations of *Enim*

Enim appears 853 times in the Vulgate New Testament. However, FORSOOTH (*forsothe*) is used only eleven times in the LV New Testament, only once for *enim* (namely, in Romans 9.28).

FORWHY (*forwhy, for why*) is used 115 times in EV, translating *enim* only four times (it usually translates *nam*). Its use in LV is usually independent of the EV usage; it appears only forty-three times, but translates *enim* twenty-six times. Here are the figures for the Gospels, the long Epistles, and Acts:

Table E.7. FORWHY in Long Books of the New Testament (Rarely as Translation of *Enim*)

	Matt.	Mark	Luke	John	Romans	1 Cor.	2 Cor.	Heb.	Acts
Vulgate *enim*	110	65	64	70	118	71	52	74	70
EV FORWHY	10	4	15	1	14	19	24	6	2
EV FORWHY as trans. of *enim*	0	0	0	0	2	1	1	0	0
LV FORWHY	1	1	1	0	6	12	6	4	2
LV FORWHY as trans. of *enim*	0	0	0	0	5	5	4	3	1

Of the four times that EV translates *enim* by FORWHY (Rom. 8.18, 14.5, 1 Cor. 12.14, and 2 Cor. 8.9), LV takes it over once, for Romans 14.5.

APPENDIX F

Simple Creature's Statement on *Ex*

A. Various Translations of *Ex* in EV and LV

According to Simple Creature, *ex* sometimes means OF, and sometimes BY. In EV and LV, *ex* is usually translated as OF, but it is also translated in several other ways, among which BY is very infrequent. One way is by A-, in "aside" (*ex latere*); another is AFTER; still another, EVENLY (in *ex equo*); also, by FOR; very commonly, FRO; more rarely IN, or ON; also OUT OF; and SITHEN (rendering *ex quo* or *ex tunc*). Table F.1 shows the incidences in Genesis, Job, Psalms, and Isaiah in the Old Testament, and Luke and the Apocalypse in the New, of a total number of 243 examples of *ex*.

Table F.1. Translations of *Ex* in Sample Books of the MEB

Trans. of Vulgate *ex* by:	Gen. (50) EV	Gen. (50) LV	Job (12) EV	Job (12) LV	Pss. (42) EV	Pss. (42) LV	Isa. (48) EV	Isa. (48) LV	Luke (52) EV	Luke (52) LV	Apoc. (29) EV	Apoc. (29) LV
A-	1	0	1	0	0	0	0	0	0	0	0	0
AFTER	1	1	0	0	0	0	0	0	1	1	0	0
BY	0	1	0	0	0	0	1	2	1	1	0	0
FOR	0	0	0	0	0	0	0	0	1	1	0	0
FRO	5	7	2	2	29	28	12	15	10	10	1	2
IN	0	1	0	1	0	0	0	0	0	0	0	0
OF	41	39	5	4	13	14	31	27	36	36	24	22
ON	0	0	0	0	0	0	0	0	0	0	1	1
OUT OF	2	1	1	1	0	0	0	1	1	1	2	3
SITHEN	0	0	2	2	0	0	4	3	2	2	1	1
(nil)	0	0	1	2	0	0	0	0	0	0	0	0

BY is substituted for a different preposition in EV only twice, once in Genesis (EV AFTER), and once in Isaiah (EV OF). But the Genesis change is to be explained by the LV policy of changing all EV AFTERs to BY (see Appendix H).

Table F.2. Rare LV Changes to BY from other EV prepositions for *Ex*

Vulgate	EV	LV
Gen. 29.24: ad quam cum, *ex* more, Jacob fuisset ingressus.	to whom whan, *after* the manner, Jacob was goon in.	and whanne Jacob had entrid to hir, *by* custome.
Isa. 47.13: ut *ex* eis adnuntiarent ventura tibi.	that *of* them they telle thingus to come to thee	that they shulde telle *by* tho thingis to cominge to thee.

B. Expansion of Use of BY in LV for Non-*Ex* Uses

In EV Genesis, BY appears only fifty times, mainly to translate *per*, "through, by," and to render Latin ablatives used without prepositions. All of these translations are carried over by LV, with two exceptions, namely, Gen. 28.20, where IN is used for *per*, and Gen. 43.34, where IN is used to render an ablative.

Table F.3. All BYs in EV Genesis

Vulgate Genesis	EV trans. with BY
ablative	17 (16 in LV)
cum	1 (= LV)
per	28 (27 in LV)
post	1 (= LV)
seorsum	3 (= LV)
Total	**BY 50 (LV 48)**

But in LV, BY appears almost three times as frequently: 148 times. One systematic use, as we will see below, is to substitute it for EV AFTER in translating Latin *secundum* and *juxta*. Here is a table of the ninety-eight added BYs:

Table F.4. Added BYs in LV Genesis

Vulgate Genesis	EV text of Genesis	LV
ablative	FOR 2	BY 2
ablative	IN 10	BY 10
ablative	INTO 1	BY 1
ablative	THROUGH 8	BY 8
ablative	TO 1	BY 1
ablative	WITH 13	BY 13
ablative	(nil) 11	BY 11
adverb	adverb 1	BY 1
cum	WITH 1	BY 1
de	AT 1	BY 1
de	OF 2	BY 2
de	ON 2	BY 2
ex	AFTER 1	BY 1
in	IN 1	BY 1
in	INTO 1	BY 1
juxta	AFTER 15	BY 15
per	THROUGH 1	BY 1
per	THROUGHOUT 3	BY 3
secundum	AFTER 9	BY 9
seorsum	ASIDE 1	BY 1
unde	OF 1	BY 1
(nil)	(nil) 12	BY 12
	Subtotal: added to EV	**BY 98**
	Total for all LV Genesis	**BY 146**

APPENDIX G

The Question of a Stylistic Break in Baruch

From a dialectal point of view, Baruch A (up to 3.20) seems to be very close to Baruch B (after 3.20). But there are some noticeable changes in style or use with prepositions and particles and pronouns and verbs. Conrad Lindberg concludes that in general B agrees more closely with LV than does A.[1] One notable feature is the plural imperative, which in Baruch A takes the form PRAYETH, as in "preyeth for the lif of Nabugodonosor" (Bar. 1.11) while in Baruch B it has the form PRAY YE (which is also the form in LV for all of Baruch).[2] There are eight instances of each in the EV manuscripts:

EV Baruch A (Douce 369.1): 1.10 (byeth, maketh, offreth), 1.11 (preyeth), 1.13 (preyeth), 2.21 (bowith doun, doth)

EV Baruch B (Douce 369.2): 4.9 (ye . . . heere), 4.19 (wandre yee, wandre), 4.21 (be yee, crie yee), 4.25 (suffre ye), 4.27 (be yee, afer-crie yee)

The EEV text (Bodley 959) is the same in Baruch A; but in EEV Baruch B (OxCCC) for the first three instances, the PRAYETH form is found:

Table G.1. Mixed Plural Imperatives in EEV and EV Baruch B

Vulgate Baruch	EEV Baruch B	EV Baruch B
4.9 *audite* confines Sion	4.9 yee neegh coestis of Sion *hereth*	4.9 *yee* nigh coostis of Syon *heere*
4.19 *ambulate* filii *ambulate*	4.19 *wandreth* yee sones *wandreth*	4.19 *wandre yee* sones *wandre*

Note that I have not italicized the YE in the EEV version; it may be that the original translator understood the YE as separate from the imperative, so that the second verse would be punctuated, "Wander, ye sons, wander"; but the EV team behind Douce 369.2 may have understood it as "Wander ye, sons, wander." Which would mean that if there was one translator for both A and B, he used the PRAYETH form only when there was no YE with the imperative. To test this question further, one should look at plural imperatives pre- and post-Baruch in all four manuscripts.

Another point of interest is that there are instances of differing translations of the same Latin word, some shown in Table G.2.[3] One inappropriate choice in B occurs in 6.61, when clouds are made to "walk" through all the world, rather than "go" or "wander" (the usage of A).

Table G.2. Different Renderings of Same Latin in Baruch A and B

Vulgate Baruch	EV Baruch A (=EEV)	EV Baruch B (=EEV)
obaudire [for *obedire*]	to well-hear (1.18, 2.5); to hear (2.29)	to obey to (3.33, 6.59)
ambulare	to go (1.18; 3.13)	to walk (4.2; 4.13; 4.26; 5.7); to wander (4.19 [twice]); *perambulare* (6.61) to walk through
signum	sign (2.11)	token (6.66)
honor	worship (2.17)	honor (4.24, 4.37; 5.1–2, 5.4, 5.6–7; cf. 6.40)
sempiternum[a]	ever-during (2.35) *as noun*: into evermore (3.3)	everlasting (4.29; 5.1) *as noun*: into without-end (4.23; 5.4)
gentes	gentiles (2.13; 3.16); folk of kind (2.29)	heathen men (4.6); folks (6.3, 6.50, 6.66) sing. (*gens*): folk (4.3; 4.15 [twice])

[a] The EV and LV copy-text of Vulgate Bar. 3.13, instead of *in pace sempiterna* had *utique in pace super terra*, "forsooth in peace upon earth" (EV); see *Biblia Sacra iuxta latinam vulgatam versionem ad codicum fidem*, 14:322, for a list of texts with this reading, starting with the thirteenth-century Parisian Bibles. Similarly, Bar. 13.25, instead of *magnus et non habet finem* must have had *magnus et non habens finem*, "gret and non havinge eende" (EV). As noted before, the EV Baruch B manuscript, Douce 369.2, uses the *-inge* form of present participle, whereas the EEV text, OxCCC, continues with the *-ende* form, as here: "gret and nott havende ende."

APPENDIX H

The Translation of *Secundum* by AFTER or UP

A. AFTER Versus UP in EV Old Testament, from Prophets to the End

In Tables H.1 and H.2, the second row records the use of the preposition *secundum* from the Prophets to the end of the Old Testament, and also the preposition *juxta* when it means the same thing, and the third row shows how it is translated in EV. First the books leading up to the break in Baruch:

Table H.1. AFTER Versus UP in EV Prophets to Baruch

	Isaiah	Jeremiah	Lamentations	Baruch A (to 3.20)
Vulgate	secundum 5 juxta 4	secundum 14 juxta 18	secundum 1 juxta 1	secundum 5 juxta 0
EV Douce 369.1	AFTER 9 UP 0	AFTER 31 UP 0 (nil) 1	AFTER 2 UP 0	AFTER 5 UP 0

Then the books after the break:

Table H.2. AFTER Versus UP in EV from Baruch to the End of the Old Testament

	Baruch B (3.20–)	Ezekiel	Daniel	Hosea	Jonah
Vulgate	secundum 1 juxta 0	secundum 23 juxta 20	secundum 11 juxta 8	secundum 4 juxta 5	secundum 0 juxta 1
EV Douce 369.2	AFTER 1 UP 0	AFTER 43 UP 0	AFTER 10 **UP 9**	AFTER 0 **UP 9**	AFTER 0 **UP 1**

	Micah	Zechariah	1 Macc.	2 Macc.
Vulgate	secundum 1 juxta 1	secundum 2 juxta 1	secundum 30 juxta 0	secundum 9 juxta 0
EV Douce 369.2	AFTER 0 **UP 2**	AFTER 1 **UP 2**	AFTER 16 **UP 14**	AFTER 9 UP 0

Note the use of UP only in the stretch between Daniel and 1 Maccabees.

EEV presents much the same picture, but one EV manuscript, Longleat 3,[1] followed largely by the last scribe of the Allanson manuscript,[2] changes six of the AFTERs to UP in 1 Maccabees, and all nine of the AFTERs in 2 Maccabees.

B. No Use of UP in EEV Gospels, but Some Inserted into EV Luke and John

Overall figures:

Table H.3. UP as Preposition in the EEV and EV Gospels

	Matthew	Mark	Luke	John
EEV	0	0	0	0
EV	1	0	10	4

The instances of UP in EV Luke occur in 1.9 and a spate in 2.22, 24, 27, 29; there is a good example in 6.23:

Table H.4. Example of UP in EV Luke

Vulgate Luke 6.23: *secundum* haec enim faciebant prophetis patres eorum.	EV: forsothe *up* thes thingis the fadris of hem diden to prophetis.	LV: for *aftir* these thingis the fadris of hem diden to prophetis.

Other instances are in Luke 12.47, 17.30, 22.22, and 23.56. This might lead us to think once again of intervention in Douce Luke by someone of Simple Creature's habits. Here are a couple of examples.

Table H.5. AFTER in EEV and LV Luke, but UP in Between in EV

Vulgate Luke 1.9: *Secundum* consuetudinem sacerdotii sorte exiit	EEV (OxCCC): *Aftir* the kustum of presthed, by sort he wente forth	EV (Douce): *Up* the custom of presthod, by sort he wente forth	LV: *Aftir* the custome of the preesthod, he wente forth bi lot
Vulgate Luke 6.23: *Secundum* haec enim faciebant prophetis patres eorum.	EEV (OxCCC): Forsothe *after* thes thingis the fadres of hem diden to prophetis.	EV (Douce): Forsothe *up* thes thingis the fadris of hem diden to prophetis.	LV: For *aftir* these thingis the fadris of hem diden to prophetis.

C. Full Use of UP in Both EEV and EV in the New Testament Epistles

Here are the figures for all of the books of the New Testament after the Gospels.

Table H.6. UP as Preposition in EEV-EV Epistles

	Rom.	1 Cor.	2 Cor.	Gal.	Eph.	Phil.	Col.	2 Thess.	1 Tim.	2 Tim.
EEV	23	6	14	8	17	6	8	3	5	5
EV	23	6	14	8	17	6	8	3	5	5

	Titus	Heb.	Acts	James	1 Pet.	2 Pet.	1 John	2 John	Jude	Rev.
EEV	6	19	14	1	8	3	1	1	2	1
EV	7	19	14	1	9	3	1	1	2	1

The only places where OxCCC (EEV) does not use the form are in Titus 1.9 and 1 Peter 4.6c (while using it in 4.6b):

Table H.7. Two Instances of EEV's Lack of UP

Vulgate Titus 1.9a: amplectentem eum qui *secundum* doctrinam est fidelem sermonem.	EEV (OxCCC): becliping that wrd trewe that is *on* doctrine.	EV (Douce): biclipping that trewe word that is *up* doctrin.	LV: takinge that trewe word that is *aftir* doctrin.
1 Peter 4.6bc: ut judicentur quidem *secundum* homines in carne, vivant autem *secundum* Deum spiritu.	that they be demed sothely *up* men in flesh, sothely that they live *in* God in spirit.	that they be demid sothely *up* men in flesch, sothely that they live *up* God in spirit.	that they be demed *by* men in fleisch, and that they live *by* God in spirit.

D. Absence of Prepositional UP in the LV Old Testament

The use of UP as a preposition never occurs in our four sample books of the Old Testament:

Table H.8. Lack of Preposition UP in LV Old Testament

Up as prep.	Gen.	1 Sam.	Job	1 Macc.
LV	0	0	0	0

But there is a cluster of uses in 2 Sam. 22:

Table H.9. Preposition UP in LV 2 Samuel

Up as prep.	2 Samuel
LV	5 1(gl)
5 in text	1) 2 Sam. 22.21a: The Lord schal yelde to me *up* my rightfulnesse. 2) 2 Sam. 22.21b: And He schal yelde to me *up*, ethir aftir, the clennesse of min hondis. 3) 2 Sam. 22.25a: And the Lord schal restore to me *upe* my rightfulnesse. 4) 2 Sam. 22.25a: And *up* the clennesse of min hondis. 5) 2 Sam. 24.19: And Dauid stiede, *upe* the word of Gad, which the Lord hadde comaundid to him.
1 in gloss	1) 2 Sam. 22.27b: And with a weyward man thou schalt be maad weyward, [gloss:] that is, in yeldinge justly peine to him *upe* his weywardnesse.

We note that in the second textual example UP is explained in a gloss as AFTER.

E. Preposition UP Absent in LV New Testament

UP as preposition is completely missing from the four Gospels and the rest of the LV New Testament:

Table H.10a. Absence of Preposition UP in LV Gospels

Up as prep.	Matthew	Mark	Luke	John
LV	0	0	0	0

Table H.10b. Absence of Preposition UP in the Rest of the LV New Testament

Up as prep.	Rom.	1 Cor.	2 Cor.	Gal.	Eph.	Phil.	Col.	2 Thess.	1 Tim.	2 Tim.
LV	0	0	0	0	0	0	0	0	0	0

Up as prep.	Titus	Heb.	Acts	James	1 Pet.	2 Pet.	1 John	2 John	Jude	Rev.
LV	0	0	0	0	0	0	0	0	0	0

F. Other Uses of UP in EV and LV

It is worthwhile to consider the ups and downs of UP in other constructions as well. First, there are the VERB + UP constructions (as in "rise up," "take up"). There is a massive rejection of it in LV Genesis and 1 Samuel, but a complete acceptance in LV Job and 1 Maccabees.

Table H.11. VERB + UP Rejected in LV Old Testament

VERB+UP	Gen.	1 Sam.	Job	1 Macc.
EV	37	36	8	16
LV	2	1	8	11

From this we should doubtless consider the likelihood that different sub-revisers are in charge of various sections of the LV Old Testament.

In the New Testament as a whole, both EV and LV are sometimes partial to VERB + UP, notably the Gospels, Acts, and Apocalypse, with avoidance elsewhere:

Table H.12. Mixed Use of VERB + UP in EV and LV New Testament

VERB+UP	Mt	Mk	Lk	Jn	Rom	1Cor	2Cor	Gal	Eph
EV	37	33	23	24	2	3	3	1	2
LV	26	27	37	24	1	2	2	2	2

VERB+UP	Col	1Tm	Heb	Acts	Jas	1Pt	Jud	Rev
EV	1	3	0	36	1	1	1	13
LV	0	3	1	48	1	1	1	13

The favor shown to VERB + UP in EV Genesis and 1 Samuel and its rejection in LV is matched in the treatment of UPON, but it does not occur in Job and only rarely in 1 Maccabees:

Table H.13. Use of UPON Drops Off in the EV Old Testament and Is Boycotted in LV

Upon OT	Gen.	1 Sam.	Job	1 Macc.
EV	107	62	0	3
LV	0	0	0	0

We see that UPON is rejected even in EV Luke and John and almost always avoided in EV Acts, and also in all of the LV New Testament:

Table H.14. Avoidance of UPON in the New Testament

Upon NT	Mt	Mk	Lk	Jn	Rom	1Cor	2Cor	Gal
EV	24	11	0	0	4	1	4	2
LV	1	0	3	1	1	0	0	0

Upon NT	Eph	Phil	Col	2Th	Heb	Acts	Jud	Rev
EV	2	1	4	1	8	4	1	18
LV	1	0	1	0	0	2	0	1

G. *Secundum* as AFTER in EV Changed to BY in LV Old Testament

There was a systematic change of AFTER to BY in the translation not only of *secundum* but also of *juxta*, used in the same sense.

Table H.15. EV AFTER for *Secundum* and *Juxta* Changed to BY in LV Genesis–Judges

Vulgate	EV	LV
Genesis *secundum* 9 *juxta* 15	AFTER 9 AFTER 15	BY 9 BY 15
Exodus *secundum* 1 *juxta* 23	AFTER 1 AFTER 23	BY 1 BY 23
Leviticus *secundum* 1 *juxta* 25	AFTER 1 AFTER 25	BY 1 BY 25
Numbers *secundum* 2 *juxta* 31	AFTER 2 AFTER 31	BY 2 BY 31
Deuteronomy *secundum* 1 *juxta* 12	AFTER 1 AFTER 12	BY 1 BY 12
Joshua *secundum* 1 *juxta* 15	AFTER 1 AFTER 14, BY 1	BY 1 BY 15
Judges *secundum* 0 *juxta* 5	AFTER 0 AFTER 5	BY 0 BY 5
Total: *secundum* 15 ***juxta* 126**	**AFTER 140, BY 1**	**BY 141**

To show the trends in the rest of the Old Testament, I track only *secundum* and not the more plentiful instances of *juxta*. We see that sometimes the imperative to eliminate AFTER flags, but in the main it is there (with a sprinkling of UPs).

Table H.16. LV Replacements of AFTER for *Secundum* from 1 Samuel to Ecclesiasticus

Vulgate	EV	LV
1 Samuel *secundum* 4	AFTER 4	BY 4
2 Samuel *secundum* 4	AFTER 4	UP 3, UP-either-AFTER 1
3 Kings *secundum* 6	AFTER 6	BY 3, UP 3
4 Kings *secundum* 5	AFTER 5	BY 4, UP 1
1 Chronicles *secundum* 9	AFTER 9	BY 9
2 Chronicles *secundum* 5	AFTER 5	AFTER 2, BY 3
1 Esdras *secundum* 8	AFTER 8	AFTER 1, BY 7
2 Esdras *secundum* 8	AFTER 8	BY 8
Judith *secundum* 5	AFTER 5	AFTER 4, BY 1
Job *secundum* 3	AFTER 3	BY 2, EVEN WITH 1
Psalms *secundum* 45	AFTER 45	AFTER 6, BY 32, UP 6, EVEN TO 1
Proverbs *secundum* 1	AFTER 1	AFTER 1
Wisdom *secundum* 3	AFTER 3	BY 3
Sirach *secundum* 39	AFTER 39	AFTER 20, BY 16, UP 2, AT THE LIKENESS OF 1
Total *secundum* 145	**AFTER 145**	**AFTER 34, BY 92, UP 16**

We now come to the portion of the Old Testament studied above when comparing the translations of *secundum* and *juxta* in EEV and EV, with some uses of UP for AFTER. Here are the figures for *secundum* for EV and LV:

Table H.17. LV Rejections of AFTER for *Secundum*, Isaiah Through Rest of Old Testament

Vulgate	EV	LV
Isaiah *secundum* 5	AFTER 5	AFTER 1, BY 4
Jeremiah *secundum* 14	AFTER 14	AFTER 6, BY 8
Lamentations *secundum* 1	AFTER 1	BY 1
Baruch A *secundum* 5	AFTER 5	BY 5
Baruch B *secundum* 1	AFTER 1	BY 1
Ezekiel *secundum* 23	AFTER 23	AFTER 2, BY 20, LIKE 1
Daniel *secundum* 11	AFTER 6, UP 5	AFTER 1, BY 10
Hosea *secundum* 4	UP 4	BY 4
Micah *secundum* 1	UP 1	BY 1
Zechariah *secundum* 2	UP 2	BY 2
1 Maccabees *secundum* 31	AFTER 15, UP 16	AFTER 2, BY 28, LIKE 1
2 Maccabees *secundum* 9	AFTER 9	BY 9
Total *secundum* 107	**AFTER 79, UP 28**	**AFTER 12, BY 93, LIKE 2**

In the New Testament, however, AFTER remains in favor in LV. Here are the figures for both *secundum* and *juxta* (the latter preposition is much more sparsely used than in the Old Testament). We have seen already that LV eliminates all of the UPs; it does so most often with BY but sometimes with AFTER.

Table H.18. *Secundum* and *Juxta* in the EV and LV New Testament

Vulgate	EV	LV
Matthew *secundum* 5	AFTER 4, UP 1	AFTER 5
Mark *secundum* 1 *juxta* 1	AFTER 1 AFTER 1	BY 1 AFTER 1
Luke *secundum* 16	AFTER 2, BY 4, UP* 10 (*AFTER in other MSS)	AFTER 15, LIKE 1
John *secundum* 5	AFTER 1, UP 3, UPON 1	AFTER 4, BY 1
Romans *secundum* 37 *juxta* 1	AFTER 16, BY 1, UP 20 UP 1	AFTER 24, BY 12, AS 1 BY 1
1 Corinthians *secundum* 14	AFTER 9, UP 5	AFTER 9, BY 5
2 Corinthians *secundum* 17 *juxta* 1	AFTER 5, UP 11, UPON 1 UP 1	AFTER 13, BY 4 AFTER 1
Galatians *secundum* 9	UP 9	AFTER 5, BY 4
Ephesians *secundum* 18	AFTER 1, UP 17	AFTER 5, BY 13
Philippians *secundum* 6	UP 6	BY 6
Colossians *secundum* 8	UP 8	AFTER 5, BY 3
2 Thessalonians *secundum* 3	UP 3	AFTER 1, BY 2
1 Timothy *secundum* 4	UP 4	AFTER 2, BY 2
2 Timothy *secundum* 6	AFTER 1, UP 5	AFTER 3, BY 3
Hebrews *secundum* 17 *juxta* 3	AFTER 1, UP 16 BESIDES 2, BY 1	AFTER 2, BY 13, LIKE 2 BY 3
Acts *secundum* 12 *juxta* 3	UP 12 UP 3	AFTER 4, BY 7, AS 1 BY 3
James *secundum* 1	UP 1	BY 1
1 Peter *secundum* 9	UP 9	BY 8, LIKE 1
2 Peter *secundum* 2 *juxta* 1	UP 2 AFTER 1	BY 2 AFTER 1
1–2 John *secundum* 2	UP 2	AFTER 2
Jude *secundum* 2	UP 2	AFTER 2
Apocalypse *secundum* 5	AFTER 5	AFTER 5
Total *secundum* 199 + *juxta* 10 = 209	**EV AFTER 48, BY 6, UP 151 (+*58) (+*141)**	**LV AFTER 109, BY 94, UP 0**

It is evident that the LV prejudice against AFTER, so visible in the Old Testament, is not to be found in the New Testament. We note that out of 48 AFTERs in the EV New Testament, LV changes only 7 to BY: once in the Gospels (Mark 6.39) and 6 times in the Epistles (Rom. 1.3, 1.4, 8.27; 1 Cor. 12.8, 14.27; Eph. 3.11).

APPENDIX I

Absolute Constructions as Discussed in GP and Actually Treated in EV/LV

Absolute Participles in the Ablative

Simple Creature starts his discussion of his translation practices[1] by taking up the ablative absolute, which, he says, can be translated into English by using one of three words, *[the] while*, *for*, or *if*, along with an appropriate verb.[2] He gives as an example of such an absolute construction, not the rather more usual type with a passive past participle, but one with an active present participle: "the master reading" (which in Latin would be *magistro legente*). This, he says, can be rephrased in English as, "while the master readeth," or "if the master readeth," or "for the master readeth"; or sometimes it would accord better with the sense to put it into the past tense, saying, "*when* the master read" or "*after* the master read," to correspond to the past tense of the main verb, or into the future tense, and here he gives another example of a present participle, Luke 21.26, "arescentibus hominibus pre timore," which he translates, "and men shall wax dry for dread."[3] Note that he adds an *and* at the beginning, whereas LV Luke adds *for*, one of the three words listed by SC. EV, of course, translates it literally, "men waxing dry for dread."

Table I.1. SC's Lucan Example of Absolute Present Participle

Vulgate Luke 21.26:	EV:	LV:	SC:
arescentibus hominibus pre timore	men waxinge drie for drede.	*for* men schulen wexe drie for drede.	*and* men shulen wexe drie for drede.

According to Charles Hunter Ross, the absolute participle is very rare in early Middle English, and it was used occasionally only in the second half of the fourteenth century, under the influence of Latin, French, and, in Chaucer's case, Italian. Chaucer uses it, sparingly, in his poetry, especially when imitating Boccaccio, but not much otherwise (however, Ross exaggerates his dependence on Boccaccio).[4] In Chaucer's prose works, it is found even less frequently: there are two instances in the Melibeus, one in the *Astrolabe,* and none in the Parson's Tale. Boethius has sixty-six uses in the *De consolatione Philosophiae*, only seven of which Chaucer renders in kind.[5] The construction is not to be seen in the English writings that used to be attributed to Wyclif.[6] The same is true of LV, as opposed to its invariable use in EV whenever an absolute construction occurs in the Latin. Here is Ross's count of incidences in the Latin Gospels and EV.[7]

Table I.2. Absolute Participles in Vulgate and EV Gospels

Vulgate		(# per chap.)	EV
Matthew (28 chaps.)	64	(2.3)	62
Mark (16 chaps.)	46	(2.9)	49
Luke (24 chaps.)	65	(2.7)	65
John (21 chaps.)	12	(0.6)	12
Total	187		188

This shows that the construction is favored mainly in the Synoptics, but even there it is comparatively rare, averaging only two or three per chapter.[8]

It is noteworthy that when a pronoun is the subject of the participle, as in John 8.30, "hec illo loquente," EV keeps it in the oblique case.

Table I.3. Pronoun as Subject of Absolute Present Participle

Vulgate John 8.30: Hec *illo* loquente, multi crededierunt in eum.	EV: *Him* spekinge thes thingis, many men bileveden into him.	LV: Whanne he spak these thingis, manye bileveden in hym.

Whereas Chaucer follows the newer custom of putting it in the nominative: "And *he* continuing ever in sturdinesse" (Clerk's Tale 700).[9] Only one example of the nominative being used in this way in EV has been found, namely, in Exodus 1:10, "we overcomen," translating "expugnatis nobis," literally, "us having been overcome" (LV "whanne we ben overcomun").[10]

Present Participle Active Absolutes in Luke 1–6

The above discussion has included all absolutes, both present and past. In studying the participles of the first six chapters of Luke, we find five examples of the present absolute in the Vulgate and EV and none in LV.

Table I.4. Present Participle Absolutes in Vulgate and EV Luke 1–6, Converted in LV

Vulgate	EV	LV
1) 2.42 *ascendentibus* illis	1) hem *stighinge* up	1) they wenten up
2) 3.1 *procurante* Pontio Pilato Judaeam	2) Pilat of Pounce *kepinge* Judee	2) whanne Pilat of Pounce governede Judee
3) 3.15 *existimante* autem populo	3) forsoth al the peple *gessinge*	3) whanne al the puple gesside
4) 3.15 et *cogitantibus* omnibus	4) and alle men *thenkinge*	4) and alle men thouyten
5) 3.21 Jesu baptizato et *orante*	5) Jhesu cristenyd and *preyinge*	5) whanne Jhesu was baptised and preyede

Perfect Passive Absolutes in Luke 1–6

When past participles are used absolutely, they are passive, except when a deponent verb is in play. There are eight such constructions in the Vulgate Luke 1–6, all eight being brought over in EV, with none in LV (which changes all to finite constructions). Observe that example 2 (Table I.5) is in the same verse as example 5 of the present absolute (Table I.4), 3.21 (Jesus *having been baptized* and *now praying*). Note too that there is no instance of either kind of absolute participle in the extra-large chapter 1, which contains eighty verses.

Table I.5. Perfect Absolutes in Vulgate and EV, Converted in LV

Vulgate	EV	LV
1) 2.43 *consummatis*que diebus	1) and the dayes endid	1) and whanne the dayes weren don
2) 3.21 Jesu *baptizato* et orante	2) Jhesu *cristenid* and preying	2) whanne Jhesu was baptised and preyede
3) 4.2 *consummatis* illis	3) tho dayes *endid*	3) whanne tho dayes weren endid
4) 4.13 *consummata* omni temptatione	4) every temptacioun *endid*	4) whanne every temptacioun was endid
5) 4.42 *facta* autem die	5) sothly the day maad	5) whanne the day was come
6) 5.11 Et *subductis* ad terram navibus	6) the bootis *led up* to the lond	6) whanne the bootis weren led up to the loond
7) 5.11 *relictis* omnibus	7) alle thingis *left*	7) they leften alle thingis
8) 5.28 *relictis* omnibus	8) alle thingis *forsaken*	8) whanne he hadde left alle thingis

Let us examine the two such absolutes in 5.11, *subductis navibus* and *relictis omnibus*:

Table I.6. Examples of Perfect Absolutes in Luke 5.11

Lk 5.11 Et *subductis* ad terram *navibus*, *relictis omnibus*, secuti sunt illum.	EV And *the bootis led up* to the lond, *alle thingis left*, they sueden him.	LV And *whanne the bootis weren led up* to the loond, *they leften alle thingis*, and they sueden hym.

We see that EV renders both literally, that is, absolutely and passively: "the boats led up" and "all things left," whereas LV changes both to finite verbs, the first passive, "when the boats were led up," and the other active, "they left all things," keeping the sequence of tenses by putting both into the past tense. We should be aware that the EV translators did not yet have available to them the use of *being* and *having been* to render such passive absolutes.[11] By this means the phrases could be rendered, "the boats being brought up" or "having been brought up" and "all things being left" or "having been left." But *having been* never occurs in EV (nor in LV), and *being* occurs only rarely in EV and LV, and never to render absolutes (see below). A familiar example in later English of absolute *being* is seen in the Second Amendment of the U.S. Constitution: "A well-regulated militia *being* necessary to the security of a free state, the right of the people to keep and bear arms shall not be infringed."[12]

Gregory Martin in his Rheims version, published in 1582, while ostensibly translating the Vulgate, actually brings over the Greek constructions, using active participles agreeing with the subject (namely, the summoned fishermen): "And having brought their shippes to land, leaving al things, they folowed him." Tyndale before him, rendering the Greek, which has active participles, uses finite active verbs.[13]

Table I.7. Luke 5.11 in the Greek Original and the Versions of Tyndale and Rheims

Luke 5.11 Greek: Kai katagagontes ta ploia epi tēn gēn, aphentes panta, ēkolouthēsan autō$_i$. (And bringing down the boats onto the land, leaving all things, they followed him.)	Tyndale 1525: And they brought the shippes to londe, and forsoke all, and followed him.	Rheims 1582: And having brought their shippes to land, leaving al things, they followed him.

Another way of resolving the Vulgate perfect absolutes would have been to use the preposition *with*: "with the boats brought up and all things left." Examples of such a construction can be seen in Chaucer and his contemporaries;[14] there is an instance in *The Romaunt of the Rose*, fragment B, line 1715: "The God of Love, *with bowe bent*," rendering *Roman de la Rose* "Li

Dex d'Amors, qui, *l'arc tendu*" ("The God of Love, who, the bow bent").[15] But I have not observed its use in EV or LV.

We can conclude, then, that it is the practice of EV to take over absolutes literally, and the practice of LV to do away with the participles by transforming them to finite constructions (see Chapter 3, the section "LV Motivations as Inferred Versus GP," for the translational implications of these practices, that is, destroying the ambiguity of the original text by choosing a definite alternative). However, Simple Creature's formulas are not verified, as Hiroshi Yonekura shows: of the three resolving conjunctions he gives (*while*, *for*, and *if*), and the two others he adds (*when* and *after*), only *while* and especially *when* are used with frequency.[16]

Table I.8. Methods of Resolving Ablative Absolutes in LV Gospels

while clause	24 (13%)
for clause	2
if clause	1
when clause	125 (68%)
after clause	0
as clause	1
prepositional phrase	1
main clause	31 (17%)
Total	185

Note the frequent resort to converting the absolute into a main clause, a procedure not mentioned by Simple Creature. We saw an example in Table I.6 above: EV "alle thingis lefte" to LV "they leften all thingis."

APPENDIX J

Other Participial Constructions in GP and EV/LV

Participles in Apposition with the Subject

Even more common than absolute participles in the Vulgate text are participles in agreement with the subject, usually present participles, and this is the second topic taken up by Simple Creature. He says that a past or present participle, whether active or passive, can be rendered with a verb of the same tense, giving the example of the Latin *dicens*, "saying," which can be given as "and says" or "that says."[1] This is in fact the way in which LV almost always transforms EV's literal rendering of appositional participles.[2]

Present Participles Agreeing with the Subject of the Sentence

By far the most instances of subject-apposition participles in the Vulgate are the present-tense forms. For instance, Luke 23.1 has the participle *surgens* agreeing with the subject, *multitudo* (but note that the verb for *multitudo* is put in the plural, *duxerunt*). EV renders the absolute phrase literally, "all the multitude rising," which in LV becomes "all the multitude arise"—in this case using the present tense and violating sequence.[3]

Table J.1. Present Nominative Participle Kept in EV and Changed Against Tense in LV

Vulgate Luke 23.1: Et surgens omnis multitudo eorum, duxerunt illum ad Pilatum.	EV: And *al the multitude risinge* of hem, ledden him to Pilat	LV: And al the multitude of hem arysen, and ledden hym to Pilat.

Sequence is kept a bit later, when EV Luke 23.3 translates *dicens*: "Forsoth, Pilate asked him, *saying*, 'Art thou the King of the Jews?' " becomes LV "And Pilate asked him *and said*, 'Art thou King of the Jews?' "

Table J.2. Present Nominative Participle Changed with Proper Tense in LV

Vulgate Luke 23.3: Pilatus autem interrogavit eum *dicens*, "Tu es rex Iudaeorum?" At ille *respondens*, ait, "Tu dicis."	EV: Forsothe Pilat axide him, *seyinge*, "Ert thou kyng of Jewis?" And he *answeringe* seide, "Thou seist."	LV: And Pilat axide hym, *and seide*, "Art thou kyng of Jewis?" And he *answeride, and* seide, "Thou seist."

Table J.3 shows the figures for the nominative appositive present participles in Luke chapters 1–6, with a total of sixty-seven instances in the Vulgate, which EV renders in kind sixty-five times, and LV only fifteen times; in addition EV adds four more on its own.

Table J.3. Present Participles Modifying Subjects in Luke 1–6

Luke	Vulgate	EV	LV
Chap. 1	12	12	4
Chap. 2	13	13 (+2)	7
Chap. 3	5	5	0
Chap. 4	12	12 (+1)	0
Chap. 5	19	18 (+1)	2
Chap. 6	6	5	2
Total	67	65 (+4)	15

As noted above, the present participle *being* is rare in the time of the MEB, there being only one instance in all of Chaucer.[4] *Having* is also rare in Chaucer, with only three instances, all in a similar formula.[5] But while both EV and LV use *having* frequently to translate the Latin *habens*, there is no Latin participle for the verb *esse*, "to be," and as a result *being* is scarce in both EV and LV. In the FM text of EV, *being* occurs fifteen times,[6] and seventeen times in LV, overlapping EV only four times (Wisdom 8.12, Hab. 2.19, 1 Cor. 15.58 and Heb. 9.11). The last two are the only instances that LV uses *being* in the New Testament (EV has three others: 2 Cor. 4.15 and 5.6 and Gal. 1.14). None of them, of course, are used absolutely.

Past Participles Agreeing with the Subject of the Sentence

The use of past participles in apposition with the subject, which Simple Creature speaks of, is much rarer. In the first six chapters of Luke, there are only three examples, all deponent (active), and all in chapter 1.

Table J.4. Lack of Past Participles Modifying Subjects in Luke 1–6

Luke	Vulgate	EV	LV
Chap. 1	3	3	1
Chap. 2	0	0	0
Chap. 3	0	0	0
Chap. 4	0	0	0
Chap. 5	0	0	0
Chap. 6	0	0	0

Table J.5. Past Participles Modifying Subjects in Luke 1

Vulgate (3)	EV (3)	LV (1)
1) 1.9: sorte exiit ut incensum poneret, *ingressus* in templum Domini	1) 1.9: by sort he wente forth, that he, *entrid* into the temple of the Lord, schulde putte ensence.	-) 1.9: he wente forth by lot, and entride into the temple, to encense.
2) 1.28: et *ingressus* angelus ad eam, dixit	2) 1.28: and the aungel, *gon* in to hir, seide	-) 1.28: and the aungel entride to hir and seide
3) 1.54: suscepit Israel puerum suum, *memoratus* misericordiae	3) 1.54: he, *havinge minde* of his mercy, took vp Israel, his child	1) 1.54: he, *havinge minde* of his mercy, took Israel, his child

In the third example, the Vulgate reading followed is clearly *memoratus* (rather than *memorari*), and LV keeps the EV translation, using the present participle *having* with a noun object (*mind*); nowadays, we would say, *being mindful*.

Other Uses of Present Participles

Progressive Participles

In Vulgate Luke 1–6, there are sixteen instances of the progressive tense, using a form of *esse*, "to be," and the present participle,[7] which EV renders literally almost always (all but once) and LV more often than not (ten of sixteen).

Table J.6. Progressive Participles in Luke 1–6

	Vulgate	EV	LV
Chap. 1	4	3	1
Chap. 2	3	3	3
Chap. 3	1	1	1
Chap. 4	2	2	1
Chap. 5	5	5	3
Chap. 6	1	1	1
Total	16	15	10

Here are three examples in quick succession, showing use by neither EV and LV (no. 1), by both EV and LV (no. 2), and by EV alone (no. 3):

Table J.7. Examples of Progressive Participles in Luke

Vulgate (3)	EV (2)	LV (1)
1) 1.20 et ecce, *eris tacens*	-) 1.20: and loo, thou shalt be stille, or doumbe	-) 1.20: And lo, thou schalt be doumbe
2) 1.21: et *erat* plebs *expectans* Zachariam	1) 1.21: and the peple *was abidinge* Zacharie	1) 1.21: and the puple *was abidinge* Zacarie
3) 1.22: et ipse *erat innuens* illis	2) 1.22: and he *was bekeninge* to hem	-) 1.22: and he bikenide to hem

Adjectival (or Pseudo-Substantive) Participles

There are a good number of present participles in the Vulgate that simply modify a noun or pronoun adjectivally, and when the pronoun is only implicit, they look like substantives, like *clamantis* in Luke 3.4: "vox clamantis in deserto," which EV renders as a participle and LV as a noun.

Table J.8. An Adjectival/Substantive Participle in Luke

Vulgate Luke 3.4: vox *clamantis* in deserto	EV: the vois of oon cryinge in desert	LV: the voice of a crier in desert

In the other two genitive adjectival participles that occur in the first six chapters of Luke, both in 2.13, "laudantium Deum et dicentum" ("of [those] praising God and saying"), LV keeps EV's participles, which, however, agree with "multitude"; if the Latin construction agreed with the English, the text would read, "multitudo militiae caelestis *laudans* Deum et *dicens*."

Table J.9. Other Adjectival/Substantive Participles in Luke

Vulgate Luke 2.13: et subito facta est cum angelo multitudo militiae caelestis *laudantium* Deum et *dicentium*	EV: and sudenly ther is maad with the aungel a multitude of hevenly knighthod, *heryinge* God and *seyinge*	LV: And sudenly ther was maad with the aungel a multitude of hevenly knighthod, *heryinge* God and *seyinge*

Here is a summary of the instances of such participles in Luke 1–6 in the five noun/pronoun cases of Latin and the EV and LV renderings. We see that LV follows suit in using EV's participles in more than half of the instances.

Table J.10. All Adjectival Participles in Luke 1–6

Vulgate		EV	LV
Nominative:	6 (2.23, 3.9, 4.28, 4.33, 5.18, 6.43)	5	3
Genitive:	3 (2.13 [2x], 3.4)	3	2
Dative:	6 (1.50, 3.11, 6.28, 6.30, 6.48, 6.49)	5	2
Accusative:	7 (2.46 [3x], 5.2, 5.27, 6.32, 6.38)	7 (+2)	6
Ablative:	2 (2.5, 6.28)	1	0
Total	24	21 (+2)	13

The extra adjectival participles supplied by EV occur in 5.1 and 5.2.

Table J.11. Adjectival Participles Added by EV

Vulgate Luke 5.1, 5.2: secus stagnum	EV: bisidis the *stondinge* watir	LV: bisidis the pool

Present Participle Representing Latin Past Participle

In one case in Luke 1–6, EV and LV translate an adjectival past participle (deponent) with a present participle, namely, in Luke 1.3.

Table J.12. Deponent Past Participle Rendered with Present Participle in EV and LV

Vulgate Luke 1.3: visum est et mihi, *assecuto* a principio omnibus diligenter ex ordine	EV: it is seen also to me, *havinge* alle thingis diligently by ordre	LV: it is seen also to me, *havinge* alle thingis diligently by ordre

In contrast, the Douai-Rheims, instead of "*having* all things," uses *having* with a past participle: "*having attained to* all things."

Note: Gerunds as Opposed to Participles

I should make it clear that I am not treating the other class of *-ing* word known as gerunds, or verbal nouns, which LV uses almost as much as EV. Usually the EV/LV gerunds do not correspond to a Latin gerund, but sometimes they do. For instance, EV/LV Luke 1.1 "the telling of things" translates Latin *narratio*, and "the beginning" of 1.2 renders *initium*; but in 1.57 "the time of bearing child" corresponds to *tempus pariendi*. In Luke 5.9–10 we see LV accepting EV's gerund but not its progressive participle.

Table J.13. LV Accepts Gerund, Rejects Participle

Vulgate Luke 5.9: in captura piscium quam ceperant	*Gerund:* EV: in the *takinge* of fisches whiche they tooken	*Gerund:* LV: in the *taking* of fischis whiche they token
Participle: Vulgate Luke 5.10: ex hoc jam homines eris *capiens*	*Participle:* EV: now fro this time thou schalt be *takinge* men	LV: now fro this time thou schalt take men

One use of gerunds invariably found in EV is rendering the Latin future participle, like *futurum*, with *to* and gerund: *to coming*. Occasionally LV does the same, as in the first example in Table J.14, and sometimes it uses a simple participle (participial adjective), as in the second example, but most frequently it puts the infinitive, *to come*, the modern usage, as in example 3.

Table J.14. Treatments of Latin Future Participles

Vulgate Luke	EV	LV
1) 3.7: a *ventura* ira	1) fro wraththe *to cominge*	1) fro the wraththe *to cominge*
2) 13.9: in *futurum* succides eam	2) in time *to cominge* thou schalt kitte it doun	2) in time *cominge* thou schalt kitte it doun
3) 22.49: videntes autem hii qui circa ipsum erant quod *futurum* erat	3) forsoth they that weren aboute hym, seinge the thing that was *to cominge*	3) and they that weren aboute him, and sain that that was *to come*

The Vulgate does not employ the postclassical use of the gerund in the ablative as an equivalent of the present participle, whereby *sedet flendo* has the same meaning as *sedet flens*, "he sits weeping."[8]

APPENDIX K

Summary of Participle Usage in Luke 1–6 (Vulgate, EV, and LV)

Table K.1. Present Participles of All Kinds in Luke 1–6

	Vulgate	EV	LV
1) Absolute:	5	5	0
2) Apposition with subject:	67	65 (+4)	15
3) Progressive:	16	15	10
4) Adjectival:	24	21 (+2)	13
5) (Past Deponent)	1	1	1
Total	113	113	39

Table K.2. Past Participles of All Kinds in Luke 1–6

Vulgate		EV	LV
1) Absolute:	8	8	0
2) Apposition with subject (deponent):	3	3	1
3) Adjectival (deponent):	1	0	0
4) Adjectival (nondeponent):	0	0	0
Total	12	11	1

We see that there are no examples in Luke chapters 1–6 of the last category in Table K.2, of past participles used adjectivally; but let me give a couple of examples from later in Luke. First, in Luke 23.11, where Herod makes fun of Jesus clothed in a white garment: EV "scorned him *clothed* with a white cloth." LV tries to change it, "and scorned him *and clothed* with a white cloth." Neither gets the grammar quite right, since each omits a necessary "him" in different places (which the Latin does not need), thus:

Table K.3. A Latin Adjectival Past Participle, with EV and LV Efforts

Vulgate Luke 23.11: Sprevit autem illum Herodes cum exercitu suo et illusit, *indutum* veste alba, et remisit ad Pilatum.	EV: Sothly Eroude with his oost dispiside him, and scornide him, *clothid* with a whit cloth, and sente [him] ayen to Pilate.	LV: But Eroude with his oost dispiside hym, and scornede hym, *and clothide* [him] with a white cloth, and sente him ayen to Pilat.

They both get it right a little later: EV Luke 23.16, "Therefore I shall deliver him *amended*"; and LV, "And therefore I shall amend him and deliver him."

Table K.4. Another Adjectival Past Participle, with Better Results

Vulgate Luke 23.16: *Emendatum* ergo illum dimittam.	EV: Therfore I schal delivere him *amended.*	LV: And therfor I schal *amende* hym, *and* delivere him.

APPENDIX L

Other Constructions Discussed in GP

Because of the still confused and partial understanding of the manuscript traditions in the MEB, my findings will necessarily be tentative and approximate but, I hope, still indicative of general trends.[1]

Relatives

The next point that SC makes is that a sentence beginning with a relative pronoun like *which* in English can be rendered by substituting its antecedent preceded by *and* or some other copulative conjunction.[2] For example, EV Luke 1.29 "*Which*, when she had heard was troubled in his word" becomes LV "*And*, when she had heard, *she* was troubled in his word."

Table L.1. Relative-Pronoun Beginnings Eliminated in LV

Vulgate Luke 1.29: *Quae* cum audisset, turbata est in sermone ejus.	EEV: *The which*, whan she hadde herde, is troublid in his word	EV: *Which*, whanne she had herd, was troublid in his word	LV: *And* whanne sche hadde herd, *sche* was troublid in his word.

LV could have put the supplied antecedent earlier, thus: "*And she*, when she had heard . . ."

Narrative Particles or Discourse Markers

Then SC takes up the frequent Vulgate postpositive narrative particles *autem* and *vero*, which we examined above in Chapter 2 and Appendix E. As noted there, the discrepancy between the abundant use of FORSOOTH in the LV Old Testament and its virtual boycotting in the LV New Testament is one of the criteria used for doubting Simple Creature's claims that he was responsible for translating the whole Bible.

Word Order

The next topic concerns the flexible word order in Latin, which regularly allows, for instance, the sequence OVS (object-verb-subject). SC gives the example of 1 Samuel 2.10, "Dominum formidabunt adversarii ejus," which he says would be translated literally, "The Lord his adversaries shall dread"—that is, OSV. EV, however, follows the Latin sequence. Preferable, SC says in effect, is to put the subject first: "The adversaries of the Lord shall dread him,"[3] and we see that that is the way it is found in LV.

Table L.2. SC's Example of Reversing Inverted Word Order

Vulgate 1 Sam. 2.10: Dominum formidabunt adversarii ejus (OVS)	EV: The Lord shulen drede the adversaries of him (OVS) SC literal: The Lord hise adversaries shulen drede (OSV)	LV: Adversaries of the Lord schulen drede him (SVO) SC improved: The adversaries of the Lord shulen drede him (SVO)

We note that in LV and SC, adversaries no longer fear "the Lord" but rather "adversaries *of the Lord* fear *him*. We observe too that SC, unlike LV, specifies *the* adversaries (emphasizing that it is *all* his adversaries).

It is only rarely, however, that LV Luke has occasion to switch EV word order, and it is usually a matter of displacing prepositional phrases. For instance, EV Luke 1.9 "by sort he wente forth" becomes "he wente forth by lot" in LV.

Table L.3. LV Switches Around a Prepositional Phrase

Vulgate Luke 1.9: secundum consuetudinem sacerdotii sorte exiit	EEV: aftir the kustum of presthed by sort he wente forth	EV: up the custom of presthod, by sort he wente forth	LV: aftir the custome of the preesthod, *he wente forth bi lot*

It has been remarked that GP shows no OV (object-verb) word order,[4] but the same is true generally of both EV and LV Luke. Further study would be needed to see how frequent or infrequent it is in both the New Testament and the Old Testament. Simple Creature's example comes from the Old Testament, and it may be that such inversion is less common in the Latin New Testament than in the Latin Old Testament. Most of the Old Testament was translated afresh by the learned scholar St. Jerome (except for books that he deemed apocryphal), though it is clear that he did not impose sophisticated diction and form on the texts. Jerome did not retranslate the New Testament, but at Pope Damasus's request he edited the current translations of the Gospels.[5] It may be that the Latin New Testament simply follows the word order of the Greek, but once again one would need to investigate the incidence of word inversion in the Greek.[6]

Ambiguous Words

Simple Creature nears the end of his treatise by referring to a couple of examples of ambiguity discussed by Augustine in his *De doctrina Christiana* that had produced faulty translations, not really relevant for anything he has found himself, but he says that the best way for a translator to deal with such problems is to "live a clean life and be full devout in prayers and have not his wit occupied about worldly things," thus allowing the Holy Spirit to help him.[7]

Prepositions and Conjunctions

Finally, we have seen, as a kind of afterthought SC adds three stylistic notes, on translating the prepositions *ex* and *secundum*, and the conjunction *enim*, which we have studied in Chapter 2 and Appendixes F, H, and E, respectively.

APPENDIX M

Some Features Not Dealt With in GP

Awkward Latinisms in EV Changed in LV

Awkward Latin-based language in EV changes in LV. For instance, Luke 1.7 "non erat illis filius" is rendered "A son was not to them" by EV, whereas LV has "They hadden no child."

Table M.1. Awkward Dative Abandoned by LV

Vulgate Luke 1.7: Non erat illis filius.	EV: A sone was not to hem.	LV: They hadden no child.

An accusative with infinitive, usually very common in Latin, but rare in the Gospels (which normally follow the Greek construction of *that* with indicative), occurs in Luke 9.18, literally followed by EV, "whom do they say me to be," but converted by LV—which fails however to convert the accusative "whom" to nominative "who."

Table M.2. LV Conversion of Accusative with Infinitive

Vulgate Luke 9.18: Quem me dicunt esse turbae?	EV: Whom seyn the cumpanies me to be?	LV: Whom seyen the puple *that I am*?

One amusing EV literal rendering comes in Luke 13.8, where the tiller of the vineyard urges his master to hold off cutting down a barren fig tree "till the while I delve about it and send turds." This answers slavishly to the Latin *et mittam stercora*, but LV changes it to a more decorous and fluent "and I shall dung it."

Table M.3. From EV "Sending Turds" to LV "Dunging"

Vulgate Luke 13.8: Domine, dimitte illam et hoc anno, usque dum fodiam circa illam et mittam stercora.	EV: Lord, suffre also this yeer, til the while I delve aboute it, and *sende toordis.*	LV: Lord, suffre it also this yeer, the while I delve aboute it, and *I schal donge it.*

"The while" is also more idiomatic than "till the while," as well as "suffer it" rather than just "suffer" (here LV is following the Latin strictly, *dimitte illam*).

The verse following this also raises a difficulty about the results of the delving and dunging, in expressing the possible continued negative results even after the tiller's pampering. EEV and EV say "and if it shall make fruit," which does not do the trick, and neither does LV's "if it shall make fruit."

Table M.4. Failure of Idiom in Latin and English

Vulgate Luke 13.9: Et si quidem fecerit fructum; sin autem in futurum succides eam.	EEV: And if it shul make frut; if noen, in time comende thou shalt kitten it doun.	EV: And if it schal make fruit; ellis in tyme to cominge thou schalt kitte it doun.	LV: If it schal make fruit; if nay, in tyme cominge thou schalt kitte it doun.

Clearly, this clause, which is similar in the Greek (*kan men poiēsē*$_i$ *karpon eis to mellon*, "and if indeed it makes fruit in the future") means something like "and perhaps it will produce fruit." The sixteenth-century translators fared no better, beginning with Tyndale, who did indeed capture the meaning, but by changing the grammar: "to see whether it will bear fruit." Geneva 1560 went back to the grammatical construction, but added a word: "and if it bear fruit, well"—a solution taken over by King James 1611, the Revised Version 1881, and the Revised Standard Version 1946. Bishops 1568 added even more: "and if it bear fruit, thou mayest let it alone." Rheims 1582 adds "happily": "and if happily it yield fruit"—which is as ineffective as EV and LV.

Table M.5. Later Renderings with the Greek in View

Luke 13.9 Tyndale 1525: To se whether it will beare frute	Geneva 1560: and if it beare frute (wel)	Bishops 1568: And it if beare frute, *thou mayest let it alone*	Rheims 1582: and if happily it yeld fruite
King James 1611: and if it bear fruit, *well*	Challoner 1752: and if happily it bear fruit	Revised Version 1881: and if it bear fruit thenceforth, *well*	Challoner rev. 1941: perhaps it may bear fruit

This sort of problem is encountered more frequently in the often elliptic style of the Pauline Epistles.

Vocabulary and Idioms (Word Choices)

In most cases, but not all, the LV word choice sits better with the way that the language is to develop. We can start with the example above of *sending* turds; in Luke 23.34, EV translates the same Latin word the same way and speaks of *sending* lots, whereas LV has the soldiers *casting* lots. Another example: Instead of EV's partitive genitive, following the Latin, "what of evil," LV puts simply "what evil" (Luke 23.22).

Table M.6. Partitive Genitive Abandoned

	Vulgate	EEV	EV	LV
Luke 23.22	quid enim mali?	sothly what *of* evel thing?	sothly what *of* ivel?	for what ivel?

In translating the Latin *quidem*, "a certain man," EV says "some man" but LV puts "a man" (Luke 13.6).

Table M.7. From SOME to the Indefinite Article

	Vulgate	EV	LV
Luke 13.6	quidem	*sum* man	*a* man

When the owner of the vineyard dealt with above came looking for fruit on the fig tree and "found not" (EV), LV puts "found none."

Table M.8. From NOT to NONE

	Vulgate	EV	LV
Luke 13.6	et non invenit	and fond *not*	and foon *noon*

In EV Luke 23.55, Jesus's body was "put," but in LV it was "laid."

Table M.9. From PUT to LAID

	Vulgate	EV	LV
Luke 23.55	quemadmodum corpus ejus positum est	and hou his body was *put*	and hou his body was *laid*

Other examples are LV's use of "also" for "and" in rendering *et*; and "people" instead of "companies" for Latin *turbae*.

Table M.10. *Et* from AND to ALSO; From COMPANIES to PEOPLE

	Vulgate	EV	LV
Luke 12.54	Dicebat autem *et* ad *turbas*	Forsoth he seid *and* to the *cumpanies*	And he seide *also* to the *puple*

Then the up-and-coming "come up" replaces "stigh up."

Table M.11. From STIGH UP to COME UP

	Vulgate	EV	LV
Luke 24.38	cogitationes ascendunt in corda vestra	and thouitis *stiyen* up in to youre hertis	and thouitis *comen* up in to youre hertis

In Luke 1.25, LV puts "reproof" for "shenship," but lets the latter stand in Luke 6.22.

Table M.12. From SHENSHIP to REPROOF, or Not

	Vulgate	EV	LV
Luke 1.25	auferre obprobrium meum inter homines	for to take awey my *schenschip* among men	to take awey my *repreef* among men
Luke 6.22	et exprobraverint [vos]	and schulen putte *schenschip* on you	and putte *schenschip* to you

Sometimes we see in the EV text (Douce 369.2) an attempt to change EEV to a reading that we might find more modern, which does not appear in LV. The rich young man in Luke 18.23 who is *contristatus* appears as SORROWFUL in EEV, EV, and LV, but when he is *tristis* in the next verse, EEV makes him SORRY, and so does LV, but EV thinks he should be as before, SORROWFUL. In the following verse, EEV says it is LIGHTER for the camel to pass through the needle, and so does LV, but EV prefers EASIER, and so do we.

Table M.13. EV Improvements of EEV, Not Appearing in LV

Luke	Vulgate	EEV	EV	LV
18.23	contristatus est	he was soreweful	he was sorwful	he was soreful
18.24	videns autem illum Iesus tristem factum	sothly Jesus seende him mad *sory*	sothly Jhesu seinge him maad *sorwful*	and Jhesus seynge hym maad *sorie*
18.25	*facilius* est enim camelum per foramen acus transire	forsothe it is *lightere* a camaile to passen thurgh a nedlis eghe	forsoth it is *esier* a camel to passe thurgh a nedlis ighe	for it is *lighter* a camel to passe thorou a nedlis ighe

More Relatives

Some relative particles in LV mark an improvement, viewed retrospectively. For instance, where EV takes the Vulgate *quoniam* and *quia* to mean FOR, "because," when they are simple synonyms for quotative *quod*, "that," LV goes with THAT.

Table M.14. LV Adopts Quotative THAT

Luke	Vulgate	EV	LV
21.31	scitote *quoniam* prope est regnum Dei	wite ye, *for* the kingdom of God is niy	wite ye *that* the kingdom of God is niy

When we see restrictive THAT in LV instead of WHICH in EV, we find that EV has deviated from EEV.[1]

Table M.15. EEV and LV Favor Restrictive THAT Against EV WHICH

Luke	Vulgate	EEV	EV	LV
12.44	supra omnia *quae* possidet	on alle thingis *that* he weldeth	on alle thingis *which* he weldith	on alle thingis *that* he weldith
21.37	in monte *qui* vocatur Oliveti	in the mount *that* is clepid of Olivete	in the hil *which* is clepid of Olivete	in the mount *that* is clepid of Olivet

LV Luke 1.26 changes dative TO WHOM or TO WHICH to possessive WHOSE and adds a missing verb, "a city of Galilee *whose* name *was* Nazareth."

Table M.16. LV Changes TO WHOM/WHICH to WHOSE

Luke	Vulgate	EEV	EV	LV
1.26	in civitatem Galilaeae *cui* nomen Nazareth	into a cite of Galilee *to whom* the name Nazareth	into a citee of Galilee, *to which* the name Nazareth	into a citee of Galilee, *whos* name *was* Nazareth

Sometimes, however, as with other constructions, EV modernizations of EEV relatives do not make it to LV, as in Luke 12.57, where EV changes WHAT to WHY, and THAT THAT to THIS THING THAT.

Table M.17. EV Improvements of EEV Relatives, Not Passed on to LV

Luke	Vulgate	EEV	EV	LV
12.57	*Quid* autem et a vobis ipsis non judicatis *quod* iustum est	Sothly *what* and of youself demen yee not *that that* is just?	Forsothe *why* and of yousilf deme ye not *this thing that* is just?	But *what* and of yousilf ye demen not *that that* is just?

Articles

Latin has neither definite nor indefinite articles, so that it is always incumbent on a translator to decide when to use them in English. In the first example in Table M.18, EV suppresses a THE that finds favor with EEV and LV, and in the next two examples LV adds an A.

Table M.18. Judgment Calls on the Use of Articles

Luke	Vulgate	EEV	EV	LV
23.44	tenebrae factae sunt in universa terra	derknesses ben mad in al *the* world	derknessis weren maad in al erthe	derknessis weren maad in al *the* erthe
23.46	clamans voce magna	criende with gret vois	cryinge with greet vois	cryinge with *a* greet vois
23.50	vir bonus et justus	a good man and just	a good man and just	a good man and *a* just

Tenses

Since English is much different from Latin in the formation of time concepts, there is a lot of uncertainty about how to express the literal sense accurately. I will simply give some illustrations of the solutions arrived at by each of the three major sources studied here, EEV, EV, and LV.

There seems to have been an uncertainty about how to render the Latin future and future perfect (or perfect subjunctive, which was identical in form). The future in this era was still "in the making," so to speak. Thus, we have three different renderings of *cum veneris*, "when thou hast come"/"when thou shalt have come"/"when thou comest." LV seems to be riding the wave of the future when it uses the third option, the present instead of the future (as we now call *shall* forms) to render the Latin future perfect (Luke 23.42).

Table M.19. Different Renderings of the Future

Luke	Vulgate	EEV	EV	LV
23.42	Memento mei cum *veneris* in regnum tuum	Have minde of me when thou *art comen* into thy kingdam	Have minde on me, whanne thou *schalt come* into thy kingdom	Have minde of me, whanne thou *comest* into thy kingdom

In a case of the Latin pluperfect, *positus fuerat*, we see LV using the past perfect "had been laid" instead of the EV simple past "was put," in speaking of the tomb where Jesus was to be buried.

Table M.20. LV Use of Past Perfect for Simple Past

Luke	Vulgate	EV = EEV	LV
23.53	in quo nondum quisquam *positus fuerat*	in which not yit ony man *was put*	in which not yit ony man *hadde be leid*

In one sequence of tenses, where the Latin goes from perfect subjunctive (or future perfect indicative) to future, EV uses future-to-future and LV present-to-future.

Table M.21. Different Sequences of Tenses

Vulgate Luke 20.13: cum hunc *viderint, verebuntur*	EV = EEV: whanne they *schulen se* him, they *schulen be aschamyd*	LV: whanne they *seen* hym, they *schulen drede*

But in the next verse, where the Latin sequence is pluperfect subjunctive to perfect indicative, EV has pluperfect-to-past and LV uses past-to-past.

Table M.22. Other Sequences of Tenses

Vulgate Luke 20.14: quem cum *vidissent*, coloni cogitaverunt inter se	EV = EEV: whom whanne the tilieris *hadden seyn*, they *thouiten* withinne hemselve	LV: and whanne the tilieris *sayn* hym, they *thouiten* withinne hemsilf

In verbs of motion, LV constantly retrogresses in changing EV's HAVE auxiliaries to BE auxiliaries.

Table M.23. EV's HAVE GONE Replaced by LV's IS GONE

Vulgate Luke 22.45: cum *surrexisset* ab oratione et *venisset* ad discipulos suos	EEV: whan he *hadde* risen fro pregheer and comen to his disciples	EV: whanne he *hadde* rise fro preier, and *hadde* come to his disciplis	LV: whanne he *was* risun fro preyer, and *was* comun to hise disciplis

Sometimes the Latin future periphrastic *-urus* forms are translated by a *TO gerund*, sometimes by a **TO infinitive** (the idiom destined to survive).

Table M.24. Periphrastic Future: Infinitive or Gerund

Luke	Vulgate	EEV	EV	LV + LLV
18.30	in saeculo *venturo*	in the world **to comen**	in the world *to cominge*	in the world *to cominge*
19.4	inde *erat transiturus*	he was **to passe** thenes	he was *to passinge* thennis	he was **to passe** fro thennus
22.23	quis esset ex eis qui hoc *facturus esset*	who it was of hem that was **to do** this thing	who it was of hem that was *to doinge* this thing	who it was of hem that was **to do** this thing

Existential *There*

EV follows the Latin construction in statements of being like *nemo est*, putting NO MAN IS, even where EEV has gone existential with the dummy subject THERE: "There is no man."[2]

Table M.25. Use and Nonuse of Dummy Subject THERE

Luke	Vulgate	EEV	EV	LV + LLV
7.28	major inter natos mulierum propheta Johanne Baptista *nemo est*	*no man is* more prophete than Jon Baptist	*no man is* more than John Baptist prophete	**there is no man** more prophete among children of wimmen than is Joon
14.22	et adhuc *locus est*	and yit **ther is place**	and yit *place is*	and yit **there is a void place**
18.29	*nemo est* qui reliquit domum, aut parentes	**ther is no man** that shal forsaken hous, or fader and moder	*no man is* that schal forsake hous, ether fadir, ethir modir	**there is no man** that schal forsake hous, or fadir, modir

Overtranslating and Undertranslating

EEV decided to translate *tetrarcha* as "prince of the fourth part," while LV was satisfied first simply with "prince," and then brought over the term from Latin as a new word, "tetrarch." EV went in another direction, with "the fourth prince."

Table M.26. Decisions About *Tetrarcha*

Luke	Vulgate	EEV	EV	LV
3.1	tetrarcha autem Galilaeae Herode	sothly Eroude *prince of the ferthe part* Galilee	sothli Eroude *prince* of Galilee	and Eroude was *prince* of Galilee
3.19	Herodes autem tetrarcha	sothly Eroude *prince of the ferthe part*	sothli Eroude, *the forthe prince*	but Eroude, *tetrark*
9.7	audivit autem Herodes tetrarcha omnia	forsothe Eroude *prince of the ferthe part*	forsoth Eroude, *the fourthe prince*, herde alle the thingis	and Eroude *tetrak* herde alle thingis

But when it comes to Caesar Augustus, EEV brings over the Latin terms "Caesar" and "August," and EV adds the internal gloss "or Noble" to the second term, while LV translated "Caesar" as "the emperor."

Table M.27. Problems with the Emperor

	Vulgate	EEV	EV	LV
Luke 2.1	exiit edictum a Caesare Augusto	A maundement wente out fro *Cesar August*	a maundement went out fro *Cesar August*, or Noble	a maundement wente out fro *the Emperour August*

In Luke 16.6, we see an effort of EV to make sense of an opaque literalism, the rendering of *cautio* as "caution," by substituting "obligation"; but, as usual, EV's improvement did not make it into LV.

Table M.28. EV's Sensible OBLIGATION Versus EEV/LV's Import CAUTION

	Vulgate	EEV	EV	LV
Luke 16.6	accipe *cautionem* tuam et sede cito scribe quinquaginta	tac thy *kaucion* and sit soone and writ fifty	taak thin *obligacioun*, and sitte soon, and writ fifty.	take thi *caucioun*, and sitte soone, and write fifty.

New Words

David Crystal reports that the *Oxford English Dictionary* has over 1,100 entries of words, many derived from the Latin, that first appear either in the EV or the LV, whether new words or new applications of older words.[3] An example of the latter is "caution," just treated, but it was a nonstarter: its appearance in this Gospel passage is the only instance cited of this sense. An example quoted by Crystal of a new word is "actor," meaning "manager, guardian," which EEV takes straight from the Latin, but which LV rejects.

Table M.29. EV New Word ACTOR Rejected by LV

Vulgate Gal. 4.2: sub tutoribus et actoribus	EEV/EV: under tutouris and *actouris*	LV: under keperis and tutoris

A similar case is "miseration," which appeared in EV but not in LV; the word limped along elsewhere until the sixteenth century, when it was mainly replaced by "commiseration."

Table M.30. EV New Word MISERATION Rejected by LV

Vulgate Neh. 9.31: Deus miserationum	EEV/EV: God of miseraciouns	LV: God of merciful doinges

Further Directions

There are other features that would be profitable to study in analyzing the differences between EV and LV. It would be good to apply to the New Testament, and to the Gospel of Luke in particular, the aspects that Lilo Moessner studies in the Psalms. Notably, she looks at the translation of prefixed Latin verbs, emphasizing that the LV decision not to use compound verbs in English (verb + particle) results in loss of meaning.[4] However, this feature seems to have been reduced even later in the Old Testament. I have found only six such cases in all of Baruch.

Table M.31. EV Baruch Compound Rendering of Prefixed Latin Verbs

Vulgate	EV (= EEV)	LV
Bar. 1.18 non *obaudivimus* vocem Domini Dei nostri	(A) wee *wel herden* not the vois of the Lord oure God	we obeiden not **to** the vois of oure Lord God
Bar. 2.5 non *obaudiendo* vocem ipsius	(A) not *wel herende* the vois of him	in not obeyinge **to** the vois of him
Bar. 2.8 non *sumus deprecati* faciem Domini Dei nostri	(A) wee *louly preyeden* not the face of the Lord oure God	we bisoughten not the face of oure Lord God
Bar. 2.21 *inclinate* umerum vestrum	(A) *bowith doun* youre shuldris	bowe ye youre schuldur
Bar. 6.42 *circumdatis* funibus	(B) *yoven aboute*, or bounden, with coordis	gird with roopis
Bar. 6.48 cum *supervenerit* illis prelium et mala	(B) whenne bataile *shal above cum* to hem, and evil thingis	whanne batels and ivels comen on hem

But in the New Testament they seem to be almost nonexistent—perhaps partially because of a diminished number of Latin prefixed verbs? The study of this feature should be correlated with the VERB + UP feature treated in Appendix H, section F. I have found only two instances of compound rendering of prefixed Latin verbs in all of Luke, with LV following suit in the second case.

Table M.32. Rare Examples of Compound Rendering of Prefixed Verbs in Luke

Vulgate	EV	LV
2.23: omne masculinum *adaperiens* vulvam	2.23: ech male kinde *openinge* the wombe *to go out*	2.23: every male kinde openinge the wombe
23.21: at illi *succlamabant*	23.21: and they *undercrieden*	23.21: and they *undurcrieden*

Another feature studied by Moessner is the use of verbal predicates with genitive and dative objects, that is, followed by "of" and "to" respectively.[5] Other topics are the question of how the missing linking verbs in Latin were dealt with in English, the treatment of relative clauses, and further work on present-participle constructions, and on word order.[6] Furthermore, serious assessments should be made of the import of the myriad features and examples given by Conrad Lindberg in the book he has produced on some of Jerome's epistles, his eight volumes on EEV, and the four on LLV.[7]

APPENDIX N

Preface to the *Longleat Sunday Gospels*
Longleat House MS 4

[fol. 1ra]

(1) As we finden in the laste ende of the Gospel of Matheu and of Mark, whanne Crist Jesus, infinighte God and very man, schulde steyin up abovin alle hevenis and alle aungelis in oure manhod and in oure kende, he seide to hese disciplis, "Goth and techith alle naciounis, and baptisith hem in the name of the Fader and of the Son and of the Holy Gost, and techith hem to kepin alle thinge that I have bodin yow, and goth into al the world (that is to seighe, into every lond in this world) and prechith the Gospel to every creature (that is to seighe, to every man and womman)." And that they schulde connith [*marg* techin] the Gospel to every man and womman and in every language, that the peple mighte connin the Gospel and understonden it.

(2) Therfore the tenthe day after his ascencioun, that was Pentecost Sonday, he sente doun to hem the Holy Gost in liknesse of brenninge tunggs for to techin the Gospel in alle tunggs and in alle languagis. And as Seint Luk tellith in his book, *Actuum* 2 cap., onon they spokin with alle tunggis and alle languagis, in so mechil that ther were men of religioun dwellinge in Jerusalem of every nacioun under hevene, and alle they herdin the disciplis of Crist spekinge in here language. But they that understodin hem nat seidin that they were drunke.

(3) But now some folis sein that Crists disciplis spokin non languge in here prechinge to ony peple but Ebrw, and that every man and womman in every lond understode hem in Ebrw as thoghu they haddin spokin to hem in here language. But this opinion and this seighinge is fals. For as Seint Luuk seight, "Every man herde hem spekin in his owene language." And for they

spokin in so manie divers languags the Jewis that understode hem nat seidin that they were dronke and thoghu alle the Jewis understode Ebrw.

(4) Wherefore, leve frend, wetith it wel that the Holy Gost taughte hem to spekin every language to techin the Gospel in every language. And therfore Seint Jon and the Book of Goddis Privites tellith that he say an aungil flighinge be the middis of hevene, havinge the endeles Gospel for to prechin it to hem that dwellin and sittin upon erthe, and to prechin it on every nacioun and kinrede and on every language and on every peple, and seide with a gret vois, "Dredith God and gevith worschepe to him, for the howre and the time comight of his Doom, and worschepith him that made hevene and erthe and see and alle thing that is therinne and the wellis of watris" (*Apoc.*, 14 cap.). This aungil, whanne [fol. 1rb] he schulde prechin the Gospel, fleghy be the middis of hevene and cride with a gret vois to alle naciounis in tokene that the Gospel scholde not ben hid but ben taught opinly to the peple, and therfore the Gospel is red in heghy place and in heghy voys in holy cherche in tokene that alle men schulde herin it and understonden it besily whanne it is red to hem and taught hem. And therfore, leve frend, sitthe Crist bad hese disciplis and othere prechouris and techeris of Godis lawe techin the Gospel to every man and womman in every language, ther may non prelat artin ne lettin preching and teching of the Gospel in Englich, but every prelat and prechour is boundin to prechin and techin the Gospel of Crist and his lawe to the peple aftir the conning that God hath sent to hem.

(5) And therfore thoghu it be these dayis defendit and inhibight be somme prelatis that men schulde techin the Gospel in Englich, I answere and sey to hem, as the Apostelis seidin to Annas and Caiphas and to the prelatis and to the buschoppis and the maistris of the Jewis whiche defendedin the Apostelis for to prechin the Gospel, *Obedire oportet deo magis quam hominibus*, "It behovith in this cas more to obeighin to God thanne to men" (*Actuum*, 5 cap.). And, leve frend, sitthe it is leful to prechin the Gospel in Englich, it is leful to writin it in Englich, bothin to the techere and to the herere, yif he conne writin, for be writinge is mest sekir examinacioun of mannis speche. And be writinge, Goddis lawe may best ben cowd and best kept in mende. And therfore, leve frend, althoghu somme prelatis han defendit me to techin the Gospel and to writin it in Englich, yet non of hem hath defendit you, ne may defendin you, to connin the Gospel in Englich, that is youre kendely language.

(6) And as Crist bad us prechin and techin the Gospel to every man and womman, so every man and womman is boundin for to don his devir to connin the Gospel of Crist and Godis lawe aftir the techinge that God sent

him. And therfore, leve frend, I preighe yow that ye wele acceptin, for Cristis seke, my travaile and my writing to you in the name of Crist. And sitthe I have wretin the Gospel to you in wol gret drede and persecucioun, ye that ben in swich sekirnesse that non prelat may lettin you ne dishesin you for conninge ne for kepinge of the Gospel, connith it and kepith it with good devocioun, as ye wele answere to Crist at the Day of Doom.

(7) And as ye moun [fol. 1va] herin, now prechinge and techinge of the Gospel and of Goddis lawe is artid and lettid more than it was wone to ben, therfore takith goodly the techinge that comith to you frely. And thoghu the persecucion of Deoclician and Maximian be now newly begonnin to lettin techinge and preching of Goddis word and Goddis lawe and to compellin men to wurschepin gravin imagis of ston and of tre, stonde ye stif in the feith, and worschepith ye yonde God abovin alle thinge. And thinkith that imagerie and peinte is but a book to the lewd peple forto stere hem to thinkin on God and othere seints and to worschepin God abovin alle thinge, and seints in here degre, as the Lawe schewith weel ([Gratian, *Decretum*], De Cons., D. 3. cap. [27], *Perlatum*).

(8) Also, be ye besy to connin and to maintenin Goddis lawe, and takith example of Seint Katerine, of Seint Lucie, and of Seint Margarete, of Seint Agneis, and of many othere whiche in here yougthe were wol conning in Cristis lawe. And take heed of Seint Cecilie, that holy maidin, whiche, as we redin in here Lif, baar alwey the Gospel of Crist in here brest, in here herte, and in here mende, and cesid neither be day ne be night for to spekin of God and of Goddis lawe, and bothe night and day sche gaf here to holy praighers. And so, leve frend, I preighe you that ye don. Havith the Gospel of Christ in meende, and whanne ye moun, spekith of Cristis Gospel and of Goddis lawe, as ye ben wone to done. And somtime, whanne ye moun, redith of the Gospel and of Goddis lawe, that ye moun the more knowe youre God and the more lovin him and wetin the betere whanne ye don weel and whanne omis. Therfore redith in bokis of Goddis lawe, for nought only they ben blissd that herin Goddis word and kepin it, but also the techeris and the rederis of Goddis word ben blissid of God. And therfore Seint Jon seight in the Book of Goddis Privites, *Beatus qui legit et qui audit verba prophecie hujus et servat ea que in ea scripta sunt*, "Blissid be he that redith and herith the wordis of this prophecie and of Goddis lawe and kepith things that ben wrete therinne" (*Apoc.*, 1 cap.).

(9) And therfor, leve frend, whanne ye moun, redith in Goddis lawe besily and herith it devoughtly and kepygtht taightly [joyfully] and preighith to Crist that I and alle othere moun con the same. For al my travaile, leve frende, I aske nought of yow but youre gode wil and youre preighere.

APPENDIX O

The Oxford Committee of Twelve, 1410–11

My reason for saying that Arundel at the February–March 1410 convocation ordered an Oxford Committee of Twelve established is that he says so in a letter of December 1410, *Meminimus*, to Oxford University. But the purpose of this committee—unlike that of the committees called for in the 1407 constitution, which was to vet the books of Wyclif and others for publication—is to cull Wyclif's books for erroneous or heretical conclusions and condemn them.[1] It was therefore sometime well after March 1410 but well before December 1410 that Arundel rebuked Oxford for its failure to form the committee and that the university replied, saying that it was sending a representative to explain the reasons for the delay. The purpose of the projected committee is here stated as "purging suspected errors from the books of John Wyclif and whatever other books are submitted" ("qui libros Magistri Johannis W. et quoslibet alios offerendos suspectis purgarent erroribus").[2]

But the university statute that was passed at Oxford (March 1410) to set up the committee gave a still different purpose: lest the university be further suspect of heresy, the committee is to have full power to condemn heresies and errors "of whatever books, lectures, and works" ("de libris, lecturis, et opusculis quibuscumque"), and any decision of the twelve, or a majority of them, was to have the force of statute.[3] We note that nothing in the statute indicates that the committee is being established in response to a requirement of the archbishop or provincial council.

In the statement made by John Wittenham and the other (elected) doctors and masters, they say they stand ready to defend a sentence they pass "against all heretics or Lollards of whatever degree" ("contra omnes hereticos seu Lollardos cujuscumque gradus"), indicating persons still among the living and not only Wyclif.[4] Although this statement is headed "Potestas XII electorum Oxonie" ("Power of the twelve electees of Oxford"), it is by no means certain that when the statement was first made, or always during the course of its operation, the group had its full complement of twelve members. The reason for doubt is not only that the university reported a delay in forming the committee, but also that when a theology student, Richard Fleming, was accused of holding a faulty proposition, there were only six masters who made the determination, a number that Fleming declared "excessively diminished."[5] He said (as reported by Henry IV in recounting the matter) that as soon as his class presentation was finished, his proposition was reprehended by "the number of six masters, which was, to be precise, excessively diminished" ("per numerum sex magistrorum precise nimis diminutum"); it was reported to him that five of them condemned it outright, while the sixth declared it wrong only according to the common understanding of the words.[6]

However, in spite of the delay in appointing the full board of censors, at least one early appointee got to work early and made notes on his progress some time in April or May of 1410, and on June 26 a convocation of regent and nonregent masters at Oxford condemned many extracts of Wyclif's *Opus evangelicum*, *Trialogus*, and other works.[7]

Since Fleming himself was a member of the Committee of Twelve who condemned Wyclif's propositions in March 1411 (one of the four students in theology on the panel),[8] Andrew Larsen concludes that he was already a member of the committee when six of them condemned him, and that he was alleging they did not constitute the majority required for such a decision.[9] I think it more likely that Fleming was complaining that the size of the committee as presently constituted was too small, and that Fleming himself was appointed only after being exonerated by the committee of eight arbitrators the king ordered to be set up. The spokesman of the committee of six who responded to the king in answer to Fleming's charge[10] was the commissary of the chancellor of Oxford.[11] This must have been John Langdon, monk of Canterbury Priory, one of the four doctors of the Committee of Twelve in 1411.[12]

The king was writing on behalf of Fleming in early December 1410, but earlier in the year, on October 22, he had written in support of the committee of doctors and other graduates elected "to examine certain articles that were being held" ("ad examinandum certos articulos et conclusiones que tenebantur") against Gospel and Church and to condemn them and the persons holding them; he ordered those opposing their judgments to be arrested and imprisoned until they submitted.[13]

In Arundel's letter of December 1410, *Meminimus*, sent at the very time that Henry IV was writing in favor of Fleming, the archbishop was writing against him, saying that his appeal was not allowable.[14] At the same time Arundel wrote two other letters to Oxford, one, *Fidedigna relatione*, denouncing four masters of arts reported as opposing the recently issued constitutions against heresy. One of the four men is John Luke, who also turns up on the 1411 Committee of Twelve, as one of the four bachelors of theology on the board.[15] The other letter, *Licet in nostris constitucionibus*, is a general rebuke against opposers of the 1407/9 Canterbury constitutions. He says that even though the constitutions against heresy and error were issued and duly published in the university and throughout the whole province, among them the fifth and sixth, beginning *Quod magistri* and *Quodque* respectively, there are some at the university who neglect and contemn them.[16] *Quodque* is the same as *Quia insuper*, ordering the committees of twelve, while *Quod magistri* is the same as *Similiter quia*, the constitution that limits the teaching of Scripture to the exposition of the text.

APPENDIX P

Wyclif's Works and the 267 Condemned Propositions, 1411

The works from which the Oxford Committee of Twelve extracted the 267 propositions they presented in 1411 for condemnation (printed in Wilkins, *Concilia*, 3:339–49) are confusingly given in Williell R. Thomson, *The Latin Writings of John Wyclyf: An Annotated Catalog* (Toronto 1983), especially p. 7 n. 5; Anne Hudson, *The Premature Reformation* (Oxford 1988), pp. 84–85; and Anne Hudson, "Notes of an Early Fifteenth-Century Research Assistant, and the Emergence of the 267 Articles Against Wyclif," *English Historical Review* 118 (2003) 685–97, reprinted as chapter 13 in her Ashgate Variorum volume *Studies in the Transmission of Wyclif's Writings* (Aldershot 2008).

I present a list here, followed by Thomson's numbering of the work (when he does not identify condemned articles, I give his number in brackets).

1. Articles 1–74: *Opus evangelicum* (Thomson nos. 374–77)
2. Articles 75–98: *De simonia* (Thomson no. 35)
3. Articles 99–107: *De perfectione statuum* (Thomson no. 426)
4. Articles 108–20: *De ordine christiano* (Thomson no. 414)
5. Articles 121–40: *Trialogus* (Thomson no. 47)
6. Articles 141–55: *Dialogus* (Thomson no. 408)
7. Articles 156–75: *De logica*, book 3 (Wilkins, *De arte sophistica*) (Thomson no. 3)
8. Articles 176–219: *De civili dominio* (Thomson nos. 28–30)
9. Articles 220–24: *De diabolo et membris ejus* (Thomson no. 430)
10. Articles 225–38: *De dotatione ecclesie* (*Supp. Trialogi*) (Wilkins, *De dotatione cesarea*) (Thomson no. 48)

11. Articles 239–49: *Responsiones ad 44 conclusiones* (Thomson no. 384)
12. Articles 250–58: *Responsiones ad Strode* (Thomson no. 386)
13. Articles 259–63: *De confessione* (Wilkins) [cf. Thomson no. 40, *De fide sacramenti*?]
14. Articles 264–67: *De versuciis pseudocleri* (Wilkins) [cf. Thomson no. 420, *De versutiis antichristi* (?)] (Hudson, "Notes," p. 696, identifies the latter with *Contra versucias pseudoclerum* [*sic*])

Thomson finds articles 117–18, 123, 125–26, and 129 somewhat derived from no. 39, *De eucharistia minor confessio* (p. 70 n. 8). On p. 7 n. 5, he also lists no. 410, *De scismate*, as excerpted by the committee, and refers to p. 274 n. 8 for documentation, but none such is to be found there. Anne Hudson, "Books and Their Survival: The Case of English Manuscripts of Wyclif's Latin Works," in *Medieval Manuscripts, Their Makers and Users: A Special Issue of Viator in Honor of Richard and Mary Rouse* (Los Angeles 2011), pp. 225–44, using a different system of counting, reduces the number of Wyclif's surviving works from Thomson's 435 to some 150. In this essay she deals with the fifty-two manuscripts produced in England that preserve some of his writings.

APPENDIX Q

William Lyndwood's Commentary on the Constitution *Periculosa*

William Lyndwood, *Provinciale; seu, Constitutiones Angliae* (Oxford 1679, repr. Farnborough 1968), p. 286.

Liber V, Titulus 4: De magistris et potestate docendi [Capitulum 3]

Scriptura Sacra non transferatur in linguam vulgarem, nec translata interpretetur, donec rite fuerit examinata, sub pena excommunicationis et nota hereseos.

Idem [Thomas Arundell in Concilio Oxoniense]

[1] [c]PERICULOSA res est, testante Beato Hjeronymo, [d]textum [e]Sacre Scripture de uno in aliud [f]idioma transferre, [g]eo quod in ipsis translationibus [h]non de facili idem sensus in omnibus retinetur, prout idem Beatus Hjeronymus, etsi inspiratus fuisset, se [i]in hoc sepius fatetur errasse.

---

[c]*PERICULOSA*: ista constitutio est ejusdem cujus et precedens, et habet quatuor dicta. [1] In primo ponit causam motivam sui statuti. [2] In secundo, ibi, *Statuimus*, statuendo prohibet Scripturam Sacram transferri in linguam Anglicanam vel aliam, auctoritate propria ipsius transferentis. [3] In tertio, ibi, *nec legatur*, prohibet usum sive lecturam certorum librorum translatorum. [4] In quarto, ibi, *Qui contra fecerit*, adjicit decretum punibile premissorum.

[d]*textum*: "textus" est liber doctorum continens tractatum sine litere vel sententie expositione. Vel *textus* est ipse tractatus libri sine expositione litere vel sententie, secundum Januensem.

[e]*Sacre Scripture*: id est, Bibliorum, que continent Vetus et Novum Testamentum [citing Gratian, *Decretum*, Dist. 9, cap. 8, *Quis nesciat*, *CIC* 1:17].

[f]*idioma*: id est, proprietatem loquendi.

[g]*eo quod*: versus [usually followed by a mnemonic hexameter].

[h]*non de facili*: simile habes, *ff De excusationibus tutorum*, lex 1 [citing Justinian Digest 27.1.1], primo responso in Glossa, ubi patet quod propter difficultatem transferendi, aliquando dictio Greca ponitur in legibus Latinis [see p. 300 n. 1]. Et facit ad hoc [citing Gratian, *Decretum*, Dist. 3, cap. 14, *Locutio*, *CIC* 1:144: "Locutio divinarum Scripturarum secundum cujusque linguae proprietatem accipienda est. Habet enim omnis lingua quedam propria genera locutionum, que cum in aliam linguam transferentur videntur absurda"].

[i]*in hoc*: scilicet, translatione Scripture.

Book V, title 4:
On masters and the authorization to teach [Chapter 3]

Sacred Scripture is not to be translated into the common tongue, nor expounded after being translated, until it is properly examined, under pain of excommunication and suspicion of heresy.

The same [i.e., Thomas Arundel in the Council of Oxford]

[1] IT IS DANGEROUS,[c] as St. Jerome says,[d] to translate a text of Sacred Scripture[e] from one idiom[f] to another, because[g] in these translations the same sense is not easily[h] kept, as St. Jerome himself admits, even though he was inspired, saying that he many times made mistakes in this matter.[i]

---

[c]*IT IS DANGEROUS*: this constitution is from the same [metropolitan] as the previous one [i.e., *Quia insuper*, Oxford Const. 6, treated by Lyndwood on pp. 284-85], and it has four parts. [1] In the first he gives the motive of his statute. [2] In the second, at *Therefore we enact*, by legislating he forbids Sacred Scripture to be translated into English or other languages on the translator's own authority. [3] In the third, at *And any such . . . is not to be read*, he prohibits the use of or lecturing on certain translated books. [4] In the fourth, at *Whoever acts against this*, he adds the decree of punishment for [contravening] the above.

[d]*text*: "text" means a book of doctors containing a treatise without explication of letter or sense. Or, according to James of Genoa [in his *Catholicon*], it refers to the content itself of a book, not including explanations of letter or sense.

[e]*Sacred Scripture*: that is, the Bible, which contains the Old and New Testament, as in Gratian's canon *Quis nesciat*.

[f]*idiom*: that is, a particular way of speaking.

[g]*because*: verse: [missing].

[h]*not easily*: you have a similar statement in the Digest, *On the Excuses of Tutors*, the first response in the Gloss to the first law, where it is clear that because of the difficulty of translation, Greek words are sometimes included in Latin laws. Gratian's canon *Locutio* is also relevant ["The language of the divine Scriptures is to be received according to the proper nature of each tongue. For every tongue has its own ways of speaking, which when translated into another tongue seem absurd"].

[i]*in this matter*: that is, in translating Scripture.

[2] [k]Statuimus igitur et ordinamus ut nemo deinceps textum aliquem Sacre Scripture [l]auctoritate sua in linguam Anglicanam vel aliam transferat per viam [m]libri, vel libelli, [n]aut tractatus.

[3] [o]Nec legatur aliquis [p]hujusmodi liber, libellus, aut tractatus jam [q]noviter tempore dicti Johannis Wickliff sive citra compositus, aut in posterum componendus, in parte vel in toto, publice vel occulte, sub pena majoris [r]excommunicationis, quousque per loci [s]diocesanum, seu, si [t]res exegerit, per [u]concilium provinciale, ipsa translatio fuerit [x]approbata.

---

[k]*Statuimus*: secunda pars.

[l]*auctoritate sua*: i.e., judicio suo. Secus si auctoritate episcopi, ut patet infra, eodem [capitulo], versu *Nec legatur*.

[m]*libri*: scilicet, de novo compilandi, ut patet infra, versu sequenti. Secus si hoc fiat per modum sermonis publici, exponendo textum in lingua vulgari. Et quod dicit, "per viam libri," intelligere potes sic, videlicet, ut inde conficiat librum continentem tota Biblia. Appellatione namque *libri* simpliciter sumpti continetur liber completus et integer, et non secundum partes numerales, prout sepius unum volumen dividitur in plures libros, ut patet in Biblia. Ad quod facit [citing Digest 32.52, *Librorum*: "Librorum appellatione continentur omnia volumina . . ."]. Vel potes intelligere sic, ut, scilicet, unum librum particularem textus Bibiorum transferat. Nam talis particularis poterit dici *libellus*, ut sequitur.

[n]*aut tractatus*: sic, videlicet, quod de dictis doctorum, vel propriis, aliquem tractatum componat applicando textum Sacre Scripture, et illius sensum transferendo in Anglicum vel aliud idioma. Et eodem modo potest intelligi quod dicit de "libro" vel de "libello," ut scilicet textum Sacre Scripture in tali libro vel libello applicet, et textum ipsum tranferat in aliud idioma.

[o]*Nec legatur*: tertia pars.

[p]*hujusmodi liber*: Scilicet, translatus de textu Sacre Scripture.

[q]*noviter*, sume quod est infra, *compositus*, et ex hoc quod dicit, *noviter compositus*, apparet quod libros, libellos, vel tractatus in Anglicis vel alio idiomate prius translatos de textu Scripture legere non est prohibitum; concordat supra, eodem [titulo], capitulo proximo, §1 [referring to Constitution 6, *Quia insuper*, the words "suo tempore vel citra noviter compositus," Lyndwood, p. 284].

[r]*excommunicationis pena*: scilicet, ferenda, et sic comminatio est.

[s]*diocesanum*: non igitur potest hoc fieri per inferiorem, nisi de ipsius mandato.

[t]*res exegerit*: quia forsan materie in tali libro, libello, vel tractatu contente requirunt altiorem indaginem et plurium sapientium investigationem. Vel quia concernunt fidem vel Ecclesiam universalem et ipsius regimen, vel alia hujusmodi.

[u]*concilium provinciale*: Quod singulis annis ad minus debet celebrare [citing *X* 5.1.25, *Sicut olim*, canon 6 of the Fourth Lateran Council, 1215, *CIC* 2:747].

[x]*approbata*: Ratio est quia, licet nudus textus Scripture fuerit translatus, potest tamen transferens in translatione errare. Vel si librum, libellum, aut tractatum compilaverit, potest, ut frequenter accidit, cum veris falsa et erronea admiscere.

[2] Therefore we enact[k] and ordain that no one from now on translate any text of Sacred Scripture on his own authority[l] into English or any other language by way of book,[m] booklet, or treatise.[n]

[3] And any[o] such book, booklet, or treatise now newly[q] composed in the time of the said John Wyclif [see p. 300 n. 2] or later, or to be composed in the future, is not to be read, in part or in whole, publicly or secretly, under pain of major excommunication,[r] until the translation itself is approved[x] by the local diocesan [bishop],[s] or, if the matter requires,[t] by a provincial council.[u]

---

[k]*Therefore we enact*: part 2.

[l]*by his own authority*: that is, his own judgment. It would be otherwise if it were by the authority of the bishop, as is clear below ("And any such book," etc.).

[m]*book*: that is, newly composed, as is clear in the next part. It would be otherwise if it were done by way of a public sermon, explaining the text in the native tongue. And when it says, "by way of a book," you can understand it thus: making a book containing the whole Bible. For the word "book," simply taken, means a whole and complete book, not referring to numbered parts, as when a volume is often divided into many books (the Bible being an obvious case). The Digest law *Librorum* is relevant ["All volumes are contained under the term "books"]. Or you can take it thus: translating a single book of the biblical text. But such a limited translation could be called a "booklet" (*libellus*), the word that follows.

[n]*treatise*: that is, when compiling a treatise using the words of doctors or one's own, to apply the text of Sacred Scripture by translating it into English or some other idiom. And what he says about "book" and "booklet" can be understood in the same way, that is, applying the text of Sacred Scripture in a book or booklet and translating the text into another idiom.

[o]*And any*: part 3.

[p]*such book*: that is, newly translated from the text of Sacred Scripture.

[q]*newly* to be taken with *composed*: and from this it appears that it is not forbidden to lecture on books, booklets, or treatises in English or another language translated before this time, which render the text of Scripture. This concords with the first part of the previous constitution ["newly composed in his time or since"].

[r]*excommunication*: that is, to be passed in the future; and so it is a threat.

[s]*diocesan*: therefore this cannot be done by an inferior, unless at the bishop's command.

[t]*matter requires*: because the contents of such a book, booklet, or treatise might require a deeper examination and the investigation of many experts. Or because they concern the faith of the universal Church and its discipline, or other suchlike.

[u]*provincial council*: which should be celebrated at least every year, as required by the Fourth Lateran Council.

[x]*approved*: the reason is that, even though the bare text of Scripture is translated, the translator can make mistakes in his translation. Or, if he compiles a book, booklet, or treatise, he can, as frequently happens, mix in the false and erroneous with the true.

[4] [y]Qui vero contra hoc fecerit, ut [z]fautor hereseos et [a]erroris similiter [b]puniatur.

[y]*Qui contra fecerit*: quarta pars.

[z]*fautor heresis*: hic habes alium casum preter eos de quibus dixi supra, capitulo proximo, eodem titulo, versu in quo aliquis dicitur *fautor heresis* [again citing Constitution 6, *Quia insuper*, referring to his note g on p. 283].

[a]*erroris*: quia prestat occasionem alios inducendi in errorem, qui ex talis libri, libelli, vel tractatus lectura inficerentur.

[b]*puniatur*: Fautor enim heresis reddit se vehementer suspectum de heresi. Et ex tali suspicione potest inquiri contra tales [citing *Decretum* C. 13 q. 3 c. *Hi qui*, which does not exist; perhaps a mistake for C. 5 q. 1 c. 3 *Hi qui*, *CIC* 1:545: "Hii qui inventi fuerint libros famosos in ecclesia ponere, anathematizentur"], et potest eis purgatio indici ad arbitrium iniquirentis; in qua si defecerint, tanquam heretici poterunt condemnari [citing *X* 5.7.13, *Excommunicamus*, §2, *Qui autem*, *CIC* 2:787–88; 2.23.14, *Litteras*, col. 357; 5.34.10, *Inter sollicitudines*, cols. 872–74]. Item talis subjacet pene excomunicationis ipso jure [citing *X* 5.7.8, *Sicut ait*, *CIC* 2:779–80]. Et postquam fuerit sic excommunicatus, efficitur infamis et intestabilis active et passive, et tali omnes actus legitimi sunt penitus interdicti [citing *X* 5.7.13, *Excommunicamus*, §3, *Credentes*, *CIC* 2:788]. Item nullum beneficium ecclesiasticum potest assequi [citing *Liber Sextus* 5.2.2, *Quicunque*, and 5.2.10, *Statutum*, *CIC* 2:1069–70, 1073]. Item non est tradendus ecclesiastice sepulture si talis decedat, ut dicto capitulo *Statutum*, in principio, et dicto capitulo *Sicut ait*. Item tales sic excommunicati et in suo excessu persistentes sunt de jure civili in perpetuum deportandi, publicatis omnibus eorum bonis, prout traditur in quadam constitutione Frederici Imperatoris que incipit, *Et patrimonium*, et est servanda, sicut patet [citing *Sext.* 5.2.18, *Ut inquisitionis*, *CIC* 2:1076–77].

[4] Whoever[y] acts against this is to be similarly punished[b] as a favorer of heresy[z] and error.[a]

[y] *Whoever*: part 4.

[z] *favorer of heresy*: here you have another case besides those I spoke of above, where there is mention of a favorer of heresy in the previous constitution.

[a] *error*: because one presents an occasion of inducing into error others who might be infected by lectures from such a book, booklet, or treatise.

[b] *punished*: because a favorer of heresy renders himself vehemently suspect of heresy. Inquisitions can be held against those who are so suspect, according to Gratian, and purgation can be ordered at the discretion of the inquisitor; if they fail it, they can be condemned as if they were heretics, according to the Fourth Lateran decree *Excommunicamus* and the decretals *Litteras* and *Inter sollicitudines*. Likewise such a person is automatically excommunicated in virtue of the decretal *Sicut ait*, and after being so excommunicated, he is rendered infamous and incapable of making a will or inheriting, and all lawful acts are denied to him, again according to *Excommunicamus*. Likewise, he can acquire no ecclesiastical benefice, as provided by *Quicunque* and *Statutum* in the *Sext*. Moreover, if such a person dies, he is not to be given ecclesiastical burial, according to *Statutum* and *Sicut ait*. In addition, those who are thus excommunicated and who persist in their offense are by civil law to be deported permanently, with all of their goods confiscated, as is provided in a constitution of the Emperor Frederick, *Et patrimonium*, which, according to the *Sext* (in the decretal *Ut inquisitionis*), is to be followed.

APPENDIX R

The Admonition *Periculum animarum* of John Stafford, Bishop of Bath and Wells, 1441

The Register of John Stafford, Bishop of Bath and Wells, 1425–1443, ed. Thomas Scott Holmes, 2 vols. (London 1915–16), 2:267–69, no. 834.

April 10, 1441, Dogmersfield Manor

Et incontinenti tunc ibidem monitus erat in specie Thomas Oke, brewer, de Tauntonia, qui alias detectus erat de et super scriptorum conduccione librorum suspectorum in vulgari translatorum et ipsorum retencione penes eum, ne amplius tales libros procuraret scribi neque penes eum retinere publice nec occulte, sub pena in monitorio publice in mercato recitato comprehensa, cujus quidem monitorii tenor sequitur et est talis:

And then and there forthwith Thomas Oke, brewer, from Taunton, who had been elsewhere detected concerning the hiring of scribes of suspect books translated into the vernacular and keeping them, was admonished specifically against the further procuring of such books for copying and keeping them, publicly or secretly, on the pain given in the admonition recited in the marketplace, the text of which admonition reads as follows:

In Dei nomine, amen. Nos, Johannes, etc.,

In God's name, amen. We John, etc.,

[1]
Periculum animarum subditorum nostrorum quantum cum Deo possumus removere cupientes, et attendentes quam periculosa res est, prout testatur Beatus Jeronimus, textum Sacre Scripture de uno in aliud idioma transferre, eo quod ex ipsis translationibus non de facili idem sensus in omnibus retinetur, prout idem Jeronimus, licet inspiratus fuisset, se in hoc sepius fatetur errasse, prout in concilio provinciali dudum Oxonie celebrato novimus esse cautum, sentenciam igitur provincialis concilii prosequentes:

[2]
Injungimus et monemus primo, secundo, et tercio peremptorie in hiis scriptis, [ut] nemo deinceps nostrarum civitatum et diocesis aliquem textum Sacre Scripture in linguam Anglicanam transferre per viam libri, libelli, aut tractatus, nec aliquem hujusmodi librum, libellum aut tractatum de lingua Anglicana conscriptum jam noviter in tempore Johannis Wyclif sive citra compositum aut imposterum componendum, in parte vel in toto, publice vel occulte, infra nostras civitates et diocesim antedictas legere, retinere, vel possidere presumat, sub majoris excommunicationis pena, quousque per nos seu, si res exigerit, per concilium provinciale hujusmodi

Desiring to remove as much as we can with God's help danger to the souls of our subjects, and being attentive to how dangerous it is, as Blessed Jerome testifies, to translate the text of Sacred Scripture from one language into another, because in such translations the same sense is not easily kept, as Jerome himself admits, even though he was inspired, he made frequent mistakes, as we know ourselves to have been warned in the provincial council held some time ago at Oxford, we therefore follow up on the sentence of the provincial council:

We enjoin and peremptorily admonish for the first, second, and third time in this writing, that from this time onward no one in our cities and diocese presume to translate any text of Sacred Scripture into the English tongue by way of book, booklet, or treatise, or to read, keep, or possess any such book, booklet, or treatise composed in English during the time of John Wyclif or later, or to be composed hereafter, in part or in whole, publicly or secretly, in our said cities and diocese, under pain of major excommunication, until such time as any such book, booklet, or treatise shall have been approved by us, or if need be, through a provincial council; declaring that if anyone

liber, libellus, aut tractatus fuerit approbatus; declarantes ut si quis huic nostre monicioni amodo contrafecerit, tanquam fautor heresis et erroris et ut suspectus de heresi merito punietur.

from now on should contravene this admonition of ours, he shall be justly punished as a supporter of heresy and error and as suspect of heresy.

[3]

Et quoniam per inquisicionem aut scrutinium in nostra diocese nuper facta aliquos libellos seu tractatus hujusmodi [inventi sunt], nedum a textu Sacre Scripture in linguam Anglicanam translatos, sed et alios, per fidei et ecclesie inimicos, ut evidenter apparet, sub palliata quadam et maliciosa ficcione callide compositos, et addicionatos, hereses et errores publice continentes, quorum aliqui presencialiter hic existunt, ipsos quidem libros in sui detestacionem et enervacionem, ac in ruborem ipsorum qui apud se retinere presumpserint, necnon in exemplum et terrorem aliorum ne libros hujusmodi penes se amodo retinere contendant, decrevimus atque decernimus de concilio confratrum nostrorum necnon in sacra theologia magistrorum ac aliorum juris peritorum nobis assistencium, publica execucione corrumpi et in presentis congregationis conspectu incendio consummari, etc.

And because through an investigation or search recently made in our diocese some booklets or treatises of this sort [were found], not only translated from the text of Sacred Scripture in English, but also others, written, as clearly appears, by enemies of Faith and Church, craftily composed under a cloaked and malicious fiction, publicly containing errors and heresies, some of which books are here present, we have decreed and here decree, on the advice of our brethren, and of masters of theology and others learned in the law assisting us, that these books be torn up here in public and in the sight of the present congregation consumed by fire, in detestation of the books themselves and for their destruction, and to the shame of those who presumed to keep them among themselves, and as an example and lesson of terror to others who strive to hold on to such books henceforth. (Etc.)

Execucio monicionis supradicte directa singulis archidiaconis:

The Execution of the above admonition, directed to each archdeacon:

Johannes, etc., archidiacono nostro Wellensi et ejus officiali, Salutem, etc.

John, etc., to our archdeacon of Wells and his official, Good health, etc.

[1]

Nuper fidedignorum instancia pulsati, immo urgente necessitate compulsi, inquisicioniem atque scrutinium per nostras civitates et diocesim fieri fecimus pro requirendis libellis, libris, ac tractatibus si qui reperiri potuissent scripti et retenti apud nostrorum aliquos subditorum translati saltem a Sacra Scripture in linguam Anglicanam in tempore Johannis Wyclif sive citra compositi, quoniam in talibus errores et hereses indubie continebantur qui, dum simplicibus legerentur, ipsi callide sic seducti, a fide et vera doctrina Sancte Matris Ecclesie recedere sunt inducti, non sine gravissimo periculo animarum.

Recently, at the instance of trustworthy persons, and compelled by urgent necessity, we ordered an investigation and search to be made throughout our cities and diocese seeking for booklets, books, and treatises, if any were to be found written and kept among some of our subjects, at least those translated from Sacred Scripture into English in the time of John Wyclif and later, because in such books heresies and errors would indubitably be contained, which, when read to simple persons, they, being thus craftily seduced, are induced to recede from the Faith and Holy Mother Church, not without the gravest peril to souls.

[2]

Quapropter, feria quarta ante Dominicam in Ramis ultimo preteritam processionem fieri fecimus solennem apud ecclesiam nostra[m] cathedralem Wellensem, vocata ad hanc et ibi presente cleri et populi multitudine copiosa. In cujus progressu quoddam monitorium nostrum ex causa premissa publice legi et intelligibiliter declarari in loco mercati publici, et quosdam libros sive libellos hujusmodi suspectos

Therefore, on the Thursday before Palm Sunday last [April 6, 1441] we put on a solemn procession at our cathedral church of Wells, to which a great multitude of clergy and people had been summoned and were present. During its course, an admonition of ours was read for the above reason, and intelligibly explained in the public marketplace, and certain suspect books or booklets of that sort that had been found then we

tunc repertos per incendium annichilari mandavimus; cujus quidem monitorii tenor sequitur et est talis, "In Dei nomine, amen." (ut supra).

ordered to be destroyed by fire. The text of the admonition is as follows: "In God's name, amen" (as above).

[3]

Et quia nedum perquam necessarium sed et dignum arbitramur dicti monitorii continenciam ad omnium subditorum nostrorum ex causis in ipso monitorio deductis perduci noticiam, vobis mandamus, in virtute obediencie firmiter injungentes, quatinus monitorium predictum tam in generalibus et aliis capitulis, accessionibus vestris, necnon parochialibus ecclesiis archidiaconatus vestri Wellensis, cum omni celeritate publicetis, et publicari faciatis intelligibiliter in vulgari, inquirentesque et continuo a[u]sculcantes de contravenientibus monicioni predicte, de quorum nominibus et cognominibus nos student[e]s statim sub pena contemptus efficere cerciorem, sicut vestro volueritis periculo respondere et quemadmodum canonicam vitare volueritis ulcionem.

And because we think it not only very necessary but also a worthy thing for the contents of the said admonition to be brought to the attention of all of our subjects for the causes given in the said admonition, we order you, enjoining you firmly in virtue of obedience, that you publish the aforesaid admonition with all speed in both general and other chapters at your comings, and also in the parish churches of your archdeaconry of Wells, and see to it that it is published understandably in the vernacular; and that you inquire and constantly listen for contraveners of the said admonition, taking care to let us know immediately their names and surnames, under pain of being in contempt, just as you would wish to respond to your own peril and as you would wish to avoid canonical retribution.

Data in manerio nostro de Dogmersfeld, decimo die mensis Aprilis, 1441, etc.

Given in our manor of Dogmersfield, April 10, 1441, etc.

Consimiliter mandatum fit decano et singulis archidiaconis.

A mandate is similarly made for the dean and each archdeacon.

Notes

I normally modernize the spelling and punctuation of texts, unless special circumstances require otherwise. In citing medieval Latin texts from classicized editions, I remedievalize *ae* and *oe* to *e*, and I regularize *i/j* and *u/v* according to vowel and consonant, as in *DMLBS*.

Preface

1 Leslie K. Arnovick and Henry Ansgar Kelly, "Bishop Challoner's Ecumenical Revision of the Douai-Rheims Bible by Way of King James," *Review of English Studies* 66 (2015) 698–722.

2 This designation appears in the title of the first chapter, "The Problem of the Middle-English Bible," of Margaret Deanesly, *The Lollard Bible and Other Medieval Biblical Versions* (Cambridge 1920; reprinted in 1966 with a "Prefatory Note" by Deanesly, pp. vii–viii). The name has been used by Conrad Lindberg, *The Middle English Bible: Prefatory Epistles of St. Jerome* (Oslo 1978), p. 9. He has produced two more volumes under this title: vol. 2, *The Book of Baruch* (1985); and vol. 3, *The Book of Judges* (1989). See also Lindberg, "Who Wrote Wiclif's Bible?" *Stockholm Studies in Modern Philology* n.s. 7 (1984) 127–35, p. 127; and Lindberg, "The Alpha and Omega of the Middle English Bible," in *Text and Controversy from Wyclif to Bale: Essays in Honour of Anne Hudson*, ed. Helen Bart and Ann M. Hutchison (Turnhout 2005), pp. 191–200.

3 Josiah Forshall and Frederic Madden (FM), *The Holy Bible, Containing the Old and New Testaments, with the Apocryphal Books, in the Earliest English Versions Made from the Latin Vulgate by John Wycliffe and His Followers*, 4 vols. (Oxford 1850; repr. New York 1982).

4 Rita Copeland, "Lollard Writings," in *The Cambridge Companion to Medieval English Literature, 1100–1500*, ed. Larry Scanlon (Cambridge 2009), pp. 111–22, at p. 113.

5 Ibid., p. 114.

Chapter 1. History of Judgments on the Middle English Bible

1 David C. Fowler, "John Trevisa and the English Bible," *Modern Philology* 58 (1960) 81–98, p. 81; repeated in Fowler, *The Bible in Early English Literature* (Seattle 1976),

p. 157; and Fowler, *The Life and Times of John Trevisa, Medieval Scholar* (Seattle 1995), p. 213.

2 [Miles Smith,] "The Translators to the Readers," in *The Holy Bible: 1611 Edition, King James Version*, intro. A. W. Pollard (1911; repr. Peabody MA 2003), [p. 5]. See David Daniell, *The Bible in English: Its History and Influence* (New Haven CT 2003), pp. 91–95.

3 John Bale, *Index Britanniae Scriptorum: John Bale's Index of British and Other Writers*, ed. Reginald Lane Poole and Mary Bateson (1902), repr. with intro. by Caroline Brett and James P. Carley (Cambridge 1990): [John Trevisa] "totam bibliam transtulit" (p. 260); [John Wyclif] "tota Biblia transtulit de Latino in Anglicum" (p. 263). The *Index*, prepared ca. 1548–52, was the basis of Bale's published *Catalogus* (1557–59); see n. 8 below.

4 Bale, *Index*, p. 266: "Bibliorum libros omnes in Anglicum idioma transtulit, adhibitis praefationibus. Prologus universalis de tota Bibliorum summa, qui continet 15 capita; incipit: *Viginti quinque libri Veteris Testamenti sunt libri fidei*, etc."

5 FM 1:1–60, "Prologue."

6 Mary Dove, *The First English Bible: The Text and Context of the Wycliffite Versions* (Cambridge 2007), pp. 41–43: Princeton, Princeton University Library MS Scheide 12 = FM MS no. 154 (1:lxi–lxii).

7 Dove, *First English Bible*, p. 70. See John Leland, *De uiris illustribus / On Famous Men*, ed. and trans. James P. Carley with Caroline Brett (Toronto 2010); his treatment of Wyclif's life and works is on pp. 635–39.

8 John Bale, *Scriptorum illustrium Majoris Britanniae . . . catalogus*, 2 vols. (Basel 1557–59) 6.1 (1:456): "Transtulit in Anglicum sermonem Biblia tota, adhibitis praefationibus atque argumentis cuique libro suis."

9 Dove, *First English Bible*, pp. 42–44, 70–71; Mary Dove, ed., *The Earliest Advocates of the English Bible: The Texts of the Medieval Debate* (Exeter 2010), p. xxix.

10 Bale, *Catalogus* 7.18 (1:518). On Bale's treatment of Trevisa, see Fowler, "John Trevisa," pp. 81–83.

11 Cambridge University Library (CUL) MS Mm.2.15; see FM 1:liv–lv, MS no. 112; Dove, *First English Bible*, p. 241.

12 Dove, *First English Bible*, p. 72, referring to Oxford, Bodleian MS Laud misc. 33, fol. 2v (statement by the new owner, Andrew Cook); fol. 145 (date); see FM 1:xlvi, MS no. 54 (mistakenly giving the date as 1635). See also H. O. Coxe, *Laudian Manuscripts* (Oxford 1973), p. 71. Dove also singles out Oxford, St. John's College MS 7 (FM 1:liii, MS no. 103), donated in 1620 by Humphrey Haggat and attributed to Wyclif. Dove thinks the attribution is by Haggat, but Forshall and Madden say that the note is in a hand of ca. 1700 and is of no authority.

13 Dove, *First English Bible*, pp. 72–73, of Oxford, Bodleian Fairfax 11; FM 1:xlviii, MS no. 72.

14 Henry Wharton, *Auctarium* (Supplement) to his edition of James Ussher, *Historia dogmatica de Scripturis et sacris vernaculis* (London 1689; I use the identical 1690 edition), pp. 307–468, at p. 435. For Thomas James's catalog of 1600, *Ecloga*, see below.

15 Wharton, *Auctarium*, p. 426.

16 Dove, *First English Bible*, p. 257, of Oxford, Bodleian Fairfax 2. The original date, "mcccc & viii," was later altered by erasing the final *c*, making it 1308, perhaps to avoid the examination of recent Bible translations required in a Canterbury constitution of 1409 (see Chapter 5 below).

17 FM 1:lx–lxi, MS no. 151.

18 Dove, *First English Bible*, p. 73.

19 Thomas James, *A Treatise of the Corruption of Scripture, Councils, and Fathers by the Prelates, Pastors, and Pillars of the Church of Rome, for the Maintenance of Popery and Irreligion* (London 1612), part 2, p. 74 (item 24).

20 Conrad Lindberg, ed., *King Henry's Bible, MS Bodley 277: The Revised Version of the Wyclif Bible* (LLV), 4 vols. (Stockholm 1999–2004).

21 Dove, *First English Bible*, p. 73. She admits that the Queen's Bible is LV, and she is puzzled by the fact.

22 Thomas James, *Ecloga Oxonio-Cantabrigiensis* (London 1600), book 2, p. 60. The New College MSS listed by Dove, *First English Bible*, p. 302, do not include a complete Bible. In his *Ecloga* at this point James names two complete Bibles in Cambridge: "Bib. Ben. 156" and one at Emmanuel College; the latter is the LV Bible later identified as by Wyclif and dated 1383, as reported by Wharton. See Dove, *First English Bible*, pp. 237–38. James in his *Ecloga* also mentions three English New Testaments and two Gospel books at Cambridge (none at Oxford).

23 Ussher, *Historia dogmatica*, p. 155. Dove, *First English Bible*, p. 73, mistakenly believes that Ussher independently viewed the manuscripts that he repeats from James.

24 Ussher, *Historia dogmatica*, pp. 159–60.

25 British Library Cotton Claudius E.II; see Dove, *First English Bible*, pp. 245–46.

26 Thomas Fuller, *The History of the Worthies of England* (London 1662), p. 204.

27 Wharton, *Auctarium*, entry on *1290, Anglicanus Interpres*, p. 426: "Wiclevum quidem S. Scripturam Anglice convertisse extra dubium est: ut Balei etenim auctoritatem taceam, id confirmat Joannes Hussus, cujus testimoniam Clarus Ussserius supra adduxit" ("There is no doubt that Wyclif translated Holy Scripture; for, not to mention Bale's authority, John Hus confirms it, whose testimony the Honorable Ussher cited above"), with a reference to p. 162 of the *Historia dogmatica* (mistake for p. 160).

28 Ibid., pp. 426–27. He gives an example of Luke 2.7, citing EV as Wyclif's and LV as by the "other translator" (whom he goes on to identify as Trevisa). He gives the EV reading as "For place was not to him in the common stable" and LV as "For there was no place to him in no chamber." In Wharton's entry on Wyclif in his *Auctarium*, pp. 432–38, for some reason he reprints his previously published assessment of Wyclif as the LV translator, and adds to it; but then refers us to "more certain conclusions" in the previous treatment: "De hac autem re vide certiora supra ad Annum 1290" (p. 436). In the following entry on Trevisa, pp. 438–39, he does not refer back to his previous identification of him as the LV translator and prologuist, but only cites Trevisa's sentiments in favor of translating the Bible in his *Dialogue*, and he notes that Ussher was misled by Caxton in dating Trevisa so early (1360), adding that Selden hallucinates more grossly ("crassius adhuc hallucinatur Seldenus") in dating him to 1460. For Dove's remarks on Wharton, see *First English Bible*, p. 73.

29 Wharton, *Auctarium*, p. 436: "Hinc patet aut antiquiorem fuisse quandam S. Scripturae translationem Anglicam, aut duplicem fuisse translationis Wiclevianae editionem." See FM 4:438; and Dove, *First English Bible*, pp. 95 (n. 53) and 293 for the Lambeth copy in question (FM MS no. 47).

30 John Lewis, *The History of the Life and Sufferings of . . . John Wicliffe* (London 1720), p. 149, referring notably to CUL MS Kk.1.8 (Prologue and LV New Testament); see Dove, *First English Bible*, p. 75.

31 John Lewis, "A History of the Several Translations of the Holy Bible," preface to *The New Testament of Our Lord and Saviour Jesus Christ Translated out of the Latin Vulgat by John Wiclif*, p. 9.

32 Dove, *First English Bible*, pp. 75–79.

33 [Humfrey Wanley et al.], *A Catalogue of the Harleian Collection of Manuscripts*, 2 vols. (London 1759[–63]), vol. 1, no. 1666. This manuscript was used by Forshall and Madden for the main text of their edition of the prologue.

34 John Wyclif, *Latin Works*, 22 vols. in 35 (London 1883–1922; repr. New York 1966).

35 Reginald Lane Poole, preface to his edition of Wyclif's *Tractatus de civili dominio*, 3 vols. (London 1895; *Latin Works* [1966], 18:1–3), 1:xviii.

36 Thomas Arnold, ed., *Select English Works of John Wyclif*, 3 vols. (Oxford 1869–71); F. D. Matthew, *The English Works of Wyclif, Hitherto Unpublished*, EETS o.s. 74 (London 1880; rev. ed. 1902).

37 On Forshall and Madden's edition (FM), see Sven L. Fristedt, *The Wycliffe Bible*, part 1, *The Principal Problems Connected with Forshall and Madden's Edition* (Stockholm 1953); part 2, *The Origin of the First Revision as Presented in "De salutaribus documentis"* (Stockholm 1969); part 3, *Relationships of Trevisa and the Spanish Medieval Bibles* (Stockholm 1973). Fristedt's comments on the FM edition, 1:13–38, deal mainly with misstatements made about some of the manuscripts. At 3:lix he says: "Without their monumental and magnificent edition, which is remarkably correct for a work of this magnitude, research on the Lollard Bible would have been well-nigh impossible." See further Appendix A below ("A Note on the Manuscripts, Versions, and Dates of the MEB").

38 Francis Aidan Gasquet, "The Pre-Reformation English Bible," *Dublin Review* 115 (1894) 122–52, reprinted with additions and a further essay in *The Old English Bible and Other Essays* (London 1897); see below for details.

39 [Arthur Ogle,] "Dr. Gasquet and the Old English Bible," *Church Quarterly Review* 51 (1900–1901) 138–46, 265–98.

40 See Appendix B below ("Cardinal Gasquet and His Critics").

41 Gasquet, "The Pre-Reformation English Bible," pp. 141–42; in *Old English Bible*, p. 137, instead of "the English pre-Reformation Scriptures," the text reads, perhaps by mistake, "the extant pre-Reformation Scriptures."

42 Gasquet, *Old English Bible*, pp. 102–3. This was the Egerton EV Bible, discussed in Chapter 4 below.

43 Gasquet, *Old English Bible*, p. 110.

44 Ibid., p. 113.

45 See Michael Wilks, "Misleading Manuscripts: Wyclif and the Non-Wycliffite Bible," *Studies in Church History* 11 (1975) 147–61, pp. 154–55; and Anne Hudson, "Lollardy: The English Heresy?" *Studies in Church History* 18 (1982) 261–83, pp. 264–65;

this article is reprinted in Hudson's *Lollards and Their Books* (London 1985) as chap. 9, pp. 141–63; see pp. 144–45.

46 Alastair Minnis, *Translations of Authority in Medieval English Literature: Valuing the Vernacular* (Cambridge 2009), p. 10. He continues: "Furthermore, not a scrap of Middle English survives which can with any confidence be attributed to him, despite the fact that his followers generated a vast corpus of vernacular theology."

47 Ibid., p. 11, citing Anne Hudson, "Wyclif and the English Language," in *Wyclif in His Times*, ed. Anthony Kenny (Oxford 1986), pp. 85–103, at p. 90. For Minnis's more expanded comments on Wyclif and the English Bible, see *Translations*, pp. 107–11 (revised from an article published in 2003).

48 Gasquet, *Old English Bible*, pp. 113–14. He discusses Knighton's attribution to Wyclif in his second article, pp. 171–74. On this question, see Anne Hudson, *The Premature Reformation: Wycliffite Texts and Lollard History* (Oxford 1988), pp. 240–41 and see below, Chapter 4, pp. 61–62.

49 Gasquet, *Old English Bible*, pp. 166–67; Gasquet, like many scholars today, dates Arundel's 1411 letter to the Pisan pope John XXIII as 1412; I take it up in Chapter 5 below.

50 Gasquet, *Old English Bible*, p. 114.

51 F. D. Matthew, "The Authorship of the Wycliffite Bible," *English Historical Review* 10 (1895) 91–99, p. 93.

52 Ogle, "Dr. Gasquet," pp. 284–86.

53 Gasquet, *Old English Bible*, p. 109.

54 See Minnis, *Translations of Authority*, p. 10 (cited above, n. 46). However, Conrad Lindberg, *English Wyclif Tracts 1–3* (Oslo 1991), p. 11, says that the three tracts he edits here, namely, *De officio pastorali*, *De Papa*, and *Of the Church and Her Members*, "are the most certain to be Wyclif's of all the sixty or more earlier attributed to him."

55 Gasquet, *Old English Bible*, p. 116. Fristedt, *Wycliffe Bible*, 1:119–21 (cf. p. 31) refutes Waterland's identification of Purvey's name in Dublin, Trinity College 75 (A.1.10).

56 Ogle, "Dr. Gasquet," pp. 269–70.

57 Anne Hudson, "John Purvey: A Reconsideration of the Evidence," *Viator* 12 (1981) 355–80, incorporated into her *Lollards and Their Books*, chap. 6, pp. 85–110. She does not mention Gasquet.

58 Gasquet, *Old English Bible*, p. 115.

59 Ogle, "Dr. Gasquet," p. 269.

60 Conrad Lindberg, *The Earlier Version of the Wycliffite Bible* (EEV), 8 vols. (Stockholm 1959–97), 5:95–96. Hudson, *Premature Reformation*, chap. 5, "Lollard Biblical Scholarship," pp. 228–77, says (p. 241 n. 76) that Deanesly, *Lollard Bible*, p. 254, speaks of the possible reinvolvement of Hereford after his return from Rome; but I can see no such suggestion on Deanesly's part; she simply says that Purvey most likely took over.

61 See Dove, *First English Bible*, pp. 256–57: dated before 1390 by Forshall and Madden and Christopher de Hamel, *The Book: A History of the Bible* (London 2001), p. 172, and before 1400 by Lindberg.

62 FM 1:xlvii; see Dove, *First English Bible*, pp. 355–56: she dates it ca. 1380–90; FM, "certainly before 1390"; Lindberg, ca. 1400. Scribe 5 of Bodley 959 went on finish Douce 369.1 (as Scribe 3), but the final inscription, "Explicit translationem Nicholay de herford," is not in his hand (FM 1:xlii, MS no. 65; and 1:l, MS no. 87).

63 See Hudson, *Premature Reformation*, pp. 241–42.

64 Ibid., p. 242. One can still find recent scholars accepting the roles assigned to Purvey and Hereford; see, for instance, James Morey, *Book and Verse: A Guide to Middle English Biblical Literature* (Urbana IL 2000), p. 11.

65 Gasquet, *Old English Bible*, p. 141.

66 Gasquet, *Old English Bible*, p. 117.

67 *FTB* (GP), chap. 15 (FM 1:57).

68 Gasquet, *Old English Bible*, p. 118.

69 This is Lindberg's position, *Earlier Version*, 8:70.

70 Gasquet, *Old English Bible*, pp. 128–29; cf. pp. 139 and 164.

71 Francis Aidan Gasquet, "What, Then, Was the English Reformation?" (a lecture given at Notre Dame University in 1905), printed in *England Under the Old Religion and Other Essays* (London 1912), pp. 86–112, at pp. 95–96. In "England Under the Old Religion," a paper written in 1903, but not printed until the publication of this 1912 volume (pp. 1–56), he explains the lack of an early printed Bible in England as not due to an alleged hostility to such an enterprise on the part of the ecclesiastical authorities: "It was rather that the need was not considered so pressing, than that the Church was determined to thwart the endeavors of a people eager to possess the Bible in their own tongue. It seems certain that some people at least were then in possession of the Scriptures in English with the approval of ecclesiastical authorities" (p. 14).

72 Herbert Thurston, "Dr. G. G. Coulton and Cardinal Gasquet," *Month* 172 (July–December 1938) 493–503, p. 498.

73 Thurston says, after the statement quoted above, "Personally I am inclined to think that the Cardinal was mistaken regarding this Catholic authorship," and adds: "but controversialists who possess any elementary sense of decency do not use such language as 'dishonesty,' 'the Gasquet scandal,' 'this truth-robber,' etc., so long as even the plain lapses of an opponent, who is respected by all the world, are consistent with good faith" (ibid., p. 498).

74 Anne Hudson, ed., *Selections from English Wycliffite Writings* (Cambridge 1978), p. 173.

75 Herbert B. Workman, *John Wyclif: A Study of the English Medieval Church*, 2 vols. (Oxford 1926), 2:195.

76 Gasquet, *Old English Bible*, pp. 137–38.

77 Fowler, "John Trevisa," p. 98. He considers Wyclif to be "the prime mover of this project," but hesitates to say how much he "involved himself in the actual task of translation." In *The Bible in Early English Literature*, pp. 156–57, he says: "I suggest that among the scholars at Queen's in the 1370s were the men who translated the Early Version of the Wyclif Bible: at the very least these would include Wyclif, Hereford, [William] Middleworth, and Trevisa." In *Life and Times of John Trevisa*, he adds a postscript, dated 1993 (pp. 231–34), in which he maintains his "conclusions as to Trevisa's probable role as a translator of the Early Version of the Wycliffite Bible."

78 Fristedt, *Wycliffe Bible*, 3:88.

79 Conrad Lindberg, "Revising the Wyclif Bible," in *Beowulf and Beyond*, ed. Hans Sauer and Renate Bauer (Frankfurt 2007), pp. 197–204; Lindberg believes that John Purvey is probably the author of the so-called General Prologue, and when he "mentions four steps taken by someone he refers to as *he*" (i.e., "a simple creature"), in setting out the process of translating the Bible, the reference is "not improbably [to] Wyclif himself" (p. 197). See also Lindberg, *Earlier Version*, 8:69–71. On p. 69 n. 3, he says that "the change of subject pronouns, from 'he' in the four points, to 'I' elsewhere, suggests a man writing on Wyclif's behalf."

80 Lindberg, *Earlier Version*, 5:92.

81 Lindberg, *Earlier Version*, 8:70; see Appendix A. Lindberg thinks that John Purvey may have worked on a later version of LV, which I call LLV (Lindberg, *King Henry's Bible*, 1:47).

82 Wilks, "Misleading Manuscripts."

83 Hudson, "Lollardy: The English Heresy?" pp. 264–65 (144–45) n. 16. Dove, *First English Bible*, joins Hudson in finding Wilks's case (that there is no evidence linking EV with Wyclif) unconvincing (p. 55). But she, like Hudson, presents Wilks as speaking of the entire Bible, whereas he only specifies the New Testament.

84 Wilks, "Misleading Manuscripts," p. 160.

85 J. Patrick Hornbeck, *What Is a Lollard? Dissent and Belief in Late Medieval England* (Oxford 2010), p. 6, drawing on Jeremy Catto, "Fellows and Helpers: The Religious Identity of the Followers of Wyclif," in *The Medieval Church: Universities, Heresy, and the Religious Life; Essays in Honour of Gordon Leff*, ed. Peter Biller and Barrie Dobson (Woodbridge 1999), pp. 141–61. Hornbeck does not deal with the subject of Bible translation in his book, except to say that the Wycliffite Bible "betrays little about the theological conviction of its translators," adding: "The prime and perhaps the only exception to this claim is the highly polemical General Prologue to the Later Version" (p. 41 and n. 62). His promise to return to GP later in his book is not fulfilled. He interprets *Periculosa* as a blanket prohibition against translating and copying (p. 25).

86 Ian R. Johnson, "The General Prologue to the Wycliffite Bible," in *The Idea of the Vernacular: An Anthology of Middle English Literary Theory, 1280–1520*, ed. Jocelyn Wogan-Browne et al. (University Park PA 1999), pp. 91–97, at p. 91. After asserting that the text of the Bible translations was banned by the constitutions of 1409, Johnson adds: "But how far it was thought of as 'Wycliffite' by most of its readers is unclear" (p. 92).

87 David Lawton, "The Bible," in *The Oxford History of Literary Translation in English*, vol. 1, *To 1550*, ed. Roger Ellis (Oxford 2008), pp. 193–233, at 199, 221, 222, 229.

88 Anne Hudson, *Doctors in English: A Study of the Wycliffite Gospel Commentaries* (Liverpool 2015), p. cliii. For earlier treatments of the *Glossed Gospels*, see Hudson's *Premature Reformation*, esp. pp. 248–61; and Hudson, "The Variable Text," in *Crux and Controversy in Middle English Textual Criticism*, ed. A. J. Minnis and Charlotte Brewer (Woodbridge 1992), pp. 49–60, at pp. 51–55.

89 Hudson, *Doctors in English*, pp. cxxxviii–cxl (the section, "Lollard Commentaries?").

90 Henry Hargreaves, "Popularising Biblical Scholarship: The Role of the Wycliffite *Glossed Gospels*," in *The Bible and Medieval Culture*, ed. W. Lourdaux and D. Verhelst

(Leuven 1979), pp. 171–89, is hardly justified in saying that the instinct to popularize biblical scholarship in English was as sound as the impulse to popularize the biblical text itself (p. 189).

91 One might refer to this co-option effort as an attempted "hijacking"; but Elizabeth Schirmer, "Canon Wars and Outlier Manuscripts: Gospel Harmony in the Lollard Controversy," *Huntington Library Quarterly* 73 (2010) 1–36, pp. 4–5, has already seized upon this term to characterize Ralph Hanna's view of the Lollards as "staging a hostile takeover" of previous vernacular biblicism, and then non-Lollards in turn taking over and using Lollard productions (specifically the Wycliffite Bible). See Hanna, *London Literature, 1300–1380* (Cambridge 2005), pp. 305–13.

92 Fiona Somerset, *Feeling Like Saints: Lollard Writings After Wyclif* (Ithaca NY 2014), p. 180.

Chapter 2. *Five and Twenty Books* as "Official" Prologue, or Not

1 Hudson, *Selections*, pp. 173–74; *Premature Reformation*, pp. 237–38.

2 Nine of these manuscripts, all but Princeton, are listed in FM 1:xxxvii with their Greek sigla (the last two sigla, ϰ, λ refer to the Prologue to Matthew). For discussion of each, see Dove, *Earliest Advocates*, pp. xxv–xxviii. The treatise is edited as "Prologue" in FM 1:1–60. Chapter 15 is also edited by Anne Hudson, in *Selections*, pp. 67–72, with notes on pp. 173–77. In *Premature Reformation*, p. 237, Hudson concludes that the prologue was definitely not provided until after the LV was completed, whereas Forshall and Madden believe that it may have been written before the LV New Testament was finished. The whole treatise has also been edited by Dove, *Earliest Advocates*, pp. 1–85, with introduction on pp. xx–xxx and notes on pp. 188–200. Dove uses as her base text Princeton University Library MS Scheide 12, a copy of the entire GP and LV Bible, described by Forshall and Madden (1:lxi–lxii, MS no. 154, owned at the time by Peregrine Acland) but not used by them. See Dove, *First English Bible*, pp. 235–37. I use the FM edition in this study, since Dove does not include all of the variants that they record.

3 Dove, *First English Bible*, pp. 248–49; see also Kathleen E. Kennedy, *The Courtly and Commercial Art of the Wycliffite Bible* (Turnhout 2014), pp. 166–71.

4 Dove, *Earliest Advocates*, p. xxix.

5 FM, "Preface," 1:xxv–xxvii.

6 GP, title (FM 1:1).

7 Dove, *Earliest Advocates*, p. 3; Hudson, *Selections*, says, "Prologue to Wycliffite Bible."

8 Gasquet names it thus on p. 141 of *The Old English Bible*: "the prologue, 'Five and Twenty Books,' so freely attributed to Wyclif."

9 In what follows, I have added the boldface; page numbers refer to FM (GP) vol. 1. He first refers to himself in the first person in chap. 1: "Therfore **I translatide** not the thridde neither the fourthe book of Esdre, that ben apocrifa, but onely the first, and of Neemie" (p. 2). The next time is in chap. 11, when claiming authorship of the gloss to Job: "For **I have declarid** in party in the glos hou the harde sentensis of Job schulen be undirstonden, therfore **I passe over** lightly now" (p. 37). The Job gloss is mainly in MS C (Cotton Claudius E.2), like the gloss to Isaiah. Forshall and Madden do not notice the author's comment on Job when they say that the author

(whom they identify as Purvey) alludes twice to his glosses, the first in chap. 11: "The prophetis han a general prologe for alle, and for **I declaride** sumdel the grete profetis, and in party the litil prophetis, and thenke soone to make an ende, with Goddis help, of the glos on the smale prophetis, **I thenke now to passe over** withouten eny tarying" (p. 41). I will treat of the author's Prologue to Isaiah at the end of this chapter. The second passage they cite is his statement about the Psalms in chap. 15: "**I have set** in the margin, by maner of a glose, what the Ebru hath, and hou it is undurstondun in sum place" (p. 58). He also uses the first person when commenting on his present lack of books in chap. 12: "Isidre, in the first book of *Souerein Good*, touchith these reulis schortliere, but **I have him not now**, and Lyre, in the biginning of the Bible, touchith more opinly these reulis, but **I have him not now**, and Ardmacan, in the biginning of his book *De questionibus Armenorum*, yeveth many goode groundis to undirstonde Holy Scripture to the lettre, and goostly undirstonding also, but **I have him not now**" (p. 48).

After he speaks of himself in the third person as a simple creature, he gives some examples of translation principles and soon reverts to the first person (pp. 57–58): "Also whanne oo word is oonis set in a reesoun, it may be set forth as ofte as it is undurstonden, either as ofte as reesoun and nede axen; and this word *autem*, either *vero*, may stonde for *forsothe*, either for *but*, and thus **I use** comounly; and sumtime it may stonde for *and*, as elde gramariens seyn. Also whanne rightful construccioun is lettid by relacion, **I resolve** it openly, thus, where this reesoun, *Dominum formidabunt adversarij ejus*, shulde be Englisshid thus by the lettre, *the Lord Hise adversaries shulen drede*, **I Englishe** it thus by resolucioun, *the adversaries of the Lord shulen drede Him*; and so of othere resons that ben like. At the biginning **I purposide**, with Goddis helpe, to make the sentence as trewe and open in English as it is in Latin, either more trewe and more open than it is in Latin; and **I preye**, for charite and for comoun profit of Cristene soulis, that if ony wiis man finde ony defaute of the truthe of translacioun, let him sette in the trewe sentence and opin of Holy Writ, but loke that he examine truly his Latin Bible, for no doute he shal finde ful manie Biblis in Latin ful false, if he loke manie, namely newe; and the comune Latin Biblis han more nede to be correctid, as manie as **I have seen** in my lif, than hath the English Bible late translatid; and where the Ebru, by witnesse of Jerom, of Lyre, and othere expositouris discordith fro oure Latin Biblis, **I have set** in the margin, by maner of a glose, what the Ebru hath, and hou it is undurstondun in sum place; and **I dide** this most in the Sauter, that of alle oure bokis discordith most fro Ebru; for the Chirche redith not the Sauter by the laste translacioun of Jerom out of Ebru into Latin, but another translacioun of othere men, that hadden miche lasse kunning and holinesse than Jerom hadde; and in ful fewe bokis the Chirche redith the translacioun of Jerom, as it mai be previd by the propre originals of Jerom, whiche he gloside. And where **I have translatid** as opinly or opinliere in English as in Latin, late wise men deme, that knowen wel bothe langagis, and knowen wel the sentence of Holy Scripture. And wher **I have do** thus or nay, ne doute, they that kunne wel the sentence of Holy Writ and English togidere, and wolen travaile with Goddis grace theraboute, moun make the Bible as trewe and as opin, yea, and opinliere in English than it is in Latin."

10 GP, chap. 15, p. 57. For the Lollard use of "simple creature," see especially Christina von Nolcken, "A 'Certain Sameness' and Our Response to It in English Wycliffite Texts," in *Literature and Religion in the Later Middle Ages: Philological Studies in Honor of Siegfried Wenzel*, ed. Richard G. Newhauser and John A. Alford (Binghamton NY 1995), pp. 191–208, at p. 198.

11 We should recall Lindberg's idea that the "he" refers to Wyclif himself ("Revising the Wyclif Bible," p. 197).

12 GP, chap. 15, p. 58: "Late the Chirche of Engelond appreve the trewe and hool translacioun *of simple men*, that wolden for no good in erthe, by here witing and power, putte awey the leste truthe, yea, the leste letter either title of Holy Writ that berith substaunce either charge. And dispute they not of the holinesse of men now livinge in this deadly lif, for they kunnen not theron, and it is reservid onely to Goddis doom. If they knowen ony notable defaute by the *translatouris* either helpis of hem, lete hem blame the defaute by charite and mercy." (Dove in her edition, line 2897, has "translatouris or helperis of hem.") Just above this, he answers the objections of those who would hold that "simple men that translaten now into English" are not of sufficient holiness and knowledge.

13 GP, chap, 1, p. 2; chap. 3, p. 3; chap. 11, p. 35; chap. 13, p. 52. See Matti Peikola, *Congregation of the Elect: Patterns of Self-Fashioning in English Lollard Writings* (Turku 2000), pp. 259–60.

14 GP, chap. 15, p. 57, citing Luke 21.26, "arescentibus hominibus pre timore," as an example of the present participle. Forshall and Madden overlook this reference to the NT when they say that the NT is mentioned only once, in one sentence in the first chapter (FM 1:xxviii).

15 A different interpretation of Simple Creature's statement is given by Lindberg, *Earlier Version*, 8:68; he believes that "the correcting of the translacioun" refers to the whole EV (discussed below).

16 Thomas Francis Knox, ed., *The First and Second Diaries of the English College, Douay* (London 1878; repr. Westmead 1969), marginal note to October 1578; for text and translation see James G. Carleton, *The Part of Rheims in the Making of the English Bible* (Oxford 1902), p. 16; beginning around October 16, Martin was to translate two chapters a day, and the college president William Allen and moderator Richard Bristow were to check and emend the text. In "The Rheims Annual Report, 1579–80," ed. Edwin H. Burton and Thomas L. Williams, in *The Douay College Diaries, Third, Fourth, and Fifth, 1598–1654, with the Rheims Report, 1579–80*, vol. 2, Catholic Record Society 11 (London 1911), pp. 553–59 (translated, pp. 559–66), which covers events from June 14, 1579, to July 22, 1580, the project is announced as finished: "Finita quoque est sed nondum edenda vernacula translatio catholicissima Bibliorum, quam selectissimis annotationibus ex commentariis praecipuorum patrum sic exornamus contra haereses hujus temporis" (p. 558); that is, "There is also finished but not yet to be put to press a very Catholic vernacular translation of the Bible, which we have adorned with well considered annotations from the commentaries of chief Fathers against the heresies of this time" (my trans.). See George Bruner Parks, "The Life and Works of Gregory Martin," in Parks's edition of Martin's *Roma sancta (1581)* (Rome 1969), pp. xi–xxxii, at p. xvi; see also Thomas M. McCoog's entry on Martin in *OxDNB*. There are by my count some 1,322 chapters in the Vulgate, and keeping to the schedule of two a day would go just under twenty-two months. The Rheims report was written twenty-one months after the work on the Bible began, but the comment on its completion does not give the impression that the work was finished only at the last minute. It is preceded by the announcement that Martin's *Treatise of Schism* had been published (which took place at the end of 1578—see Parks's ed. of *Roma sancta*, p. 273), and it is followed by the remark that some other books written both in Latin and English are ready for the press, but there is no

opportunity for printing them ("Sunt et alii nonnulli libri tam latine quam anglice scripti jamque ad praelum parati, sed non est opportunitas excudendi"). The New Testament was published at Rheims in March 1582, or perhaps early April; see A. C. Southern, *Elizabethan Recusant Prose, 1559–1582* (London [1950]), pp. 234–35, 454–56; and the Old Testament, at Douai in 1610 not 1609/10); see Arnovick and Kelly, "Bishop Challoner's Ecumenical Revision," pp. 698–99.

17 Fowler, 'John Trevisa," p. 95.

18 Daniell, *Bible in English*, pp. 91–95: "Appendix: The Enigma of John Trevisa." See also Hudson, *Premature Reformation*, pp. 241–42; and Dove, *First English Bible*, pp. 80–81. Trevisa is a "J" candidate in the attribution to "J and others" in MS Cambridge Ee.1.10 (ca. 1430; see Dove, *First English Bible*, pp. 239–41). The manuscript notation says that the translation of N ends here and the translation of J and others begins now. Forshall and Madden overlooked the note (FM 1:liv). It was discovered by Henry Hargreaves; see "An Intermediate Version of the Wycliffite Old Testament," *Studia Neophilologica* 28 (1956) 130–47, p. 133, where he first read "N" as "H*er*," which he corrected in "The Wycliffite Versions," in *The Cambridge History of the Bible*, vol. 2, ed. G. W. H. Lampe (Cambridge 1969), pp. 387–415, at p. 400. Nicholas Hereford is the only "N" candidate that has been put forward.

19 See Lilo Moessner, "Translation Strategies in Middle English: The Case of the Wycliffite Bible," *Poetica* (Tokyo) 55 (2001) 123–54, esp. p. 134. Moessner limits her study to the first fifty psalms, which are in a part of the EV that uses the *-ende* form for the present participle, without realizing that most of the FM EV text uses the *-inge* form (Forshall and Madden do not report the variants *-inge* and *-ende*). For both EV and LV they chose primary manuscripts that use *-inge*, except for the middle part of the EV Old Testament, where the manuscript, Douce 369.1, uses *-ende*. It is interesting to note that the final scribe of this manuscript, Scribe 3, had (according to FM) the previous job of being the final copyist, Scribe 5, of Bodley 959, the manuscript that preserves the earliest version of EV, which I call EEV. As Scribe 5 of EEV, he gradually changed from using the *-inge* form to the *-ende* form, perhaps grooming himself for his next assignment. See Appendix C, "Present Participles in *-inge* and *-ende* in EV."

20 Fristedt, *Wycliffe Bible*, 3:7–58: "Trevisa and the Wycliffite Bible." See A. S. G. Edwards, "John Trevisa," in *A Companion to Middle English Prose*, ed. Edwards (Cambridge 2004), pp. 117–26, esp. p. 121; and Anne Hudson, "Wycliffite Prose," in Edwards's earlier edited volume *Middle English Prose: A Critical Guide to Major Authors and Genres* (New Brunswick NJ 1984), pp. 249–70, at pp. 263–64.

21 GP, chap. 1, p. 2.

22 John Wyclif, *De veritate Sacrae Scripturae*, ed. Rudolph Buddensieg, 3 vols. (London 1905–7; *Latin Works* 18:1–3), chap. 11 (1:242, 246–47); see the translation of Ian Christopher Levy, *On the Truth of Holy Scripture* (Kalamazoo 2001), pp. 163, 167. Gustav Adolf Benrath, *Wyclifs Bibelkommentar* (Berlin 1966), only treats at length three books of the Old Testament (Psalms, Canticles, and Lamentations); but his Scripture index has the Apocrypha separated out at the end, as in modern Protestant Bibles (unlike the MEB). One of Wyclif's favorite passages was the story of Susanna, which falls outside the Hebrew canon, at the end of Daniel (as Wyclif notes in *De veritate* 11, 1:232, Levy p. 155). See Jonathan Stavsky, "As the Lily Among Thorns: Daniel 13 in the Writings of John Wyclif and His Followers," *Viator* 46:1 (Spring 2015) 249–76. Dove, *First English Bible*, p. 95, is mistaken in claiming that Jerome's

position was that of "the whole of the western medieval church," as is Hudson, *Premature Reformation*, p. 230, when she says that "the General Prologue to the Wycliffite translation of the bible explains at its outset the difference between the apocrypha and the canonical books in terms that not even Arundel could have found offensive."

23 GP, chap. 1, p. 2: "Therfore Cristen men and wimmen, olde and yonge, shulden studie fast in the Newe Testament, for it is of ful autorite, and opin to undirstonding of simple men, as to the pointis that be moost nedeful to salvacioun; and the same sentence is in the derkiste placis of Holy Writ, whiche sentence is in the opin placis; and ech place of Holy Writ, bothe opin and derk, techith mekenes and charite; and therfore he that kepith mekenes and charite hath the trewe undirstonding and perfectioun of al Holy Writ, as Austin previth in his sermoun of the preising of charite. Therfore no simple man of wit be aferd unmesurably to studie in the text of Holy Writ, forwhy tho ben wordis of everlasting lif."

24 GP, chap. 2, p. 3: "It semith opin heresie to seye that the Gospel with his treuthe and fredom suffisith not to salvacioun of Cristen men without keping of ceremonies and statutis of sinful men and unkunninge, that ben maad in the time of Sathanas and of Antecrist" (cf. posthumous charge no. 1 against Richard Hunne, 1514; see below, Chapter 7).

25 GP, chap. 10, pp. 29–30: "But alas, alas, alas! . . . Summe Cristene lordis senden general lettris to alle her ministris and leegemen, eithir tenauntis, that the pardouns of the bisschopis of Rome, that ben opin leesingis, for they graunten many hundred yeeris of pardoun aftir Domesday, be prechid generaly in her rewmes and lordschipis" (cf. charge 2 against Hunne).

26 GP, chap. 10, p. 30: "Summe Cristen lordis in name not in dede preisen and magnifien freris lettris, ful of disceit and leesingis, and make hire tenauntis and meyne to swere bi herte, boonis, nayles, and sides, and other membris of Crist, and pursuen ful cruely hem that wolden teche treuly and freely the Lawe of God" (cf. charge 4 against Hunne). For more citations of Simple Creature's polemics here, see Somerset, *Feeling Like Saints*, pp. 178–79.

27 GP, chap. 10, p. 33: "Ech lord and greet prelat comynly makith to him an ydole of sum seint, whom he worschipith more than God; for comunly they sweren bi oure Lady of Walsingham, seint Joon Baptist, seint Edward, seint Thomas of Caunterbury, and such othere seintis" (cf. charge 8 against Hunne).

28 GP, chap. 10, p. 33: "To absteine fro oothis nedeles and unleeveful, and to eschewe pride, and speke onour of God and of his lawe, and repreve sinne bi weye of charite, is matir and cause now why prelatis and summe lordis sclaundren men and clepen hem Lollardis, eretikis, and riseris of debate and of tresoun ayens the king."

29 GP, chap. 10, p. 34: "By withdrawing of almes, and in yevinge it to dede stockis either stoonis, either to riche clerkis and feined religiouse, were to speke now, if a man hadde the spirit of goostly strengthe; now men knelin and preyen and offren faste to dede imagis, that han neither hungir neither coold" (cf. charge 10 against Hunne).

30 GP, chap. 13, p. 51; cf. charge 12 against Hunne.

31 Lewis, "History of the Several Translations," p. 9.

32 Hudson, *Premature Reformation*, p. 247, says, "Internal references within the General Prologue have suggested to most critics that LV was completed some time between

1395 and 1397," citing FM, Deanesly, and Fristedt. See also J. I. Catto, "Wyclif and Wycliffism at Oxford, 1356–1430," in *HUO* 2:175–261, at p. 223 n. 158. Others, notably Dove, *First English Bible*, pp. 110–13, hold for 1387, as we will see in Chapter 3.

33 Dove, *First English Bible*, pp. 110–13, citing the *Historia vitae et regni Ricardi secundi*, ed. George B. Stow, Jr. (Philadelphia 1977), p. 135. The master, John Bloxham, was dead by July 1387, and the latest parliament in which he could have been charged was that of 1386. However, the chronicler may have mistaken the official involved. Bloxham's successor as warden was John Wendover; see A. B. Emden, *A Biographical Register of the University of Oxford to A.D. 1500* (*BRUO*), 3 vols. (Oxford 1957–59), 3:2014.

34 GP, chap. 12, pp. 44–45. A note in Harley 1666, printed in the FM text (1:45), emphasizes the passage: "How men schulden ete Cristis flesch and His blood."

35 See charge 11 against Hunne.

36 Augustine, *De doctrina Christiana* 3.16 (PL 34:74–75).

37 See "Wyclif's Confessions on the Eucharist," in Hudson, *Selections*, pp. 17–18, and notes on pp. 141–44. Wyclif emphasizes, however, that Christ is present in the sacrament in a way different from his physical presence when he was alive on earth and from his current physical presence in heaven (Hudson, *Selections*, p. 143). This conforms to the doctrine espoused in *Thirty-Seven Conclusions*, ed. Josiah Forshall, under title *Remonstrance Against Romish Corruptions in the Church* . . . (London 1851), art. 15, pp. 40–43; see Appendix D, note 13, below.

38 FM 1:xxii. Fristedt, *Wycliffe Bible*, 1:10, agrees with them; as does Hargreaves, "Wycliffite Versions," p. 410; and Lindberg, *Earlier Version*, 8:68, 70.

39 GP, chap. 15, p. 58: "The comune Latin Biblis han more nede to be correctid, as manie as I have seen in my lif, than hath the English Bible late translated."

40 Lindberg, *Earlier Version*, 8:68, finds another reference, when he speaks of the fourth step, "the correcting of the translacioun" (GP, chap. 15, p. 57).

41 GP, chap. 1, p. 1.

42 I do not include the first *either* of an *either* + *either* construction, corresponding to *either* + *or* (one instance, GP, chap. 3, p. 4: "*Either* foryive thou this trespas to hem, *either* do me out of thy book in which thou hast writen me," citing Exod. 32.32; cf. LV: "Ethir foryive thou this gilt to hem, ether if thou doist not, do awey me fro thy book which thou hast write").

43 One of the manuscripts that Forshall and Madden collate, Dublin, Trinity College A.1.10, consistently changes *either* to *or*. The manuscript that Dove chooses as a base text, Princeton, Scheide 12 (FM no. 154, Acland MS, not collated by them), regularly uses *either* (*ether*) at first, but on p. 12 (middle of chap. 3, FM p. 6), it shifts mainly to *or*. The last *either* in the Princeton MS occurs in chap. 13, line 2550 (p. 73), "fattest kiin, *ether* ful of shenschipe (FM p. 52: "fattest kiin, *either* kiin ful of schenshipe").

44 For the one instance in which *ne* is used, on the first page of the treatise, "*ne* the prayer of Manasses," the Princeton text has *nether* (ed. Dove, line 26). I do not count the sole use of *ne* in chap. 15, which can be seen in the quotation given above (GP, chap. 15, p. 58), "ne doute, they that kunne . . ."; it is a negative imperative, which is not a contrast with *neither*. In the sentence that follows in the text, *no* is used:

"And no doute to a simple man . . ." The Princeton text has *no* in both places (lines 2865, 2868).

45 GP, chap. 15, p. 58; two manuscripts, however, namely, Oxford U. Col. G 3 and Cambridge, Corpus Christi Col. 147, have *either* (*ether*) in both places. In his earlier statement of intent, also on p. 58, cited above, *either* is used.

46 See *LALME*, the dot maps, 1:427; and the County Dictionary for *or*, 4:229. But the one MS listed as having only the forms *ether* and *ethir*, LP 6660 (Bck), viz., Royal 1.C.8, is the FM LV copy text, which, as we will see below, rarely uses these forms in the New Testament. The MS used for GP chap. 15, CUL Mm.2.15, using *either*, is located in Bedfordshire (*LALME* 3:3–4). Another indication can be seen in John H. Fisher, Malcolm Richardson, and Jane L. Fisher, eds., *An Anthology of Chancery English* (Knoxville TN 1984). Of the 70,000 words in the texts provided, *or* is used 376 times, and there are no occurrences of other forms of the conjunctions.

47 See Appendix D, Part A, "EV Old Testament Preference for OR, LV Old Testament Preference for EITHER."

48 Appendix D, Part B, "OR Preference in EV Gospels—Except Luke."

49 Appendix D, Part C, "OR Preference in EEV Luke, as Opposed to EV Luke."

50 Appendix D, Part D, "OR Preference in All EEV and LV Gospels."

51 Lindberg, *Earlier Version*, 7:21.

52 Fristedt, *Wycliffe Bible*, 2:lv.

53 Ibid., 3:29. For a list of eighteen other First Revision characteristics, see 2:xlv. The tables that Fristedt gives here show that at least by this time Fristedt does not hold for a second revision of EV before LV. Lindberg attributes the second-revision notion to Fristedt as a constant; see Lindberg, "Who Wrote Wyclif's Bible?" pp. 131, 135.

54 Appendix D, Part E, "OR Preference in EV and LV Pauline Epistles."

55 Appendix D, Part F, "OR Preference in Later EV and LV New Testament—Except for Four LV Books."

56 Appendix D, Part G, "EVER-EITHER Usage in GP and LV Old Testament."

57 GP, Chap. 15, p. 57: "Also whanne oo word is oonis set in a reesoun, it may be set forth as ofte as it is undurstonden, either as ofte as reesoun and nede axen; and this word *autem*, either *vero*, may stonde for 'forsothe,' either for 'but,' and thus I use comounly; and sumtime it may stonde for 'and,' as elde gramariens seyn." The first part of this sentence is cited in the *Oxford English Dictionary* (*OED*) under "reason" to illustrate sense 4.b, "*Grammar*. A sentence; (also) a main or dependent clause. *Obs*."

58 See Appendix E, Part A, "FORSOOTH for *Autem/Vero* in Both EV and LV Old Testament."

59 Appendix E, Part B, "FORSOOTH for *Autem/Vero* in EV New Testament, Not in LV New Testament."

60 GP, chap. 15, p. 60: "And this word *enim* signifieth cominly 'forsothe,' and, as Jerom seith, it signifieth cause, thus: 'forwhy.'"

61 Appendix E, Part C, "FORSOOTH and FORWHY as Translations of *enim*."

62 GP, chap. 15, p. 60: "Also this word *ex* signifieth sumtime 'of,' and sumtime it signifieth 'by,' as Jerom seith."

63 Appendix F, Part A, "Various Translations of *ex* in EV and LV."

64 Appendix F, Part B, "Expansion of Use of BY in LV for Non-*Ex* Uses"; see also Appendix H, Part G, on changing *after* to *by*.

65 GP, chap. 15, p. 60 "And this word *secundum* is taken for 'aftir,' as manie men seyn, and cominly, but it signifieth wel 'by,' eithir 'up,' thus 'by youre word,' either 'up youre word.'"

66 GP, chap. 15, p. 57.

67 FM 1:xviii, note s.

68 Fristedt, *Wycliffe Bible*, 1:9, 104.

69 Appendix G, "The Question of a Stylistic Break in Baruch."

70 Appendix H, Part A, "AFTER Versus UP in EV Old Testament, from Prophets to the End."

71 Appendix H, Part B, "No Use of UP in EEV Gospels, but Some Inserted into EV Luke and John."

72 Appendix H, Part C, "Full Use of UP in Both EEV and EV in the New Testament Epistles."

73 Similar changes of translators are indicated by the vicissitudes of other uses of *up* in EV and LV, specifically VERB + UP and UPON. See Appendix H, Part F.

74 Appendix H, Part D, "Absence of Prepositional UP in the LV Old Testament."

75 Appendix H, Part E, "Preposition UP Absent in LV New Testament."

76 Appendix H, Part G, "*Secundum* as AFTER in EV Changed to BY in LV Old Testament."

77 FM 1:xxviii.

78 FM 1:xv–xvi.

79 See Hudson, *Premature Reformation*, pp. 248–59.

80 Lindberg, "Revising the Wyclif Bible," p. 197; and see the writings of Fristedt and Lindberg cited in Chapter 1 above.

81 FM 1:xvii.

82 FM 1:l–li, description of MS no. 87 (Douce 369.1); cf. pp. xlvii–xlviii, description of MS no. 65 (Bodl. 959). Lindberg, *Earlier Version*, 1:24, has found innumerable corrections by *prima manus* and *alia manus* not mentioned in FM.

83 Lindberg, *Earlier Version*, 5:91–96. See also Simon Forde, "Hereford, Nicholas (b. ca. 1345, d. after 1417)," in *OxDNB*; Forde says that Hereford appears to have made his peace with Archbishop Courtenay in 1391. I would put it earlier, since he held the rectorship of a parish in Kent from January 22 of 1391.

84 See Hudson, *Premature Reformation*, pp. 241–42.

85 FM 1:xvii–xviii, note s, reproduced in Fristedt, *Wycliffe Bible*, 1:4–6.

86 Lindberg, *Earlier Version*, 5:51, 66–67, 71. See below, Appendix G.

87 Deanesly, *Lollard Bible*, esp. pp. 260–97; she says on p. 266: "It is thus clear that but one person wrote the *General Prologue*, and that he edited also the second version of the Wycliffite Bible. This person was Wycliffe's secretary and literary executor, the leader of the remnant of his sect, the 'eximius doctor' John Purvey. . . . Moreover,

the *General Prologue* is but one of a series of tracts written in the years about 1387 by Purvey."

88 Hudson, "John Purvey."

89 It is interesting that Mary Dove must have started out believing that Purvey wrote GP, since there are two relics of this identification in her studies: "Wyclif and the English Bible," in *A Companion to John Wyclif, Late Medieval Theologian*, ed. Ian Christopher Levy (Leiden 2007), pp. 365–406, at p. 396 n. 168 (where she says that chap. 10 of GP shows that Purvey had Guy of Baysio's *Rosarium*); and *First English Bible*, p. 94 n. 51 (which says that Purvey cites the *Catholicon* in GP).

90 See Emden, *BRUO*, 3:1526–27.

91 Maureen Jurkowski, "New Light on John Purvey," *English Historical Review* 110 (1995) 1180–90. See also her "Lollard Book Producers in London in 1414," in *Text and Controversy from Wyclif to Bale: Essays in Honour of Anne Hudson*, ed. Helen Barr and Ann M. Hutchison (Turnhout 2005), pp. 201–26, at pp. 209–10. She identifies Parisiensis as William Peraldus ("New Light," p. 1185), which is indeed the name sometimes given in these circles to Peraldus and his *Summa de viciis*; see, for instance, Dove's edition of *Five and Twenty Books* (GP), *Earliest Advocates*, p. 192, note to lines 1743–45 on p. 51 (FM 1:32). But the designation commonly refers also to William of Auvergne, bishop of Paris; see Siegfried Wenzel, *Latin Sermon Collections from Later Medieval England: Orthodox Preaching in the Age of Wyclif* (Cambridge 2005), pp. 54 (Peraldus), 111, 114, 320 (Auvergne); neither author is reported to have written a commentary on the New Testament epistles, but both wrote popular sermons on the Sunday liturgies.

92 Hudson, *Premature Reformation*, pp. 250, 257–58; Hudson, *Doctors in English*, pp. cxxxviii–cxl.

93 Prologue to *Short Matthew*, ed. Dove, labeled GG1, in *Earliest Advocates*, pp. 172–73, using as main text London, BL MS Add. 41175; the other copy is in Cambridge, Trinity College B.1.38. Dove shows the presence of four *eithers*; but in a portion of the text edited by Hargreaves, "Popularising Biblical Scholarship," p. 181, one *either* is given as *other* ("*other* 'Gregor in his omeli,'" Dove's line 34), and has another *either* that is omitted by Dove in line 38 ("what euer doctour *ether* glos y alegge").

94 Hudson, *Doctors in English*, texts of *Short Matthew*: 1(a)ii (pp. 8–9), 1(c)ii (pp. 17–19), citing Add. 41175; and 5(b)i (p. 38), 5(b)ii (p. 39), citing York Minster Library XIV.D.2.

95 Prologue to *Short Luke*, ed. Dove as GG4, *Earliest Advocates*, pp. 184–85 (only in Oxford Bodley 143).

96 Ibid., p. 184: "Herfore a *pore caitif*, lettid fro preching for a time, for causis knowun of God, writith the Gospel of Luk in English, with a short exposicioun of olde and holy doctouris, to the pore men of his nacioun whiche kunnen litil Latin *ether* noon, and ben pore of wit and of worldly catel, and netheles riche of good wille to plese God. First, this *pore caitif* settith a ful sentence of the text . . . afterward he settith a sentence of a doctour. . . . Whanne I alegge 'Ambrose here' *ether* 'Bede here,' understonde on the same text expowned."

97 *Long Luke*: Hudson, *Selections*, pp. 51–52; *Doctors*, texts 2(a)i (pp. 20–29), 2(b)i (pp. 34–35), 6(b)i (pp. 67–71), citing Cambridge University Library Kk.2.9. *Short Luke*: Hudson, *Selections*, pp. 49–50; *Doctors*, texts 2(a)ii (pp. 30–33), 2(b)ii (p. 36),

6(b)ii (pp. 72–73), citing Bodley 243. In the last-named selection, *Long Luke* has one *or* (*Doctors*, p. 71, line 135), kept in *Short Luke* (p. 73 line 46).

98 *Short Mark*: Hudson, *Doctors*, texts 4(a) (pp. 42–43), 4(b)i (pp. 44–45), 4(c) (pp. 50–55), all from Add. 41175, and 4(b)ii (pp. 46–49), from York MS. The passage at 7(c)ii (pp. 97–98) shows *Short Mark* seemingly abbreviating what may be a *Long Mark* passage preserved in the York MS, 7(c)i (pp. 92–96), both using *either*, notably in changing EV Romans 2.15 "accusinge *or also* defending" or LV "accusynge *or* defendynge" to "accusynge *either* defendynge." The version in *Short Mark* is farther away from the EV/LV texts than the York text:

EV: "A witnessinge and bitwixe hemselve of thoughtis accusinge *or* also defendinge."

LV: "A witnessyng bytwixe hemsilf of thoughtis that ben accusynge *or* defendynge."

York: "And thoughtis accusynge *either* defendynge bitwixe hemsilf togidere."

Short Mark: "Thoughtis schulen accuse *ether* defende bitwixe hemsilf togidere."

99 Hudson, *Doctors*, pp. cli–clii.

100 Ibid., text 6(c)i, *Long John* as found in York MS, fols. 113rb–117ra: thirty-nine *or*s; thirteen *either*s; one *either-either*.

101 Prologue to *Short John*, Bodley 243 (Dove, *Earliest*, p. 186); body of *Short John*, Hudson, *Selections*, pp. 60–64, and *Doctors*, text 3(a) (Bodley 243): only *or*. However, in *Premature Reformation*, p. 257 at n. 155, Hudson cites a sentence of *Short John* using *either* (the *either* cited on p. 251 n. 124 is not from *Short John* but from *Short Matthew*).

102 Prologue to *Long Matthew* (or *Intermediate Matthew*), Dove, *Earliest*, p. 174–79; Epilogue to *Intermediate/Long Matthew* (Dove, *Earliest*, pp. 180–83): all *or* (except that there are two instances of *either-either* alongside two cases of *either* + *or* in the Epilogue). Hudson, *Doctors*: *Long Matthew*, 1(a)i (pp. 5–7), 1(b) (pp. 10–12), 1(c) (pp. 13–16), 6(a) (pp. 6–66), Add. 28026; and 5(a) (pp. 56–57), York MS. In the last selection, the York MS uses *or* when drawing on *Long Matthew* and *either* when using *Long Luke*. It seems to follow its exemplars in this matter throughout (to judge from the selections given by Hudson). Similarly, the scribe of Bodley 243 follows *Short Luke* in using *either* and *Short John* in using *or*. By the way, Hudson, *Doctors*, pp. liv–lv (cf. p. xx), wishes to withdraw the label *Intermediate Matthew* as inaccurate, assimilating it to *Long Matthew*.

103 Hudson, *Doctors*, p. clii, says that the *Glossed Gospels* "originated in Oxford relatively early, certainly before 1400 and probably before 1390 or even 1385, in close association with the work on both versions of the Wycliffite Bible." On p. cxlix she cites Knighton's account of William Smith of Leicester in 1389: "Libros eciam solempnes quos in materna lingua de Evangelio, de epistolis Pauli, et aliis epistolis et doctoribus conscripserat, et, ut fatebatur, per octo annos studiose conscribere laboraverat, archiepiscopo coactus tradidit" (*Knighton's Chronicle, 1337–1396*, ed. and trans. G. H. Martin [Oxford 1995], p. 534). She says that the reference to the Gospel and doctors would be appropriate to the *Glossed Gospels*, but the rest of it is not. Martin translates thus: "He had written out solemn texts of the Gospels in his own language, and others from St. Paul's and other epistles, and works of the doctors of the church, which, as he confessed, he had labored over for eight years, and which he was made to surrender to the archbishop." He suggests that his companions William Parmenter

and Michael Scrivener may have helped him when he was writing (*Knighton's Chronicle*, p. 535 and n. 4). Perhaps this is the force of the verb *conscribere*, "write with." Earlier, Knighton said that Smith was a blacksmith who had taught himself the ABCs and writing (p. 292). K. B. McFarlane, *John Wycliffe and the Beginnings of English Nonconformity* (London 1952), says that Smith "spent eight years compiling English books based on the New Testament and the writings of the Fathers" (p. 141). Writing to Fristedt in 1953, McFarlane says, "Can you translate Knighton's words to mean that he *translated* the gospels and epistles? I should have said that it meant that 'he had compiled (or 'put together') long-winded books in the mother tongue *about* the epistles and gospel.'" See Fristedt, *Wycliffe Bible*, 3:88. By the way, McFarlane, *John Wycliffe*, p. 139, names "Parchmener" (parchment-maker) rather than "Parmenter" (tailor) for Smith's companion.

104 Christina von Nolcken, "Lay Literacy, the Democratization of God's Law, and the Lollards," in *The Bible as Book: The Manuscript Tradition*, ed. John L. Sharpe III and Kimberly van Kampen (London 1998), pp. 177–95, says that when the translators of EV began work on producing LV, they were "perhaps now located somewhere outside Oxford" (pp. 179–80), but presumes that the same persons produced both EV and LV.

105 LV Prologue to Isaiah (FM 3:226).

106 Dove, "Wyclif and the English Bible," p. 400; Dove, *First English Bible*, pp. 106–7, 121, 129.

107 GP, chap. 11, p. 42.

108 I should add that the prologue also uses *ever-either*, but in the same context as the EV prologue, saying that Isaiah prophesied "of *ever-either* realm." EV Prologue to Isaiah, FM 3:224; LV Prologue to Isaiah, FM 3:225.

109 *The Holy Prophet David*, ed. Dove, in *Earliest Advocates*, pp. 150–59, as *The Holi Prophete Dauid*, contained in only one manuscript, Cambridge University Library Ff.6.31; introduction on pp. liv–lvii; notes on pp. 218–19.

110 *Holy Prophet*, p. 159; Dove, *Earliest Advocates*, p. lv. Cf. FM GP, chap. 10, p. 32; in Dove's edition in *Earliest Advocates*, pp. 50–51, lines 1703–36.

111 Mary Dove, "The Lollards' Threefold Biblical Agenda," in *Wycliffite Controversies*, ed. Mishtooni Bose and J. Patrick Hornbeck II (Turnhout 2011), pp. 211–26, at p. 221. She sees this focus as a response to "the Church's opposition to the English Bible."

112 LV Prologue to Isaiah (FM 3:226).

113 For an analysis of the content of GP, see Dove, *First English Bible*, pp. 120–21.

114 Rita Copeland, "Wycliffite Ciceronianism? The General Prologue to the Wycliffite Bible and Augustine's *De doctrina Christiana*," in *Rhetoric and Renewal in the Latin West, 1100–1540: Essays in Honour of John O. Ward*, ed. Constant J. Mews, Cary J. Nederman, and Rodney M. Thomson (Turnhout 2003), pp. 185–200, at p. 193. She says that nothing that the author says is new to interpretive tradition but his use of it "as part of a defiant polemic on behalf of lay access to Scripture" is new (pp. 193–94). If it were not for Simple Creature's vigorous Wycliffitism, I would suggest using the term "determined" rather than "defiant," since advocating the translation of the Scriptures at this time was a perfectly orthodox position. The sections based on *De doctrina Christiana*, in chaps. 12 and 13, are excerpted in Rita

Copeland and Ineke Sluiter, eds., *Medieval Grammar and Rhetoric: Language Arts and Literary Theory, AD 300–1475* (Oxford 2009), pp. 845–53.

115 GP, chap. 12, p. 48: "Austin writith al this in the thridde book of *Cristen Teching*, aboute the middil, and in the ende. Isidre, in the firste book of *Soverein Good*, touchith these reulis schortliere, but I have him not now, and Lyre, in the biginning of the Bible, touchith more opinly these reulis, but I have him not now, and Ardmacan [Richard Fitzralph, archbishop of Armagh], in the biginning of his book *De questionibus Armenorum*, yeveth many goode groundis to undirstonde Holy Scripture to the lettre, and goostly undirstonding also, but I have him not now."

116 Dove, *Earliest Advocates*, p. lxii. She edits Prologue to *Intermediate Matthew* on pp. 174–79. She cites the conclusion of Simon Hunt, "An Edition of Tracts in Favour of Scriptural Translation and of Some Texts Connected with Lollard Vernacular Biblical Scholarship" (D.Phil. thesis, 2 vols., University of Oxford, 1994), 1:192–96. The Prologue to *Intermediate Matthew* uses *or* seventeen times and *other* one time; *either* occurs three times, but only in *either* + *or* combinations.

117 See Dove, *First English Bible*, pp. 106–7.

118 GP, chap. 15, p. 57.

119 For other grammatical matters taken up by Simple Creature, see Appendix H, and for further comparisons between EV and LV, see Appendices I–M.

Chapter 3. The Bible at Oxford

1 G. R. Evans, *John Wyclif: Myth and Reality* (Oxford 2005), p. 113.

2 Beryl Smalley, "The Biblical Scholar," in *Robert Grosseteste, Scholar and Bishop: Essays in Commemoration of the Seventh Centenary of His Death*, ed. D. A. Callus (Oxford 1955), pp. 70–97, at 95; J. A. Robson, *Wyclif and the Oxford Schools: The Relation of the "Summa de ente" to Scholastic Debates at Oxford in the Later Fourteenth Century* (Cambridge 1961), pp. 26–27.

3 There was also a small faculty at Toulouse from the thirteenth century.

4 William J. Courtenay, "The Bible in the Fourteenth Century: Some Observations," *Church History* 54 (1985) 176–87, p. 185. See also his "Franciscan Learning: University Education and Biblical Exegesis," in *Defenders and Critics of Franciscan Life: Essays in Honor of John V. Fleming*, ed. Michael F. Cusato and Guy Geltner (Leiden 2009), pp. 55–64.

5 Beryl Smalley, "Problems of Exegesis in the Fourteenth Century," *Antike und Orient im Mittelalter*, ed. Paul Wilpert (Berlin 1962), pp. 266–74, pp. 266, 274. She takes "exegesis" here to mean specifically "the teaching of the Bible in schools and universities" (p. 266).

6 Courtenay, "Bible in the Fourteenth Century," p. 186.

7 Ibid. Smalley, "Problems," p. 274, says the dry spell was broken in France by Gerson, seemingly forgetting about Wyclif's coeval John of Hesdin; see her article on him, "Jean de Hesdin O.Hosp.S.Ioh.," *Recherches de théologie ancienne et médiévale* 28 (1961) 283–330.

8 Eric Doyle, "William Woodford, O.F.M. (c. 1330–c. 1400): His Life and Works, Together with a Study and Edition of His *Responsum contra Wiclevum et Lollardos*," *Franciscan Studies* 23 (1983) 17–187: if it were not for his controversies with Wyclif,

Woodford "would very probably have continued to compose commentaries on scripture and no doubt would have completed his *Postilla super Matthaeum*" (p. 17); Woodford speaks of when "I did the course of lectures" (*concurrebam*) with Wyclif on the *Sentences* (*cum eo in lectura Sententiarum*) (p. 26 n. 19). He kept the responses that Wyclif wrote to his arguments (Robson, *Wyclif*, p. 193; Doyle, "William Woodford," p. 34). Woodford refers to many articles that he himself wrote *in lectura Sententiarum*, but no trace of them has been found (Doyle, p. 55).

9 Cornelia Linde, *How to Correct the Sacra Scriptura? Textual Criticism of the Latin Bible Between the Twelfth and Fifteenth Century* (Oxford 2012), pp. 64, 159–70, 258–59. Fitzralph composed the *Summa . . . in questionibus Armenorum* while in Avignon, 1337–44, but the last five books, in which the material on Scripture is contained, may have been added after the mid-1340s. He died in 1360.

10 Linde, *How to Correct*, p. 158.

11 *Statuta antiqua Universitatis Oxoniensis*, ed. Strickland Gibson (Oxford 1931), p. 49: *De theologis licenciandis ad incipiendum* (1253), "nisi legerit aliquem librum de canone Biblie vel librum *Sentenciarum* vel *Historiarum*."

12 Ibid., pp. 49–50: *Forma lecta licenciandis ad incipiendum in theologis* (before 1350), "et aliquem librum de canone Biblie vel *Sentenciarum* Oxonie in scolis theologie publice legant" (probably taken to mean all four books of the *Sentences*).

13 Ibid., p. 50: "Bibliam biblice per triennium audisse . . . ac aliquem librum de canone Biblie legisse, teneatur." Evans, *John Wyclif*, p. 35, says that secular students spent four years hearing lectures on the Bible, while friars spent six years (no source cited). William J. Courtenay, "The Bible in Medieval Universities," in *The New Cambridge History of the Bible*, vol. 2, *From 600 to 1450*, ed. Richard Marsden and E. Ann Matter (Cambridge 2012), pp. 555–78, at p. 571, says that the requirement of lecturing on a book of the Bible could be satisfied in a single year, or even over the summer; see also his "Franciscan Learning," p. 61. In a private communication, he tells me that he has come to this conclusion from working on individual lives of mendicants who went through the theology course.

14 *Statuta antiqua*, p. 50: "Post lecturam insuper libri *Sentenciarum*, ad minus per biennium vel fere studio incepturus insistat, antequam scandat cathedram magistralem."

15 J. A. Weisheipl, "Ockham and the Mertonians," in *HUO* 1:607–58, at p. 642.

16 Ibid., citing *Statuta antiqua*, p. 117 lines 7–12. The 1314 agreement begins with a question of disputations "antequam bachalarii incipiant legere in theologica facultate" (p. 116). A statute passed just before this, ca. 1311, stipulates that no one but a bachelor of theology could lecture publicly on the Bible (*Cui licet legere Bibliam et cui non*, p. 52), which contradicts the statutes that say that lecturing on a book of the Bible is one of the requirements for becoming a bachelor.

17 Catto, "Wyclif and Wycliffism," p. 179.

18 Henry Osborn Taylor, *Thought and Expression in the Sixteenth Century*, 2nd ed., 2 vols. (New York 1930), 2:24: "When reasoning and writing in Latin, Wyclif's style and method never cast off the scholastic bands. But in English he is another man." Of course, nowadays, he is credited with nothing in English.

19 Reginald Lane Poole, preface to his edition of Wyclif's *Tractatus de civili dominio*, 1:xviii; Poole goes on to give some examples of Wyclif's English-based Latin. See also Rudolf Buddensieg, introduction to *John Wiclif's Polemical Works in Latin*, 2 vols. (London 1883; *Latin Works* [1966], 11:1–2), 1:lxxxvi: "What still more renders

his perusal difficult is the writer's habit of following the construction of his mother language in the rules of syntax and in his general mode of expressing his thoughts."

20 See Williell R. Thomson, *The Latin Writings of John Wyclyf: An Annotated Catalog* (Toronto 1983), pp. 192–215.

21 Ibid., p. 193; Evans, *John Wyclif*, pp. 114–17.

22 John R. H. Moorman, *Church Life in the Thirteenth Century* (Cambridge 1945; corr. repr. 1955), p. 96. Some rectors of parishes, designated as "Master," would already have finished the seven-year arts course (usually begun at the age of fourteen), which Moorman describes on p. 95. See also James A. Weisheipl, "Curriculum of the Faculty of Arts at Oxford in the Early Fourteenth Century," *Mediaeval Studies* 26 (1964) 143–85. On the length of the arts course as seven years of study plus two of regency, see J. M. Fletcher, "Developments in the Faculty of Arts, 1370–1520," in *HUO* 2:315–45, pp. 329–30, 333.

23 Moorman, *Church Life*, p. 96 nn. 1–3. The last-named was in combination with canon law ("in Sacra Scriptura et canonibus") early in the thirteenth century (Bishop Wells of Lincoln, 1209–35). The other examples cited are from the end of the thirteenth century: theology, Canterbury (Archbishop Peckham, 1279–92), Hereford (Bishop Cantilupe, 1275–82), and Worcester (Bishop Giffard, 1268–1302); Sacred Page, Winchester (Bishop Pontoise, 1282–1304).

24 F. Donald Logan, *University Education of the Parochial Clergy in Medieval England: The Lincoln Diocese, c. 1300–c. 1350* (Toronto 2014). On this subject see also William J. Courtenay, "The Effect of Papal Provisions to Oxford and Paris Scholars on the Pastorate and Care of Souls," in *Christianity and Culture in the Middle Ages: Essays to Honor John Van Engen*, ed. David C. Mengel and Lisa Wolverton (Notre Dame IN 2015), pp. 358–86. Logan's study of rector-students ends with 1350 and the plague. It is often asserted that their numbers declined afterward; see, for instance, R. N. Swanson, "Learning and Livings: University Study and Clerical Careers in Later Medieval England," *History of Universities* 6 (1986–87) 81–103, at pp. 86, 98. But Professor Logan cautions in a letter to me that such conclusions are for the most part only surmises, and firm conclusions must await studies of bishops' registers. I have examined the registers of Salisbury and Lincoln at the beginning of the fifteenth century: *The Register of Robert Hallum, Bishop of Salisbury, 1407–1417*, ed. Joyce M. Horn (Torquay 1982), with only eighteen licenses (I do not count no. 1150, granted by Hallum's successor in 1419); *The Register of Philip Repingdon, 1405–1419*, ed. Margaret Archer, 3 vols. (Hereford 1963–82), with ninety-seven licenses. None of them specify any particular place of study.

25 Logan, *University Education*, p. 76. Logan assumes that the MA was not necessary for getting a degree in canon law or civil law, but the point does not seem to be altogether clear. Leonard E. Boyle, "Canon Law Before 1380," in *HUO* 1:531–64, p. 543, says that having an MA was not a prerequisite for completing a doctorate in civil law, though it would shorten studies by two years. Describing a somewhat later period, Fletcher, "Developments," p. 320, would seem to suggest that the same was true of canon as well as civil law, since he speaks only of law in general. He says that "the formal academic educational pyramid where all students proceeded to a higher faculty only after obtaining a qualification from the faculty of arts" had little relevance by the fifteenth and early sixteenth centuries, when "students were frequently proceeding to the study of law after only a token period in the faculty of arts, despite the promise of a somewhat shorter law course if they first incepted in arts." But Boyle

also states later ("Canon Law," pp. 552–53) that a study leave for a rector with no MA was an opportunity to obtain one, while those with MAs would be able to seek "a degree in a higher faculty such as theology or canon law (and of civil law if he were not a priest)." The idea that only clerics who had not yet been ordained to the priesthood could study civil law is belied, I suggest, by William Lyndwood's account given below, in which he indicates that those on study leave had a choice of studying canon or civil law (without cautioning that the latter was not available to priests).

26 T. A. R. Evans, "The Number, Origins, and Careers of Scholars," in *HUO* 2:485–538, pp. 497–98.

27 Unfortunately, however, these "amateur" students do not seem to have left much of a record of their presence. There is no place for them in T. H. Aston, "Oxford's Medieval Alumni," *Past and Present* 74 (February 1977) 3–40. See also Alan B. Cobban, *The Medieval English Universities: Oxford and Cambridge to c. 1500* (London 1988), esp. 209–56.

28 Boniface VIII, *Cum ex eo*, *Liber Sextus* 1.6.34, in *Corpus iuris canonici* (*CIC*), ed. Emil Friedberg, 2 vols. (Leipzig 1879–81; repr. Graz 1959), 2:964–65: "Sancimus . . . ut episcopi . . . dispensare possint libere quod usque ad septennium *literarum studio* insistentes promoveri minine teneantur, nisi ad ordinem subdiaconatus duntaxat" ("We allow bishops to freely dispense [rectors] undertaking *the study of letters* from being bound to promotion except to the order of subdeacon for up to seven years").

29 John Andrew (Johannes Andreae), *Apparatus in Librum Sextum* (ca. 1304) = Ordinary Gloss to *Liber Sextus*, in *Corpus Juris Canonici* (*CJC*), 3 vols. (Rome 1582) (http://digital.library.ucla.edu/canonlaw/index.html), 1.6.34 (3:164, lines 57–59): ad v. *litterarum*: "Cum non distinguat, intelligo generaliter: sive in grammatica, sive in jure canonico, vel civili, vel scientia theologie studeat" ("Since he does not distinguish, I understand it generally: 'whether he studies in grammar, in canon law, or civil law, or in the science of theology'").

30 Ibid., ad v. *septennium*: "Nota in septennio scholarem esse debere provectum; studens in theologia, in quinquennio [*Decretales Gregorii IX* (1534) 5.5.5, Honorius III, *Super specula* (1219), *CIC* 2:770–71], et etiam studens in jure civili."

31 Logan, *University Education*, p. 76.

32 William Lyndwood, *Provinciale; seu, Constitutiones Angliae* [1434] (Oxford 1679; repr. Farnborough 1968).

33 Repingdon, *Register*, 1:2, May 13, 1405: "Concessa fuit littera non residencie Willelmo Lyndewode diacono, rectori ecclesie parochialis de Walton' Lincoln' diocesis, *litterarum studio* insistendo ubicumque, etc., ac dimittendo fructus ad firmam per idem tempus; et dispensatum fuit cum eodem juxta capitulum *Cum ex eo* quod non teneatur promoveri ad ordinem presbyteratus duraturum biennium [i.e., duraturo biennio]" ("A letter of non-residence was granted to William Lyndwood, deacon, rector of the parochial church of Walton in the diocese of Lincoln for engaging in *the study of letters* anywhere, etc., and putting the fruits to farm during the same time; and he was dispensed with the said chapter *Cum ex eo* from his obligation to be promoted to the order of priesthood for a period of two years"). See Emden, *BRUC*, pp. 379–81; and Emden, *BRUO*, 2:1191–93: Lyndwood became rector of Walton-le-Wolds in November 1403; he was ordained subdeacon on February 23, 1404, and deacon the following month, March 15, 1404; he had become bachelor of canon law

by 1403, and proceeded as JUD (doctor of both laws) by 1407; he was ordained priest on March 12, 1407.

34 Lyndwood, *Provinciale* 1.17.2, *Veloces ad audiendum*, p. 76, notes *c*, *d*, *l*. A similar statute for the Court of Arches (where Lyndwood served as judge from 1417 to at least 1431) was enacted in 1295 by Archbishop Winchelsey, requiring at least four or five years of study of "civil and canon law" in the schools of some university or city and one year in the Arches itself. See F. Donald Logan, ed., *The Medieval Court of Arches* (Woodbridge 2005), pp. xxvii, 7–8.

35 Lyndwood, *Provinciale* 1.17.2, *Veloces ad audiendum*, p. 76, note *f* s.v. *et civile*: "Cum principalis intentio statuentis, ut apparet in integra sub parte decisa, versetur circa advocatos in causis ecclesiasticis, puto quod sufficit ut talis audiverit jus civile secundum remissiones que ponuntur in glossa juris canonici, et sine quibus jura canonica, presertim in judicialibus, non possunt bene intelligi nec sciri. Alioquin si studium suum divideret, nunc unum, nunc reliquum audiendo, non posset in scientia unius vel alterius proficere; quia dum ad utrumque festinaverit, neutrum bene perageret" ("Since the principal intention of the statute-maker, as is evident in the whole decree in the omitted portion, concerns advocates in ecclesiastical cases, I believe that it suffices for such a student to audit civil law according to the responses placed in the gloss of canon law, without which the canons cannot be well comprehended or understood. Otherwise, if he were to divide his study, attending now to one thing, now the other, he could not become proficient in the one science or the other; for while he would hasten to both, he would traverse neither one well").

36 GP, chap. 13, p. 51; cf. charge 12 against Hunne.

37 As Mary Dove points out ("Scripture and Reform," in Marsden and Matter, *New Cambridge History of the Bible*, vol. 2, pp. 579–95), SC is drawing on Jerome's exegesis of Amos 1.3, "a verse which threatens that although God will cause Damascus to repent of three great sins he will have no mercy when Damascus commits a fourth" (p. 594).

38 GP, chap. 13, pp. 51–52.

39 Wyclif, *De veritate Sacrae Scripturae*, chap. 26 (3:39): "Verumptamen licet rectori ad tempus colligere semen fidei in scholis theologicis extra parochiam, ad finem ut ipsum seminet 'in tempore oportuno' [Ps. 31.6; 144.15]." He gives the year of writing in chap. 11 (1:258). Neither of these passages is included in Levy's abridged translation.

40 *Why Poor Priests Have No Benefice* (Matthew, *English Works*, pp. 244–53), chap. 2, p. 250; here is the original spelling: "Yif siche curatis ben stired to gone lerne Goddis Lawe and teche here parischenis the Gospel, cominly they schullen gete no leve of bischopis but for gold; and whanne they schullen most profite in here lerninge, than schulle they be clepid hom at the prelatis wille."

41 Lewis, "History of the Several Translations, p. 9.

42 The operative portion of the statute, *De theologis licenciandis ad incipiendum*, is found just before the provision cited on required lecturing; it reads: "Quod nullus in eadem universitate incipiat in theologia nisi prius rexerit in artibus in aliqua universitate" (*Statuta antiqua*, p. 49; see the introduction, pp. xlii–xliii, cxiii).

43 Lewis, "History of the Several Translations," p. 9. Citing Anthony Wood, *Historia et antiquitates Universitatis Oxoniensis*, 2 vols. (Oxford 1674; ECCO), 1:194; see also the English translation, *The History and Antiquities of the University of Oxford*, trans.

John Gutch, 2 vols. (Oxford 1792; ECCO), 1:517–18. In the cited entry, Wood quotes Adam Marsh's contemporary report of the purport of the 1253 statute: "quod in posterum nullus incipiat in theologia nisi prius inceperit in liberalibus, et unum librum canonis aut *Sententias* legerit et publice in universitate predicaverit." See *Epistolae fratris Adae de Marisco de ordine Minorum*, ed. J. S. Brewer, in *Monumenta franciscana*, vol. 2, Rolls Series 4.1 (London 1858), pp. 77–489, Epistle 192, p. 346. Brewer characterizes the incident thus: Marsh "has to stand up for the rights of his scholars against the jealousy of the Convocation at Oxford . . . who are by no means inclined to depart from the ancient usages of the University in favour of the new students, or allow them to proceed in theology without biding their due time at the established resting-places in Arts" (preface, p. lxxxiii). The requirement of lecturing on one book of the canon of the Bible or on the *Sentences* and giving a public sermon refers to theology requirements, not the MA regency.

44 FM 1:xxiii–xxiv; Dove, *First English Bible*, pp. 110–13. Forshall and Madden rightly characterize the attempted enforcement of the full statutory requirements as "an impediment to students for a degree in divinity" (p. xxiv), but do not notice Simple Creature's mischaracterization of it; whereas Dove joins Simple Creature in misrepresenting it as a requirement of "students to become regents in Arts before beginning the study of Divinity" (p. 110). In "Scripture and Reform," p. 595, she says that the "unforgivable sin" for the author "was not the church's persecutions of Wyclif's followers but a university regulation aimed at ensuring that all students would receive a thorough grounding in logic, grammar and rhetoric." For Richard's mandates to the university, see *Calendar of Close Rolls: Richard II*, 6 vols. (London 1914–27), 3:378–79, 511.

45 GP, chap. 15, p. 57.

46 Contrary to Catto, "Wyclif and Wycliffism," p. 222, who sees here an account of the production of EV and the provision of EV Gospels with glosses, answering to the *Glossed Gospels*.

47 GP, chap. 10, p. 37, and chap. 11, p. 41; see Hudson, *Premature Reformation*, p. 236.

48 GP, chap. 15, p. 58. Henry Hargreaves, "The Latin Text of Purvey's Psalter," *Medium Aevum* 24 (1955) 73–90, notes that this claim is belied concerning the Psalter. He finds this to be the only case in which Simple Creature's presentation is not accurate (p. 90).

49 Dove, "Scripture and Reform," p. 590.

50 Hudson, *Doctors in English*, p. cxlvi.

51 Ibid., p. lii.

52 Hudson, *Premature Reformation*, p. 243.

53 Appendix I, "Absolute Constructions as Discussed in GP and Actually Treated in EV/ LV." See especially Table I.8.

54 Catto, "Wyclif and Wycliffism," p. 222. On one occasion, in *De veritate Sacre Scripture*, book 6 (ed. Buddensieg, 1:109–10, tr. Levy, p. 98), Wyclif speaks of the wording "Scriptura *quem* Pater sanctificavit" in correct codexes of John 10.35–36, rather than "*quam* sanctificavit"; but there is no reported variant of *quam*: see *Biblia Sacra iuxta Vulgatam versionem*, ed. Robert Weber et al., ed. 5, ed. Roger Gryson (Stuttgart 2007), p. 1878; *Novum Testamentum latine*, ed. Kurt Aland and Barbara Aland, ed. 2 (Nördlingen 1992), p. 284.

55 See Dove, *First English Bible*, pp. 175–88, esp. 177–78.

56 Fristedt, *Wycliffe Bible*, 2:xlix. Lindberg, *Earlier Version*, 5:70, notes that some of the corrections added to MS Bodley 959 (EEV) "make the translation conform with the (presumedly) best text of the Vulgate."

57 Fristedt, *Wycliffe Bible*, 2:liii.

58 We must remember, however, Adam Easton's Hebrew biblical studies, and there may well have been some acquaintance with Greek at the university.

59 Albert C. Baugh, "The Middle English Period," in *A Literary History of England*, ed. Baugh (New York 1948), pp. 109–312, at p. 271. The second edition of 1967 adds a supplement with additional discussion and bibliography.

60 Moessner, "Translation Strategies," pp. 150–51.

61 Cf. the first definition of "calque" in *Random House Dictionary of the English Language*, 2nd ed. unabridged (New York 1987): "Loan translation, esp. one resulting from bilingual interference in which the internal structure of a borrowed word or phrase is maintained but its morphemes are replaced by those of the native language." Take the Los Angeles place name "Mar Vista," a Spanish calque of "Seaview" (instead of the more idiomatic "Vista del Mar"). Ungrammatical Latin calques are to be found in abundance among the new names imposed on planetary surfaces; see, for instance, "Mars Revealed: A New Look at Forces That Shape the Desert Planet," map supplement, *National Geographic*, February 2001, e.g., "Olympus Mons" (instead the more idiomatic "Olympus," or "Olympi Mons," or "Mons Olympicus").

62 Moessner, "Translation Strategies," p. 149, citing David Lawton, "Englishing the Bible, 1066–1549," in *The Cambridge History of Medieval English Literature*, ed. David Wallace (Cambridge 1999), chap. 17, pp. 454–82, at 470.

63 See Lawton, "Englishing," p. 470, describing a similar process in Richard Rolle's approach to the Psalms.

64 Lindberg, "Alpha and Omega," p. 191.

65 Dove, "Scripture and Reform," p. 590.

66 Lawton, "Englishing," p. 470.

67 Fristedt, *Wycliffe Bible*, 3:7–40. He compares the two translations of book 6, chaps. 15, 25–26, on pp. 41–58. In dealing with the MEB, of course, Fristedt sees that there were two complete revisions: from EEV (my designation) to EV, and from EV to LV.

68 The author of this translation was "a (Lollard) versionist well acquainted with the making of the Wycliffite Bible. . . . This author can be no other than Trevisa, whose relations with the Lollards were far from being strained. It is conceivable, however, that by a vocabulary differing also in non-literalisms he wished to alienate his writings from theirs in order to avoid the suspicion of heresy" (Fristedt, *Wycliffe Bible*, 3:38–40).

69 Fowler, "John Trevisa," p. 94.

70 Fristedt, *Wycliffe Bible*, 3:11.

71 Fristedt says that Trevisa goes beyond LV by introducing "a free form of translation unknown to the Wycliffe Bible" (*Wycliffe Bible*, 3:38), but assumes that he did participate in producing LV in the 1380s when he returned to Queen's (3:40 n. 41).

72 Jane Beal, *John Trevisa and the English Polychronicon* (Tempe AZ 2012), pp. 146–47.

73 John Trevisa, *Dialogus inter dominum et clericum*, ed. Roger Waldron, "Trevisa's Original Prefaces on Translation: A Critical Edition," in *Medieval English Studies Presented to George Kane*, ed. Edward Donald Kennedy, Ronald Waldron, and Joseph S. Wittig (Woodbridge 1988), pp. 285–99. Alfred W. Pollard edits it from Caxton's edition, *Dialogue Between a Lord and a Clerk upon Translation*, from Trevisa's translation of Higden's *Polychronicon*, in *Fifteenth Century Prose and Verse* (Westminster 1903), pp. 203–10. Both editions include Trevisa's epistle to Lord Berkeley, briefly explaining his translation procedures.

74 Deanesly, *Lollard Bible*, p. 250. Fowler responds: the most that can be said is that Trevisa does not refer explicitly to any Middle English translation ("John Trevisa," p. 88 n. 35).

75 Trevisa, *Dialogus*, p. 292; Caxton by eyeskip omitted the portion in brackets (Pollard, p. 206).

76 Ibid., pp. 292–93 (Pollard, pp. 206–7).

77 Lawton, "Englishing," p. 472; Moessner, "Translation Strategies," p. 151. See McFarlane, *John Wycliffe*, p. 118: "The literate laity, important as they were, were not the only class to whom a vernacular Bible was likely to be welcome. It is doubtful how many of the inferior clergy had a sufficient knowledge of Latin to be able to make anything of the Vulgate; certainly not all. It may well be that the Lollards, when they undertook the production of an English translation, had them rather than the laity principally in mind." Dove, *First Engish Bible*, p. 65, suggests the same thing.

78 Lewis Brewer Hall, *The Perilous Vision of John Wyclif* (Chicago 1983), pp. 141–43. Hall cites the English version of Wyclif's *De officio pastorali* as urging that priests have the Bible in English, since the rulers of England have it in French; but he must be citing it from memory, since the author calls for "Englishmen," not priests, to have the Bible in English. The English *De officio pastorali* was published by Matthew, *English Works*, pp. 405–57; I follow the new edition by Conrad Lindberg in *English Wyclif Tracts 1–3*, pp. 29–81. The English adapter of the treatise has added a chapter, no. 15 (Matthew, pp. 429–30; Lindberg, pp. 51–53), condemning friars for opposing vernacular Scripture. It begins (I modernize), "And here the friars with their fautors say that it is heresy to write thus God's Law in English, and make it known to lewd men." Wyclif's Latin treatise was written in 1379 (see Stephen E. Lahey, *John Wyclif* [New York 2009], p. 21); I have seen no speculation about the date of the English version except for Lindberg, who thinks it likely that Wyclif himself produced it. It is the added chapter of the English version of *De officio pastorali* that James Gairdner, *Lollardy and the Reformation in England: An Historical Survey*, 4 vols. (London 1908–13), 1:107–8, cites to establish that Wyclif wished to translate the Bible for the common people.

79 See R. N. Swanson, *Church and Society in Late Medieval England* (Oxford 1989), p. 261: "Although the English Bible is traditionally associated with the Lollards, its readers were not all heretics. For many, access to the scriptures in English aided comprehension of the Latin, and it was presumably for this purpose that it was used by (say) the nuns of Syon, who also possessed English translations of their religious offices to aid comprehension of their services."

80 Richard Ullerston speaks of the obligation of helping the "slightly literate" (*exiliter litterati*) to improve by translating the Bible: "Non solum licitum est sed expediens

est talia transferre in linguam nativem ad profectum exiliter literatorum et laicorum" ("It is not only allowed but advisable to translate such things into the native language for the advancement of the slightly lettered and lay persons"): the sixth of the supplementary reasons given at the end of his treatise on translating the Bible, *Tractatus de translacione Sacre Scripture in vulgare*, Vienna, Österreichische Nationalbibliothek, MS 4133, fols. 195–207v, at fol. 207vb.

81 McFarlane, *John Wycliffe*, pp. 118–19.

82 Hudson, *Premature Reformation*, p. 246: "As further investigation is carried out by modern scholars, the existence of 'intermediate' stages is coming to be recognized. Perhaps most remarkable of all is the fact that it is so hard to discern in the LV text any discrepancies of translational method between one part of the bible and another. The LV seems stylistically homogeneous, and amazingly stable from one manuscript to another."

83 See esp. Chapter 2 and Appendixes D–M.

84 Lindberg, *King Henry's Bible*, 4:34.

85 Lawton, "Englishing," p. 472: "The standard explanation . . . has to do, irrelevantly, with the development of an English prose-style."

86 Nicholas Watson, "Theories of Translation," in Ellis, *Oxford History of Literary Translation in English*, 1:73–91, p. 73.

87 Ibid., p. 74: "Even where 'literalism' is most desirable, especially in Bible translation, the translation policies labeled 'word for word' and 'sense for sense' are conceived as interlocking pragmatic resolutions of this conflict [between fidelity and clarity], not as differing theoretical positions." "Literal" has another meaning in biblical studies, of course, a contrast to "figurative" or "spiritual" senses. SC discusses this in chapter 12 of GP, and it is in his warning not to interpret Scripture as figurative when the clear meaning is literal, or literal when it is figurative, where he makes what has been taken to be his most heterodox sentiment, insisting on the figurative meaning of Christ's command to eat his flesh and drink his blood (pp. 44–45); but, as we saw in Chapter 2 above, it is simply a direct quotation from St. Augustine.

88 See David Norton, *A History of the English Bible as Literature* (Cambridge 2000), p. 8, commenting on Simple Creature's statement about making the English "openlier" in English than it is in Latin: "The principle that the translation should be as clear as or clearer than the original is at odds with some ideas of faithful translation, for it involves a kind of correction of the original. Nevertheless, the Protestants, or proto-Protestants, preferred to emphasise the comprehensibility of the text and to play down ambiguity and difficulty." This echoes what Norton says in his *History of the Bible as Literature*, 2 vols. (Cambridge 1993), 1:82.

89 Norton, *History of the Bible as Literature*, 1:33–37.

90 See Appendix I.

91 See Hudson's discussion of this point, *Selections*, p. 175 (at lines 41–51). She gives an example from Mark 16.20: "In LV the Latin present participial construction is interpreted as implying a causal connection between the two clauses; but the relation could merely be one of attendant circumstances, not correctly translated as *for* plus a finite verb."

92 Copeland and Sluiter, *Medieval Grammar and Rhetoric*, p. 316.

93 GP, chap. 15, p. 58: "Where I have translatid as opinly or opinliere in English as in Latin, late wise men deme, that knowen wel bothe langagis and knowen wel the sentence of Holy Scripture; and wher I have do thus, or nay, ne doute, they that kunne wel the sentence of Holy Writ and English togidere and wolen travaile with Goddis grace theraboute, moun make the Bible as trewe and as opin, yea, and opinliere in English than it is in Latin."

94 GP chap. 15, p. 60: "Manie such adverbis, conjunccions, and preposiciouns ben set ofte oon for another, and at fre chois of autouris sumtime; and now tho shulen be taken as it acordith best to the sentence. By this maner, with good living and greet travel, men moun come to trewe and cleer translating, and trewe undurstonding of Holy Writ, seme it nevere so hard at the biginning. God graunte to us alle grace to kunne wel, and kepe wel Holy Writ, and suffre joyefully sum peine for it at the laste. Amen."

95 See Ian Christopher Levy, "A Contextualized Wyclif: *Magister Sacrae Paginae*," in Bose and Hornbeck, *Wycliffite Controversies*, pp. 33–57, at pp. 45–46.

96 Catto, "Fellows and Helpers," pp. 152–53.

97 Matti Peikola, "The Wycliffite Bible and 'Central Midland Standard': Assessing the Manuscript Evidence," *Nordic Journal of English Studies* 2 (2003) 29–51, p. 30, citing a forthcoming paper by Merja Black (Merja Black Stenroos, "A Variationist Approach to Middle English Dialects," University of Stavanger Collections of Articles, 2008) as showing "the possible association of Type I with Oxford University"; in n. 1 he says that this "well-argued association of the origins of CMS with Oxford introduces a meaningful contextual link between the seemingly disparate Wycliffite and medical/scientific textual components of Type I." Dove, *First English Bible*, p. 148, citing Lindberg, *Earlier Version*, 1:18–19, finds a certain dialectal uniformity in LV manuscripts (Central Midlands or South-East Midlands, or a mix of the two), whereas EV manuscripts show more variance, including West, East, and North Midlands features.

98 Anne Hudson, "Five Problems in Wycliffite Texts and a Suggestion," *Medium Aevum* 80 (2011) 283–306, pp. 292–98.

99 Anne Hudson, ed., *Two Revisions of Rolle's English Psalter Commentary and the Related Canticles*, EETS o.s. 340–41 (Oxford 2012–13).

100 The sermon cycle has been edited by Hudson and Pamela Gradon as *English Wycliffite Sermons*, 5 vols. (Oxford 1983–96).

101 Hudson, "Five Problems," p. 297.

102 GP, chap. 15, p. 57.

103 William Tyndale, *The New Testament: The Text of the Worms Edition of 1526 in Original Spelling*, ed. W. R. Cooper (London 2000), p. 554 (I, of course, have modernized the spelling).

104 See Chapter 2 at n. 50; Appendix C, Parts B–D.

105 Dove, *First English Bible*, pp. 246–48.

106 Lindberg, *Earlier Version*, 8:71.

107 See p. 98 below.

Chapter 4. Oxford Doctors, Archbishop Arundel, and *Dives and Pauper* on the Advisability of Scripture in English

1 Cornelia Linde, "Arguing with Lollards: Thomas Palmer, OP, and *De translatione scripture sacre in linguam barbaricam*," *Viator* 46:3 (Autumn 2015) 235–54.

2 Deanesley, *Lollard Bible*, pp. 418–37: Palmer, *De translatione sacrae scripturae in linguam Anglicanam.* The treatise appears in a Dominican manuscript made in 1430, in Cambridge, Trinity College MS B.15.11, fols. 42vb–47va. The treatise is presented anonymously, but identified as Palmer's by another hand of the same time. See Anne Hudson, "The Debate on Bible Translation, Oxford 1401," *English Historical Review* 90 (1975) 1–18 (repr. in *Lollards and Their Books*, pp. 67–84), pp. 1–2 (67–68). I wish to thank Dr. Linde for helping me decipher various puzzling points of the manuscript.

3 Linde, "Arguing," pp. 240, 246–54.

4 Emden, *BRUO* 3:1421–22. While provincial, Palmer was accused of various kinds of misconduct, as Linde recounts, including using "prison tortures" (*questiones carcerales*) to elicit information about offenses by friars. He was dismissed from office in 1396, but in the next year he was elected prior of the London Blackfriars, a post held until 1407.

5 The incipit of the response is *Singulis Cristi fidelibus*; it is preserved in the register of John Trefnant, *Registrum Johannis Trefnant, Episcopi Herefordensis [1389–1404]*, ed. W. W. Capes (London 1916), pp. 396–401. According to the heading, it is by Palmer—*Responsio fratris T. Palmer, ad litteras superscriptas* (p. 396)—but it is signed by Hereford—"Per magistrum Nicholaum Hereford quem Spiritus Sanctus ab erroribus revocavit" (p. 401); and the responder says that the Lollard's letter, *Cum nemo mittens manum*" (given here on pp. 394–96), was addressed to him. The letter is headed *Sequitur copia unius littere misse magistro Nicholao Hereford per unum Lollardum* (p. 394). Emden identifies the Lollard who wrote the letter as Walter Brit (Brute), *BRUO* 3:1422 (entry on Palmer), but I find this ascription doubtful. The letter cites Scripture only once (Psalm 138.22) and Gratian four times, whereas Brute's long self-defense (in Trefnant, *Registrum*, pp. 285–358) constantly cites Scripture but refers to Gratian only once, mistakenly: "in *Decretis* Dist. 23 q. primo, cap. *Paratus*" (p. 309); "Dist." is wrong, since the reference is to Cause 23, not Distinction 23 (C. 23 q. 1 c. 2 *Paratus*, *CIC* 1:891–92)—though the content of the canon is reported accurately. Neither letter nor response is dated, but they appear in the register after the records of Brute's trial, which ended on October 3–6, 1393, in the presence of many masters, including Hereford (pp. 359–60). See H. A. Kelly, "Lollard Inquisitions: Due and Undue Process," in *The Devil, Heresy and Witchcraft in the Middle Ages: Essays in Honor of Jeffrey B. Russell*, ed. Alberto Ferreiro (Leiden 1998), pp. 279–303; repr. in Kelly, *Inquisitions and Other Trial Procedures in the Medieval West*, Variorum Collected Studies (Aldershot 2001), chap. 6 (with the same pagination), at pp. 283–85.

6 Hudson, *Premature Reformation*, p. 93.

7 Palmer, *De trans.* 1.1–18: *Quod sic videtur* (fols. 42vb–43rb; cf. Deanesly, *Lollard Bible*, pp. 418–21). Deanesly thinks that the scribe misnumbered by calling no. 9 "10," and she renumbers it as "9," and so with the rest, ending with "17." But Linde shows that the scribe's fault was to incorporate no. 9 at the end of no. 8, by reading

"Sed multi in tanto sunt muti," etc., instead of "9 Sic: Multi in tanto sunt muti," etc. The scribe correctly calls the next one no. 10, and so on to the end.

8 Palmer, *De trans.* 2.1–18: *Ad oppositum* (fols. 43rb–44va; Deanesly, pp. 421–25).

9 Palmer, *De trans.* 3.1–13: *Pro responsione: Alie veritates* (fols. 44va–46ra; Deanesly, pp. 425–31: "Additional reasons for and against vernacular scriptures"). For instance, 3.12 reads: "Laicis utilia ad salutem et non alia de Sacra Scriptura sunt eis tradenda" ("What is useful to the laity for salvation is to be translated for them from Sacred Scripture, and not other matter"; fol. 45vb; Deanesly, p. 430).

10 Palmer, *De trans.* 4 [*Contra veritates*] (fol. 46rab; Deanesly, pp. 431–33: "Pro-Vernacular-Bible Rejoinder").

11 Palmer, *De trans.* 5: *Responsio* (fol. 46rb–vb; Deanesly, pp. 433–34: "Anti-Vernacular-Bible Rejoinder").

12 Palmer, *De trans.* 6.1–18 (fols. 46vb–47va; Deanesly, pp. 434–47: "Further answers to the principal arguments of those who desire translations").

13 Palmer, *De trans.* 1.18 (fol. 43rb): "18. Sic. Secundum regulam racionis omnia intelliguntur esse concessa que expresse non sunt prohibita; sed non invenitur in tota Sacra Scriptura prohibitum quod ipsa sic transferatur in idioma barbaricum." Cf. Deanesly, pp. 420–21; she, of course, numbers it as 17. For *intelliguntur* she has *intelligimus*.

14 Palmer, *De trans.* 6.18 (fol. 47va): "[Ad] 18. Arguebatur sic: 'Principalis causa quare non potest transferri in linguam barbaricam videtur esse quod illa non regulatur regulis grammaticalibus et figuris, cum [= sine] quibus non potest Sacra Scriptura a falsitate et incongruitate salvari. Sed propter ha[n]c causam non deberet ea transferri secundum aliquam partem ejus, nec quoad necessaria saluti nec quoad alia, quia hec regule, tropi, et figure sunt omnibus partibus Scripture Sacre eque communes.' Cujus oppositum dicendum est." Cf. Deanesly, p. 437; at the end, for *eque communes* she has *aequivocationes*, and for *dicendum* she reads *dictum*.

15 Palmer, *De trans.* 6.18 (fol. 47va; Deanesly, p. 437): "Ad istud dico negando quod omnibus partibus Scripture sunt ille regule, tropi, et figure eque communes, quia alique partes quoad sensum litteralem verificantur sine ipsis, et alique aperta sunt et plana. 'Jugum enim meum suave est et onus meum leve' [Matt. 11.30]. Et que moralia sunt quasi de jure naturali et facilia ad credendum, unde Psalmista, 'Testimonia tua credibilia facta sunt nimis' [Ps. 92.5]. Et ideo non indiget figuris et tropis vel aliis a falsitate ac incongruitate salventur, ut alia difficilia ibidem contenta."

16 Palmer, *De trans.* 2.1 (fol. 43rb; Deanesly, p. 421).

17 Palmer, *De trans.* 2.2 (fol. 43va; Deanesly, p. 421): "Non omnis veritas est scribenda in Anglico, quia multe sunt inutiles. Sed omnis veritas continetur in sacra scriptura, secundum Lollardos, quia continet primam veritatem, que continet omnes alias veritates."

18 See Linde, "Arguing," p. 247.

19 As Hudson, *Premature Reformation*, pp. 377–78, points out, Wyclif himself and his followers in general allowed for some valid early traditions.

20 A sentiment expressed by Simple Creature in *Five and Twenty Books*; GP, chap. 12, FM 1:49: "Holy Scripture containeth all profitable truth and all other sciences privily in the virtue of wits either understandings, as wines be contained in grapes," etc., attributing it to Grosseteste.

21 Palmer, *De trans.* 2.18 (fol. 44va): "Quomodo ergo non errarent simplices idiote circa Scripturam, si eam haberent in vulgari? Nonne modo, propter malum intellectum

Lollardorum et simplicium, grammaticam solum intelligentes Christi discipulos illam spiritualiter et exponentes persequuntur? Constat quod sic." Deanesly, p. 425, changes *nonne* for *idiomate* and puts *[qui]* before *Christi*. She corrects the manuscript reading *gramaticarrm* to *grammaticam*, which I accept.

22 Butler incepted as doctor of theology around 1401; see Emden *BRUO* 1:329.

23 William Butler, *Determinacio contra translacionem*, ed. Deanesly, in *Lollard Bible*, pp. 399–418; the date in the colophon, p. 418, is "Anno Domini MCCCC° primo," meaning between March 25, 1401, and March 24, 1402. When Archbishop Ussher reports on this, *Historica dogmatica*, pp. 162–63, he says that the determination is against the translation identified by Thomas James as by Wyclif, and he says that Purvey testifies that after this there was a general mandate in England that the translation be burned. When Ussher deals with Purvey under the date of 1420, he mentions only the heretical and erroneous sentiments collected by the Carmelite Richard Lavinham (which are in *Fasciculi zizaniorum magistri Johannis Wyclif cum tritico*, ed. Walter Waddington Shirley, Rolls Series 5 [London 1858], pp. 383–99), where there is no such report.

24 Butler, *Determinacio*, p. 411: "Quinto, arguo contra prefatam assertionem per subtilitatem ipsius Scripture spiritualis artificii, et contra unum quod ita dicunt assertores prefati, qui, *ut mihi relatum est*, [dicunt quod] . . ." ("Fifth, I argue against the aforesaid assertion because of the subtlety of the literal artifice of Scripture itself, and against one thing that the aforesaid assertors thus say, who, *as it was related to me*, [say that] . . ."). The point made by the assertors is that not only is it useful and profitable that Scripture be translated for the people to read but the same would also be true of the expositions of the holy doctors.

25 Butler, *Determinacio*, p. 418.

26 Ibid., p. 408: "Cur debet aliquis murmurare quod nostri intronizati pontifices non permittunt suis infimis lecturam Sacre Scripture, per cognitionem inflammantium ad pietatem, cum hoc in celesti hierarchia, ubi videtur esse conformis, nullatenus sit repertum?" ("Why should anyone complain that our enthroned pontiffs do not permit lecturing on Sacred Scripture to their lowest subjects, to become aware of what inflames them to piety, since this is not to be found in the celestial hierarchy, which is seen to be parallel?").

27 Catto, "Wyclif and Wycliffism," pp. 239–40.

28 Kantik Ghosh, *The Wycliffite Heresy: Authority and the Interpretation of Texts* (Cambridge 2002), pp. 105–10. Ghosh suggests that Ullerston's treatise may have been produced in the early 1390s, and *editus* (in the sense of revived) in 1401 (p. 109).

29 Deanesly, *Lollard Bible*, pp. 290–91.

30 Hudson, "Debate on Bible Translation," p. 10 (76). For Ullerston, see Emden, *BRUO*, 3:1928–29; Margaret Harvey, "Ullerston, Richard," in *OxDNB*. Around 1401, he wrote a defense of Church endowments against the Lollards, and in 1408, at the prompting of Bishop Hallum of Salisbury he compiled propositions for Church reform in anticipation of the Council of Pisa. For an account of the Latin letter that he wrote to Prince Henry on the duties of knighthood, sometime between 1404 and 1408, titled *De officio militari*, see Jeanne E. Krochalis, "The Books and Reading of Henry V and His Circle," *Chaucer Review* 23 (1988–89) 50–77, at pp. 61–62. The complete manuscript of Ullerston's Latin treatise on Bible translation

is in Vienna. The fragment that Hudson found is at Cambridge, Gonville and Caius College MS 803/807 frag. 36.

31 *Against Them* is edited by Deanesly, in *Lollard Bible*, pp. 439–45. It is also edited by Curt F. Bühler, "A Lollard Tract: On Translating the Bible into English," *Medium Aevum* 7 (1938) 167–83; and by Dove, who titles it, from the incipit following the title, *First Seith Bois*, in *Earliest Advocates*, pp. 143–49.

32 Hudson, "Debate," p. 9 (75).

33 With the "yardarm" of the digit extending to the right rather than to the left, as in our current form of "7." The form of the "7" in the numbering added in a later hand to the left margin of this page is in the usual form of an inverted *V*. For clearer images of the date, see middle-english-bible.com.

34 Richard Ullerston, *Tractatus de translacione Sacre Scripture in vulgare*, chap. 1, fol. 195ra, lines 1–11 (I regularize u/w/v as well as i/j): "Stabilita siquidem translacione Jeronimi tamquam vera in duobus articulis prelibatis, superest ad tercium procedendum, istum videlicet: 'Utrum, sicut Jeronimo licuit ab Hebreo et Greco in Latinum transferre sacrum canonem, ita liceat ipsum in alias linguas minus principales et famosas transferre.'" That is, "It having been established in the previous two articles that the translation of Jerome is true, it remains to proceed to the third, viz., 'Whether, as it was allowed to Jerome to translate the sacred canon from Hebrew and Greek into Latin, just so, it is allowable to translate it into other languages less important and celebrated.'" Hudson, "Debate," pp. 5–6 (71–72), also reproduces the opening sentences of the treatise. In Deanesly's translation, p. 291, she puts "less principal and beautiful," showing that the Latin transcription she was following had *formosas* rather than *famosas*. She was relying on excerpts given by M. Denis in his catalog of the library; see Hudson, "Debate," p. 3 (69) n. 2.

35 Christopher Ocker, "The Bible in the Fifteenth Century," in *Christianity in Western Europe, c. 1100–c. 1500*, ed. Miri Rubin and Walter Simons, vol. 4 of *Cambridge History of Christianity* (Cambridge 2009), pp. 472–93, speaking of western Europe, says, "Apart from Wycliffites, no one seems to have advocated unrestricted Bible reading" (p. 485). In so saying, he designates all advocates of English Scriptures as Wycliffites.

36 Ullerston, *Tractatus*, chap. 1, fol. 195ra, lines 11–21: "Et quamvis iste articulus in temporibus patrum nostrorum nullatenus in dubium vertebatur, modo vero tam grandis dubitacio oritur super illo quod duo valentes doctores hujus kathedre quasi in ista materia totum tempus lecture sue consumebant; quorum unus ad articuli partem negativam arguebat per aliquot argumenta, alter vero succedens ad articuli partem affirmativam arguebat nescio per quot argumentorum vigenarios. Neuter tamen apparuit scole quid voluit ultimate in materia articuli diffinere" ("And although this article in the times of our fathers in no way came into doubt, now however such a great doubt arises about it that two valiant doctors of this *cathedra* consumed the whole time of their lecture on a similar question. One of them argued for the negative side by various arguments, while the other coming after him argued for the affirmative side of the article, using I know not how many scores of arguments. It appeared to the School, however, that neither of them succeeded in the end in making a definitive case for his position"). The use of *kathedra/cathedra* to refer to a university is otherwise unrecorded in England, to judge by (*DMLBS*); Hudson, "Debate," p. 9 (75), cites such a meaning as being in Charles du Cange, *Glossarium mediae et infimae latinitatis*, new ed., 10 vols. (Niort 1883–87), 2:226, but I cannot see it.

37 Ullerston, *Tractatus*, chap. 1, fol. 195ra, lines 22–28: "In pertractando igitur hunc articulum, sic procedam: primo quidem recitabo quedam argumenta primi doctoris; secundo, adjiciam plura de propriis ad partem articuli negativam; et tercio pro modulo meo solvam argumenta que fiunt ad oppositum articuli antedicti, per que luculenter patebit quid velim sentire circa articulum pretaxatum" ("Therefore, in treating this article I shall proceed thus: first I will recite some of the arguments of the first doctor; second, I will add some of my own arguments to the negative side; and third, according to my capacity, I will solve the arguments made against the aforesaid article, whereby it will clearly appear what I wish to hold concerning the stated article").

38 Deanesly, *Lollard Bible*, p. 291.

39 Hudson, "Debate," pp. 6–7 (72–73). The same is true of Ghosh, *Wycliffite Heresy*, p. 87; Ghosh analyzes the treatise extensively on pp. 87–92, 102–11.

40 Dove, *Earliest Advocates*, p. xlix.

41 Ullerston, *Tractatus*, chap. 1, fol. 195ra, lines 29–32: "Querit enim primus doctor, 'Utrum Scriptura Sacra est in omnes linguas interpretanda,' que quidem questio aliqualiter coincidit cum articulo meo."

42 Ibid., fol. 195ra, lines 48–50: "Ista siquidem argumenta cūdit [ēudit, ōudit, eiīdit, ēūdit, ōūdit?] vir quidam amicus de manu prefati doctoris scripta." The verb used is not certain, though the meaning is fairly obvious; perhaps *condit/condidit* is meant.

43 Ibid., fol. 195ra, line 50: "Sed contra articulum arguitur sic" ("But against the article it is argued thus").

44 Ibid., chap. 11, fol. 200rb, lines 43–44: "Et per hoc patet aliqualis solucio ad argumenta doctoris reverendi."

45 As suggested by Fiona Somerset, "Professionalizing Translation at the Turn of the Fifteenth Century: Ullerston's *Determinacio*, Arundel's *Constitutiones*," in *The Vulgar Tongue: Medieval and Postmedieval Vernacularity*, ed. Somerset and Nicholas Watson (University Park PA 2003), pp. 145–57, at pp. 148–49. On p. 148, she says, "No less than thirty arguments for and against are considered," which obscures the actual format, which is that he presents thirty arguments against the article, and then he proceeds to refute them.

46 I give an example in my *Satan: A Biography* (Cambridge 2006), pp. 253–55, from *Summa* 2.2.95.4, where the obviously false position being debated is this: "It seems to be the case that there is nothing wrong with divination that involves invoking demons."

47 There are relics of another capitulation system, which are crossed out, reaching to chapter 38 just before the current chapter 23, on fol. 206ra.

48 Ullerston, *Tractatus*, chap. 6, fol. 197va, lines 34–42; given by Hudson, "Debate," p. 7 (73).

49 Ullerston, *Tractatus*, chap. 6, fol. 197va, lines 42–53: "Sed quoniam, ut dicit Salomon, 'Qui cito credit, levis est corde' [Ecclus. 19.4], recitabo aliqua motiva que me movent in hac parte ad partem affirmativam sustinendum; et signanter dico 'motiva,' quia revera, quantum estimo, non possunt fieri valide demonstraciones ad unam partem seu ad aliam, sed grosse et figuraliter oportet hic procedere secundum quod racio materie moralis exigit, ut vult Aristoteles, primo *Ethicorum*; consequenterque ponam que credo aut saltem conjecturo esse motiva aliorum qui favent parti questionis negative" ("But because, as Solomon says, 'He who believes easily is slight of heart,' I will list some of the motives that move me in this matter to uphold the affirmative side;

and I take 'motives' in a general way, because, in truth, I think that no valid demonstrations can be given favoring the one side or the other, but one must proceed here roughly and figuratively, in accord with what moral reason requires in the matter, as Aristotle says in the first book of his *Ethics*; and after this, I will set out what I believe or at least conjecture to be the motives of others who favor the negative side of the question"). Hudson overlooks the first part of this statement, and wonders if the setting forth of positive motives is an interpolation.

50 Ibid., chap. 24, fol. 207va, lines 4–9: "Istud tamen quod premissum est, viz., de publicacione legis Christi in quocumque ydiomate, est cum moderamine faciendum, ut superius dictum erat, quod bene notat Dominus Altissiodorensis" etc. ("But that which was premised, viz., concerning the publication of the Law of Christ in every language, is to be done with moderation, as was stated above, which the lord [bishop, William] of Auxerre, says well," leading to an interminable and seemingly irrelevant quotation from Augustine's *Soliloquies*).

51 Ibid., fol. 207vb, lines 22–35.

52 Ibid., [Supplement], fol. 207vb. The nine reasons are as follows: (1) there is no command of the Lord against it; (2) English is as worthy as other modern languages; (3) as it was allowable for the hermit Richard (Rolle) to translate the Psalter, it is allowed to others to do similarly; (4) difficulty in translating Scripture, like difficulty in practicing virtue, does not mean that it is impossible or should not be attempted; (5) in spite of natural difficulties like equivocal tropes and synonyms, Scripture can be translated idea for idea—the Fathers did it; (6) it is expedient to help the insufficiently literate; (7) bishops' counsel is needed; (8) some things are not appropriate to laypersons, whether in Latin or English; (9) as the just should not be damned with the unjust, so well-composed English works should not be condemned. For the text of no. 6, see above, Chapter 3 n. 80.

53 Ibid., fol. 207vb, lines 59–63, Reason 7: "Sicut predicacionis verbi Dei, ministracionis sacramentorum ecclesie, exercicium est taxandum per sanum concilium prelatorum, ita eciam de usu translacionis, quantumlibet licite est censendum; patet hoc ex fidelitate et prudencia servi quem constituit dominus super familiam suam, ut det illis in tempore tritici mensuram" ("Just as the exercise of preaching the Word of God and ministering of the sacraments is to be regulated by the sane counsel of prelates, so too concerning the use of translation: it is to be licitly judged in just the same way; as is clear from the faithfulness and prudence of the servant whom his master set over his family, to give them their measure of wheat in due season" [Luke 12.42]). I am not certain of the meaning of the abbreviation *qúīlz* or *qmlz*, which I render *quantumlibet*.

54 Hudson, "Debate," pp. 1, 9, 15 (67, 75, 81).

55 Ullerston, *Tractatus*, chap. 1, fol. 195ra, lines 36–40: "Item, si aliqui deberent [interpretari Scripturam], precipue deberent esse sacerdotes, et inter eos illi qui magis obligantur ad noticiam Sacre Scripture, qui sunt episcopi; sed illi pro hiis diebus fuerint insufficientes; ergo, etc." ("Again, if anyone should [interpret Scripture], it should be priests, and among them those who have the greatest obligation to the understanding of Sacred Scripture, that is, bishops; but these days they would be insufficient for it; therefore, etc.").

56 Ibid., chap. 10, fol. 199va, lines 45–55, to 199vb, lines 1–4: "Ad secundum, cum assumit si aliqui deberent sic transferre, essent episcopi, qui pro hiis diebus sunt insufficientes, dico quod non sequitur; quamvis enim bene deceret statum episcopalem circa talia grandia solertem esse, non tamen sequitur, etsi illi non sufficerent ad

talia ded[ica]nda per industriam propriam, quod ceteri omnes tamquam insufficientes relinquerentur; sed sufficit quod sint electi viri qui singulariter sufficient ad talia peragenda. Quando enim missi fuerant 72 interpretes Alexandriam, non legitur aliquem eorum fuisse pontificem, sed probi et ellecti viri fuerant, de qualibet tribu sex" ("To the second argument, when he assumes that if some persons should thus translate, they should be bishops, I say that it does not follow; for even though it would be fitting for the episcopal rank to be expert concerning such great matters, it does not follow that, even if they were not sufficiently capable of such accomplishments through their own industry, all others would also be left insufficient for it; it suffices that upright men are chosen who are especially able to fulfill this task. For when the seventy-two interpreters were sent to Alexandria, we do not read that any of them was a pontiff, but they were upright and chosen men, six from each tribe"). He adds the example of a cathedral chancellor who sets up grammar schools, but does not teach them himself, and an emperor who rules through his consuls.

57 Deanesly, *Lollard Bible*, pp. 437–38; as noted above, she edits it on pp. 439–45.

58 Hudson, "Debate," pp. 14–15 (80–81).

59 *Against Them*, ed. Dove, p. 147, lines 133–34.

60 Dove, *Earliest Advocates*, p. li.

61 Ibid., p. 217.

62 Ibid., pp. li, liii.

63 Ian Johnson, "Vernacular Theology/ Theological Vernacular: A Game of Two Halves?" in *After Arundel: Religious Writing in Fifteenth-Century England*, ed. Vincent Gillespie and Kantik Ghosh (Turnhout 2011), pp. 73–88, taking *Against Them* as definitely Lollard, discusses the supposed implications of the collocation of texts in Morgan (pp. 86–87).

64 Dove, *Earliest Advocates*, p. li; she describes the contents of the Trinity MS on p. lii.

65 Ibid., p. 217.

66 *Against Them*, ed. Dove, p. 147, lines 135–38: "We that han moche comined with the Jewis knowen wel that all mighty men of hem, in wat londe they ben born, yit they han in Ebrew the Bible, and they ben more actif in the Olde Lawe thane any Latin man comonly, yhe, as wel the lewde men of the Jewes as prestis."

67 M. Reddan, "Domus Conversorum," in *The Victoria History of London*, ed. William Page, vol. 1 (London 1909), pp. 551–54; cf. R. G. Davies, "Wakering, John," in *OxDNB*. Wakering's predecessor as warden was Nicholas Bubwith, serving from 1402 to 1405; in 1407 he became bishop of Bath and Wells. See Emden, *BRUO* 1:294–96.

68 Michael Adler, *Jews of Medieval England* (London 1939), pp. 323–24, 368–70, 372–73; H. A. Kelly, "Jews and Saracens in Chaucer's England: A Review of the Evidence," *Studies in the Age of Chaucer* 27 (2005) 125–69 (repr. in *Law and Religion in Chaucer's England* [Farnham 2010], chap. 7), pp. 136–37, 140–41, 157, 160, 168.

69 Dove, *Earliest Advocates*, pp. xlix–l, 214–18.

70 Minnis, *Translations of Authority*, pp. 25–26.

71 *Against Them*, ed. Dove, p. 148, lines 147–49: "Friar Tille . . . said before the bishop of London, hearing a hundred men, that Jerome said he erred in translating of the Bible." Spelling modernized, here and below.

72 Emden, *BRUO*, 3:1876. Emden says that Tille was "prior of London Convent in 1402; still in 1408"; but under Thomas Palmer, p. 1422, he says that Palmer was elected prior in 1397 and vacated the office in 1407.

73 David Wilkins, *Concilia Magnae Britanniae et Hibernieae*, 4 vols. (London 1737), 3:314–20.

74 *Against Them*, ed. Dove, p. 148, lines 147–52, citing Acts 13.6–12.

75 Ibid., pp. 148–49, lines 171–79 (spelling modernized).

76 Ralph Hanna, "The Difficulty of Ricardian Prose Translation: The Case of the Lollards," *Modern Language Quarterly* 51 (1990) 319–40, pp. 322 n. 7, 339 n. 34.

77 Dove, *Earliest Advocates*, p. 218; cf. p. li.

78 *The Statutes of the Realm*, 12 vols. (London 1810–28; repr. 1963, 1993), 2:25–26: 5 Richard II c. 5. For the Blackfriars meeting, see p. 78 in the text.

79 Ibid., 2:125–28: 2 Henry IV, c. 15 (1401): *Contra Lollardos*. The statute was not titled *De heretico comburendo*; this was the name of the writ ordering such execution. John A. F. Thomson, *The Later Lollards, 1414–1520* (London 1965), pp. 221–22, reports that a roll of writ formulas compiled around 1430 contain copies of writs *De heretico comburendo* and *De Lollardis arrestandis*. That *Contra Lollardos* was the name of the statute is shown in the copy contained in the bishop of Exeter's register, cited by F. C. Hingeston-Randolph, *The Register of Edmund Stafford (A.D. 1395–1419): An Index and Abstract of Its Contents* (London 1886), p. xi: "Statutum regium contra Lollardos" (text to be found on fols. 322–323v of vol. 2 of the register). A similar title is given for the constitution of the Canterbury Province of 1401, "Constitucio Provincialis contra Lollardos" (on fols. 318–21 of vol. 2 of the register), which in the *Rotuli Parliamentorum*, 6 vols. (London 1767–77), 3:467–68, is called *Petitio cleri contra hereticos*; cf. the new edition, *The Parliament Rolls of Medieval England, 1275–1504*, ed. Chris Given-Wilson, 16 vols. (Woodbridge 2005), 8:122–25; and in Wilkins, *Concilia*, 3:252–54. Thomas Walsingham speaks of it similarly: *Statutum de Lollardis et Lollardo combusto* (rubric); "editum est statutum de Lollardis"; "statutum editum fuit de Lollardis," in *The St. Albans Chronicle: The Chronica Maiora of Thomas Walsingham*, ed. and trans. John Taylor, Wendy R. Childs, and Leslie Watkiss, 2 vols. (New York 2003–11), 2:308, 590 (the editors refer to it by its spurious title, 2:39 n. 435, and in their introduction, 2:lxxx, lxxxiii, xcv). Jeremy Catto, "Shaping the Mixed Life: Thomas Arundel's Reformation," in *Image, Text, and Church, 1380–1600: Essays for Margaret Aston*, ed. Linda Clark, Maureen Jurkowski, and Colin Richmond (Toronto 2009), pp. 94–108, for some reason gives the title in French, "contre les Lollardes" (p. 95).

80 See the previous note.

81 *The Westminster Chronicle, 1381–1394*, ed. and trans. L. C. Hector and Barbara F. Harvey (Oxford 1982), pp. 318–20, 330.

82 Emden, *BRUO*, 3:1733 s.v. "Southam, Thomas." Another named member of the tribunal is William Bottlesham, OP, bishop of Llandaff, a doctor of theology (see R. G. Davies, "Bottlesham, William," in *OxDNB*; Emdem, *BRUC*, p. 76).

83 *Knighton's Chronicle, 1337–1396*, ed. and trans. G. H. Martin (Oxford 1995), pp. 242–45: "Magister Johannes Wyclif Evangelium, quod Cristus contulit clericis et ecclesie doctoribus, ut ipsi laicis et infirmioribus personis secundum temporis exigenciam et personarum indigenciam cum mentis eorum esurie dulciter ministrarent, transtulit de Latino in Anglicam linguam, non angelicam; unde per ipsum fit vulgare

et magis apertum laicis et mulieribus legere scientibus, quam solet esse clericis admodum literatis et bene intelligentibus, et sic evangelica margarita spargitur et a porcis conculcatur" ("The Gospel, which Christ gave to the clergy and the doctors of the church, that they might administer it to the laity and to weaker brethren, according to the demands of the time and the needs of the individual, as a sweet food for the mind, that [Gospel] Master John Wyclif translated from Latin into the language not of the angels but of the English, so that he made them to be common and open to the laity, and to women who were able to read, which used to be for literate and perceptive clerks, and scattered about the Evangelists' pearls to be trampled by swine"). A bit later, in speaking of the signs of the end of the world, he attributes the translation effort to all Lollards (pp. 248–49): "[que allegaciones] magis tamen congruunt istis novis populis Lollardis, qui mutaverunt Evangelium Christi in evangelium eternum, id est, vulgarem linguam et communem maternam et sic 'eternam,' quia laicis reputatur melior et dignior quam lingua Latina" ("[but these citations] better apply to those new people, the Lollards, who have changed the Gospel of Christ into 'the eternal Gospel,' that is into the vulgar and common mother tongue, which laymen believe to be better and more worthy than the Latin tongue"). Martin omits rendering *et sic "eternam."* My own translation of the last clause ("id est vulgarem . . . lingua Latina") is as follows: "that is, into the vernacular and common maternal—and thus 'eternal'—tongue, because it seems to the laity to be better and more worthy than the Latin tongue." He is punning on the maternal/eternal Gospel.

84 Ibid., pp. 438–43. The commission is dated May 23, 1388. On Brightwell and this commission, see Hudson, *Premature Reformation*, pp. 77–78.

85 The March 30 commission is given by Gerald Bray, *Records of Convocation*, 20 vols. (Woodbridge 2005–6), 4:118–19; and Wilkins, *Concilia*, 3:204. See H. G. Richardson, "Heresy and the Lay Power Under Richard II," *English Historical Review* 51 (1936) 1–28, pp. 11–12, citing the *Calendar of the Patent Rolls: Richard II*, 7 vols. (London 1895–1909), vol. 3 (*1385–1389*), pp. 427, 430, 448, 468, 536. The last such commission he cites is in vol. 4 (*1388–1392*), p. 172: December 16, 1389, to Archbishop Courtenay for John Trefnant, the new bishop of Hereford, and his commissaries, mentioning Wyclif, Hereford, Aston, and Purvey, and specifying both English and Latin books.

86 Richardson, "Heresy," p. 10.

87 Gasquet, *Old English Bible*, p. 150. For John Foxe's edition of *Against Them*, see *The Acts and Monuments*, ed. 4, ed. Josiah Pratt, 8 vols. (London [1877]), 4:672–74. Foxe misread *bylle* as *byble*. See the 1530 printing of *A Compendious Olde Treatyse* (Marlborow = Antwerp), EEBO image 5. Cf. Dove, *Earliest Advocates*, p. liv. The Pratt edition of Foxe is based primarily on Foxe's fourth English edition of 1583, with some additions from his earlier editions (like this treatise, found on pp. 452–54 of the 1563 edition, preceded and followed by later additions to the treatise; EEBO images 264–65). See Thomas Freeman, "Texts, Lies, and Microfilm: Reading and Misreading Foxe's 'Book of Martyrs,'" *Sixteenth Century Journal* 30 (1999) 23–46, p. 24. The fourth edition of 1877 is a reprinting of the third edition, 1853–70, except for the biography of Foxe (Freeman, pp. 23–24 n. 3). Unlike Freeman, I consider Pratt's edition generally reliable.

88 British Library MS Egerton 617–18.

89 Dove, *First English Bible*, pp. 58–59, 64–65, 141–42, 246–47; and see Sven L. Fristedt, "A Weird Manuscript Enigma in the British Museum," *Stockholm Studies in Philology* n.s. 2 (1964) 116–21. Dove, *First English Bible*, pp. 58–59, cites A. I. Doyle

as saying that the Bible "must be meant for display and use on a lectern." See Doyle, "English Books In and Out of Court from Edward III to Henry VII," in *English Court Culture in the Later Middle Ages*, ed. V. J. Scattergood and J. W. Sherborne (London 1983), pp. 163–81, at p. 168.

90 See Gasquet, *Old English Bible*, pp. 102–3, 141–42.

91 An example is Jill C. Havens, "A Curious Erasure in Walsingham's Short Chronicle and the Politics of Heresy," *Fourteenth Century England* 2 (2002) 95–106, at pp. 104–5. In keeping with current orthodoxy she says that "possession of a Wycliffite bible was not illegal until after Arundel's Constitutions in 1409"—a statement that I dispute, following Gasquet.

92 FM 1:xliii, no. 32. The passage is discussed by Matti Peikola, "The Sanctorale, Thomas of Woodstock's English Bible, and the Orthodox Appropriation of Wycliffite Tables of Lessons," in Bose and Hornbeck, *Wycliffite Controversies*, pp. 153–74, esp. pp. 155–63.

93 Peikola, "Sanctorale," p. 173. He also cites the dedication to the Duke of Gloucester of the Wycliffite *Dialogue Between a Friar and a Secular*, ed. Fiona Somerset, in *Four Wycliffite Dialogues*, EETS o.s. 333 (Oxford 2009), pp. 32–42. Somerset, pp. xlvii–xlviii, considers the next duke, Humphrey, to be a possible recipient of the dedication, but agrees that Woodstock is more likely.

94 Peikola, "Sanctorale," p. 160.

95 Ibid., pp. 157–59. He says that the lectionary seems to have been written in another hand from that of the scribe who wrote the main text, but that the lectionary (including the Wycliffite passage) was not composed by either scribe. The passage had been interpolated into the readings for St. Nicholas, to make it less conspicuous, Peikola thinks; but since a correction to the passage was added by the main scribe, both scribes clearly adverted to the content of the passage.

96 Anne Hudson, "'Who Is My Neighbour?' Some Problems of Definition on the Borders of Orthodoxy and Heterodoxy," in Bose and Hornbeck, *Wycliffite Controversies*, pp. 79–96, at pp. 80–83.

97 Gasquet, *Old English Bible*, pp. 151–54. Gasquet here refutes the idea that the Wycliffite "poor priests" would have concerned themselves with marking or using the English Bibles for liturgical purposes. See Elizabeth Solopova, "Manuscript Evidence for the Patronage, Ownership, and Use of the Wycliffite Bible," *Form and Function in the Late Medieval Bible*, ed. Eyal Poleg and Laura Light (Leiden 2013), pp. 333–49, for examples of LV Bibles fitted out for public liturgical use. One of them, Bodleian Fairfax 2, has the date, "M.ccc[ ] & viij," with the brackets representing an erasure. The usual assumption is that a *c* has been erased, changing the date from 1408 to 1308, perhaps, as Solopova puts it, "in order to avoid censorship by making the book appear pre-Wycliffite and therefore legal" (p. 337). However, apart from the fact that *Periculosa* only called for episcopal inspection of recent *translations* (not copies of translations), Andrew Watson, *Catalogue of Dated and Datable Manuscripts c. 435–1600 in Oxford Libraries*, 2 vols. (Oxford 1984), 1:76 no. 485, says that ultraviolet examination suggests that it was an ampersand that was erased, meaning that it was a botched correction (the scribe put the *&* farther away and forgot to add the fourth *c*); Solopova responds by saying that UV examinations are notoriously fallible (p. 337 n. 13).

98 Peikola, "Sanctorale," p. 164.

99 Ibid., p. 168.

100 Ibid., pp. 155, 169–71.

101 R. B. Dobson, "Neville, Alexander," in *OxDNB*.

102 Margaret Aston, *Thomas Arundel: A Study of Church Life in the Reign of Richard II* (Oxford 1967), p. 349.

103 Peers were required to be in attendance in London by July 29 to accompany the funeral cortege from Sheen to Westminster on the day before interment, which was August 3. Richard, Earl of Arundel, the archbishop's brother, was "conspicuously late," and King Richard in a fury struck him in the face. See Nigel Saul, "Anne," in *OxDNB*. According to the *Historia vitae et regni Ricardi secundi*, ed. Stow, p. 134, King Richard put off the date of her burial until the feast of St. Anne, ordinarily July 26; but since he buried her on August 3, the saint's feast must have been celebrated with an octave in England. Solemn celebration of St. Anne in England was undoubtedly initiated by Richard himself at the time of his betrothal to Anne of Bohemia in May of 1381; the letter of authorization by Pope Urban VI, *Splendor paterne glorie*, is dated June 21, 1381 (22 Kal Jul, fourth year of his pontificate). See the appendix to Lyndwood's *Provinciale*, p. 60; J. D. Mansi, *Sacra concilia*, 54 vols. (Paris 1901–27), 26:617–618; and John Richard Magrath, ed., *The Obituary Book of Queen's College, Oxford* (Oxford 1910), p. xiii. The correct date of 1381 is noted by Ann W. Astell, "Chaucer's 'St. Anne Trinity': Devotion, Dynasty, Dogma, and Debate," *Studies in Philology* 94 (1997) 395–416, at p. 397 n. 7. The mistaken dates of 1378, 1382, and 1383 are cited elsewhere, for example in Nigel Saul, *Richard II* (New Haven CT 1997), p. 324 (1383) and pp. 455–56 (1382). The last-named date, 1383, is the year in which the pope's letter was promulgated and put into effect in England. See Wilkins, *Concilia*, 3:178–79, for the mandate of the archbishop of Canterbury, dated May 18, 1383, ordering the pope's letter (repeated here and properly dated June 21, 1381) to be carried out. For the dates of Richard's betrothal on May 2 and presumed ratification on May 3, 1381, see H. A. Kelly, *Chaucer and the Cult of St. Valentine* (Leiden 1986), pp. 123–27. For other indications of Richard's and Anne's devotion to St. Anne, see Wendy Scase, "St. Anne and the Education of the Virgin: Literary and Artistic Traditions and Their Implications," in *England in the Fourteenth Century: Proceedings of the 1991 Harlaxton Symposium*, ed. Nicholas Rogers (Stamford CT 1993), pp. 81–96.

104 *Against Them*, ed. Deanesly, in *Lollard Bible*, p. 445; cf. Dove, *Earliest Advocates*, p. 149, lines 180–90.

105 Dove, *Earliest Advocates*, p. 218. Cf. H. Leith Spencer, *English Preaching in the Late Middle Ages* (Oxford 1993), p. 37, who characterizes this account as a "well-known story, even if it is no more than Lollard make-believe," according to which "no less a man than Archbishop Arundel (better known from hostile sources as a notorious suppressor of the scriptures and stifler of evangelical preachers) was said to have commended the late Queen Anne." Spencer does not justify her allegation that Arundel was seen as a "suppressor of the scriptures" in hostile sources of his time; that would seem to be more characteristic of *modern* historians of Lollardy.

106 Hanna, "Difficulty," p. 323, who accepts the same reading of *best*, says that the Lollard author is writing here with "heavy-handed irony," having presented Arundel "as a representative of those negligent men he attacked, as a worldling prelate."

107 Gasquet, *Old English Bible*, pp. 149–50, citing Strype (d. 1737), *Memorials of Cranmer*, edition of 1812, 1:3 (it also appears there in the original edition of 1694). Gasquet says that Strype found it in an old manuscript apparently written at the time of the death of Anne in 1392 (Strype's date, for 1394), rather than as found in the

tract printed by Foxe, which Gasquet goes on to cite for the story of the parliament of Richard's time, as we saw above.

108 Workman, *John Wyclif*, 2:193.

109 Fristedt, *Wycliffe Bible*, 2:lxvii.

110 Jonathan Hughes, "Arundel [Fitzalan], Thomas," in *OxDNB*. Saul, *Richard II*, p. 456, also accepts the account as real: "Archbishop Arundel praised her at her funeral 'for notwithstanding her foreign birth, having in Engish all the four gospels together' with vernacular glosses on them." He admits, however, that "there are problems in interpreting this account, which may well be embroidered." Others who see possible historical value in the anecdote are Doyle, "English Books," p. 168; Andrew Taylor, "Anne of Bohemia and the Making of Chaucer," *Studies in the Age of Chaucer* 19 (1997) 95–119, at pp. 115–16; and, more cautiously, J. W. Sherborne, "Aspects of English Court Culture in the Later Fourteenth Century," in Scattergood and Sherborne, *English Court Culture*, pp. 1–27 at p. 23.

111 Katherine Walsh, "Wyclif's Legacy in Central Europe in the Late Fourteenth and Early Fifteenth Centuries," in *From Ockham to Wyclif*, ed. Anne Hudson and Michael Wilks (Oxford 1987), pp. 397–417, at p. 416. Note that Gasquet, who puts the funeral in 1392, is not the only historian who can get dates wrong. I should mention here that Lynne Long, *Translating the Bible: From the Seventh to the Seventeenth Century* (Aldershot 2001), p. 84, acknowledges that Arundel approved of Anne's English Gospels in 1394, but changed his mind in 1408 [*sic*], when he forbade further translations and the reading of any translation made in Wyclif's time or since.

112 Walsh, "Wyclif's Legacy," pp. 416–17. In 1396 Arundel was appointed archbishop of Canterbury, succeeding William Courtenay (d. July 31, 1396).

113 Wyclif, *De triplici vinculo amoris*, in *Latin Works*, vol. 1 (*Polemical Works*), p. 168: "et ex eodem patet eorum stulticia, qui volunt dampnare scripta tamquam heretica propter hoc, quod scribuntur in Anglico et acute tangunt peccata que conturbant illam provinciam. Nam possibile est, quod nobilis regina Anglie, soror Cesaris, habeat evangelium in lingua triplici exaratum, scilicet Boemica, in lingua Teutonica, et Latina, et hereticare ipsam propterea implicite foret luciferina superbia. Et sicut Teutonici volunt in isto racionabiliter defendere linguam propriam, sic et Anglici debent de racione in isto defendere linguam suam" ("and it is evident from this [he has just explained that rulers who are legitimate according to God's laws cannot be impugned by contrary human laws] the foolishness of those who wish to condemn writings as heretical because they are in English and sharply touch on the sins that disturb that province [i.e., England]. For it is possible that the noble queen of England, Caesar's sister, might possess the Gospels produced in triple tongue, that is, the Bohemian tongue, the German tongue, and the Latin tongue, and to declare her a heretic on this account would be pride like Lucifer's. And, just as the Germans reasonably desire to defend their own language there [in Germany], so the English should with reason defend their language here").

114 Johann Loserth, *Wiclif and Hus* (London 1884), pp. 260–62. Later scholars who make this mistake include Deanesly, *Lollard Bible*, p. 248, who translates "possibile est quod nobilis regina . . . habeat" as "it is lawful for the noble queen . . . to have," which indicates actual possession; and Dove, *First English Bible*, p. 69, who accepts Anne's ownership of the trilingual Gospels.

115 Workman, *John Wyclif*, 2:193 n. 1.

116 Loserth, *Wiclif and Hus*, 262. He says that the misinsertion must have been done at an early stage, since Hus in 1411 says that he took these words from this treatise.

117 *Dives and Pauper* (*DP*), ed. Priscilla Heath Barnum, EETS 275, 280, 323, 2 vols. in 3 (Oxford 1976–2004), 1:1:ix; 2:xviii–xx.

118 *DP* Commandment 1, chap. 47 (1:1:182–83): He says that in 1400 the Calends of January fell on a Thursday, and this year they also fell on a Thursday. This works out to be 1405. Earlier, chap. 29 (1:1:147–48), he refers to a comet that appeared in 1402.

119 *DP* Commandment 4, chap. 11 (1:1:327).

120 Ibid.

121 *DP*, Commandment 6, chap. 3 (1.2:64; cf. 2:xx, 197).

122 See Barnum's introduction, in *Dives and Pauper*, 2:xix–xx, and her notes to the passages (2:149, 197).

123 The work is described by Anne Hudson and H. L. Spencer, "Old Author, New Work: The Sermons of MS Longleat 4," *Medium Aevum* 53 (1984) 220–38. They admit that "the designation *postils* is perhaps rather more apt than 'sermons'" (p. 224), but since "postil" is more appropriate to piecemeal glossing I suggest that "commentary" is preferable. As is evident from my arguments above, I disagree with their conclusions that the work definitely refers to the constitutions (p. 222), and that the "Wycliffite translation of Scripture" was "banned" (p. 233). Of the four places cited as showing knowledge of the constitutions (p. 234 n. 12), one is the prologue and another is fol. 90vb, cited below. The other two, fols. 69rb and 88vb, are not discussed (I find nothing relevant there). I should note, too, that the six places cited for Reginald Pecock's references to the constitutions (p. 237 n. 62) do not bear out the claim that he is citing them or referring to them.

124 *Longleat Sunday Gospels*, preface, fol. 1rb (cited by Hudson and Spencer, "Old Author," p. 231). For the complete preface in its original spelling, see Appendix N below. This passage is in ¶5.

125 Ibid., fol. 1rb, ¶5 (Hudson and Spencer, pp. 231–32). We may note that canon law, by way of a decree of the Fourth Lateran Council in 1215, ordered that, when there is diversity of languages, instruction be given in the appropriate languages: *Quoniam in plerisque*, canon 9 of Fourth Lateran, *Decretales Gregorii IX* [1234], 1.31.14 (*CIC* 2:191–92).

126 Hudson and Spencer, "Old Author," p. 233.

127 *Longleat* preface, fol. 1rb, ¶6 (cited by Hudson and Spencer, p. 232, except for the last clause).

128 Ibid., fol. 1rb–va, ¶7 (partially cited by Hudson and Spencer, p. 232).

129 Gratian, *Decretum*, part 3 (*De consecratione*), Dist. 3, cap. 27, *Perlatum* (*CIC* 1:1360); here is Gregory's text in PL 75:146CD: "Perlatum ad nos fuerat quod, inconsiderato zelo succensus, sanctorum imagines sub hac quasi excusatione, ne adorari debuissent, confregeris. Et quidem, quia eas adorari vetuisses, omnino laudavimus; fregisse vero, reprehendimus. Dic, frater, a quo factum sacerdote aliquando [vel] auditum [est] quod fecisti? . . . Aliud est enim picturam adorare, aliud per picture historiam quid sit adorandum addiscere. Nam quod legentibus scriptura, hoc idiotis prestat pictura cernentibus: quia in ipsa ignorantes vident quod sequi debeant, in ipsa legunt, qui litteras nesciunt. Unde et precipue gentibus pro lectione pictura est."

130 *Longleat* preface, fol. 1va, ¶8.

131 *Longleat*, fol. 90vab (cf. Hudson and Spencer, p. 232), Thirteenth Sunday after Trinity.

132 *The Chastising of God's Children*, ed. Joyce Bazire and Eric Colledge, in "*The Chastising of God's Children" and "The Treatise of Perfection of the Sons of God*" (Oxford 1957), chap. 27, p. 221 (respelled). Another author, a monk, probably a Kentishman, who around the end of the 1300s set about translating parts of the Bible for a fellow monk and a nun, feared that he might be putting his very life in danger. See Anna C. Paues, *A Fourteenth Century English Biblical Version* (Cambridge 1904), pp. 4–5. He says that Christ's law obliges him to do it, but in doing it he might perchance undergo death, since "we" (that is, the current times) have fallen far away from Christ's law. The text reads: "Brother, I knowe wel that I am holde by Cristis lawe to parforme thin axinge; bote natheles we beth now so fer yfallen awey from Cristis lawe that yif I wolde answere to thin axinges I most in cas underfonge the deth—and thou wost wel that a man is yholden to kepe his lif as longe as he may." It is hard to imagine what the source of his concern was.

Chapter 5. The Provincial Constitutions of 1407

1 Bray, *Records of Convocation*, 4:307–18 (text of the constitutions of Oxford, 1407, without variants); 4:349 (letter of April 14, 1409, recounting the discussion and confirmation of the constitutions in the 1409 convocation). The constitutions are also found in Wilkins, *Concilia*, 3:314–19; an edition without variants (which are very few in Wilkins) is given in Lyndwood, *Provinciale*, appendix, pp. 64–68. *Periculosa* is accurately translated by Workman, *John Wyclif*, 2:194; and Deanesly, *Lollard Bible*, p. 296. See Dove, *First English Bible*, pp. 35–36, 38–39. The translation given by Nicholas Watson, "Censorship and Cultural Change in Late-Medieval England: Vernacular Theology, the Oxford Translation Debate, and Arundel's Constitutions of 1409," *Speculum* 70 (1995) 822–64, pp. 828–29 n. 15 is also accurate; but, as I have had occasion to note before, he is mistaken in saying that the ordinance prohibited unlicensed *ownership* of new translations, and I question his interpretation of *translatio* to include commentary (Kelly, "Lollard Inquisitions," p. 288 n. 38). Confirming the narrow (and correct) meaning of *translatio* in the constitution is Kathryn Kerby-Fulton, *Books Under Suspicion: Censorship and Tolerance of Revelatory Writing in Late Medieval England* (Notre Dame IN 2006), p. 400.

2 Rita Copeland, *Pedagogy, Intellectuals, and Dissent in the Later Middle Ages: Lollardy and Ideas of Learning* (Cambridge 2001), p. 202, citing only the first part of the constitution.

3 De Hamel, *The Book*, p. 166. Cf. Graham D. Caie, "Chaucer and the Bible," in *Chaucer and Religion*, ed. Helen Phillips (Woodbridge 2010), pp. 24–34: "Such translations were forbidden in the later-medieval period" (p. 24).

4 Ralph Hanna, "English Biblical Texts Before Lollardy and Their Fate," in *Lollards and Their Influence in Late Medieval England*, ed. Fiona Somerset, Jill C. Havens, and Derrick G. Pitard (Woodbridge 2003), pp. 141–53, at p. 151; part of this essay appears as "The End of Early London Literature" in Hanna's *London Literature*, pp. 305–13; for this passage, see p. 309.

5 Copeland, "Lollard Writings," p. 114; cf. p. 112: the constitutions "prohibited unlicensed possession of vernacular Bibles." Cf. Judy Ann Ford, *John Mirk's Festial:*

Orthodoxy, Lollardy, and the Common People in Fourteenth-Century England (Cambridge 2006), p. 118: "The possession of English translations of the Bible was declared unlawful by Archbishop Arundel." Richard Marsden, "The Bible in English in the Middle Ages," in *The Practice of the Bible in the Middle Ages*, ed. Susan Boynton and Diana J. Reilly (New York 2011), pp. 272–95, says that the constitution "forbade the translation of any text of Scripture into English and the ownership of any translation made in the time of Wyclif or later, without the express permission of a bishop, which would be granted only after inspection of the translation" (p. 290).

6 Christina von Nolcken, "Another 'Lollere in the Wynd'? The Miller, the Bible, and the Destruction of Doors," in *Through a Classical Eye: Transcultural and Transhistorical Visions in Medieval English, Italian, and Latin Literature in Honour of Winthrop Wetherbee*, ed. Andrew Galloway and R. F. Yeager (Toronto 2009), pp. 238–66 at pp. 250–51: it was "legislation against the further translation of any biblical texts as well as against the reading of such texts in any book, booklet, or tract made in or after the time of Wyclif."

7 David Lawton, *Faith, Text, and History: The Bible in English* (New York 1990), p. 52; see also Lawton's "The Bible," p. 219: "after 1401 . . . owning English Bibles became a capital offense"; p. 223: during the fifteenth century, "Power pretended that the people had no English Bible, and burned a minatory few of those who violated the pretence."

8 Kerby-Fulton, *Books Under Suspicion*, p. 399: "It is, as Workman says, largely the possession of Bibles, tragically, that sent people to the flames," referring to Workman, *John Wyclif*, 2:196 and his note 3 for a list of persons so punished. But what Workman actually says is that there is abundant evidence of persecution of the Lollards for possessing copies of the vernacular Scriptures, referring to accounts in Foxe. I will take up these references to Foxe below. Workman also refers to *Knighton's Chronicle*, which I discussed in Chapter 4 above.

9 Michael Livingston, ed., *The Middle English Metrical Paraphrase of the Old Testament* (Kalamazoo MI 2011), p. 32. Moreover, "the Wycliffite Bible was declared heretical"; "just possessing a copy could, at times, warrant the branding of heresy upon one's person regardless of personal beliefs" (p. 33).

10 Ghosh, *Wycliffite Heresy*, p. 86.

11 Lynne Long, "Vernacular Bibles and Prayer Books," in *The Oxford Handbook of English Literature and Theology*, ed. Andrew Hass, David Jasper, and Elisabeth Jay (Oxford 2007), pp. 54–78, at p. 57; cf. p. 58: the Wycliffite Bible was "a direct challenge to the established hierarchy." As for *Periculosa*, Long takes the view that since the Wycliffite Bible needed episcopal approval, it was automatically proscribed (p. 61). As noted above (Chapter 4 n. 111), in her later study, *Translating the Bible*, p. 84, she takes the view that the constitution forbade all English translations.

12 Thomas More, *A Dialogue Concerning Heresies* 3.14, ed. Thomas M. C. Lawler, Germain Marc'hadour, and Richard C. Marius, in *The Complete Works of St. Thomas More*, vol. 6, in 2 parts (New Haven CT 1981), 1:314.

13 Constitutions of Oxford, 1407, const. 7, in Bray, *Records of Convocation*, 4:315; cf. Lyndwood, *Provinciale* 5.4 (title *De magistris*), [c. 3], p. 286. The text in the Lyndwood appendix, p. 66, has *excommunicationis majoris* and *recognita et approbata*.

14 Gasquet, *Old English Bible*, pp. 122–23. The *similiter* omitted by Gasquet refers to the same penalty in the previous constitution, *Quia insuper*. A faulty translation is

given by Frans van Liere, *An Introduction to the Medieval Bible* (Cambridge 2014), who says that the edict banned translation. Instead of interpreting *diocesanus* as "diocesan bishop" he takes it to mean "diocesan Council" (p. 201). The same is true of Robert Tombs, *The English and Their History* (London 2014), p. 131. Morey, *Book and Verse*, p. 39, likewise mistranslates, rendering *per loci diocesanum* as "in every place of the diocese," with the result that no one can translate afresh or read a new translation unless approval is forthcoming from the provincial council. Fiona Somerset, "Censorship," in *The Production of Books in England, 1350–1500*, ed. Alexandra Gillespie and Daniel Wakelin (Cambridge 2011), pp. 239–58, also interprets the constitution as meaning that only a provincial council can authorize a translation (p. 242), and furthermore she believes that the MEB is specifically mentioned in the constitution (p. 252), the implication being that it was denied approval both in 1407 and 1409.

15 Gasquet, *Old English Bible*, p. 123,

16 Even Anne Hudson slips in saying that the edict forbade "the possession of vernacular scripture unless the owner had received prior permission from his bishop" (*Selections*, p. 163). Elsewhere, she says that the constitutions "notoriously forbade the dissemination or ownership of vernacular biblical texts unless they and their owners had received episcopal licence." See her "*Laicus litteratus*: The Paradox of Lollardy," in *Heresy and Literacy, 1000–1530*, ed. Peter Biller and Anne Hudson (Cambridge 1994), pp. 222–36, at p. 232. Again, in "Lollard Literature," in *The Cambridge History of the Book in Britain*, vol. 2 (1100–1400), ed. Nigel Morgan and Rodney M. Thomson (Cambridge 2008), pp. 329–39, she says that episcopal approval was needed for "both version and owner" (p. 330), and speaks of "the *Constitutions*' crippling restrictions on ownership" (p. 337).

17 *Statuta antiqua Universitatis Oxoniensis*, p. 49.

18 *Quia insuper*, ed. Bray, *Records of Convocation*, 4:314; Lyndwood, *Provinciale*, 5.4.[2], pp. 284–85.

19 Hudson, "Debate," p. 1 (67); cf. p. 3 (69): "the legitimacy of biblical translation" is "a closed argument, settled by recent legislation." In her more recent book *Doctors in English*, Hudson says simply that Arundel banned the Wycliffite Bible (p. cxxxviii) and outlawed the vernacular translation of Scripture (p. cliv).

20 Constitution no. 5, *Similiter quia*, given in Lyndwood, *Provinciale* 5.4.[1], pp. 282–84; comm. ad v. *consuevit* (p. 284 note i): "Scilicet grammaticaliter, et sic secundum sensus mysticos vel morales non debent eam exponere, quia hoc non pertinet ad ipsorum facultatem sive doctrinam." See Copeland, *Pedagogy*, pp. 119–22.

21 Nicholas Love, *Mirror of the Blessed Life of Jesus Christ*, ed. Michael G. Sargent (New York 1992), p. 7: "Memorandum quod circa annum Domini millesimum quadringentesimum decimum, originalis copia hujus libri, scilicet *Speculi vite Christi in Anglicis*, presentabatur Londoniis per compilatorem ejusdem N. reverendissimo in Christo patri et domino, Domino Thome Arundell, Cantuarie archiepiscopo, ad inspiciendum et debite examinandum antequam fuerat libere communicata. Qui post inspeccionem ejusdem per dies aliquot, retradens ipsum librum memorato ejusdem auctori, proprie vocis oraculo ipsum in singulis commendavit et approbavit, necnon et auctoritate sua metropolitica, utpote catholicum publice communicandum fore decrevit et mandavit, ad fidelium edificacionem et hereticorum sive Lollardorum confutacionem. Amen." A. I. Doyle, "The Study of Nicholas Love's *Mirror*, Retrospect and Prospect," in *Nicholas Love at Waseda: Proceedings of the International Conference, 20–22 July 1995*, ed. Shoiochi Oguro, Richard Beadle, and Michael G. Sargent

(Cambridge 1997), pp. 163–74, at p. 169, has argued that Love's work circulated before Arundel gave his approval. Cited by Michelle Karnes, "Nicholas Love and Medieval Meditations on Christ," *Speculum* 82 (2007) 380–408, p. 402 n. 89. The real question is, however, whether it circulated in the province of Canterbury before this, as well as in the province of York.

22 Karnes, "Nicholas Love," pp. 403–5. She infers that Hudson believes that the *Mirror* is implicitly opposed to the English Bible in *Premature Reformation*, p. 439, and she cites Ghosh, *Wycliffite Heresy*, p. 148, and Nicholas Watson, "Censorship," p. 855, as holding Love's explicit opposition. Ghosh, *Wycliffite Heresy*, p. 147, says that Love's work "was licensed by Archbishop Thomas Arundel in 1410 as an official alternative to the Lollard Bible, the use of which had been severely restricted." Schirmer, "Canon Wars," holds that Love's *Mirror* is intended to replace Scripture, in keeping with Arundel's desire to provide alternatives to "Wycliffite biblical canons" (pp. 15–16).

23 Karnes, "Nicholas Love," p. 403. Karnes is speaking of Love's program for meditation. She notes, p. 402, with Kantik Ghosh, "Nicholas Love," in Edwards, *Companion to Middle English Prose*, pp. 53–66, at p. 55, that Love avoids exact citations of Scripture.

24 Love, *Mirror* [Proem], pp. 9–10.

25 E.g., Hudson, *Premature Reformation*, p. 240; Dove, *First English Bible*, p. 36; and Dove, "Wyclif and the English Bible," p. 385. Both Hudson and Dove cite the date as 1412 (as does Gasquet, which is Wilkins's conjecture; Wilkins did not know about the meeting of bishops on March 17, 1411, or the response of the pope to the letter, dated November 20, 1411 [Workman, *John Wyclif*, 2:366, 372]).

26 Constitution no. 6 (*Quia insuper*), given in Lyndwood, *Provinciale* 5.4.[2], pp. 284–86; Bray, *Records of Convocation*, 4:314.

27 H. E. Salter, "Documents from Faustina C.vii and Other Sources, Dealing in Particular with the Years 1409 and 1411," in *Snappe's Formulary and Other Records*, Oxford Historical Society, vol. 80 (Oxford 1924), pp. 90–193, p. 99; Workman, *John Wyclif*, 2:359–60, agrees. The letter from the university is given by Salter on pp. 117–18 (treated below).

28 See Appendix O, "The Oxford Committee of Twelve, 1410–11."

29 Convocation of February–March 1410 at St. Paul's, Bray, *Records*, 4:355–72. Bray, pp. 372–74, has misplaced Arundel's letter to Oxford, dated June 23, 1411, taking it to refer to this convocation, altering the date of March 17, 1411, to March 17, 1410, on grounds that no convocation was held in March of 1411 (as we will see, it was not a convocation but a committee of bishops that was held in March 1411). The constitution on heresy trials is no. 2, p. 371. Bray, *Records*, 19:83, tells us that these constitutions "are remarkable chiefly for the fact that they were little copied and now survive only in one rather obscure manuscript."

30 Salter, "Documents," pp. 119–20, doc. 6.

31 The 267 articles are given in Wilkins, *Concilia*, 3:339–49, dated 1412. Catto, "Wyclif and Wycliffism," p. 248, dates their report to March 17, 1411, but, as we will see, this is the date on which the bishops acted against the propositions.

32 The works from which the propositions were extracted are listed in Appendix P, "Wyclif's Works and the 267 Condemned Propositions, 1411."

33 Salter, "Documents," pp. 128–30, doc. 13; addressed to Arundel "aliisque venerabilibus patribus et prelatis provincie Cantuariensis" and "tam venerando cetui prelatorum, et ad defensionem percelebrem catholice fidei firmiter et feliciter adunari [*lege* adunato]." Salter's edition of the letter omits the 267 propositions (p. 130 n. 3). "By some extraordinary blunder," Salter says, Wilkins had already printed the letter earlier, under 1382, as taken from Archbishop Sudbury's register, and followed it with the names of the twelve Oxford censors from 1411 (*Concilia*, 3:171–72). Wilkins gives the letter again here, on p. 339, but omits the names of the censors at the end of the list of 267 propositions on p. 349.

34 Salter, "Documents," pp. 156–58, doc. 24, *Quia nos certas conclusiones*; edited also by Bray, *Records of Convocation*, 4:372–73, and interpreted as referring to the 1410 convocation.

35 By Salter, "Documents," p. 100; followed by Workman, *John Wyclif*, 2:359–66.

36 By Bray, *Records*, 3:372 n. 883; 19:83.

37 Wilkins, *Concilia*, 3:157: "Nos, Willelmus . . . archiepiscopus Cantuariensis . . . quosdam venerabiles confratres suffraganeos nostros et alios, ac quamplures sacre pagine, juris canonici et civilis doctores et bacalarios, quos famosiores et peritiores de regno credidimus et sanctius in fide catholica sentientes, quorum nomina inferius continentur, convocavimus." In the archbishop's letter *Ecclesiarum prelati*, of May 28, 1382, included in *Fasciculi zizaniorum*, pp. 275–82, he says that the meeting was only of the scholars, convened on the advice of some of his bishops: "De quamplurimum fratrum et suffraganeorum nostrorum consilio et assensu, convocavimus plures sacre theologie doctores" (p. 276). But in fact eight of his suffragans were in attendance, and also another bishop from the province of York, namely, John Fordham, bishop of Durham (*Fasciculi*, p. 286).

38 Arundel, *Quia nos*, June 23, 1411 (Salter, "Documents," pp. 156–57): "Quia nos certas conclusiones, tam in sacra theologia quam in philosophia, ut hereticas et erroneas, male sonantes et piarum aurium offensivas, ac determinationi sancte matris Ecclesie repugnantes, quas vobis sub sigillo nostro clausas in rotulo presentibus annexo transmittimus, prius per duodecim personas Universitatis predicte, seu saltem majorem et saniorem partem earundem, per dictam Universitatem auctorititate nostri provincialis consilii alias ad hoc electas, a libris et libellis et aliis codicibus, exactissimis examinatione et scrutinio extractas, elicitas, et damnatas, una cum libris et libellulis, juxta sanctiones orthodoxorum patrum, in quibus eedem conclusiones vel aliqua earundem assertive et conclusionaliter sunt contente, nuper, die viz. XVII[e] Marcii ultimi preteriti, in domo capitulari ecclesie London, visis perantea, ex decreto nostro et plurimorum confratrum et suffraganeorum nostrorum tunc ibidem existencium, ac diligentissime examinatis conclusionibus antedictis per venerabiles fratres nostros Philippum Lincolniensem et Robertum Saresbiriensem Dei gracia episcopos, de unanimi consensu et assensu ipsorum Lincolniensis et Saresbiriensis necnon Ricardi Londoniensis, Henrici Wintoniensis, Roberti Herefordensis, Nicholai Bathoniensis et Wellensis, Henrici Menevensis, et aliorum venerabilium confratrum nostrorum et suffraganeorum nostre provincie tunc ibidem personaliter existencium, hec fieri instantissime postulantium, auctoritate sancte matris Ecclesie et dicti nostri provincialis concilii damnavimus; . . . vobis . . . mandamus . . . quatenus . . . omnes . . . jurare faciatis et compellatis quod prefatas conclusiones . . . ac libros et libellos . . . arctius evitare studeant." That is, "Since we condemned certain conclusions both in

sacred theology and in philosophy as heretical and erroneous, ill-sounding and offensive to pious ears, and repugnant to the determination of Holy Mother Church, which we are sending to you under our seal in a roll attached to this present letter, conclusions that were beforehand extracted and excerpted from books and booklets and other codices through careful examination and scrutiny by twelve persons of the foresaid University elected for this purpose by the said University on authority of our provincial council, and condemned by them, or at least by the greater and saner number of them, along with the books and booklets in which the said conclusions or some of them were assertively or affirmatively contained, according to the sanctions of orthodox fathers; and since recently, namely on the seventeenth day of March last, in the chapter house of the church of London, the said conclusions, first seen and diligently examined, upon our decree and that of several of our confreres and suffragans, by our venerable brothers Philip of Lincoln and Robert of Salisbury, were condemned by the unanimous consent and assent of the said Lincoln and Salisbury and also of Richard of London, Henry of Winchester, Robert of Hereford, Nicholas of Bath and Wells, Henry of St. David's, and of other venerable confreres and suffragans of ours there present in person, on the authority of Holy Mother Church and our said provincial council; . . . we command . . . you . . . that . . . you make . . . all . . . swear . . . and compel them, to strenuously strive to avoid the foresaid conclusions . . . and books and booklets."

39 Salter, "Documents," pp. 133–35, doc. 15, *Miserator et misericors Dominus*; Wilkins, *Concilia*, 3:350–51. Salter, p. 100, suggests a date of about March 20, 1411. For the condemnation of Wyclif in Rome in 1412–13 and later at the Council of Constance, see my essay, "Trial Procedures Against Wyclif and Wycliffites in England and at the Council of Constance," *Huntington Library Quarterly* 61 (1999) 1–28, pp. 20–21.

40 Arundel, *Miserator et misericors Dominus* (Salter, "Documents," p. 134).

41 GP, chap. 15 (p. 57).

42 Deanesly, *Lollard Bible*, p. 238.

43 Lindberg, *Earlier Version*, 8:69–71, interprets *nove translationis* to refer to LV, as opposed to EV, meaning that Arundel is affirming that Wyclif himself was involved in producing LV. He presumes that the increased glossing in LV would have been found to be objectionable to the Church authorities. Fristedt, for his part, thinks that Arundel is referring to the First Revision (that is, EV, as opposed to EEV) as well as to LV: "The rigidly literal and frequently unintelligible nude text Englished by Hereford and others was not objectionable to the Church when in the hands of clerks and temporal lords, whereas the revised text of the Earlier Version, whose originator was Wycliffe, could not be tolerated since teeming with glosses and other explicatory matter intended for the laity and the unlettered; and consequently his offence was the introduction of this *new* way of translation, which led to the production of the yet more odious Later Version" (*Wycliffe Bible*, 2:lxvii).

44 Deanesly, *Lollard Bible*, p. 238.

45 Gasquet, *Old English Bible*, p. 123 n. 1 and p. 170.

46 Ibid., p. 170.

47 Ibid., p. 167.

48 Ibid., 126–27. On this subject, see my "Lollard Inquisitions," pp. 301–2.

49 Gasquet, *Old English Bible*, p. 167. I cannot see where Gasquet is getting his material from in Kenyon, who seems only to allude to Arundel's letter, referring to "contemporary evidence of Archbishop Arundel," p. 205. See Frederic G. Kenyon, *Our Bible and the Ancient Manuscripts, Being a History of the Text and Its Translations*, 2nd ed. (London 1896), pp. 204–8, at p. 205. Matthew, "Authorship," translates this passage of the letter on p. 98.

50 Gasquet, *Old English Bible*, pp. 167–68.

51 Kenyon, *Our Bible*, p. 207.

52 Gasquet, *Old English Bible*, pp. 167–68 n. 2.

Chapter 6. Treatment of the English Bible in the Fifteenth Century

1 Hanna, "English Biblical Texts," p. 151 (*London Literature*, p. 310).

2 Dove, *First English Bible*, pp. 37–67.

3 Michael Sargent, "Censorship or Cultural Change? Reformation and Renaissance in the Spirituality of Late Medieval England," in *After Arundel: Religious Writing in Fifteenth-Century England*, ed. Vincent Gillespie and Kantik Ghosh (Turnhout 2011), pp. 55–72, p. 60 n.15.

4 Ibid., p. 65.

5 Kennedy, *Courtly and Commercial Art*, pp. 1, 4. She makes a nearly identical statement in "Reintroducing the English Books of Hours, or 'English Primers,'" *Speculum* 89 (2014) 693–723, at 697.

6 Kennedy, *Courtly and Commercial Art*, p. 5, cites Hudson's "Lollard Book Production," in *Book Production and Publishing in Britain, 1375–1475*, ed. Jeremy Griffiths and Derek Pearsall (Cambridge 1989), pp. 125–42, for noting both the concern for display copies and the desire for anonymity and fear of prosecution. In this essay, Hudson interprets *Periculosa* as permitting ownership only of pre-Wyclif translations, and requiring that copies even of such translations needed the bishop's permission (p. 131). She considers the "Wycliffite Bible" to be forbidden, but says that high-ranking persons (such as Henry VI and Henry VII) could doubtless have obtained permission to own their copies (pp. 131–32).

7 Kennedy, *Courtly and Commercial Art*, pp. 4–13. See also her *Medieval Hackers* (Brooklyn 2015), esp. pp. 70–71.

8 Eric Colledge, "Introduction," in Bazire and Colledge, *Chastising of God's Children*, p. 35.

9 Ogle, "Dr. Gasquet," p. 286; Dove, *First English Bible*, p. 45 and n. 49.

10 Repingdon, *Register*, ed. Archer, 1:7–9; and see Archer's introduction, 1:xxxiv.

11 Ibid., 1:xxxii.

12 Catto, "Fellows and Helpers," pp. 152–53.

13 Repingdon, *Register*, 1:101–4; Archbishop Arundel in his mandate characterizes Satan as the *inimicus homo* of the parable of the sower, Matt. 13.28 (p. 102 Bray, *Records of Convocation*, 4:307).

14 Repingdon, *Register*, 1:140; for the text, see Wilkins, *Concilia* 3:311–12; Bray, *Records of Convocation*, 4:338–41.

15 Repingdon, *Register*, 1:153; the text of the constitutions is given on folios 37–39.

16 Logan, *University Education*, p. 2.

17 Ian Forrest, "Anti-Lollard Polemic and Practice in Late Medieval England," in *The Fifteenth Century*, vol. 3, *Authority and Subversion*, ed. Linda Clark (Woodbridge 2003), pp. 63–74, at p. 70. In *The Detection of Heresy in Late Medieval England* (Oxford 2005), p. 116, Forrest makes the point that licenses in Repingdon's dioceses and other dioceses increased in frequency after the constitutions were promulgated.

18 Repingdon, *Register*, 1:58, 126.

19 Ibid., 2:293–94. Unfortunately, the part of the text of this commission referring to the constitution is badly transcribed (I italicize the obvious mistakes): "quod nullus a iure scripto *misericordie auctoritatas privilegia ve speciali munitas* predicet verbum Dei nisi primo de *diocesani* loci." I conjectually edit the beginning of the commission (addressed to Richard Fleming and to a canonist) as follows: "Licet doctorum ordo sit quasi precipuus in ecclesia, non debet sibi quisquam indifferenter predicacionis officium usurpare; nam secundum Apostolum, 'Quomodo predicabunt nisi mittantur?' [Rom. 10.15], et Veritas ipsa dicit, 'Rogate D[ominum] messis ut mittat operarios in messam suam' [Luke 10.2]. Horum siquidem [+ auctoritate?] ac cujusdam constitutionis provincialis ('Quod nullus a jure scripto mi[nime] auctori[zatus], privilegi[o]ve speciali munit[u]s, predicet verbum Dei, nisi primo de diocesan[o] loci, debite examinatus, licenciam ad hoc obtinuerit specialem'), in hac parte edire [+ modum?] consideracione provida [+ volumus?]. Nonnulli, ut accepimus, doctores et scolares," etc. ("Although the order of doctors is as it were foremost in the Church, no one should thrust himself into the office of preaching at random; for, according to the Apostle, 'How shall they preach unless they are sent?'—and Truth itself says, 'Ask the Lord of the harvest that He send laborers to His harvest.' [On the authority] of these, therefore, and [on that] of a certain provincial constitution ('That no one not authorized by written permission, or not possessing a special privilege, is to preach the word of God, unless he first obtains, after being duly examined, a special license for it from the diocesan of the place'), [we wish] with prudent consideration to produce [a mode of proceeding]. Several doctors and scholars, as we have heard," etc. The relevant text of *Quod nullus* reads: "Quod nullus . . . ad predicandum verbum Dei a jure scripto minime auctorizatus, privilegiove speciali munitus, officium . . . in se assumat . . . nisi primo . . . diocesano illius loci . . . se presentet et examinationem subeat" (Bray, *Records*, 4:311).

20 Repingdon, *Register*, 3:152–53, no. 295. The commission begins in the same way, "Licet doctorum ordo . . . officium usurpare," and then goes on to speak of the need to send laborers to the harvest. The examiners are to proceed "juxta et secundum formam in constitutione provinciali nuper contra detractores evangelicos proinde edita."

21 See Forrest, "Anti-Lollard Polemic," pp. 69–74.

22 Repingdon, *Register*, 2:367–69; Bray, *Records*, 4:411–13.

23 Repingdon, *Register*, 2:371–72. At the same time that he issued the summons for the convocation, Arundel sent around orders for prayers and processions for peace and against plague and against Lollardy (*Lollardria*), which was on the increase (pp. 362–63).

24 Ibid., 2:379–80; see Archer's introduction, 1:xxxv. Oldcastle's trial of 1413 is given on 3:10–13, no. 24. See 3:185, no. 346: a commission in 1417 to proceed against the supporters of Oldcastle.

25 Ibid., 3:117 no. 193. A year earlier, Repingdon had uncovered some heresy suspects in his visitation of the archdeaconry of Leicester (Archer's introduction, p. xxxiv).

26 See Maureen Jurkowski, "Heresy and Factionalism at Merton College in the Early Fifteenth Century," *Journal of Ecclesiastical History* 48 (1997) 658–81, p. 659.

27 *The Register of Henry Chichele, Archbishop of Canterbury, 1414–1443*, ed. E. F. Jacob, 4 vols. (Oxford 1937–47), 3:18–19; Bray, *Records*, 5:33–34. See John Thomson, *Later Lollards*, pp. 222–23.

28 Repingdon, *Register*, 3:128, no. 224; p. 141, no. 249; pp. 156–59, no. 299; p. 193, no. 365.

29 Ibid., 3:130–31, no. 227; see also pp. 118–19, no. 201, commission to inspect Bagworth's books, dated August 5, 1416. Bagworth had earlier done penance for protecting Lollards (3:69–70, no. 110).

30 Chichele, *Register*, 1:cxxxix.

31 Repingdon, *Register*, 2:328–61; for fol. 83, see pp. 331–33.

32 Jacob, in Chichele, *Register*, 1:cxxxix.

33 Repingdon, *Register*, 3:193–94, no. 365 (fols. 176v–177). I have had occasion before to find fault with Jacob in his preface; see H. A. Kelly, "English Kings and the Fear of Sorcery," *Mediaeval Studies* 39 (1977) 206–38, pp. 222–23 n. 64.

34 As noted by Deanesly, *Lollard Bible*, pp. 6–7 n. 2, such "episcopal licenses may have been verbal."

35 For the dates of the bishops, see *Handbook of British Chronology*, ed. E. B. Fryde et al., 3rd ed. (London 1986); for the extant registers, see David M. Smith, *Guide to Bishops' Registers of England and Wales* (London 1981). A good list of relevant registers with proceedings against Lollards is to be found in Hornbeck, *What Is a Lollard?* pp. 215–16. The registers of Bangor, Bath and Wells, Chichester, Hereford, Lincoln, and Salisbury for the time of the constitutions of 1407/9 have been printed; those of Canterbury (Archbishop Arundel), Coventry, Ely, London, Norwich, and Exeter have not, though a calendar of the Exeter register has been published (see below). No registers survive from Llandaff, Rochester (except for six folios), St. Asaph, St. David's (Henry Chichele), Winchester (Henry Beaufort), and Worcester. The register of the vicar-general of St. David's survives and has been printed, but there is nothing in it of interest to us.

36 *Registrum Roberti Mascall, Episcopi Herefordensis, A.D. MCCCCIV–MCCCCXVI*, ed. Joseph H. Parry (London 1917), pp. 105–6. The gathering is called *congregitio* and *convocatio*.

37 Hallum, *Register*, pp. 141–142, nos. 954–55. Before this, on p. 131, no. 920, is the record of publishing the constitutions against heresy of 1416.

38 See ibid., p. 211, no. 1126, where there is reference in 1410 to the Committee of Twelve at Oxford appointed to reprove errors in Wyclif's books, and this group and the chancellor of the university examined a university scholar, Peter Clerk, suspected of holding dissident views; Clerk convinced his examiners of his orthodoxy.

39 *The Episcopal Register of Robert Rede, Ordinis Predicatorum, Lord Bishop of Chichester, 1397–1415*, ed. Cecil Deedes, 2 vols., Sussex Record Society, vols. 8, 11 (Lewes 1908–10), 1:145–46.

40 Only a calendar has been published, Hingeston-Randolph, *Register of Edmund Stafford*.

41 *The Register of Nicholas Bubwith, Bishop of Bath and Wells, 1407–1424*, ed. Thomas Scott Holmes, 2 vols. (London 1914). The summons to the heresy convocation issued by Archbishop Arundel in October 1413 is included, 1:151–54.

42 Thomas Netter of Walden, *Doctrinale antiquitatum fidei catholicae ecclesiae*, ed. Bonaventura Blanciotti, 3 vols. (Venice 1758–59; repr. Farnborough 1967). See Anne Hudson, "Netter [Walden], Thomas (c.1370–1430)," in *OxDNB*.

43 Mishtooni Bose, "Orthodoxy and the Theory of Scriptural Translation" (paper given at the conference "Transforming Scripture: Biblical Translations and Adaptations in Old and Middle English," St. Anne's College, Oxford, May 29–31, 2014), a preliminary version of the chapter "Orthodox Agenda for Vernacular Translation," in *The Wycliffite Bible: Origin, History and Interpretation*, ed. Elizabeth Solopova (forthcoming from Brill, Leiden 2017).

44 When discussing characteristics of Wycliffites, he says that they condemn everything said by the pope or Church that is not contained in Scripture, quoting Wyclif (Netter, *Doctrinale* 1:11, *Doctrina Wiclevistarum prima*), but he does not mention any concern on their part for people to read Scripture for themselves; rather, they urge the reading of Wyclif's books (1:19, *Doctrina sexta*).

45 Netter, *Doctrinale*, 3:12; my translation, in antique style. Here is the original: "Judicio ergo meo, mi Wicleff, corrumpendo sensum Scripture Scripturas negaveras, et eo penalius quo eis per hypocrisim falsum osculum spopondisti, quod non fecerat Manichaeus. Non credunt forsan plurimi quod sis falsarius. Quot locis monstravi jam superius corruptiones Scripturarum per te ipsum immissas, et ipsas Dei leges praesumptionibus tuis pessime vitiatas?"

46 Ibid., cols. 12–13. He follows with another five examples of his getting the literal meaning of Scripture wrong.

47 See, for example, Hudson, *Selections*, p. 164.

48 Chichele, *Register*, 3:190: "Adductus fuit eciam eodem die quidam dominus Johannes Galle, capellanus de civitate Londoniense, de heresi et errore notatus; qui tamen, interrogatus, nichil mali fatebatur, sed credidit, ut dixit, bene et catholice, et ut sancta mater ecclesia docet. Apud quem tamen inventus fuit quidam liber in vulgari de evangeliis bene scriptus, vocatus *Liber Nove Legis* in Anglico" ("There was also brought forth on the same day a certain Sir John Galle, chaplain of the city of London, suspect of heresy and error. But when interrogated, he confessed nothing wrong, saying that he believed well and Catholically and as Holy Mother Church teaches. However, there was found on him a book in the vernacular of the Gospels, well written, called in English *Book of the New Law*"). Bray, *Records*, 5:247, reads the name as "Gale." See below, pp. 109–110, for use of "New Law" among the suspects of Norfolk and Suffolk at this time.

49 Above, p. 83.

50 On Lyndwood, see C. R. Cheney, "William Lyndwood's *Provinciale*," in his *Medieval Texts and Studies* (Oxford 1973), pp. 158–84; and Brian Edwin Ferme, *Canon Law in Late Medieval England: A Study of William Lyndwood's "Provinciale" with Particular Reference to Testamentary Law* (Rome 1996). See also Emden, *BRUO*, 2:1191–93; Emden, *BRUC*, pp. 379–81; and R. H. Helmholz, "Lyndwood, William," in *OxDNB*. Lyndwood began acting as official by 1417, still in 1431 (Emden). The court was called "the Court of Arches," but Lyndwood did not hold the title of dean of St. Mary of the Arches (de Arcubus, i.e., Bow Street); it was held rather by

Thomas Bekington from at least 1423 to 1434. At this time, Bekington was the archbishop's chancellor, and official of Canterbury later (1433–38), and eventually bishop of Bath and Wells (1443–65) (Emden, *BRUO* 1:157–59). At one point during the convocation of 1428, both Master Lyndwood and Master Bekington were said to be busy *in curia de Arcubus* (Chichele, *Register*, 3:192).

51 Repingdon, *Register*, 1:2.

52 Hallum, *Register*, p. 139, no. 945.

53 See Helmholz, "Lyndwood."

54 Henry Chichele was admitted as bachelor of civil law at Oxford in 1389. He served as chancellor of Salisbury from 1404, vacated by May 1409, having in the meantime (October 4, 1407) been papally provided as bishop of St. David's; he became archbishop of Canterbury in 1414. See Emden, *BRUO* 1:410–12.

55 John Southam achieved his licentiate in civil law at Oxford by 1389; he took over as archdeacon of Oxford in 1404 from his uncle Thomas Southam (who chaired the parliament committee in 1388 examining Lollard preachers; see above), until his death in 1441. He was official of Lincoln from 1412 to 1417. He left a Latin Bible to Lincoln College upon his death. See Emden, *BRUO*, 3:1732–33.

56 Richard Fleming received his MA at Oxford by 1403 and he was a student in theology by 1408; he was on the committee that condemned the 267 propositions of Wyclif in 1411 (see Appendix O below); he was bishop of Lincoln until his death in 1431. In 1427 he founded Lincoln College at Oxford to help counteract the spread of heresy. See Emden, *BRUO* 3:697–99.

57 Chichele had been absent from England at the time of the synod or council of Oxford in 1407, but present, as bishop of St. David's, for the convocation of London in January 1409, where he was appointed delegate to the Council of Pisa; see Jeremy Catto, "Chichele, Henry," in *OxDNB*. The same is true of Bishop Hallum of Salisbury, who was also a canonist (he achieved a doctorate in canon law at Oxford by 1403); see Emden, *BRUO* 2:854–55; and R. N. Swanson, "Hallum, Robert," in *OxDNB*.

58 January "1408" means "1409" in modern usage, since our new year begins on January 1, whereas in the Middle Ages it started only on March 25.

59 Chichele, *Register*, 3:190: "Qui quidem dominus Johannes Galle missus fuit venerabili patri episcopo Londoniensi per ipsum et clericos suos examinandus" ("This Sir John Galle was sent to the venerable father bishop of London to be examined by him and his clerics"). Cf. Bray, *Records*, 5:247.

60 Chichele, *Register*, 3:191–92; see Kelly, "Lollard Inquisitions," p. 300 and n. 71.

61 See Kelly, "English Kings," pp. 222–23 n. 64.

62 Chichele, *Register*, 3:195–96; Bray, *Records*, 5:253.

63 Chichele, *Register*, 3:196–97; Bray, *Records*, 5:255

64 For this ad hoc position, see H. A. Kelly, *The Matrimonial Trials of Henry VIII* (Stanford CA 1976, repr. Eugene OR 2004), pp. 23, 80, 89–90.

65 Chichele, *Register*, 3:198–99: "Item quod idem dominus Radulphus postquam venit ad civitatem Londoniensem habuit penes se, ministravit, et tradidit diversis personis libros diversos Johannis Wyclif et alios in anglicis conscriptos doctrinam et opiniones erroneas dicti magistri Johannis Wyclif et dicti magistri Petri [Clerk] continentes.

Super quo articulo interrogatus dixit quod habuit unum librum vocatum *Trialogum* et eciam *Evangelia* Wyclif per duodecim annos elapsos, quos, ut dixit, vendidit cuidam capellano de comitatu Suth. vocato Johanni Botte, et aliter non credidit contenta in dicto articulo fore vera" ("Next, that the same Sir Ralph after he had come to the city of London had with him various books of John Wyclif and others written in English containing the erroneous teaching and opinions of the said Master John Wyclif and the said Master Peter, and that he provided and gave them to various persons. On being interrogated on this article, he said that during the past twelve years he had a book called *Trialogus* as well as Wyclif's *Evangelia*, which, he said, he sold to a chaplain of the county of Suffolk named John Botte; otherwise he did not believe the contents of the article to be true"). Cf. Bray, *Records*, 5:257 (which for *alios in anglicis conscriptos* mistakenly has *alias in anglicis conscriptos*). Article 7 has a different expression of elapsed time: Because of the foregoing and other causes "per viginti annos proximo jam elapsos et continue citra" Mungin is said to be suspected and publicly "infamed" of as a Lollard. I translate: "through the twenty years now elapsed before last year and continually since."

66 Chichele, *Register*, 3:198; Bray, *Records*, 5:257.

67 Chichele, *Register*, 3:205: Insuper [invenimus] quod publice asseruisses, tenuisses, et affirmasses quod non est licitum alicui Christiano bellare seu pugnare contra hereticos de regno Bohemie, item quod omnia essent communia et nulli liceret habere proprietatem, sufficienter et legitime contra te probatum fuisse et esse; teque [invenimus] libros diversos nonnullos hereses et errores continentes penes te scienter habuisse et detinuisse, ipsosque nec ordinario loci revelasse aut liberasse nec aliter eos secundum juris exigenciam destruxisse" ("Moreover [we have found] that it was and is sufficiently and legitimately proved against you that you publicly asserted, held, and affirmed that it is not licit for any Christian to war or fight against the heretics of the kingdom of Bohemia; also that [you asserted, etc.] that it is allowed to no one to have property; and [we have found] that you knowingly had and kept about your person divers books containing not a few heresies and errors, without revealing them to the ordinary of the place, or turning them over or destroying them in accord with the requirements of the law"). Cf. Bray, *Records*, 5:264 (for *ordinanio* read *ordinario*).

68 H. A. Kelly, "Inquisitorial Deviations and Cover-Ups: The Prosecutions of Margaret Porete and Guiard de Cressonessart, 1308–1310," *Speculum* 89:4 (2014) 936–73, n. 63. See Hostiensis (Henry of Susa, d. 1271), *In primum-sextum Decretalium librum commentaria*, 6 vols. (Venice 1581, repr. Turin 1965) on *Decretales Gregorii IX* 5.7.13 *Excommunicamus* §3 "velut heretici" [*CIC* 2:788] 5:38A no. 4: "Licet in veritate possit esse quod non est hereticus, tamen ac si esset, propter tantum contemptum ecclesie et clavium; ex quo sic condemnatus est, penas heretici incurrit" ("Although in truth it could be that he is not a heretic, nevertheless he is [treated] as if he were, because of such great contempt for the Church and the keys; on this account he is thus condemned, [and] he incurs the punishments of a heretic").

69 Chichele, *Register*, 3:205; Bray, *Records*, 5:264. Jacob, in his edition of Chichele, *Register*, 1:cxxxv, raises the question why Thomas Bagley was handed over to the secular court and Mungin was not. The answer, in my view, is not simply a matter of judicial discretion, but also of the nature of the charges. Bagley persistently denied the real presence (saying that the consecrated host is bread in nature and Christ *in figura*), among other things (Convocation of 1431, in Bray, *Records*, 5:285–86). In contrast, the two opinions of Mungin proved against him by witnesses, that it was

not lawful to take up arms against heretics in Bohemia, and that property could not lawfully be held privately, would not rate as heresies but as errors, and classify him as a favorer of heresy rather than a heretic; and the same is true of keeping the wrong kind of books. At the 1382 Blackfriars meeting, one can readily see the differences between the ten propositions denominated as heresies and the fourteen ranked as errors. See the English version given in Foxe, *Acts and Monuments*, ed. Pratt, 3:21–22. I take up the charge of vehement suspicion below when dealing with Lyndwood.

70 Wyclif, *Latin Works*, vol. 8, *Latin Sermons*, part 1, *Super Evangelia dominicalia*; part 2, *Super Evangelia de sanctis*.

71 For the *Opus*, see Anne Hudson and Anthony Kenny, "Wyclif, John (d. 1384)," in *OxDNB*.

72 See Beryl Smalley, "John Wyclif's *Postilla super totam Bibliam*," *Bodleian Library Record* 4 (1953) 186–205.

73 See Appendix O.

74 Kelly, "Trial Procedures," p. 20.

75 Workman, *John Wyclif*, 2:319.

76 Bray, *Records*, 5:281–91.

77 *The Register of John Stafford, Bishop of Bath and Wells, 1425–1443*, ed. Thomas Scott Holmes, 2 vols. (London 1915–16).

78 Repingdon, *Register*, 1:57 (December 1405); see Emden, *BRUO*, 3:1750–52.

79 R. G. Davies, "Stafford, John," in *OxDNB*.

80 John Stafford, *Register*, 1:103–8, no. 332. The heading reads: "Mandatum contra sortilogos, falsos juratores sive perjuros, atque Lollardos, vel libros Lollardie vel alios in lingua vulgari conscriptos."

81 Ibid., p. 105. Here is the context, pp. 105–6: "hujusmodi reatu culpabiles sanctorum patrum constitutionibus et generalium consiliorum auctoritate sunt majoris excommunicacionis vinculo innodati" ("those guilty of such a crime are bound by the bond of major excommunication from the constitutions of the holy fathers and the authority of general councils"), and every prelate is required both by canon law and the deliberation of the general council last celebrated at London to eradicate such crimes in his own diocese: "labem tam odibilem apud Deum piacolorum terribili ulcioni (quam avertat Altissimus) verissimiliter proximorum quilibet tenetur prelatus, tam ex canonis precepto quam ex deliberacione consilii generalis Londonii ultimo celebrati, in sua diocesi purgare et cum omni diligencia tollere festinanter" ("this offense, so hateful to God, [liable] to the terrible vengeance of punishments likely soon to come (which may the Most High avert), every prelate is bound, both by the precept of the canon and the deliberation of the general council last held at London, in his own diocese to purge and with all diligence to speedily remove").

82 Ibid., p. 107.

83 De Hamel, *The Book*, p. 178. Deanesly, *Lollard Bible*, p. 328, says much the same thing, by omitting the words *ad examen*, perhaps because it was not supplied to her by her correspondent. This correspondent apparently did not know of the 1441 entry in Stafford's register (see below).

84 Emden, *BRUO* 2:1192.

85 Lyndwood, *Provinciale* 5.4 (*De magistris*), [chap. 3] (*Periculosa*), p. 286. See Appendix Q for the entire constitution and commentary.

86 Lyndwood, *Provinciale* 5.4.[3], p. 286, note c.

87 Ibid.

88 See *DMLBS*. The earliest citation is 1302, meaning "lecture."

89 Lyndwood, *Provinciale* 5.4.[2], *Quia insuper*, s.v. *legatur*: "Per viam doctrinationis, secus per viam examinationis" (p. 284, note g).

90 Ibid.: "Vel potes intelligere de simplici lectura, secundum ea que continentur, *Extra.*, e cap. *Cum ex injuncto* in principio sub parte decisa [i.e., in the excised part of *Decretales Gregorii IX* 5.7.12, *CIC* 2:784–85], ubi recitatur quod in urbe et diocesi Metensis laicorum et mulierum multitudo non modica evangelium, epistolas Pauli, psalterium, *Moralia Job*, et plures alios libros sibi fecit in Gallico sermone transferri, translationem hujusmodi adeo acceptans, ut secretis conventionibus talia inter se laici et mulieres eructare presumerent, et sibi invicem predicare." The decretal was issued by Innocent III in 1199, and forbade laypeople to preach and hold secret conventicles. It became part of general canon law in 1234 by being included in the *Decretales*.

91 *CJC* 2:1677, Innocent III, *Cum ex injuncto* (1199), *Decretales* 5.7.12, "Cum ex injuncto," *et infra*: "Licet autem desiderium intelligendi divinas Scripturas, et secundum eas studium adhortandi, reprehendendum non sit, sed potius commendendum, in eo tamen apparent quidem laici merito arguendi, quod occulta conventicula celebrant, officium predicationis Christi sibi usurpant, sacerdotum simplicitatem eludunt, et eorum consortium aspernantur qui talibus non inherent" ("Although the desire to understand the divine Scriptures and to encourage their study is not to be reprehended but rather commended, it appears that certain laymen are to be rebuked in this, that they hold secret conventicles, usurp to themselves Christ's office of preaching, ridicule the simplicity of priests, and spurn those who do not join them in such things").

92 Lyndwood, *Provinciale* 5.4.[3], p. 286, s.v. *beato Hjeronymo textum*, note d.

93 Ibid., s.v. *libri*, note m: "Scilicet, de novo compilandi, ut patet infra, versu sequente. Secus si hoc fiat per modum sermonis publici, exponendo textum in lingua vulgari."

94 Ibid.: "Et quod dicit *per viam libri*, intelligere potes sic, vicelicet, ut inde conficiat librum continentem tota Biblia. Apellatione namque *libri* simpliciter sumpti continetur liber completus et integer, et non secundum partes numerales, prout sepius unum volumen dividitur in plures libros, ut patet in Bibliis."

95 Ibid.: "vel potes intelligere sic, ut scilicet unum librum particularem textus Bibliorum transferat. Nam talis particularis translatio poterit dici *libellus*, ut sequitur." The mandate therefore does not refer to translating "any passage or phrase from the Bible," as it is taken by Tombs, *The English*, p. 131.

96 Ibid., s.v. *aut tractatus*, note n.

97 Lyndwood, *Provinciale*, 5.4.[3], s.v. *noviter . . . compositus* (p. 286 note q): "et ex hoc . . . apparet quod libros, libellos, vel tractatus in Anglicis vel alio idiomate prius translatos de textu Scripture legere non est prohibitum" ("and from this it appears that it is not forbidden to lecture on books, booklets, or treatises in English or another language translated before this time, which render the text of Scripture").

98 Ibid., 5.4.[2], s.v. *tempore suo* (p. 284): "Scilicet postquam incepit hereses suas seminare usque ad mortem ejusdem."

99 Ussher, *Historica dogmatica*, p. 164: "Unde intelligimus ante Wiclevi tempora Scripturas in linguam vernaculam translatas extitisse, neque etiam earum lectionem prohibitam esse."

100 Lyndwood, *Provinciale* 5.4.[3], s.v. *approbata* (p. 286 note x): "Ratio est, quia licet nudus textus Scripture fuerit translatus, potest tamen transferens in translatione errare. Vel si librum, libellum, aut tractatum compilaverit, potest, ut frequentur accidit, cum veris falsa et erronea admiscere."

101 Ibid., s.v. *concilium provinciale*, note u.

102 Ibid., s.v. *res exegerit*, note t.

103 Ibid., s.vv. *excommunicationis pena* and *fautor heresis*, notes r, z. For the sort of offenses that could bring conviction of vehement suspicion of heresy, see Lyndwood, *Provinciale* 5.5.[4], *Finaliter*, s.v. *vehementer suspecti* (p. 302, col. b, note n), spelled out in my essay, "Thomas More on Inquisitorial Due Process," *English Historical Review* 123 (2008) 847–94, p. 880 n. 139. Lyndwood gives a long list of persons who can be called fautors of heresy in his comments on the previous 1407 constitution, *Quia insuper*, 5.5.[2], s.v. *fautor heresis*, p. 285, note g.

104 Lyndwood on *Periculosa*, s.v. *erroris*, p. 286, note a: "Quia prestat occasionem alios inducendi in errorem, qui ex talis libri, libelli, vel tractatus lectura inficerentur" ("Because it gives occasion of inducing others into error, being infected by a lecture from such a book, booklet, or treatise").

105 Bray, *Records*, 5:341–45, 347–48. Arundel also called the 1407 Oxford council a convocation (Bray, 4:308–9).

106 Lyndwood, *Provinciale*, Appendix, pp. 73–74: "Hereticks, Lollars, and Fawtowrs of yanie [*sic*]."

107 Mandate of Archbishop Chichele from the London provincial council, October 8, 1434, in John Stafford, *Register*, 2:170–72 (no. 509).

108 Bray, *Records*, 5:347–48. The relevant article, numbered by Bray as 10, reads "wilful brenners of houses, usurers [the missing text should go here], thieves and robbers and ravishers, falsaries of the pope's letters." As far as I can see, Bray does not specify his source for this part of the record of the 1434 council.

109 John Thomson, *Later Lollards*, p. 179. Thomson's conclusion, that though we cannot tell whether the charges of Lollardy against him were proved, "his possession of vernacular Scriptures does hint that he may have had sympathies and connexions with Lollards" (p. 180), is surprising; rather it was his possession of Wyclif's works that would give rise to such a suspicion. Robert Lutton, *Lollardy and Orthodox Religion in Pre-Reformation England: Reconstruction Piety* (Woodbridge 2006), says that Boreham "admitted to owning Wycliffite books, including four vernacular Gospels" (p. 152), which, of course, holds true only if one agrees that EV and LV are Wycliffite.

110 John Stafford, *Register*, 2:267–68, no. 834. For the text and my translation, see Appendix R "The Admonition *Periculum animarum* of John Stafford, Bishop of Bath and Wells, 1441."

111 The text of the execution order is also given in Appendix R.

112 John Stafford, *Register*, 2:173–80, no. 511. For Peckham's letter, see Lyndwood, *Provinciale*, Appendix, pp. 28–30; in the margins are given the page numbers in Lyndwood's treatise where he excerpts paragraphs and comments on them.

113 Gasquet, *Old English Bible*, p. 145: it was "written probably not later than the year 1450," and printed "about the year 1530" at the wish of the current abbess.

114 *The Myroure of Oure Ladye*, ed. John Henry Blunt, EETS e.s. 19 (London 1873), p. viii. Workman, *John Wyclif*, 2:196, accepts 1415, but the *Middle English Dictionary* (*MED*) places it ca. 1450. This matter is treated by Deanesly, *Lollard Bible*, pp. 339–40. See also Vincent Gillespie, "The Mole in the Vineyard: Wyclif at Syon in the Fifteenth Century," in *Text and Controversy from Wyclif to Bale: Essays in Honour of Anne Hudson*, ed. Helen Bart and Ann M. Hutchison (Turnhout 2005), pp. 131–61; Gillespie speaks of "the Arundelian prohibition" against "owning" and "producing" vernacular Scripture (pp. 159–60).

115 *Myroure*, p. 71. Cited by Gasquet, "Pre-Reformation English Bible," p. 147; Gasquet, *Old English Bible*, pp. 145–46. Here is the text in the original spelling: "Forasmuch as it is forboden under paine of cursinge that no man shulde have ne drawe eny texte of Holy Scripture into Englisshe without license of the bishop diocesan, and in diverse places of youre service ar suche texts of Holy Scripture, therefore I asked and have license of our bishop to drawe such thinges into Englisshe to your gostly comforte and profit, so that both our consience in the drawinge and youres in the havinge may be the more sewre and clere."

116 *Myroure*, p. 3. Cited by Gasquet in the *Old English Bible*, p. 146, in a section added to the 1894 article.

117 Reginald Pecock, *The Repressor of Over Much Blaming of the Clergy*, ed. Churchill Babington, 2 vols., Rolls Series no. 19 (London 1860), 1:xxviii. Exceptions, Babington says, occur when Pecock seems to be quoting from memory, as in the first sixty pages of the *Repressor*. There is an extended quotation of LV Romans 2.1, 11–23 in part 1, chap. 12, pp. 63–64; and Babington singles out part 5, chap. 1, 2:476–84, where there are extensive citations of LV: James 1.27; 2 Pet. 2.1–3; 1 Tim. 4.1–7; 2 Tim. 3.1–10; Titus 1.10–14; 2 Pet. 3.3–5; Jude [2.]11–13, 16–23; Col. 2.8, 16–23; Matt. 24.9–11; Mark 13.5–7; Matt. 24.21–29; Mark 13.19–24.

118 Pecock, *Repressor* 1.20, 1:119. Here is the original spelling, except for i/y, u/v, i/j: "Also thou schalt not finde expressely in Holy Scripture that the Newe Testament schulde be write in Englisch tunge to laymen, or in Latin tunge to clerks; neither that the Oold Testament should be write in English tunge to laymen or in Latin tunge to clerkis; and yit ech of these governauncis thou wolte hold to be leeful and to be a meritorie, vertuose, moral deed for to thereby deserve grace and glorie, and to be the service of God, and therefore to be the lawe of God." The first part of this passage is cited by Deanesly, *Lollard Bible*, p. 362, as if from the *Book of Faith*. Some of her other citations of Pecock are faulty as well. On p. 361, n. 2 should refer to p. 174 of the *Book of Faith*; the quotation at the bottom of p. 361 has a note indicator ("2" instead of "4") but no corresponding note, and I have not yet found the source of the text. On p. 362, n. 3 should be to the *Repressor*, not to the *Book of Faith*.

119 Sarah James, "'Langages, whose reules ben not writen': Pecock and the Uses of the Vernacular," in *Vernacularity in England and Wales, c. 1300–1550*, ed. Elisabeth Salter and Helen Wicker (Turnhout 2011), pp. 101–17, notes Pecock's similarities to the author of *Five and Twenty Books* (GP) on this score (p. 107–9).

120 Pecock, *Repressor* 1.7, 1:37; Gasquet, *Old English Bible*, p. 148. Here is the original spelling: "This what I have now seid of and to Bible-men, I have not seid undir this entent and meening, as that I schulde feele to be unleeful laymen for to reede in the Bible and for to studie and leerne therin, with help and counseil of wise and weel leerned clerkis and with licence of her governour the bischop."

121 Reginald Pecock, *The Reule of Crysten Religioun*, ed. William Cabell Greet, EETS o.s. 171 (London 1927), prologue, p. 17 (respelled, like the next passage).

122 Ibid., p. 18.

123 See Kirsty Campbell, *The Call to Read: Reginald Pecock's Books and Textual Communities* (Notre Dame IN 2010), p. 211.

124 For an excellent summary, see Wendy Scase, "Pecock, Reginald," in *OxDNB*.

125 Nothing pertinent is to be found in the surviving records of convocations held under Archbishop Stafford. See Bray, *Records*, 6:1–60.

126 Hudson, *Premature Reformation*, p. 443, citing F. Donald Logan, "Archbishop Thomas Bourgchier Revisited," in *The Church in Pre-Reformation Society: Essays in Honour of F. R. H. Du Boulay*, ed. Caroline M. Barron and Christopher Harper-Bill (Woodbridge 1985), pp. 170–88; the text of the *monicio* is given on pp. 187–88. I have emended the beginning words of the mandate, *Inter solitudines*, to *Inter solicitudines*, with confirmation from Professor Logan that this is the correct reading.

127 FM 1:lxiii, MS no. 158 (at the time owned by Lord Ashburnham); Gasquet, *Old English Bible*, pp. 148–49. The Bible in question is now at Manchester, John Rylands University Library MS 77; described by N. R. Ker, *Medieval Manuscripts in British Libraries*, 5 vols. (Oxford 1969–2002), 3:404; and Dove, *First English Bible*, p. 295, and see her discussion, pp. 47–53.

128 Hanna, "English Biblical Texts," pp. 150–51, expanded in his *London Literature*, pp. 308–10; cf. Deanesly, *Lollard Bible*, p. 336. Somerset, "Censorship," 255–56, discusses the fact that the statement was subsequently inked out.

129 Gasquet, *Old English Bible*, p. 149.

130 Hanna, *London Literature*, p. 308.

131 Caroline Barron, review of *London Literature*, by Ralph Hanna, in *Journal of British Studies* 45 (2006) 876–78. She suggests as a possibility for the woman who bought the Bible Jane Boughton, the second wife of the mayor of London John Yonge, whom he married in 1466/7; Jane's mother Joan was later condemned as a heretic, admirer of John Wyclif, and burned in 1494. See Henry Summerson, "Boughton, Joan (c.1414–1494)," in *OxDNB*.

132 Contrary, then, to Anne Hudson, "Wyclif Texts in Fifteenth-Century London," in her *Studies in the Transmission of Wyclif's Writings* (Aldershot 2008), chap. 15, pp. 3–4, who suggests that the vetting occurred after Ive succeeded Eborall as master.

133 Sheila Lindenbaum, "London After Arundel: Learned Rectors and the Strategies of Orthodox Reform," in *After Arundel: Religious Writing in Fifteenth-Century England*, ed. Vincent Gillespie and Kantik Ghosh (Turnhout 2011), pp. 187–208, at p. 192.

134 Richard Rex, *Henry VIII and the English Reformation*, 2nd ed. (Houndmills 2006), p. 86, citing Imogen Luxton, "The Lichfield Court Book: A Postscript," *Bulletin of the Institute of Historical Research* 44 (1971) 120–25, p. 124.

135 Shannon McSheffrey and Norman Tanner, *Lollards of Coventry, 1486–1522* (Cambridge 2003), p. 157: "Dicit quod vicarius jam mortuus, videlicet Doctor Preston, habuit librum ab ea de Nova Lege, quem restituit eidem denuo. Et favebat eidem et ceteris, ut asserit" (they give a translation on p. 160). See their introduction, pp. 25–30. They observe that "neither wills nor the ownership of English scriptures and devotional works are good indicators of heretical leanings in this period" (p. 30). See also Shannon McSheffrey, "Heresy, Orthodoxy and English Vernacular Religion,

1480–1525," *Past and Present* 186 (February 2005) 47–80, who notes that, while there was some official opposition to the use of English, shown notably by Bishop Hales of Coventry in 1486, when he forced two men to abjure the use of English prayers (p. 52), she agrees with Eamon Duffy's assessment that in general the use of the vernacular was being encouraged by the authorities in the years around 1500 (p. 51), citing Duffy, *The Stripping of the Altars: Traditional Religion in England, 1400–1580* (New Haven CT 1992), pp. 53–87. Duffy wrongly reports that there had been an earlier ban on English versions of the New Testament (p. 79), and he concludes that English Bible reading required an episcopal license (p. 80). It is true, however, that at least some persons believed the latter to be the case, as we have seen in the case of Syon Abbey.

136 Rex, *Henry VIII*, p. 86.

137 Gasquet, *Old English Bible*, p. 142.

138 Stephen Morrison, *A Late-Fifteenth-Century Dominical Cycle*, EETS o.s. 337–38 (London 2012), pp. lvii–lx.

139 Ibid., p. lx.

140 Gasquet, *Old English Bible*, pp. 143–44.

141 Diarmaid MacCulloch, *A History of Christianity: The First Three Thousand Years* (London 2009; repr. 2010), p. 569.

142 Ibid., p. 1061 n. 30.

143 Workman, *John Wyclif*, 2:196.

144 Foxe, *Acts and Monuments*, 3:538–39.

145 Ibid., 3:587–88, 595; see Deanesly, *Lollard Bible*, p. 358.

146 Foxe, *Acts and Monuments*, 3:596–97; see Deanesly, *Lollard Bible*, p. 358.

147 Foxe, *Acts and Monuments*, 3:599–600.

148 Ibid., 4:133–35; for these cases, see McSheffrey and Tanner, *Lollards of Coventry*, pp. 63–87.

149 Foxe, *Acts and Monuments*, 4:178

150 Ibid., 4:184, 186.

151 Ibid., 4:221–43.

152 De Hamel, *The Book*, pp. 186–87.

153 Charles Lethbridge Kingsford, ed., *Chronicles of London* (Oxford 1905), p. 211.

154 A. H. Thomas and I. D. Thornley, eds., *The Great Chronicle of London* (London 1938), p. 264.

155 Thomson, *Later Lollards*, p. 157, says that these four abjurations were among nine in all that took place in London in 1496.

156 Ibid., pp. 88–89, citing the unpublished register of Richard Fox, bishop of Winchester, 1501–28. See also Margaret Aston, *Lollards and Reformers: Images and Literacy in Late Medieval Religion* (London 1984), pp. 147, 199.

157 Foxe, *Acts and Monuments*, 4:217. Newbury is presumably the town in Berkshire, in the diocese of Salisbury. At the beginning, Foxe says that he is drawing on "the register of Sir John Longland," and at the end he says: "And thus much out of the registers of London," before turning to "the registers and records of Lincoln." John

Longland was dean of Salisbury from 1514 until his promotion to bishop of Lincoln in 1521 (papal provision of March 20, consecration on May 5).

158 Foxe, *Acts and Monuments*, 4:216. De Hamel elaborates upon this thus: Brewster "claimed (perhaps quite truthfully) that he was not even able to read the 'little book of Scripture in English . . . almost worn for age,' which was found in his possession" (*The Book*, p. 187). Foxe gives an account of Brewster and Sweeting together, pp. 180–81, and of Sweeting separately on pp. 214–15, followed by one on Brewster, pp. 215–16.

159 Foxe, *Acts and Monuments*, 4:206–7.

160 Ibid., 4:228; noted by Shannon McSheffrey, *Gender and Heresy: Women and Men in Lollard Communities, 1420–1530* (Philadelphia 1995), pp. 96 and 202 n. 96.

161 Foxe, *Acts and Monuments*, 4:229.

162 Ibid., 4:228.

163 Ibid., 4:232.

164 Ibid., 4:233.

165 Ibid.

166 Ibid., 4:232, 242. On p. 231, Butler is said to have been detected by John Clerke, though for what we are not told.

167 Ibid., 4:230. In another case, an informer named Roger Dods reported a group of people in the house of John Brabant for "reading a certain English book of Scripture" (ibid., 4:237). J. Patrick Hornbeck II, "*Wycklyffes Wycket* and Eucharistic Theology: Cases from Sixteenth-Century Winchester," in Bose and Hornbeck, *Wycliffite Controversies*, pp. 279–94, overreads this by saying that the accusation was "of reading an unauthorized English translation of a biblical text" (p. 283). He cites the incident from the 1583 edition of Foxe, p. 834, misreading the table there as limiting the accusation as against Brabant alone. See the EEBO reproduction of Foxe 1583, vol. 2, image 37.

168 Thomson, *Later Lollards*, pp. 242–43.

169 Norman Tanner, ed., *Kent Heresy Proceedings*, Kent Archaeological Society, Kent Records, 26 (Gloucester 1997), p. 53; Lutton, *Lollardy and Orthodox Religion*, pp. 159–60.

170 De Hamel, *The Book*, p. 187.

171 Dove, *First English Bible*, p. 55.

Chapter 7. The End of the Story

1 Thomas More, *Dialogue Concerning Heresies* 3.14 (pp. 314–15). I modernize the spelling throughout.

2 More, *Dialogue* 3.14 (p. 316): "And therewith I fet[ched] him forth the *Constitutions Provincial* with Lyndwood thereupon, and turned him to the place in the title *De magistris*."

3 Ibid.

4 Ibid., 3.15 (p. 317).

5 Deanesly, *Lollard Bible*, pp. 6–7 n. 2, 116, 331, 371. For the latter, which is Manchester, John Rylands Library MS Eng. 81, see Dove, *First English Bible*, pp. 53–54, 295.

6 Gasquet, *Old English Bible*, pp. 144–45.

7 More, *Dialogue* 3.15 (pp. 317–19).

8 Ibid. (p. 330).

9 Cambridge, Corpus Christi College, Parker Library MS 147 (CCCC 147; FM MS S of LV), with annotations in the margin identified by Archbishop Matthew Parker as in the hand of Geoffrey Blyth, bishop of Coventry and Litchfield (1503–30).

10 Arthur Ogle, *The Tragedy of the Lollards' Tower: The Case of Richard Hunne, with Its Aftermath in the Reformation Parliament, 1529–33: A Review of Events from the Downfall of Wolsey to the Birth of Elizabeth* (Oxford 1949), p. 128.

11 E. Jeffries Davis, "The Authorities for the Case of Richard Hunne," *English Historical Review* 30 (1915) 477–88. Miss Davis commissioned Mrs. W. J. Harrison to inspect the manuscript, and she reported that some of the implicated passages were not marked, and that there were marks against many other passages not used against Hunne; her conclusions are cited by Ogle, *Tragedy*, p. 128.

12 See Dove, *First English Bible*, pp. 235–36. She says that the passages of GP on which articles 2–4, 7–9, and 11 are based are not marked or annotated, and four of the passages that are annotated are not referred to in the articles.

13 Ogle, *Tragedy*, pp. 117–29. On inspection and reinspection, he finds that eleven of the thirteen passages are marked, all but nos. 6 and 7, and he has a plausible explanation for this. W. R. Cooper, "Richard Hunne," *Reformation* 1 (1996) 221–51, finds Ogle's case "powerfully argued" that it was the Bible used at the trial (p. 247).

14 I treat the case briefly in my essay "Thomas More on Inquisitorial Due Process," pp. 864–65, but I give far too much credence to More's recollection of it, as does Gasquet. For bibliography on Hunne, see John Fines, "Hunne, Richard," in *OxDNB*. Fines does not mention the study by J. Duncan M. Derrett, "The Affairs of Richard Hunne and Friar Standish," in *The Apology of Sir Thomas More, Knight* (1533), ed. J. B. Trapp, *Complete Works of St. Thomas More*, vol. 9 (New Haven CT 1979), pp. 215–46; or Cooper, "Richard Hunne." An important new study has come out since, G. W. Bernard, *The Late Medieval English Church: Vitality and Vulnerability Before the Break with Rome* (New Haven CT 2012), chap. 1, "The Hunne Affair," pp. 1–16. He shows that Cooper is mistaken in thinking that the coroner's inquiry extended into 1516; it lasted only two days, convening on December 5, with a verdict of murder reported on December 6, 1514. The king's council reviewed the matter in February 1515, and in November the king ordered a not guilty plea of Horsey to be accepted (see below); the order was put into movement in February 1516, and Horsey was released by the king's bench in April (Bernard, pp. 12–13, 241). The *Enquirie* pamphlet cited by Cooper (see below), at sig. c 3r–v, reproduces a letter from Bishop FitzJames to Cardinal Wolsey asking his intercession for Horsey: "my poor Chancellor now in ward and indicted by an untrue quest for the death of Richard Hunne, upon the only accusation of Charles Joseph made by pain and durance" (Cooper, "Richard Hunne," p. 242).

15 For Horsey, see Emden *BRUO* 2:967: he received his doctorate in canon law from Oxford by 1501. He had been FitzJames's official and vicar-general when he was bishop of Rochester from 1502 and bishop of Chichester from 1504, and probably performed the same functions when FitzJames became bishop of London in 1506, and certainly did so in 1510. He vacated his position as archdeacon of London in March 1514, when he probably became chancellor. Emden lists him as chancellor of

the bishop of London from 1515 to 1531, but provides no documentation; he does not treat of the Hunne affair.

16 Foxe, *Acts and Monuments*, 4:183–84.

17 Ibid., p. 184.

18 For the jury's verdict, see Bernard, *Late Medieval*, p. 12. For an English translation of the jury's verdict, see Foxe, *Acts and Monuments*, 4:196–97, taken from Hall's *Chronicle*, taken in turn from a pamphlet published in Antwerp around 1537, *The Enquirie and Verdite of the Quest panneld of the death of Richard Hune wich was founde hanged in the Lolars tower*. See the EEBO version, STC / 53:12; and see the edited version in Cooper, "Richard Hunne," pp. 237–45 (omitting the preface, "To the Reader"). The supposed narrative of the jury at the beginning is doubtless the invention of the compiler, and the depositions are probably from the hearing conducted by the king's council at Barnard's Castle in February. The first of them is dated February 14, 1515 (omitted in the Hall-Foxe version). See Bernard, *Late Medieval*, p. 8.

19 Foxe, *Acts and Monuments*, 4:186.

20 Ibid., pp. 208–13. For Man's trial, see my "Thomas More on Inquisitorial Due Process," pp. 864, 888.

21 Cooper, "Richard Hunne," p. 241, *Enquirie and Verdite*, sig. c 1v, "Master Commensarie"; corrected in Foxe, *Acts and Monuments*, 4:194, "Master Commissary." Cooper says, "The bishop's commensary at this time was Dr. Thomas Head, who had played a prominent role in John Baker's examination for heresy" (p. 251 n. 53), but he does not give a source. Foxe does not say so (4:173–78); the only official he mentions here (p. 178) is Thomas Bennet, doctor of law, as FitzJames's chancellor and vicar-general. Neither Head nor Bennet is recorded by Emden as having studied at Oxford or Cambridge.

22 Foxe, *Acts and Monuments*, 4:186–87.

23 Ibid., p. 186; Ogle, "Dr. Gasquet and the Old English Bible," pp. 292–96. Cooper, "Richard Hunne," pp. 245–47, gives generally briefer passages, citing the GP as it appears in CCCC 147.

24 As noted above, this is simply a translation of Augustine, *De doctrina Christiana* 3.16.

25 Ogle, *Tragedy*, pp. 124–25. He says that the author of GP, whom he takes to be John Purvey, was writing with the authority of St. Augustine at this point (he does not say that he was actually translating Augustine), and says that the passage in question "is so innocent that it had not occurred to Bishop Blythe as calling for animadversion" (see below), but "Head seizes upon it as offering just the thing he wants."

26 See McSheffrey and Tanner, *Lollards of Coventry*, pp. 2–11.

27 Andrew A. Chibi, "Blyth, Geoffrey," in *OxDNB*.

28 Ogle, *Tragedy*, p. 129.

29 FM 1:45. The note is not reported in Dove's edition, *Earliest Advocates*, p. 64, line 2225.

30 See J. Fines, "The Post-Mortem Condemnation for Heresy of Richard Hunne," *English Historical Review* 78 (1963) 528–31; they are analyzed by Cooper, "Richard Hunne," pp. 229–30.

31 "And that the seid Roger seid also to him this day, that the seid book was wont to lie in St. Marget Cherche in Brigstreet sometime a month togidders, when he was clerke there" (Fines, "Post-Mortem," p. 531).

32 John Davis (Fines, "Post-Mortem," p. 530): "Deponit quod legit [*Ussher*: Ricardus ex eodem Prologo] coram dicto deponente congruentiam et rationem quare Biblia potuit transferri in linguam Anglicanam: quae congruentiae et rationes continentur in fine ejusdem prologi" ("He deposes that [Richard from the same prologue] read before the said deponent the fittingness and reason why the Bible could be translated into the English tongue, which fittingnesses and reasons are contained at the end of the said Prologue").

33 See Emden, *BRUO* 3:2135–36, "Yonge, John": he was consecrated bishop *in partibus infidelium* (viz., to the extinct see of Callipolis, in Thrace) on June 13, 1513, and was collated to the archdeaconry of London on March 28, 1514. He incepted his doctorate in theology at Oxford in 1504. See also Andrew A. Chibi, "Yonge, John (1462/3–1526), Bishop and College Head," in *OxDNB*.

34 Bishop Young (Fines, "Post-Mortem," p. 530): "Depositio . . . quod Ricardus se dixit coram dicto deponente congruentiam et rationem quare Biblia illa potuit transferre in linguam Anglicanam: quae congruentiae et rationes continentur in fine hujusmodi prologi." As it stands here, Young's testimony does not hang together grammatically. To make it grammatical, we could do this: "quod Ricardus se dixit coram dicto deponente [habere] congruentiam et rationem quare Biblia illa potuit transferre in linguam Anglicanam"—that is, "Richard said that he had fittingness and reason why he could translate that Bible into the English tongue." But presumably Young intended to say the same thing as Davis.

35 It is interesting to see that John Fines in his *OxDNB* entry on Hunne says that the posthumous trial "found that he had denied transubstantiation and the veneration of saints; his abiding interest in the vernacular scriptures was incontestable circumstantial evidence."

36 Atwater was consecrated just the month before, on November 12.

37 The Latin text of the bishop's sentence is given by Foxe in a footnote, *Acts and Monuments*, 4:188–90. No notice is taken in the sentence of the fact that there were two sets of articles, and that Hunne died before the second set was leveled.

38 There is an LV New Testament (with no prologue) recently owned by Dr. Steve Sohmer of Los Angeles (passing in 2011 to an anonymous buyer), which likewise belonged to Thomas Downe, according to the inscription on the flyleaf: "Iste liber constat Thome Downe de haloghton." As de Hamel, *The Book*, p. 336, notes, the association of Downe with both Bibles is tantalizing; but in the caption that he gives to a plate of the manuscript on p. 186, no. 132, he goes too far in saying that the Sohmer Bible "was perhaps the actual manuscript described in the trial of Richard Hunne in 1514." See also Dove, *First English Bible*, p. 126 n. 113 and p. 281. The book of Gospels that was brought to Hunne in prison was not said to be in English. Downe is not to be confused with or related to Master John Downam (as is done by Cooper, "Richard Hunne," pp. 229–30), who served as FitzJames's promoter in Hunne's trial before his death and administered the articles against him, as we read in FitzJames's sentence, Foxe, *Acts and Monuments*, 4:189n (he perhaps was the John Donham, Donam, or Dounham who incepted his doctorate in theology at Oxford in 1491; see Emden, *BRUO* 1:585). A Dr. John Dowman was the vicar in spirituals for

the diocese of Winchester who served as promoter in the trial of Thomas Denis in 1512; see Hornbeck, *What Is a Lollard?* p. 3.

39 See Andrew Chibi, *Henry VIII's Conservative Scholar: Bishop John Stokesley and the Divorce, Royal Supremacy, and Doctrinal Reform* (Bern 1997), p. 100: Stokesley replying to Archbishop Cranmer in 1535, refusing to participate in the preparation of a vernacular Bible.

40 More, *Dialogue* 3.16 (p. 331).

41 Ibid. (pp. 331–32).

42 Ibid. (p. 332).

43 Ibid. (p. 339).

44 Ibid. (p. 340).

45 Ibid. (p. 341).

46 Ibid. For More's later views on the English Bible, see Brendan Bradshaw, "The Controversial Sir Thomas More," *Journal of Ecclesiastical History* 36 (1985) 535–69, at p. 560; and Eamon Duffy, "'The comen knowen multitude of crysten men': *A Dialogue Concerning Heresies* and the Defence of Christendom," in *The Cambridge Companion to Thomas More*, ed. George M. Logan (Cambridge 2011), pp. 191–215, at p. 208.

47 Martin was born around 1542 and in 1557 he became a fellow of the new St. John's College at Oxford. After obtaining his MA, he lectured there in Greek (1564–68). In 1569 he joined William Allen in his English College at Douai, and received a bachelor's degree in theology in 1573 (being also ordained priest that year), and a licentiate in theology in 1575. In May 1576 he started lecturing in Hebrew at Douai, but in November he led the first group of students to the English College in Rome, where he stayed for eighteen months, until summoned by Allen back to the northern English College (now transplanted to Rheims). He arrived in July 1578 and began his work of translation in October, finishing it in 1580. Martin's longtime classmate Edmund Campion entered the Jesuits after receiving his theology degree with Martin in 1573, but Martin himself never joined the order. See the accounts by Parks, "Life and Works"; and McCoog, "Martin, Gregory." Parks says that Allen announced the Bible project in September ("Life and Works," p. xvi), and McCoog gives September as the *terminus a quo*. But the diary entry cited above (Chapter 2 n. 16) says that he started "Octobris 16 vel circiter"; granted, the entry is in the margin so it must have been put in as an afterthought. Allen, in a letter of September 16, does not precisely announce the project, but says that they will undertake it if the pope thinks it should be done. See *The Letters and Memorials of William Cardinal Allen (1532–1594)*, ed. Fathers of the Congregation of the London Oratory, intro. Thomas Francis Knox (London 1882), no. 25, pp. 52–67, at 65–66; after outlining the great need for an orthodox vernacular Bible, he says: "Certe nos si Sua Sanctitas faciendum judicabit, id etiam agemus ut fideliter, pure, et genuine secundum approbatam ecclesiae editionem Biblia vertantur, cum ad hanc rem viros jam habeamus aptissimos" ("Certainly, if His Holiness judges that it should be done, we ourselves will see to it that the Bible be translated as faithfully, purely, and genuinely [as possible] according to the approved edition, since we now have men very capable for this task").

48 See Chapter 2 n. 16 above for different accounts of Martin's time of translation. See the *OxDNB* entries on Gregory Martin (Thomas M. McCoog), William Allen (Eamon Duffy), and Richard Bristow (Peter E. B. Harris). McCoog says that the

work of translation was Martin's, while Allen, Bristow, and William Reynolds "were involved primarily as revisers." Harris says that "Bristow was responsible, with Gregory Martin, for much of the translation." Duffy says that Allen "raised the finance and supplied many of the doctrinal notes" for Martin's translation.

49 The preface could be a joint composition by Martin, Allen, and others; it speaks of "our translation," perhaps meaning to include the annotations.

50 *The New Testament of Jesus Christ, Translated Faithfully into English out of the Authentical Latin . . . in the English College of Rheims* (Rheims 1582; *BIE*), "The Preface to the Reader," [p. iv].

51 Ibid., [p. v], citing Session 4 of Trent.

52 *Canons and Decrees of the Council of Trent: Original Text with English Translation*, ed. H. J. Schroeder (St. Louis MO 1941). The first, *Decretum de canonicis Scripturis*, establishes the number of the books of the biblical canon, as contained in the Latin Vulgate. The second, *Decretum de editione et usu sacrorum librorum*, establishes the Latin Vulgate as the authentic version, commands interpreters of Scripture not to deviate from traditional meanings, requires printers of the Bible, especially the old Vulgate, to print it correctly and not anonymously; and it requires all books on sacred matters (*de rebus sacris*) to be approved by the bishop and forbids passages of Scripture to be put to profane uses.

Conclusion

1 See Ralph Hanna and Sarah Wood, eds., *Richard Morris's "Prick of Conscience": A Corrected and Amplified Text* (Oxford 2013), pp. 378–83.

Appendix A. Note on Manuscripts

1 Dove, *First English Bible*, p. 247.

2 Kennedy, *Courtly and Commercial Art*, pp. 197–208, "Table of Copies of the Wycliffite Bible."

3 For a list of the English Books of Hours, see Kennedy's article "Reintroducing the English Books of Hours," p. 720. Only eight of the seventeen use LV for the psalms and canticles, while eight of the remaining nine use a translation that is, Kennedy claims, "EV-influenced." In so saying, she goes against the judgment of Henry Hargreaves, "The Middle English Primers and the Wycliffite Bible," *Modern Language Review* 51 (1956): 215–17, who says that the translation is independent of EV (and LV). I do not find Kennedy's demonstration of EV influence ("Reintroducing," pp. 696–701) to be persuasive.

4 All eight volumes of Lindberg's *Earlier Version* are in the series Acta Universitatis Stockholmiensis: Stockholm Studies in English. The text consists of Oxford, MS Bodley 959 (collated by FM) for Genesis to Baruch 3.20 (vols. 1–5), and Oxford, MS Christ Church 145 (FM calls it E.4), which contains the entire Bible, for the remainder (FM collates only for NT); Lindberg's vol. 7 contains *The Gospels Edited from MS Christ Church 145* (1994), and vol. 8 the rest of the New Testament. Bodley 959 is analyzed in *LALME* 3:375–76.

5 Fristedt, *Wycliffe Bible*, 1:109, gives the examples of tense modifications in Luke 1.8, 1.12, and 1.26 (present changed to past); and see 2:liii–lviii. Fristedt's overall judgment is that all of the manuscripts of EV have been revised sporadically (2:lv). See

Sven Fristedt, "The Authorship of the Lollard Bible," *Stockholm Studies in Modern Philology* (*SSMP*) o.s. 19 (1956) 28–41, p. 33, cited in full by Paul Smith, "Could the Gospel Harmony *Oon in Foure* Represent an Intermediate Version of the Wycliffite Bible?" *Studia Neophilogica* 80 (2008) 160–76 (p. 161). I find Smith's affirmative answer unconvincing. Smith cites other articles of Fristedt: "A Weird Manuscript Enigma in the British Museum"; "New Light on John Wycliffe and the First Full English Bible," *SSMP* n.s. 3 (1968) 61–86; "A Note on Some Obscurities in the History of the Lollard Bible," *SSMP* n.s. 4 (1972) 38–45. For a summary of Fristedt's arguments in his essays, stressing the question of authorship, see Lindberg, "Who Wrote Wiclif's Bible?" Fristedt died in 1980.

6 Fristedt, *Wycliffe Bible*, 2:xlv.

7 Lindberg, *King Henry's Bible*; see his conclusion about the nature of the version, 4:34. Forshall and Madden collate Bodley 277 in their edition. For a description of the work, see Anne Hudson, "The Carthusians and a Wycliffite Bible," in *Ecclesia, Cultura, Potestas*, ed. Pawel Kras et al. (Cracow 2006), pp. 731–42; she takes up the Bibles of Henry IV and Henry V on p. 736. Dove, *First English Bible*, p. 44 n. 44, suggests that this Bible may be the same as the one owned by Henry IV, for possessing which a London bookseller in 1419 was indicted. A. I. Doyle suggests the same in his review of Hanna's *London Literature* in *Medium Aevum* 76 (2007) 123–25. But the bookseller was acquitted, and therefore kept the Bible. See Henry Summerson, "An English Bible and Other Books Belonging to Henry IV," *Bulletin of the John Rylands Library* 79 (1997) 109–15.

8 See Lindberg, *Early Version*, 8:69–71.

9 Lindberg, *King Henry's Bible*, 1:47. Lindberg attributes the work on the Vulgate to Wyclif, and thinks it likely that John Trevisa worked on EEV, Nicholas Hereford on EV, Wyclif himself on LV, and perhaps John Purvey on LLV.

10 For Easton, see Linde, *How to Correct the Sacra Scriptura?*, p. 158. For the passage-to-passage method of the translators, see Dove, *First English Bible*, pp. 175–88. There is only one fourteenth-century (Latin) Bible listed at Oxford in N. R. Ker, *Medieval Libraries of Great Britain: A List of Surviving Books*, 2nd ed. (London 1964), p. 149: Oxford, Bodleian Library, Ashmole 748, originally at Staple Hall; but the earliest mention of this house seems to be the notice of its principal, John Segden, in 1440; see *The Historical Register of the University of Oxford: Being a Supplement to the Oxford University Calendar, with an Alphabetical Record of University Honours and Distinctions Completed to the End of Trinity Term 1888* (Oxford 1900), p. 29. However, we know that Latin Bibles were much sought out for reading in the libraries of religious houses, from William Woodford, O.F.M., *Responsum contra Wiclevum et Lollardos*, in Eric Doyle, "William Woodford," pp. 120–87, question 60, pp. 179–80.

Appendix B. Cardinal Gasquet and His Critics

1 Gasquet, "Pre-Reformation English Bible."

2 When the Vulgate commission started producing volumes in 1926, Gasquet as head was the only member mentioned by name: *Biblia Sacra iuxta latinam vulgatam versionem ad codicum fidem*, ed. Cardinal [Francis] Aidan Gasquet and the Benedictine monks of the pontifical commission instituted by Pius X ("iussu Pii pp. XI, cura et studio monachorum Sancti Benedicti, Commissionis Pontificiae a Pio X institutae sodalium, praeside Aidano Gasquet cardinale, edita"), 18 vols. (Rome 1926–95).

3 Dove, *First English Bible*, pp. 45–46. Another history that would need rewriting is that of the English vernacular and the credit given to the Lollards in its development. See Wendy Scase, "Re-inventing the Vernacular: Middle English Language and Its Literature," in *The Cambridge Companion to Medieval English Literature, 1100–1500*, ed. Larry Scanlon (Cambridge 2009), pp. 11–23: "Lollard writings attempt to regularize in the interests of a massive supra-regional religious agenda. A cluster of literary projects—at least two translations of the Bible (1382–95), aids to bible study, sets of sermons, and satirical and polemical tracts—was carried out by followers of the heretic John Wyclif. The Lollards developed an English prose which could communicate across dialectal boundaries; Wycliffite English is based on the dialect of the south and central Midlands, the variety which came to underpin standard English" (p. 22).

4 Dove, *First English Bible*, p. 46.

5 Ibid, p. 45 and n. 49.

6 M. D. Knowles, *Cardinal Gasquet as an Historian*, Creighton Lecture in History, 1956 (London 1957). This lecture, of twenty-six pages, was reprinted in "*The Historian and Character" and Other Essays by Dom David Knowles* (Cambridge 1963), pp. 240–63. I will give the page numbers of both publications. Here, see p. 1 (250), where he cites G. R. Elton, *England Under the Tudors* (London 1955), p. 484.

7 Knowles, *Cardinal Gasquet*, p. 26 (262).

8 Ibid., p. 14 (252).

9 Ibid., p. 19 (256).

10 Peter Marshall, "Lollards and Protestants Revisited," in Bose and Hornbeck, *Wycliffite Controversies*, pp. 295–318, at p. 296.

11 Eamon Duffy, *The Stripping of the Altars: Traditional Religion in England, 1400–1580* (New Haven CT 1992); reprinted in 2005 with a "Preface to the Second Edition."

12 Marshall, "Lollards and Protestants," p. 299.

13 Ibid., p. 314. Gairdner also agreed with Gasquet that it was not condemned by Archbishop Arundel in 1407/9, even though it was Wycliffite and recognized as such (both of which conclusions Gasquet denied). See Gairdner, *Lollardy and the Reformation in England*, vol. 1, pp. 105–11. For the epigraph from Gairdner cited at the beginning of this book, see p. 101: "I have said that Wycliffe's chief bequest to posterity was the English Bible." His earlier statement is more telling (p. 12): "Wycliffe's chief bequest to posterity was his English Bible, and the great idea that the laity too might quench their spiritual thirst directly from that well of Life." Gairdner did not, however, believe that Wyclif himself had a hand in the translation (pp. 102–3).

14 Eamon Duffy, "A. G. Dickens and the Late Medieval Church," *Historical Research* 77 (2004) 98–110, p. 101. Duffy exaggerates the seriousness of Gasquet's scholarly lapses. An example he gives is his getting the title of Gibbon's history wrong (saying *Rise and Fall* rather than *Decline and Fall*) in an essay addressed to Edmund Bishop; but in this paragraph Duffy himself makes a worse mistake, saying that Gasquet's "last book of real value was the collaborative study, with Edmund Bishop, *Edward VI and the Book of Common Prayer*, published in 1902" (pp. 99–100). As Duffy's own footnote accurately states, this book was published in 1890. Like Knowles, Duffy implicitly accepts Gasquet's wrongness on the subject of the English Bible, except for admitting that it was accepted by the faithful. He sums up his own position thus,

in *Stripping of the Altars*, "Preface to the Second Edition" (2005), p. xxvi: "The appeal of vernacular scripture was clearly a powerful one in an increasingly literate lay population. The ban imposed in 1409 was therefore pregnant with consequence for the future, leaving unsatisfied a need attested by the fact that many and perhaps most fifteenth-century owners and readers of Wycliffite bibles were impeccably orthodox Catholics."

15 Gasquet, "Pre-Reformation English Bible," p. 142 (*Old English Bible*, p. 137).

16 F. D. Matthew, "The Authorship of the Wycliffite Bible," *English Historical Review* 10 (1895) 91–99.

17 Frederic G. Kenyon, *Our Bible and the Ancient Manuscripts, Being a History of the Text and Its Translations*, 2nd ed. (London 1896); his preface is dated October 25, 1895; the first edition was published in 1895 (non vidi). He takes up Gasquet's thesis on pp. 204–8. His discussion remained the same in the 3rd edition of 1897, but in the 1898 version of the 3rd edition, he adds a "Preface to the Third Edition" and four pages of "Additions and Corrections" (pp. i–iv), repeated in the 4th edition of 1903, in which he responds (p. iv) to Gasquet's second article of 1897 (see below).

18 Gasquet, *The Old English Bible and Other Essays* (London 1897). Essay 4, "The Pre-Reformation English Bible" (erroneously giving "July, 1895" as the date of its first appearance), on pp. 102–55, adds fifteen lengthy footnotes to the original text, without indicating that they are additions; the fifteenth, n. 2 on pp. 146–47, documents added material in the text, likewise not indicated as an addition: namely, further discussion of the *Mirror of Our Lady*. Essay 5, "The Pre-Reformation English Bible (2)," appears on pp. 156–78.

19 Francis Aidan Gasquet, "The Printed English Bible," in *The Eve of the Reformation* (1899; London 1900), pp. 208–44, at pp. 208–9.

20 J. H. Lupton, "Versions (English)," in *A Dictionary of the Bible*, ed. James Hastings, Extra Volume (Edinburgh 1904; repr. 1906), pp. 236–71, at p. 241. Lupton mistakenly thinks that Gasquet was claiming that EV and LV predated Wyclif's time.

21 Ogle, "Dr. Gasquet."

22 Knowles, *Cardinal Gasquet*, p. 21 (258).

23 Francis Aidan Gasquet, *The Old English Bible and Other Essays*, new ed. (London 1908), page v; essay 4 appears on pp. 87–134 and essay 5 on pp. 135–55. On pp. 140–41, he breaks into the note originally given on pp. 161–62 of the first edition, to add to his response to Kenyon. This addition appears in the 1907 printing of his first edition, pp. 383–84, to be added to p. 161.

24 G. G. Coulton, *Ten Medieval Studies*, 3rd ed. (Cambridge 1930; repr. Boston 1959), appendix 2, p. 203. These studies were first published in 1906, but this appendix first appeared (as appendix 1) in the 2nd ed. (1915). He lists fifteen problems with *The Old English Bible*, the first twelve taken from Ogle. The first error that he contributes himself, no. 13 (p. 206), is, in my view, not valid. Gasquet held that *aliquis textus* in the 1407 constitutions referred to any "detatched" passage of Scripture, whereas Coulton says that, since "*textus* was the consecrated word for the whole volume containing the four Gospels," that is what it means here. James Gairdner's rendering, "any passage of Scripture" (*Lollardy and the Reformation*, 1:108), supports Gasquet. Coulton's item no. 14 is simply a complaint that Gasquet reprinted his previous essays in reset type, without corrections, and no. 15 is an observation that Gasquet only rarely corrects his work.

25 G. G. Coulton, *The Roman Catholic Church and the Bible*, 2nd ed. (London 1921).

26 Ibid., pp. 4–6, 23–27, 31–33, 37–38.

27 Herbert Thurston, *Some Inexactitudes of Mr. G. G. Coulton: A Sheaf of Criticisms and Rejoinders Arising Mainly Out of Mr. Coulton's Volume "The Medieval Village"* (London 1927), p. 60.

28 G. G. Coulton, *Sectarian History* (Taunton 1937), pp. 5–8. Collected in G. G. Coulton, [Controversial pamphlets] ([v.p.], [1924–39]), 16 pamphlets in 1 volume, no. 12.

29 G. G. Coulton, *The Scandal of Cardinal Gasquet: A Sequel to "Sectarian History"* (Taunton 1937).

30 Thurston, "Dr. G. G. Coulton and Cardinal Gasquet."

31 G. G. Coulton, *Details of the Gasquet Case* (Taunton 1938?); *A Premium upon Falsehood: A Postscript to "The Scandal of Cardinal Gasquet"* (Taunton 1939).

32 G. G. Coulton, *Fourscore Years: An Autobiography* (New York 1944; preface dated 1941). Chapter 34, "An Extreme Case," deals with Cardinal Gasquet, pp. 329–37. He speaks of his grievances on the subject of the Bible on p. 332.

33 Deanesly, *Lollard Bible*, preface, p. vii (cited above).

34 Ibid., p. 1; in this she is like Lupton (see n. 20 above).

35 Gairdner, *Lollardy and the Reformation*, 1:111. Speaking of the Bibles owned by Thomas, Duke of Gloucester, Henry VI, and Henry VII, he says, "Abbot Gasquet, on the contrary, contends that they must be copies of that earlier Bible which, on Sir Thomas More's authority, he believes to have existed before Wycliffe." See also Hugh Pope, *English Versions of the Bible*, rev. Sebastian Bullough (St. Louis 1952), p. 66.

36 Gasquet, *Old English Bible* (1897), pp. 116, 137.

37 Alfred W. Pollard, review of Deanesly's *Lollard Bible*, *History* 5 (1920–21) 223–26, referring to p. 300 n. 2. On Pollard's original statement and Deanesly's reaction, see Fowler, *Life and Times*, pp. 219–20.

38 Workman, *John Wyclif*, 2:149–200, "Wyclif and the Bible," esp. p. 164 n. 1.

39 Ibid., pp. 185–86.

40 Ibid., pp. 190–91.

41 Ibid., p. 185 n. 3, citing Matthew, "Authorship," p. 95. Matthew's article alone is cited by Charles Edward Mallett, *A History of the University of Oxford*, 3 vols. (London 1924–27), 1:231 n. 1, as having answered "Cardinal Gasquet's doubts in regard to the Wycliffite tradition."

42 Workman, *John Wyclif*, 2:195; the gloss Workman cites is discussed by Deanesly, *Lollard Bible*, p. 279 n. 3.

43 Ogle, *Tragedy of the Lollards' Tower*, pp. 114–18. So far as I can tell, Ogle published only two other books during his long life, namely, *The Marquis d'Argenson: A Study in Criticism, Being the Stanhope Essay* (Oxford 1893); and *The Canon Law in Mediaeval England: An Examination of William Lyndwood's "Provinciale," in Reply to the Late Professor F. W. Maitland* (London 1912). On Ogle's viewpoint in *Tragedy*, see Marshall, "Lollards and Protestants Revisited," pp. 302–3.

44 Ogle, *Tragedy*, p. 117.

45 Ogle, "Dr. Gasquet and the Old English Bible," p. 297; he quotes Gasquet's statement in *Old English Bible* (1897), p. 138—"So far as I have been able to discover, however, from an examination of the two texts, there is nothing inconsistent with their having been the work of perfectly orthodox sons of Holy Church"—and adds: "In this opinion we are glad to follow him."

Appendix C. Present Participles in *-inge* and *-ende* in EV

1 Moessner, "Translation Strategies in Middle English," p. 138 (the reason she alleges is that "Middle English forms in *-ing* . . . cannot denote a person"). On the historical development of the present participle, see Tauno F. Mustanoja, *A Middle English Syntax* (Helsinki 1960), pp. 547–48.

2 FM 2:479 to 3:490.

3 FM 1:l, MS no. 87.

4 FM 1:li, MS no. 91 (called Christ Church E.4 here).

5 An exception is in Matthew 8, where two of the twenty-six *-ende* participles in this chapter contained in Christ Church 145 are noted (using the siglum *X*), both in 8.14: "lyende" and "shakende."

6 I have found the participles by searching "ende" in EV *BIE* in the range covered (Ecclesiasticus 48 to Baruch 3, FM 2:479 to 3:490) corresponding to Scribe 5 in Bodley 959 (EEV). There is only one *-end*, namely, Isa. 28.15, "scourge flowend," 3:272, and one *-ande*, in a rare gloss, Isa. 11.8, "the faunt, *or a soukande childe*, " 3:247. In EEV (Bodley 959) *-ande* appears a few times instead of *-ende*, e.g., Jer. 13.9: "seiande." Lindberg has counted twelve such instances (*Earlier Version*, 5:44). One notable verse in EEV Isaiah is 52.7: "Hou faire up on mounteynes the feet of the, tellende and prechende pes, tellende good, prechende helthe, seiynge, 'Sion, regnen shal thi God' (5:154), with *-ende* four times and *-ynge* one time.

7 *LALME*, 3:375–76, studying fols. 288–94 of Bodley 959, that is, Ecclesiasticus 48 to Isaiah 19 (Lindberg, *Earlier Version*, 5:99–120).

8 *LALME* dot map 348, 1:391; item map 57, no. 6, 2:242; County Dictionary, 4:106 (under item 57: Present participle).

9 John Gower, *Confessio Amantis*, ed. G. C. Macaulay, 2 vols., EETS e.s. 81 (London 1900). See Macaulay's discussion of his participial use, 1:cxix–cxx. On Gower's background, see Douglas Gray, "Gower, John," in *OxDNB*.

10 FM 1:xlvii, MS no. 65 (Bodley 959); 1:l, MS no. 87 (Douce 369.1). However, de Hamel, *The Book*, pp. 172–73, taking it as probable that Nicholas Hereford is Scribe 5 of Bodley 959, judges that it is *not* probable that the hand of Scribe 3 of Douce 369.1 is the same.

Appendix D. EITHER/OR Preferences in the MEB

1 LV 1 Maccabees uses OR twice, 4.38 and 5.46, and twice more in glosses, 6.34 and 8.3. I have checked the LV variants for Genesis, and find that MSS E (Arundel 104), L (Bodl. 296), and P (Emmanuel Coll. 2) regularly change EITHER to OR.

2 I should note that the main copy text of this part of the EV New Testament, Douce 369.2 (FM 1:xvii), differs in its affiliation in Luke and John; see Fristedt, *Wycliffe Bible*, 1:6.

3 Clearly following what would become standard reading from Gutenberg to the Clementine edition of 1592; see the Nestle-Aland edition of the New Testament, *Novum Testamentum Latine*, ed. Kurt Aland and Barbara Aland, ed. 2 (Nördlingen 1992); *Biblia Sacra juxta vulgatam clementinam*, ed. Professors of Scripture of Paris and Saint Sulpice (Rome 1956). The older text has *et*: see *Biblia Sacra iuxta vulgatam versionem*, ed. Robert Weber et al., 5th ed., ed. Roger Gryson (Stuttgart 2007).

4 The other instances are 1.20 ("stille *or* doumbe"); 2.1, 3, 24; 3.6; 5.1; 10.27; 18.5; 22.5; 22.64.

5 Lindberg, *Earlier Version*, 7:21, notes that all of the twenty-nine manuscripts of EV that he collates for the Gospels, including EEV (OxCCC 145) have undergone revision—some, of course, more than others. See pp. 9–11 for the list of manuscripts, and pp. 21–25 for some specifics of revision. He finds Douce 369.2 (MS *K*) in general more revised in Luke and John than in Matthew and Mark. See 8:29–33 for more comments.

6 There are six OTHERs in Douce Luke, but one of them translates Latin *neque* "nor" (Luke 11.33).

7 One particularly interesting gloss occurs in Luke 7.22, which corresponds to Matthew 11.5. The Latin of both texts reads *pauperes evangelizantur*, "the poor are evangelized." EEV Matthew has "pore men ben preched," while EEV Luke has a more Lollard-sounding reading, "pore men ben take to prechen the gospel *or mad keperes of the gospel*," which is basically the reading of EV Matthew and Luke. Four MSS of Matthew (*BrOPeU*) have only "maad keperis of the gospel," whereas three manuscripts of Luke (*LoOQ*) have only "pore men ben take to prechen the gospel," which is the reading of LV Matthew and Luke. (Lindberg does not track EITHER variants of OR.)

8 When analyzing only OR in Luke and the other Gospels, I do not count the first particle of EITHER + OR constructions.

9 *LALME* 3:16. For accounts of MS Royal 1.C.8, see FM 1:xxxix–xl; and Dove, *First English Bible*, pp. 248–29.

10 Another striking case of a scribe who religiously follows dialectal uses in his exemplars can be seen in Ann Eljenholm Nichols, "The Illustrations of Corpus Christi College MS 32: 'Þe Glose in Englissche Tunge,'" in *Image, Text, and Church, 1380–1600: Essays for Margaret Aston*, ed. Linda Clark, Maureen Jurkowski, and Colin Richmond (Toronto 2009), pp. 37–67, at pp. 38–39: "The scribe of MS 32 was a careful transcriber, scrupulously preserving two forms of the definite article, *þee* (*þe*) in Mark and *þo* in Luke." The manuscript preserves a set of glossed Gospels using neither EV nor LV.

11 EV Luke 7.42: "He yaf freely to *ever either*." Other manuscripts have BOTH instead of EVER EITHER (*booth* AMNOQSY, bothe PWXY). The siglum for Egerton is G.

12 See *OED*, s.v. "ever," *adv.* 4.a, citing Pecock, *Repressor*, 1:8; see also 1:256; 2:391, 558; *OED*, s.v. "neither" B.1.a, and Pecock, 1:14, 52, 53, 256. For EVER EITHER the only other source cited is the Close Rolls, 1444–45.

13 FM 1:xxv. Forshall edited *Thirty-Seven Conclusions* in the next year, 1851, under the title of *Remonstrance Against Romish Corruptions in the Church, Addressed to the People and Parliament of England in 1395, 18 Ric. II* (London 1851). Forshall has no doubt that the author is John Purvey. See the discussion of this work by Anne Hudson, *Premature Reformation*, pp. 214–17; she finds it difficult to date and can offer no

conjecture as to its author. We should note that *Thirty-Seven* has the double-substance take on the Eucharist, that it is both Christ's body and bread, and not accidents without substance (Concl. 15, pp. 40–43), in contrast to the seeming stance of St. Augustine, repeated by SC (GP, chap. 12, p. 45; see above) that Christ's command to eat his flesh is purely "a figurative speche." However, there is not necessarily an opposition here, as can be seen in the 70th proposition among the 267 Wyclif statements condemned in 1411 (see below): "Sicut Christus est simul Deus et homo, sic hostia consecrata est simul corpus Christi et verus panis; quia est corpus Domini ad minimum in figura, et verus panis in natura. Vel, quod idem sonat, est verus panis naturaliter, et corpus Christi figuraliter"—taken from the *Opus evangelicum*; see Wilkins, *Concilia Magnae Britanniae et Hiberniae*, 3:342. Cf. article 121 from the *Trialogus*: "Substantia panis manet in altari post consecrationem, et non desinit esse panis"; and article 122: "Sicut Johannes fuit figuraliter Helias et non personaliter, sic panis in altari figuraliter est corpus Christi; et absque omni ambiguitate haec est figurativa locutio: 'Hoc est corpus meum,' sicut ista: 'Johannes ipse est Helias'" (p. 344). The thirty-seven conclusions themselves (without commentary and corollaries) are much less radical than the commentaries and corollaries that follow, and they seem to have been first formulated in Latin. See H. F. B. Compston, "The Thirty-Seven Conclusions of the Lollards," *English Historical Review* 26 (1911) 738–49 (the Latin text of the articles is given on pp. 741–49, lined up with the translations in *Thirty-Seven Conclusions*).

14 On p. 1, the Cotton OTHER appears as OR in the Bodley 540 copy; and on p. 13, where there are two instances of EITHER and two of OR, at the first OR Forshall notes that OR appears as OTHER passim in the Bodley copy.

15 Richard Rex, *The Lollards* (Basingstoke 2002), p. 163 n. 71, referring to *Wyclyffes Wycket* (Norenburch [London] 1546; EEBO, STC 25590), presumably at sig. [Avii] (Image 8 [p. 13]), where the author refers to Jesus as being with the Father and Holy Ghost at the creation, making things out of naught "by worde of His vertue, for He said, 'Be it do,' and it was done, as whose workes never earthly man might comprehende either make. And yet the wordes of the making of these thinges, by me written, in the beginning of Genesis, even as God spake them, and if ye can not make the worke that He made, and have the wordes by which He made it, how shal he [*lege* ye] make Him that made the works?—and you have no wordes of auctorite either power lefte you on earthe by whiche ye shulde do this, but as ye have fained this crafte of youre false errours, whiche some of you understand not."

16 He uses EITHER twelve times and OR thirty-three times. For two uses of EITHER, see the quotation just above: "comprehende *either* make," "auctorite *either* power."

Appendix E. The Uses of FORSOOTH

1 SOOTHLY appears in GP, chap. 1, p. 2: "*Catholicon* seith this on that word *apocrifa*. But **sothely** alle the bookis of the Newe Testament . . . ben fully of autorite of bileve." FORSOOTH appears in chap. 14, p. 54: "Such previnge may not be maad bi goostly sense, as Austin seith ayens Vincent Donatiste; **forsothe** the forseid autorite was fillid to the lettre in Salomon."

2 LV Luke 16.17: "*Forsothe* it is lighter hevene and erthe to passe than that o titil falle fro the lawe."

3 LV Luke 5.10: "*Sothely* in liik maner James and Joon, the sones of Zebedee, that weren felowis of Symount Petre"; 12.39: "If an hosebonde man wiste in what our the theef wolde come, *sothely* he schulde wake."

Appendix G. The Question of a Stylistic Break in Baruch

1 Lindberg, *The Middle English Bible*, vol. 2, *The Book of Baruch* (Oslo 1985), pp. 36–39. I wish to thank my assistant Dr. Claire Banchich for her valuable help in doing an independent analysis of the two parts of EV Baruch.

2 Noted briefly in Lindberg, *Book of Baruch*, p. 38.

3 Some of these are given by Conrad Lindberg, "The Break at Baruch 3.20 in the Middle English Bible," *English Studies* 60 (1979) 106–10, p. 19, namely, *ambulare*, *honor*, and *gentes*, and he lists others: *convertere*, *justus*, *infirmus*, and *projicio*. He also lists many more examples by drawing on the text pre-Baruch and post-Baruch. See also his article, "The Manuscripts and Versions of the Wycliffite Bible: A Preliminary Survey," *Studia Neophilogica* 42 (1970) 333–47, p. 345, where he notes some other differences.

Appendix H. The Translation of *Secundum* by AFTER or UP

1 The Longleat MS is treated by Lindberg, *Earlier Version*, 1:16, 6:38, 46–47; and Dove, *First English Bible*, pp. 252–53.

2 FM's MS *H*, no. 155, now CUL Add. 6681 (Dove, *First English Bible*, p. 284); Lindberg, *Earlier Version*, 6:33–35, 46.

Appendix I. Absolute Constructions as Discussed in GP

1 All of Simple Creature's translational principles are summarized and illustrated by FM 1:xxii–xxiii. See also Hudson, *Selections*, pp. 175–77; and Dove, *First English Bible*, pp. 145–48; and in more detail, Fristedt and Lindberg in their studies and editions.

2 On ablative absolutes in the MEB, see Fristedt, *Wycliffe Bible*, 3:65–66; Hiroshi Yonekura, *The Language of the Wycliffite Bible: The Syntactic Differences Between the Two Versions* (Tokyo 1985), pp. 412–21, 442. In "The Wycliffite Bible: John Purvey's Translation Method," *Linguistics and Philology* 5 (1984) 1–25, and "John Purvey's Version of the Wycliffite Bible: A Reconsideration of His Translation Method," *Studies in Medieval English Language and Literature* 1 (1986) 67–91, pp. 69–70, Yonekura looks specifically at the four Gospels.

3 GP, chap. 15, p. 57: "In translating into English, manie resolucions moun make the sentence open, as an ablatif case absolute may be resolvid into these thre wordis, with covenable verbe, 'the while,' 'for,' 'if,' as gramariens seyn; as thus: 'the maistir redinge, I stonde,' may be resolvid thus, 'while the maistir redith, I stonde,' either 'if the maistir redith,' etc., either 'for the maistir,' etc.; and sumtime it wolde acorde wel with the sentence to be resolvid into 'whanne' either into 'aftirward,' thus: 'whanne the maystir red, I stood,' either 'aftir the maystir red, I stood'; and sumtime it may wel be resolvid into a verbe of the same tens, as othere ben in the same resoun, and into this word *et*, that is, 'and' in English, as thus, *arescentibus hominibus pre timore*, that is, 'and men shulen wexe drie for drede.'"

4 Charles Hunter Ross, "The Absolute Participle in Middle English and Modern English," *Publications of the Modern Language Association* 8 (1893) 245–302, pp. 253–

54, 261–62, 298. He finds fourteen clear examples of present absolute participles in Chaucer's poems and fifteen of past absolute participles, with nine additional doubtful examples. In analyzing his references, and using Larry Benson's *Riverside Chaucer,* I find eleven present absolutes: *Parliament of Fowls* 99; *House of Fame* 796; *Troilus and Criseyde* 1.309, 1.547, 4.29–30; *Canterbury Tales*: Wife of Bath 1028; Clerk 700, 777, 1048; Canon's Yeoman 1320, 1324. And I find sixteen past absolutes: *Parliament* 82; *Troilus* 2.1290, 3.923, 3.985–96, 4.141, 4.218, 4.911, 4.1159, 4.1271, 5.1348–49; *Legend of Good Women* 1110 (2); *Canterbury Tales*: General Prologue 273, 423; Knight 2421; Squire 297. The three present-participle absolutes in *Troilus* do indeed imitate Boccaccio's constructions in the *Filostrato*, but the same is true of only one of the nine instances of past-participle absolutes in *Troilus*, namely, 4.911, "thise words seide" (*Fil.* 4.106.1, *questo detto*). And the one example of a past-participle absolute in the Knight's Tale does not depend on Boccaccio's *Teseida*. Ross does not consider absolute constructions in which no participle is expressed; for example, he counts *Canterbury Tales*' General Prologue 273, "His bootes clasped faire and fetisly," but not 272: "Upon his heed a Flaundrissh bever hat." Another example is Knight 2279: "the hornes fulle of meeth." The corresponding Italian is not absolute, being introduced by *with*, but it is attached to a past absolute in the previous line: *Teseida* 7.71.1–2, "le servienti sue tutte chiamate, / co' corni pien d'offerte "("all her handmaidens summoned, *with* horns full of offerings"). Ross wrongly counts Knight 2281, "smoking the temple," as a present absolute, taking it to mean "the temple was smoking," whereas it means "incensing the temple," the participle agreeing with Emily as subject of the sentence.

5 Ross, "Absolute Participle," pp. 254–55.

6 Ibid., p. 256. Ross examined the first volume edited by Arnold, *Select English Works of John Wyclif,* and found no example.

7 Ibid., p. 256 n. 2.

8 Yonekura, who does not know Ross's article, gives different figures for the EV Gospels: Matthew, 62; Mark, 49; Luke, 65; John, 12; for a total of 188 ("Wycliffite Bible," p. 6), but his count is clearly faulty from the fact that in three of his examples (Matt. 13.33, 21.39, 27.17) the participles are not absolute but dependent.

9 Ross, "Absolute Participle," pp. 284–85. In this case, Chaucer is inventing his own absolute construction, not translating from Petrarch's Latin or its French translation.

10 Ibid., p. 285. While I am on the subject of Chaucer, I should note that it would not be surprising if Chaucer consulted EV or LV, if he had access to them, in making his own translations from the Vulgate; but, since he never manifests any clear extended use of either translation, judgments that he did so must be considered with reserve, as, for instance, those of Craig T. Fuhrman, "Did Chaucer Read the Wycliffite Bible?" *Chaucer Review* 42 (2007–8) 111–38, esp. p. 128; and Frances McCormack, *Chaucer and the Culture of Dissent: The Lollard Context and Subtext of the Parson's Tale* (Dublin 2007), pp. 149–75 ("Chaucer and the Wycliffite Bible"). One noteworthy comment by McCormack is, "Paradoxically, the Wycliffite Bible does not tend to reproduce, in any extensive way, the vocabulary that recurs repeatedly throughout the English Lollard sermons" (p. 161).

11 In Luke 1.3, which is treated as part of a prologue and appears only in two MSS of EV (*U,V*), there is a deponent (active) past participle, *assecuto*, "having acquired," in

apposition to the dative *mihi*: "visum est et mihi, assecuto a principio omnibus diligenter ex ordine, tibi scribere"; translated simply by *having*: "It is seen also to me, *havinge* alle thingis diligently by ordre, to write to thee."

12 I modernize the capitalization, and follow the punctuation used in the form distributed to the states for ratification, which coincides with modern practice; the form written by William Lambert and presented to the House and Senate contains two "breathing commas" (nowadays diagnosed as *comma faults*), before "being necessary" and before "shall not be infringed."

13 Later translations are cited from Luther A. Weigle, ed., *The New Testament Octapla* (New York [1962]), who lists originals and editions thus: Tyndale (1525) 1535; Great Bible (1539) 1540; Geneva Bible (1560) 1562; Bishops' Bible (1568) 1602. He includes Rheims and King James, as well as RV 1881/ASV 1901 (Revised Version and American Standard Version) and RSV (1946) 1960 (Revised Standard Version).

14 Mustanoja, *Middle English Syntax*, pp. 116–17.

15 Félix Lecoy, ed., *Le Roman de la Rose*, by Guillaume de Lorris and Jean de Meun, 3 vols. (Paris 1965–70), 1:52, line 1679; *Romaunt*, in Benson, *Riverside Chaucer*, p. 705. See Ross, "Absolute Participle," p. 264.

16 Yonekura, "Wycliffite Bible," pp. 4–7.

Appendix J. Other Participial Constructions in GP and EV/LV

1 GP, chap. 15, p. 57: "Also a participle of a present tens either preterit, of actif vois eithir passif, may be resolvid into a verbe of the same tens, and a conjunccioun copulatif, as thus, *dicens*, that is, 'seyinge,' may be resolvid thus, 'and seith,' eithir 'that seith'; and this wole, in manie placis, make the sentence open, where to Englisshe it aftir the word wolde be derk and douteful."

2 On the resolution of present participles to finite forms in LV, see Fristedt, *Wycliffe Bible*, 1:110, 124–26, 128, and 3:66–67. Yonekura, "John Purvey's Version," pp. 70–74, deals with both present and past participles in apposition under the categories of time, attendant circumstance, and repeated action. See further his *Language of the Wycliffite Bible*, pp. 426–42.

3 Note that in the Latin the singular *surgens* is used, agreeing with *multitudo*, but in the main clause the plural *duxerunt* is employed. EV, in using the past tense *ledden*, does not violate number, whereas LV, using present-tense *arisen*, construes *multitudo* as plural.

4 Chaucer, *Boece*, book 2, prosa 7, line 156: "[the soule] *beinge* in hevene" translating *celo fruens* (Ralph Hanna and Traugott Lawler, the editors in Benson, *Riverside Chaucer*, pp. 419, 1154, emend the reading to "usinge," in keeping with the French version of Jean de Meun).

5 Chaucer, *Parliament of Fowls* 426: "*Havinge* reward [regard] only to my trouthe"; *Troilus* 4.85–86: "*Having* unto my tresor ne my rente / Right no resport [regard]"; ibid., 5.1735: "*Having* unto min honour ne my reste / Right no reward."

6 In the FM edition, ten times as "beynge" and five as "beende" (the latter in the Douce 369.1 *-ende* section, from 1 Esdras to Baruch).

7 W. van der Gaaf, "Some Notes on the History of the Progressive Form," *Neophilologus* 15 (1930) 201–15, traces continuity from Old English to Middle English, and

discounts the influence of Anglo-Norman; but he does not bring up the question of Latin influence.

8 See *Allen and Greenough's New Latin Grammar*, ed. J. B. Greenough et al. (1903; repr. New Rochelle NY 1979), p. 319, no. 507 n. 1: "In this use [expressing manner] the ablative of the gerund is, in later writers nearly, and in mediaeval writers entirely, equivalent to a present participle." Boccaccio uses an Italian equivalent, in *Filostrato* 7.54.4–5, "considerando al tuo affetto pio / la fede data" ("[I,] considering the faith given to your devoted affection"), which Chaucer reflects but turns into a past-participle absolute in *Troilus* 5.1348: "considered this, that . . ."

Appendix L. Other Constructions Discussed in GP

1 The main text of EV for the last sixth of the Old Testament and for the New Testament is Oxford, Bodl. Douce 369, part 2 (not analyzed in *LALME*). For a summary of the manuscripts used by FM, see Fristedt, *Wycliffe Bible*, 1:14–18.

2 GP, chap. 15, p. 57: "Also a relatif, 'which,' may be resolvid into his antecedent with a conjunccioun copulatif, as thus, 'which renneth': 'and he renneth.'" See Yonekura, "John Purvey's Version," pp. 74–76.

3 GP, chap. 15, p. 57: "Also whanne rightful construccioun is lettid by relacion, I resolve it openly, thus, where this reesoun, *Dominum formidabunt adversarij ejus*, shulde be Englisshid thus by the letter: 'The Lord hise adversaries shulen drede,' I Englishe it thus by resolucioun: 'The adversaries of the Lord shulen drede him'; and so of othere resons that ben like."

4 Susan Pintzuk and Ann Taylor, "The Loss of OV Order in the History of English," in *The Handbook of the History of English*, ed. Ans van Kemenade and Bettelou Los (Malden MA 2006), pp. 249–78, at p. 272.

5 See Jerome's letter to Damasus placed in the Vulgate at the beginning of the Gospels; other letters of Jerome are given in the Vulgate Old Testament as prologues, and these prologues were translated into English for the EV text. The Gospel prologues attributed to Jerome in EV are not by him.

6 Cf. the reminder of Fristedt, *Wycliffe Bible*, 1:103, that the Vulgate differs in style. He says that this fact is emphasized by Anna C. Paues, *A Fourteenth-Century English Biblical Version* (Cambridge 1904), pp. lxxxii–lxxxvi, but it is not apparent to me that it is so.

7 GP, chap. 15, pp. 59–60: "But in translating of wordis equivok, that is, that hath manie significacions undur oo lettre, may lightly be pereil, for Austin seith in the seconde book of *Cristene Teching* [*De doctrina Christiana* 2.12.18, PL 34:43–44], that if equivok wordis be not translatid into the sense either undurstonding, of the autour, it is errour; as in that place of the Salme, 'the feet of hem ben swifte to shede out blood,' [Ps. 13.3 expanded; Rom. 3.15], the Greek word is equivok to 'sharp' and 'swift,' and he that translatide 'sharpe feet,' erride, and a book that hath 'sharpe feet,' is fals, and mut be amendid; as that sentence 'Unkinde yonge trees shulen not yeve depe rootis,' owith to be thus, 'Plauntingis of avoutrie shulen not yeve depe rootis' [cf. Wisdom 4.3]. Austin seith this there. Therefore a translatour hath greet nede to studie wel the sentence, both bifore and aftir, and loke that suche equivok wordis acorde with the sentence, and he hath nede to live a clene lif, and be ful devout in preyers, and have not his wit ocupied about worldly thingis, that the Holi Spirit,

autour of wisdom, and kunning, and truthe, dresse him in his werk, and suffre him not for to erre."

Appendix M. Some Features Not Dealt With in GP

1 I have not done a systematic study on this point.

2 Dove, *First English Bible*, p. 149, cites Fristedt's discussion of existential *there* in the OT, as practiced by EV and followed by LV after Amos 5.2, but before that LV uses the *none is that* construction. On p. 150, she speaks of LLV (MS Bodley 277, ed. Lindberg, *King Henry's Bible*) adding existential *there*, e.g., to LV John 4.46 ("and a litil king was," changed to "and ther was a litil king"). She thinks that the reviser of this manuscript had copies of both EV and LV and was familiar with the practices of both (p. 152).

3 David Crystal, *The Stories of English* (London 2004), p. 240. Other examples he cites of new words are *leviathan, lightful, merchandising, money-changer, neckerchief, observation,* and *reprehensible*, as well as *cognation, burnt-offering, again-rise*, and *adjurement*. The one example he gives of a new meaning is *mystery*.

4 Moessner, "Translation Strategies," pp. 127–31.

5 Ibid., pp. 131–34.

6 Ibid., pp. 134–36, 136–37, 137–43, and 143–47, respectively.

7 Lindberg, *Middle English Bible*, vol. 1; *Earlier Version*; and *King Henry's Bible*.

Appendix O. The Oxford Committee of Twelve

1 Archbishop Arundel, letter of December 1410, given by Salter, "Documents from Faustina C.vii," doc. 7, pp. 121–23, at p. 121: "Meminimus nos nuper in ultima convocatione nostra celebrata Londonio de consilio suffraganeorum nostrorum inibi existentium statuisse duodecim personas industrias per predictam universitatem vestram eligendas fore, que libros damnate memorie Johannis W. diligenter rimarent, et si quas conclusiones in eisdem sapientes errores vel hereses invenirent, ipsas dicti auctoritate consilii cum cohercione contradicentium et rebellium canonice condemnarent" ("We remind you that in the last convocation celebrated in London, at the counsel of our suffragans who were there, we ordered twelve industrious persons to be chosen by your university to diligently examine the books of John Wyclif, of damned memory, and if they found any conclusions in them savoring of errors or heresies, to condemn them canonically by the authority of the said council [i.e., convocation], using coercion against those contradicting or rebelling"). The letter is dated December in the fourteenth year of Arundel's translation and the twelfth year of Henry IV, which would be 1410, but Salter dates it instead to 1409, thinking that the convocation in question was that of January 1409: "the letter cannot be of December 1410, for it states that the committee was appointed 'by the last convocation'" (p. 123 n. 1). But on p. 99, as stated in Chapter 5 above (p. 77), Salter assumed that the committee was ordered to be appointed not in 1409 but 1407.

2 Salter, "Documents from Faustina C.vii," pp. 117–18, doc. 3, *Reverendissime . . . lassatur* (Oxford to Arundel on delay in forming the committee).

3 Ibid., pp. 118–19, doc. 4, *Articulus in plena congregatione . . . concessus*: "Ne digne de cetero mater nostra universitas de errore vel heresi habeatur suspecta, placet congregacioni regencium et non regencium xii idoneas personas eligere, videlicet magistros,

quorum sex sunt australes et sex boriales, qui de libris, lecturis, et opusculis quibuscumque pro heresibus et erroribus extirpandis, inquirendis, examinandis, reprobandis, vel exceptandis, seu damnandis plenariam habeant potestatem, sic quod dictorum xii vel majoris partis eorundem decretum vim statuti habeat in premissis" ("Lest our mother the university be rightly suspected henceforth of error or heresy, the congregation of regents and nonregents is pleased to elect twelve suitable persons—namely, masters—six of them southerners and six northerners, who are to have full power of extirpating heresies and errors from whatsoever books, lectures, and works, and investigating, examining, reproving, objecting to, or condemning such, so that what is decided by the twelve or a majority of them shall have the force of statute").

4 Ibid., p. 119, doc. 5, *Potestas XII electorum Oxonie.*

5 Ibid., p. 127, doc. 12, *In Cristo carissimi* (letter of Henry IV to Oxford to set up committee of eight arbitrators [December 1410]): Fleming seeks a remedy "super certo gravamine sibi, ut asseruit, illato per sex magristros qui, ut dicit, pretendebant se judices, in numero nimis diminuto, in causa heresium et errorum" ("concerning a grievance charged against him, he states, by six masters who as he says claimed to be judges, in a number excessively diminished, in a case of heresy and error"). Salter dates this document and nos. 10 and 11, also from the king, by the sign-off of no. 10, "a Groby le quart jour de Decembre," as 1409, in keeping with the rest of the his chronology, though he admits that Henry was not only near Groby on December 4 in 1409, but also at Groby on December 6–8 in 1410 (p. 125 n. 1). Andrew E. Larsen, *The School of Heretics: Academic Condemnation at the University of Oxford, 1277–1409* (Leiden 2011), p. 225, goes along with Salter in dating Fleming's condemnation to 1409 rather than 1410, and also in his essay "Secular Politics and Academic Condemnation at Oxford, 1358–1411," in *Religion, Power, and Resistance from the Eleventh to the Sixteenth Centuries*, ed. Karen Bollerman, Thomas M. Izbicki, and Cary J. Nederman (New York 2014), pp. 37–53 at p. 41.

6 Salter, "Documents," p. 127 (doc. 12).

7 Catto, "Wyclif and Wycliffism," pp. 247–48.

8 The twelve members are listed in Salter, "Documents," p. 130.

9 Larsen, *School of Heretics*, pp. 226–27. Catto, "Wyclif and Wycliffism," p. 246, also assumes that Fleming was already a member of the committee.

10 See above at n. 6: the spokesman said that all six of them censured his proposition, although one of them specified that it was wrong only on the face value of the words.

11 Salter, "Documents," pp. 128–29 (doc. 12); the king sent his letter to "the chancellor or his commissary and the procurators" of the university, and, after the report of Fleming's original objection, we hear: "Et tarde idem commissarius universitatis nostre predicte ac alii magistri electi ad damnandum hereses et errores nobis suas litteras humiliter direxerunt," which I translate, "And later the same commissary of our said university and the other masters elected to condemn heresies and errors humbly directed their letter to us."

12 Emden, *BRUO* 2:1093–94, "Langdon, John." He is identified as the chancellor's commissary in 1410 or 1411. I should note here that the *confrater* of Oxford who carried earlier correspondence from Oxford to the king and from the king back again is identified as Master J.W. (Salter, "Documents," pp. 125–26, doc. 11), who Salter thinks may be John Wittenham or John Wells (pp. 97, 125 n. 1). John Wells is said to have called for the condemnation of eighteen Wycliffite propositions at Oxford

on July 26, 1410 (Salter, p. 100, citing Thomas Gascoigne). The articles are given by Walsingham, but assigned to the wrong year, namely, 1409 (*St Albans Chronicle*, 2:570–79). They are not the same as the eighteen articles of Wyclif sent from Oxford to convocation in 1397 (Bray, *Records*, 4:174–77).

13 Salter, "Documents," pp. 136–37, doc. 16, *Carissimi ac dilecti cum nuper*; doc. 17 (pp. 137–38) is a French version of the same letter.

14 Ibid., pp. 121–23, doc. 7, *Meminimus.*

15 Ibid., p. 123, doc. 8, *Fidedigna relatione.*

16 Ibid., p. 124, doc. 9, *Licet in nostris constitucionibus.*

Appendix Q. William Lyndwood's Commentary on the Constitution *Periculosa*

1 See the Ordinary Gloss of Accursius (d. 1263) to Digest, lib. 27, tit. *De excusationibus*, lex 1, *Herennius*, *Corpus juris civilis Justinianei*, ed. Johannes Fehius of Gailsdort, 6 vols. (Lyons, 1627; repr. Osnabrück, 1966), 2:255: s.v. *inepta*: "quia sepe non potest bene fieri translatio de una lingua in aliam" ("because often a translation cannot be well effected from one tongue into another"); s.v. *verba*: "Hoc frequenter fit quod verba Greca ponuntur in legibus Latinis" ("This frequently happens, that Greek words are put into Latin laws").

2 In his gloss to the previous constitution, *Quia insuper*, p. 284 note c, Lyndwood gives an account of Wyclif: he was a great heresiarch who revived many old heresies in England in his time, and the whole of Bohemia was intoxicated by his doctrines. It remains so to the present, to the extent that Pope Martin V has proclaimed a crusade against the Bohemians this year, 1429, under the direction of Cardinal Beaufort, Bishop of Winchester, and last year, 1428, Bishop Fleming of Lincoln on orders of the Holy See exhumed his bones from where they were buried in his parish church of Lutterworth, burning them and throwing the ashes into the nearest river.

Works Cited

MANUSCRIPTS

Cambridge, Corpus Christi College, Parker Library MS 147 (LV Bible).

Cambridge, Gonville and Caius College MS 803/807 frag. 36 (end of Ullerston treatise).

Cambridge, Trinity College MS B.15.11, fols. 42vb–47va (Thomas Palmer, *De translatione sacrae scripturae in linguam barbaricam*).

Longleat House MS 4 (*Longleat Sunday Gospels*) Vienna, Österreichische Nationalbibliothek, MS 4133, fols. 195–207v (see Ullerston).

PUBLISHED WORKS

Adler, Michael. *Jews of Medieval England* (London 1939).

Against Them That Say That Holy Writ Should Not or May Not Be Drawn into English (*First Saith Boece*). Edited by Deanesly, in *Lollard Bible*, pp. 439–45; Bühler, "A Lollard Text"; and Dove, in *The Earliest Advocates*, pp. 143–49.

Allen, William. *The Letters and Memorials of William Cardinal Allen (1532–1594)*, ed. Fathers of the Congregation of the London Oratory, intro. Thomas Francis Knox (London 1882).

Andrew, John (Johannes Andreae). *Apparatus in Librum Sextum* (ca. 1304) = Ordinary Gloss to *Liber Sextus*, *Corpus Juris Canonici*, 3 vols. (Rome 1582), vol. 3:1 (http://digital.library.ucla.edu/canonlaw/index.htm).

Arnold, Thomas, ed. *Select English Works of John Wyclif*, 3 vols. (Oxford 1869–71).

Arnovick, Leslie K., and Henry Ansgar Kelly. "Bishop Challoner's Revision of the Douai-Rheims Bible by Way of King James." *Review of English Studies* 66 (2015): 698–722.

Astell, Ann W. "Chaucer's 'St. Anne Trinity': Devotion, Dynasty, Dogma, and Debate," *Studies in Philology* 94 (1997) 395–416.

Aston, Margaret. *Lollards and Reformers: Images and Literacy in Late Medieval Religion* (London 1984).

———. *Thomas Arundel: A Study of Church Life in the Reign of Richard II* (Oxford 1967).

Aston, T. H. "Oxford's Medieval Alumni," *Past and Present* 74 (February 1977) 3–40.

Bale, John. *Index Britanniae scriptorum: John Bale's Index of British and Other Writers*, ed. Reginald Lane Poole and Mary Bateson (1902), repr., with intro. by Caroline Brett and James P. Carley. Cambridge, 1990.

———. *Scriptorum illustrium Majoris Britanniae . . . catalogus*, 2 vols. (Basel 1557–59).

Barron, Caroline. Review of *London Literature, 1300–1380*, by Ralph Hanna, in *Journal of British Studies* 45 (2006) 876–78.

Baugh, Albert C., "The Middle English Period," in *A Literary History of England*, ed. Baugh (New York 1948), pp. 109–312. The second edition of 1967 adds a supplement with additional discussion and bibliography.

Bazire, Joyce, and Eric Colledge, eds. *"The Chastising of God's Children" and "The Treatise of Perfection of the Sons of God"* (Oxford 1957).

Beal, Jane. *John Trevisa and the English Polychronicon* (Tempe AZ 2012).

Benrath, Gustav Adolf. *Wyclifs Bibelkommentar* (Berlin 1966).

Benson, Larry D., gen. ed. *The Riverside Chaucer*, ed. 3 (Boston 1987).

Bernard, G. W. *The Late Medieval English Church: Vitality and Vulnerability Before the Break with Rome* (New Haven CT 2012).

Biblia Sacra iuxta latinam vulgatam versionem ad codicum fidem, ed. Cardinal [Francis] Aidan Gasquet and the Benedictine monks of the pontifical commission instituted by Pius X, 18 vols. (Rome 1926–95).

Biblia Sacra iuxta vulgatam versionem, ed. Robert Weber et al., 5th ed., ed. Roger Gryson (Stuttgart 2007).

Biblia Sacra juxta vulgatam clementinam, ed. Professors of Scripture of Paris and Saint-Sulpice (Rome 1956).

Boccaccio, Giovanni. *Tutte le opere*, ed. Vittore Branca. Vol. 2 (Milan 1964): *Filostrato*, ed. Vittore Branca; *Teseida delle nozze di Emilia*, ed. Alberto Limentani.

Bose, Mishtooni. "Orthodoxy and the Theory of Scriptural Translation," paper given at the conference "Transforming Scripture: Biblical Translations and Adaptations in Old and Middle English," St. Anne's College, Oxford, May 29–31, 2014; a preliminary version of the chapter "Orthodox Agenda for Vernacular Translation," in *The Wycliffite Bible: Origin, History and Interpretation*, ed. Elizabeth Solopova (forthcoming from Brill, Leiden 2017).

Bose, Mishtooni, and J. Patrick Hornbeck II, eds. *Wycliffite Controversies* (Turnhout 2011).

Boyle, Leonard E. "Canon Law Before 1380," in *HUO* 1:531–64.

Bradshaw, Brendan. "The Controversial Sir Thomas More," *Journal of Ecclesiastical History* 36 (1985) 535–69.

Bray, Gerald. *Records of Convocation*, 20 vols. (Woodbridge 2005–6).

Bubwith, Nicholas. *The Register of Nicholas Bubwith, Bishop of Bath and Wells, 1407–1424*, ed. Thomas Scott Holmes, 2 vols. (London 1914).

Buddensieg, Rudolf, ed. *John Wiclif's Polemical Works in Latin*, 2 vols. (London 1883; Wyclif, *Latin Works* [1966], 11:1–2).

———, ed. *John Wyclif's De veritate Sacrae Scripturae*, 3 vols. (London 1905–7; *Wyclif's Latin Works*, 18:1–3).

Bühler, Curt F. "A Lollard Tract: On Translating the Bible into English," *Medium Aevum* 7 (1938) 167–83.

Burton, Edwin H., and Thomas L. Williams, ed. *The Douay College Diaries, Third, Fourth, and Fifth, 1598–1654, with the Rheims Report, 1579–80*, vol. 2, Catholic Record Society 11 (London 1911).

Butler, William. *Determinacio contra translacionem*, ed. Margaret Deanesly, in *Lollard Bible*, pp. 399–418.

Caie, Graham D. "Chaucer and the Bible," in *Chaucer and Religion*, ed. Helen Phillips (Woodbridge 2010), pp. 24–34.

Calendar of Close Rolls: Richard II, 6 vols. (London 1914–27).

Calendar of the Patent Rolls: Richard II, 7 vols. (London 1895–1909).

Campbell, Kirsty. *The Call to Read: Reginald Pecock's Books and Textual Communities* (Notre Dame IN 2010).

Canons and Decrees of the Council of Trent: Original Text with English Translation, ed. H. J. Schroeder (St. Louis 1941).

Carleton, James G. *The Part of Rheims in the Making of the English Bible* (Oxford 1902).

Catto, Jeremy (J. I.). "Chichele, Henry," in *OxDNB*.

———. "Fellows and Helpers: The Religious Identity of the Followers of Wyclif," in *The Medieval Church: Universities, Heresy, and the Religious

Life; Essays in Honour of Gordon Leff, ed. Peter Biller and Barrie Dobson (Woodbridge 1999), pp. 141–61.
———. "Shaping the Mixed Life: Thomas Arundel's Reformation," in *Image, Text, and Church, 1380–1600: Essays for Margaret Aston*, ed. Linda Clark, Maureen Jurkowski, and Colin Richmond (Toronto 2009), pp. 94–108.
———. "Wyclif and Wycliffism at Oxford, 1356–1430," in *HUO* 2:175–261.
The Chastising of God's Children. Ed. Bazire and Colledge, q.v.
Chaucer, Geoffrey. See Benson.
Cheney, C. R. "William Lyndwood's *Provinciale*," in his *Medieval Texts and Studies* (Oxford 1973), pp. 158–84.
Chibi, Andrew A. "Blyth, Geoffrey," in *OxDNB*.
———. *Henry VIII's Conservative Scholar: Bishop John Stokesley and the Divorce, Royal Supremacy, and Doctrinal Reform* (Bern 1997).
———. "Yonge, John (1462/3–1526), Bishop and College Head," in *OxDNB*.
Chichele, Henry. *The Register of Henry Chichele, Archbishop of Canterbury, 1414–1443*, ed. E. F. Jacob, 4 vols. (Oxford 1937–47).
Cobban, Alan B. *The Medieval English Universities: Oxford and Cambridge to c. 1500* (London 1988).
Colledge, Eric. Introduction to *The Chastising of God's Children*, ed. Bazire and Colledge (q.v.), pp. 1–90.
Compston, H. F. B. "The Thirty-Seven Conclusions of the Lollards," *English Historical Review* 26 (1911) 738–49.
Cooper, W. R. "Richard Hunne," *Reformation* 1 (1996) 221–51.
Copeland, Rita. "Lollard Writings." In *The Cambridge Companion to Medieval English Literature, 1100–1500*, ed. Larry Scanlon (Cambridge 2009), pp. 111–22.
———. *Pedagogy, Intellectuals, and Dissent in the Later Middle Ages: Lollardy and Ideas of Learning* (Cambridge 2001).
———. "Wycliffite Ciceronianism? The General Prologue to the Wycliffite Bible and Augustine's *De doctrina Christiana*," in *Rhetoric and Renewal in the Latin West, 1100–1540: Essays in Honour of John O. Ward*, ed. Constant J. Mews, Cary J. Nederman, and Rodney M. Thomson (Turnhout 2003), pp. 185–200.
Copeland, Rita, and Ineke Sluiter, eds. *Medieval Grammar and Rhetoric: Language Arts and Literary Theory, AD 300–1475* (Oxford 2009).

Coulton, G. G. [Controversial pamphlets] ([v.p.], [1924–39]), 16 pamphlets in 1 volume.
———. *Details of the Gasquet Case* (Taunton 1938?).
———. *Fourscore Years: An Autobiography* (New York 1944; preface dated 1941).
———. *A Premium upon Falsehood: A Postscript to "The Scandal of Cardinal Gasquet"* (Taunton 1939).
———. *The Roman Catholic Church and the Bible*, 2nd ed. (London 1921).
———. *The Scandal of Cardinal Gasquet: A Sequel to "Sectarian History"* (Taunton 1937).
———. *Sectarian History* (Taunton 1937).
———. *Ten Medieval Studies*, 3rd ed. (Cambridge 1930; repr. Boston 1959; first published in 1906; 2nd ed., 1915, contains the list of Cardinal Gasquet's errors as appendix 1; in subsequent editions, it appears as appendix 2).
Courtenay, William J. "The Bible in Medieval Universities," in *The New Cambridge History of the Bible*, vol. 2, ed. Richard Marsden and E. Ann Matter (Cambridge 2012), pp. 555–78.
———. "The Bible in the Fourteenth Century: Some Observations," *Church History* 54 (1985) 176–87.
———. "The Effect of Papal Provisions to Oxford and Paris Scholars on the Pastorate and Care of Souls," in *Christianity and Culture in the Middle Ages: Essays to Honor John Van Engen*, ed. David C. Mengel and Lisa Wolverton (Notre Dame IN 2015), pp. 358–86.
———. "Franciscan Learning: University Education and Biblical Exegesis," in *Defenders and Critics of Franciscan Life: Essays in Honor of John V. Fleming*, ed. Michael F. Cusato and Guy Geltner (Leiden 2009), pp. 55–64.
Coxe, H. O. *Laudian Manuscripts* (Oxford 1973).
Crystal, David. *The Stories of English* (London 2004).
Daniell, David. *The Bible in English: Its History and Influence* (New Haven CT 2003).
Davies, R. G. "Bottlesham, William," in *OxDNB*.
———. "Stafford, John," in *OxDNB*.
———. "Wakering, John," in *OxDNB*.
Davis, E. Jeffries. "The Authorities for the Case of Richard Hunne," *English Historical Review* 30 (1915) 477–88.
Deanesly, Margaret. *The Lollard Bible and Other Medieval Biblical Versions* (Cambridge 1920; reprinted in 1966 with a "Prefatory Note" by Deanesly, pp. vii–viii).

de Hamel, Christopher. *The Book: A History of the Bible* (London 2001).

De officio pastorali, expanded English rendering of John Wyclif's treatise of the same name. Ed. Matthew, *English Works*, pp. 405–57. Ed. Conrad Lindberg, *English Wyclif Tracts 1–3* (Oslo 1991), pp. 29–81.

Derrett, J. Duncan M. "The Affairs of Richard Hunne and Friar Standish," in *The Apology of Sir Thomas More, Knight* (1533), ed. J. B. Trapp, *Complete Works of St. Thomas More*, vol. 9 (New Haven CT 1979), pp. 215–46.

Dictionary of Medieval Latin from British Sources (*DMLBS*) (Oxford 1975–2013).

Dives and Pauper (*DP*), ed. Priscilla Heath Barnum, EETS 275, 280, 323, 2 vols. in 3 (Oxford 1976–2004).

Dobson, R. B. "Neville, Alexander," in *OxDNB*.

Dove, Mary, *The First English Bible: The Text and Context of the Wycliffite Versions* (Cambridge 2007).

———. "The Lollards' Threefold Biblical Agenda," in *Wycliffite Controversies*, ed. Mishtooni Bose and J. Patrick Hornbeck II (Turnhout 2011), pp. 211–26.

———. "Scripture and Reform," in *The New Cambridge History of the Bible*, ed. Richard Marsden and E. Ann Matter, vol. 2 (Cambridge 2012), pp. 579–95.

———. "Wyclif and the English Bible," in *A Companion to John Wyclif, Late Medieval Theologian*, ed. Ian Christopher Levy (Leiden 2007), pp. 365–406.

———, ed. *The Earliest Advocates of the English Bible: The Texts of the Medieval Debate* (Exeter 2010).

Doyle, A. I. "English Books In and Out of Court from Edward III to Henry VII," in *English Court Culture in the Later Middle Ages*, ed. V. J. Scattergood and J. W. Sherborne (London 1983), pp. 163–81.

———. Review of *London Literature, 1300–1380*, by Ralph Hanna, in *Medium Aevum* 76 (2007) 123–25.

———. "The Study of Nicholas Love's *Mirror*, Retrospect and Prospect," in *Nicholas Love at Waseda: Proceedings of the International Conference, 20–22 July 1995*, ed. Shoiochi Oguro, Richard Beadle, and Michael G. Sargent (Cambridge 1997), pp. 163–74.

Doyle, Eric. "William Woodford, O.F.M. (c. 1330–c. 1400): His Life and Works, Together with a Study and Edition of His *Responsum contra Wiclevum et Lollardos*," *Franciscan Studies* 43 (1983) 17–187.

du Cange, Charles. *Glossarium mediae et infimae latinitatis*, new ed., 10 vols. (Niort 1883–87).

Duffy, Eamon. "A. G. Dickens and the Late Medieval Church," *Historical Research* 77 (2004) 98–110.

———. "Allen, William (1532–1594), Cardinal," in *OxDNB*.

———. "'The Comen Knowen Multitude of Crysten Men': *A Dialogue Concerning Heresies* and the Defence of Christendom," in *The Cambridge Companion to Thomas More*, ed. George M. Logan (Cambridge 2011), pp. 191–215.

———. *The Stripping of the Altars: Traditional Religion in England, 1400–1580* (New Haven CT 1992; repr. 2005, with "Preface to the Second Edition").

Edwards, A. S. G. "John Trevisa," in *A Companion to Middle English Prose*, ed. Edwards, pp. 117–26.

———, ed. *A Companion to Middle English Prose* (Cambridge 2004).

———, ed. *Middle English Prose: A Critical Guide to Major Authors and Genres* (New Brunswick NJ 1984).

Elton, G. R. *England Under the Tudors* (London 1955).

Emden, A. B. *A Biographical Register of the University of Cambridge to A.D. 1500* (*BRUC*) (Cambridge 1963).

———. *A Biographical Register of the University of Oxford to A.D. 1500* (*BRUO*), 3 vols. (Oxford 1957–59).

Evans, G. R. *John Wyclif: Myth and Reality* (Oxford 2005).

Evans, T. A. R. "The Number, Origins, and Careers of Scholars," in *HUO* 2:485–538.

Fasciculi zizaniorum magistri Johannis Wyclif cum tritico. Ed. Walter Waddington Shirley, Rolls Series 5 (London 1858).

Fehius of Gailsdort, Johannes, ed. *Corpus juris civilis Justinianei*, 6 vols. (Lyons 1627; repr. Osnabrück 1966).

Ferme, Brian Edwin. *Canon Law in Late Medieval England: A Study of William Lyndwood's "Provinciale" with Particular Reference to Testamentary Law* (Rome 1996).

Fines, John. "Hunne, Richard," in *OxDNB*.

———. "The Post-Mortem Condemnation for Heresy of Richard Hunne," *English Historical Review* 78 (1963) 528–31.

Fisher, John H., Malcolm Richardson, and Jane L. Fisher, eds. *An Anthology of Chancery English* (Knoxville TN 1984).

Five and Twenty Books. Ed. Forshall and Madden, under title of "Prologue," in FM 1:1–60.

Fletcher, J. M. "Developments in the Faculty of Arts, 1370–1520," in *HUO* 2:315–45.
Ford, Judy Ann. *John Mirk's Festial: Orthodoxy, Lollardy, and the Common People in Fourteenth-Century England* (Cambridge 2006).
Forde, Simon. "Hereford, Nicholas (b. ca. 1345, d. after 1417)," in *OxDNB*.
Forrest, Ian. "Anti-Lollard Polemic and Practice in Late Medieval England," in *The Fifteenth Century*, vol. 3, *Authority and Subversion*, ed. Linda Clark (Woodbridge 2003), pp. 63–74.
———. *The Detection of Heresy in Late Medieval England* (Oxford 2005).
Forshall, Josiah, and Frederic Madden, eds. *The Holy Bible, Containing the Old and New Testaments, with the Apocryphal Books, in the Earliest English Versions Made from the Latin Vulgate by John Wycliffe and His Followers* (FM), 4 vols. (Oxford 1850; repr. New York 1982).
Fowler, David C. *The Bible in Early English Literature* (Seattle 1976).
———. "John Trevisa and the English Bible," *Modern Philology* 58 (1960) 81–98.
———. *The Life and Times of John Trevisa, Medieval Scholar* (Seattle 1995).
Foxe, John. *The Acts and Monuments*, 4th ed., ed. Josiah Pratt, 8 vols. (London [1877]), mainly a reprint of the 3rd ed. of 1853–70, ed. Pratt. Based on the 1583 edition, with some additions from earlier editions.
Freeman, Thomas. "Texts, Lies, and Microfilm: Reading and Misreading Foxe's 'Book of Martyrs,'" *Sixteenth Century Journal* 30 (1999) 23–46.
Friedberg, Emil, ed. *Corpus iuris canonici*, 2 vols. (Leipzig 1879–81; repr. Graz 1959).
Fristedt, Sven L. "The Authorship of the Lollard Bible," *Stockholm Studies in Modern Philology* o.s. 19 (1956) 28–41.
———. "The Dating of the Earliest Manuscript of the Wycliffite Bible," *Stockholm Studies in Modern Philology* n.s. 1 (1960) 79–85.
———. "New Light on John Wycliffe and the First Full English Bible," *Stockholm Studies in Modern Philology* n.s. 3 (1968) 61–86.
———. "A Note on Some Obscurities in the History of the Lollard Bible," *Stockholm Studies in Modern Philology* n.s. 4 (1972) 38–45.
———. "A Weird Manuscript Enigma in the British Museum," *Stockholm Studies in Modern Philology* n.s. 2 (1964) 116–21.
———. *The Wycliffe Bible*, 3 parts, part 1, *The Principal Problems Connected with Forshall and Madden's Edition* (Stockholm 1953); part 2, *The Origin of the First Revision as Presented in "De salutaribus documentis"* (Stockholm 1969); part 3, *Relationships of Trevisa and the Spanish Medieval Bibles* (Stockholm 1973).

Fuhrman, Craig T. "Did Chaucer Read the Wycliffite Bible?" *Chaucer Review* 42 (2007–8) 111–38.

Fuller, Thomas. *The History of the Worthies of England* (London 1662).

Gaaf, W. van der. "Some Notes on the History of the Progressive Form," *Neophilologus* 15 (1930) 201–15.

Gairdner, James. *Lollardy and the Reformation in England: An Historical Survey*, 4 vols. (London 1908–13).

Gasquet, Francis Aidan. "England Under the Old Religion" (1903), in *England Under the Old Religion and Other Essays*, pp. 1–56.

———. *England Under the Old Religion and Other Essays* (London 1912).

———. *The Eve of the Reformation: Studies in the Religious Life and Thought of the English People in the Period Preceding the Rejection of the Roman Jurisdiction by Henry VIII* (London 1900).

———. *The Old English Bible and Other Essays* (London 1897), containing essay 4, "The Pre-Reformation English Bible (1)" (an expanded version of the 1894 essay), pp. 102–55; and essay 5, "The Pre-Reformation English Bible (2)," pp. 156–78. In the reprinting of 1907, there is a slight expansion of essay 5. In the new edition (London 1908), essay 4 is on pp. 87–134, and essay 5 on pp. 135–55.

———. "The Pre-Reformation English Bible," *Dublin Review* 115 (1894) 122–52.

———. "The Printed English Bible," in *The Eve of the Reformation* (1899; London 1900), pp. 208–44.

———. "What, Then, Was the English Reformation?" (1905), in *England Under the Old Religion and Other Essays*, pp. 86–112.

———, ed. *Biblia Sacra iuxta vulgatam versionem*, q.v.

Ghosh, Kantik. "Nicholas Love," in *A Companion to Middle English Prose*, ed. A. S. G. Edwards (Cambridge 2004), pp. 53–66.

———. *The Wycliffite Heresy: Authority and the Interpretation of Texts* (Cambridge 2002).

Gillespie, Vincent. "The Mole in the Vineyard: Wyclif at Syon in the Fifteenth Century," in *Text and Controversy from Wyclif to Bale: Essays in Honour of Anne Hudson*, ed. Helen Bart and Ann M. Hutchison (Turnhout 2005), pp. 131–61.

Given-Wilson, Chris, ed. *The Parliament Rolls of Medieval England, 1275–1504*, 16 vols. (Woodbridge 2005).

Gower, John. *Confessio Amantis*, ed. G. C. Macaulay, 2 vols., EETS e.s. 81 (London 1900).

Gray, Douglas. "Gower, John," in *OxDNB*.

Greenough, J. B., G. L. Kittredge, A. A. Howard, and Benjamin I. D'Ooge, eds. *Allen and Greenough's New Latin Grammar* (Boston 1903; repr. New Rochelle NY 1979).

Hall, Lewis Brewer. *The Perilous Vision of John Wyclif* (Chicago 1983).

Hallum, Robert. *The Register of Robert Hallum, Bishop of Salisbury, 1407–1417*, ed. Joyce M. Horn (Torquay 1982).

Handbook of British Chronology. Ed. E. B. Fryde et al., 3rd ed. (London 1986).

Hanna, Ralph. "The Difficulty of Ricardian Prose Translation: The Case of the Lollards," *Modern Language Quarterly* 51 (1990) 319–40.

———. "The End of Early London Literature," in his *London Literature*, pp. 305–13.

———. "English Biblical Texts Before Lollardy and Their Fate," in *Lollards and Their Influence in Late Medieval England*, ed. Fiona Somerset, Jill C. Havens, and Derrick G. Pitard (Woodbridge 2003), pp. 141–53.

———. *London Literature, 1300–1380* (Cambridge 2005).

Hanna, Ralph, and Sarah Wood, eds. *Richard Morris's "Prick of Conscience": A Corrected and Amplified Text* (Oxford 2013).

Hargreaves, Henry. "An Intermediate Version of the Wycliffite Old Testament," *Studia Neophilologica* 28 (1956) 130–47.

———. "The Latin Text of Purvey's Psalter," *Medium Aevum* 24 (1955) 73–90.

———. "The Middle English Primers and the Wycliffite Bible," *Modern Language Review* 51 (1956) 215–17.

———. "Popularising Biblical Scholarship: The Role of the Wycliffite *Glossed Gospels*," in *The Bible and Medieval Culture*, ed. W. Lourdaux and D. Verhelst (Leuven 1979), pp. 171–89.

———. "The Wycliffite Versions," in *The Cambridge History of the Bible*, vol. 2, ed. G. W. H. Lampe (Cambridge 1969), pp. 387–415.

Harris, Peter E. B. "Bristow, Richard (1538–1581), Roman Catholic Priest," in *OxDNB*.

Harvey, Margaret. "Ullerston, Richard," in *OxDNB*.

Havens, Jill C. "A Curious Erasure in Walsingham's Short Chronicle and the Politics of Heresy," *Fourteenth Century England* 2 (2002) 95–106.

Helmholz, R. H. "Lyndwood, William," in *OxDNB*.

[Hereford, Nicholas.] *Singulis Cristi fidelibus*, in *Registrum Johannis Trefnant, Episcopi Herefordensis [1389–1404]*, ed. W. W. Capes (London 1916), pp. 396–401.

Hingeston-Randolph, F. C. *The Register of Edmund Stafford (A.D. 1395–1419): An Index and Abstract of Its Contents* (London 1886).

The Historical Register of the University of Oxford: Being a Supplement to the Oxford University Calendar, with an Alphabetical Record of University Honours and Distinctions Completed to the End of Trinity Term 1888 (Oxford 1900).

The History of the University of Oxford (*HUO*), gen. ed. T. H. Aston, 8 vols. (Oxford 1984–2000); vol. 1, *The Early Oxford Schools*, ed. J. I. Catto with Ralph Evans (1984); vol. 2, *Late Medieval Oxford*, ed. Catto and Evans (1992); vol. 3, *The Collegiate University*, ed. James McConica (1986).

The Holy Prophet David. Ed. Mary Dove, in *Earliest Advocates*, pp. 150–59, as *The Holi Prophete Dauid*; introduction on pp. liv–lvii; notes on pp. 218–19.

Hornbeck, J. Patrick II. *What Is a Lollard? Dissent and Belief in Late Medieval England* (Oxford 2010).

———. "*Wycklyffes Wycket* and Eucharistic Theology: Cases from Sixteenth-Century Winchester," in *Wycliffite Controversies*, ed. Mishtooni Bose and J. Patrick Hornbeck II (Turnhout 2011), pp. 279–94.

Hostiensis (Henry of Susa, d. 1271). *In primum-sextum Decretalium librum commentaria*, 6 vols. (Venice 1581; repr. Turin 1965).

Hudson, Anne. "Books and Their Survival: The Case of English Manuscripts of Wyclif's Latin Works," in *Medieval Manuscripts, Their Makers and Users: A Special Issue of Viator in Honor of Richard and Mary Rouse* (Los Angeles 2011), pp. 225–44.

———. "The Carthusians and a Wycliffite Bible," in *Ecclesia, Cultura, Potestas*, ed. Pawel Kras et al. (Cracow 2006), pp. 731–42.

———. "The Debate on Bible Translation, Oxford 1401," *English Historical Review* 90 (1975) 1–18; repr. in *Lollards and Their Books*, pp. 67–84.

———. *Doctors in English: A Study of the Wycliffite Gospel Commentaries* (Liverpool 2015).

———. "Five Problems in Wycliffite Texts and a Suggestion," *Medium Aevum* 80 (2011) 283–306.

———. "John Purvey: A Reconsideration of the Evidence," *Viator* 12 (1981) 355–80, repr. in *Lollards and Their Books*, pp. 85–110.

———. "*Laicus litteratus*: The Paradox of Lollardy," in *Heresy and Literacy, 1000–1530*, ed. Peter Biller and Anne Hudson (Cambridge 1994), pp. 222–36.

———. "Lollard Book Production," in *Book Production and Publishing in Britain, 1375–1475*, ed. Jeremy Griffiths and Derek Pearsall (Cambridge 1989), pp. 125–42.

———. "Lollard Literature," in *The Cambridge History of the Book in Britain*, vol. 2 (1100–1400), ed. Nigel Morgan and Rodney M. Thomson (Cambridge 2008), pp. 329–39.

———. *Lollards and Their Books* (London 1985).

———. "Lollardy: The English Heresy?" *Studies in Church History* 18 (1982) 261–83, repr. in *Lollards and Their Books*, pp. 141–63.

———. "Netter [Walden], Thomas (c. 1370–1430)," in *OxDNB*.

———. "Notes of an Early Fifteenth-Century Research Assistant, and the Emergence of the 267 Articles Against Wyclif," *English Historical Review* 118 (2003) 685–97, repr. as chap. 13 in *Studies in the Transmission of Wyclif's Writings*.

———. *The Premature Reformation: Wycliffite Texts and Lollard History* (Oxford 1988).

———. *Studies in the Transmission of Wyclif's Writings*, Variorum Reprint Series (Aldershot 2008).

———. "The Variable Text," in *Crux and Controversy in Middle English Textual Criticism*, ed. A. J. Minnis and Charlotte Brewer (Woodbridge 1992), pp. 49–60.

———. "'Who Is My Neighbour?' Some Problems of Definition on the Borders of Orthodoxy and Heterodoxy," in *Wycliffite Controversies*, ed. Mishtooni Bose and J. Patrick Hornbeck II (Turnhout 2011), pp. 79–96.

———. "Wyclif and the English Language," in *Wyclif in His Times*, ed. Anthony Kenny (Oxford 1986), pp. 85–103.

———. "Wycliffite Prose," in *Middle English Prose: A Critical Guide to Major Authors and Genres*, ed. A. S. G. Edwards (New Brunswick NJ 1984), pp. 249–70.

———. "Wyclif Texts in Fifteenth-Century London," in *Studies in the Transmission of Wyclif's Writings*, chap. 15.

———, ed. *Selections from English Wycliffite Writings* (Cambridge 1978).

———, ed. *Two Revisions of Rolle's English Psalter Commentary and the Related Canticles*, EETS o.s. 340–41 (Oxford 2012–13).

Hudson, Anne, and Pamela Gradon, eds. *English Wycliffite Sermons*, 5 vols. (Oxford 1983–96).

Hudson, Anne, and Anthony Kenny. "Wyclif, John (d. 1384)," in *OxDNB*.

Hudson, Anne, and H. L. Spencer. "Old Author, New Work: The Sermons of MS Longleat 4," *Medium Aevum* 53 (1984) 220–38.

Hughes, Jonathan. "Arundel (Fitzalan), Thomas," in *OxDNB*.

James, Sarah. "'Langages, whose reules ben not writen': Pecock and the Uses of the Vernacular," in *Vernacularity in England and Wales, c. 1300–1550*, ed. Elisabeth Salter and Helen Wicker (Turnhout 2011), pp. 101–17.

James, Thomas. *Ecloga Oxonio-Cantabrigiensis* (London 1600).

———. *A Treatise of the Corruption of Scripture, Councils, and Fathers by the Prelates, Pastors, and Pillars of the Church of Rome, for the Maintenance of Popery and Irreligion* (London 1612).

Johnson, Ian R. "The General Prologue to the Wycliffite Bible," in *The Idea of the Vernacular: An Anthology of Middle English Literary Theory, 1280–1520*, ed. Jocelyn Wogan-Browne, Nicholas Watson, Andrew Taylor, and Ruth Evans (University Park PA 1999), pp. 91–97.

———. "Vernacular Theology/ Theological Vernacular: A Game of Two Halves?" in *After Arundel: Religious Writing in Fifteenth-Century England*, ed. Vincent Gillespie and Kantik Ghosh (Turnhout 2011), pp. 73–88.

Jurkowski, Maureen. "Heresy and Factionalism at Merton College in the Early Fifteenth Century," *Journal of Ecclesiastical History* 48 (1997) 658–81.

———. "Lollard Book Producers in London in 1414," in *Text and Controversy from Wyclif to Bale: Essays in Honour of Anne Hudson*, ed. Helen Barr and Ann M. Hutchison (Turnhout 2005), pp. 201–26.

———. "New Light on John Purvey," *English Historical Review* 110 (1995) 1180–90.

Karnes, Michelle. "Nicholas Love and Medieval Meditations on Christ," *Speculum* 82 (2007) 380–408.

Kelly, Henry Ansgar. *Chaucer and the Cult of St. Valentine* (Leiden 1986).

———. "English Kings and the Fear of Sorcery," *Mediaeval Studies* 39 (1977) 206–38; repr. in *Inquisitions and Other Trial Procedures*, chap. 7.

———. *Inquisitions and Other Trial Procedures in the Medieval West*, Variorum Collected Studies (Aldershot 2001).

———. "Inquisitorial Deviations and Cover-Ups: The Prosecutions of Margaret Porete and Guiard de Cressonessart, 1308–1310," *Speculum* 89:4 (2014) 936–73.

———. "Jews and Saracens in Chaucer's England: A Review of the Evidence," *Studies in the Age of Chaucer* 27 (2005) 129–69; repr. in *Law and Religion in Chaucer's England*, chap. 7.

———. *Law and Religion in Chaucer's England*, Variorum Collected Studies (Farnham 2010).

———. "Letter," *Medieval Academy News*, Spring 2005, p. 6.

———. "Lollard Inquisitions: Due and Undue Process," in *The Devil, Heresy and Witchcraft in the Middle Ages: Essays in Honor of Jeffrey B. Russell*, ed. Alberto Ferreiro (Leiden 1998), pp. 279–303; repr. in *Inquisitions and Other Trial Procedures*, chap. 6.

———. *The Matrimonial Trials of Henry VIII* (Stanford CA 1976; repr. Eugene OR 2004).

———. Review of *Earliest Advocates*, by Mary Dove, *Speculum* 88 (2013) 281–82.

———. Review of *The School of Heretics*, by Andrew E. Larsen, *Renaissance Quarterly* 65 (2012) 955–56.

———. *Satan: A Biography* (Cambridge 2006).

———. "Thomas More on Inquisitorial Due Process," *English Historical Review* 123 (2008) 847–94.

———. "Trial Procedures Against Wyclif and Wycliffites in England and at the Council of Constance," *Huntington Library Quarterly* 61 (1999) 1–28; repr. in *Inquisitions and Other Trial Procedures*, chap. 5.

———. "Uniformity and Sense in Editing and Citing Medieval Texts," *Medieval Academy News*, Spring 2004, pp. 8–9.

Kennedy, Kathleen E. *The Courtly and Commercial Art of the Wycliffite Bible* (Turnhout 2014).

———. *Medieval Hackers* (Brooklyn 2015).

———. "Reintroducing the English Books of Hours, or 'English Primers,'" *Speculum* 89 (2014) 693–723.

Kenyon, Frederic G. *Our Bible and the Ancient Manuscripts, Being a History of the Text and Its Translations*, 2nd ed. (London 1896); 3rd ed. (1897); 3rd ed. (1898), with added "Preface to the Third Edition" and four pages of "Additions and Corrections" (pp. i–iv), repeated in 4th ed. (1903).

Ker, N. R., *Medieval Libraries of Great Britain: A List of Surviving Books*, 2nd ed. (London 1964).

———. *Medieval Manuscripts in British Libraries*, 5 vols. (Oxford 1969–2002).

Kerby-Fulton, Kathryn. *Books Under Suspicion: Censorship and Tolerance of Revelatory Writing in Late Medieval England* (Notre Dame IN 2006).

King James Version. *The Holy Bible: 1611 Edition, King James Version*, intro. A. W. Pollard (1911; repr. Peabody MA 2003).

Kingsford, Charles Lethbridge, ed. *Chronicles of London* (Oxford 1905).

Knighton's Chronicle, 1337–1396. Ed. and trans. G. H. Martin (Oxford 1995).

Knowles, M. D. *Cardinal Gasquet as an Historian*, Creighton Lecture in History, 1956 (London 1957); repr. in *"The Historian and Character" and Other Essays by Dom David Knowles* (Cambridge 1963), pp. 240–63.

Knox, Thomas Francis, ed. *The First and Second Diaries of the English College, Douay* (London 1878; repr. Westmead 1969).

Krochalis, Jeanne E. "The Books and Reading of Henry V and His Circle," *Chaucer Review* 23 (1988–89) 50–77.

Lahey, Stephen E. *John Wyclif* (New York 2009).

Larsen, Andrew E. *The School of Heretics: Academic Condemnation at the University of Oxford, 1277–1409* (Leiden 2011).

———. "Secular Politics and Academic Condemnation at Oxford, 1358–1411," in *Religion, Power, and Resistance from the Eleventh to the Sixteenth Centuries*, ed. Karen Bollerman, Thomas M. Izbicki, and Cary J. Nederman (New York 2014), pp. 37–53.

Latin Vulgate Bible (*Biblia sacra vulgata*). Douay-Rheims Bible website, http://www.drbo.org/lvb/.

Lawton, David. "The Bible," in *The Oxford History of Literary Translation in English*, vol. 1, *To 1550*, ed. Roger Ellis (Oxford 2008), pp. 193–233.

———. "Englishing the Bible, 1066–1549," in *The Cambridge History of Medieval English Literature*, ed. David Wallace (Cambridge 1999), chap. 17, pp. 454–82.

———. *Faith, Text, and History: The Bible in English* (New York 1990).

Lecoy, Félix, ed. *Le Roman de la Rose*, by Guillaume de Lorris and Jean de Meun, 3 vols. (Paris 1965–70).

Leland, John. *De uiris illustribus / On Famous Men*, ed. and trans. James P. Carley with Caroline Brett. Toronto, 2010.

Levy, Ian Christopher. "A Contextualized Wyclif: *Magister Sacrae Paginae*," in *Wycliffite Controversies*, ed. Mishtooni Bose and J. Patrick Hornbeck II (Turnhout 2011), pp. 33–57.

———, trans. Wyclif, *On the Truth of Holy Scripture* (q.v.).

Lewis, John. *The History of the Life and Sufferings of . . . John Wicliffe* (London 1720).

———. "A History of the Several Translations of the Holy Bible," preface to *The New Testament of Our Lord and Saviour Jesus Christ Translated out of the Latin Vulgat by John Wiclif* (London 1731).

Lindberg, Conrad. "The Alpha and Omega of the Middle English Bible," in *Text and Controversy from Wyclif to Bale: Essays in Honour of Anne Hudson*, ed. Helen Bart and Ann M. Hutchison (Turnhout 2005), pp. 191–200.

———. "The Break at Baruch 3.20 in the Middle English Bible," *English Studies* 60 (1979) 106–10.

———, ed. *The Earlier Version of the Wycliffite Bible*, 8 vols. (Stockholm 1959–97) (EEV). NB: the first five volumes are titled *Ms. Bodley 959: Genesis-Baruch in the Earlier Version of the Wycliffite Bible.*

———, ed. *English Wyclif Tracts 1–3* (Oslo 1991).

———, ed. *King Henry's Bible, MS Bodley 277: The Revised Version of the Wyclif Bible*, 4 vols. (Stockholm 1999–2004) (LLV).

———. "The Manuscripts and Versions of the Wycliffite Bible: A Preliminary Survey," *Studia Neophilogica* 42 (1970) 333–47.

———, ed. *The Middle English Bible*, 3 vols.; vol. 1, *Prefatory Epistles of St. Jerome* (Oslo 1978); vol. 2, *The Book of Baruch* (Oslo 1985); vol. 3, *The Book of Judges* (Oslo 1989).

———. "Revising the Wyclif Bible," in *Beowulf and Beyond*, ed. Hans Sauer and Renate Bauer (Frankfurt 2007), pp. 197–204.

———. "Who Wrote Wiclif's Bible?" *Stockholm Studies in Modern Philology* n.s. 7 (1984) 127–35.

Linde, Cornelia. "Arguing with Lollards: Thomas Palmer, OP, and *De translatione scripture sacre in linguam barbaricam*," *Viator* 46:3 (Autumn 2015) 235–54.

———. *How to Correct the Sacra Scriptura? Textual Criticism of the Latin Bible Between the Twelfth and Fifteenth Century* (Oxford 2012).

Lindenbaum, Sheila. "London After Arundel: Learned Rectors and the Strategies of Orthodox Reform," in *After Arundel: Religious Writing in Fifteenth-Century England*, ed. Vincent Gillespie and Kantik Ghosh (Turnhout 2011), pp. 187–208.

Livingston, Michael, ed. *The Middle English Metrical Paraphrase of the Old Testament* (Kalamazoo MI 2011).

Logan, F. Donald. "Archbishop Thomas Bourgchier Revisited," in *The Church in Pre-Reformation Society: Essays in Honour of F. R. H. Du Boulay*, ed. Caroline M. Barron and Christopher Harper-Bill (Woodbridge 1985), pp. 170–88.

———. *The University Education of the Parochial Clergy in Medieval England: The Lincoln Diocese, c. 1300–c. 1350* (Toronto 2014).

———, ed. *The Medieval Court of Arches* (Woodbridge 2005).

Long, Lynne. *Translating the Bible: From the Seventh to the Seventeenth Century* (Aldershot 2001).

———. "Vernacular Bibles and Prayer Books," in *The Oxford Handbook of*

English Literature and Theology, ed. Andrew Hass, David Jasper, and Elisabeth Jay (Oxford 2007), pp. 54–78.

Loserth, Johann. *Wiclif and Hus* (London 1884).

Love, Nicholas. *Mirror of the Blessed Life of Jesus Christ*, ed. Michael G. Sargent (New York 1992); cf. the revised edition (Exeter 2004).

Lupton, J. H. "Versions (English)," in *A Dictionary of the Bible*, ed. James Hastings, Extra Volume (Edinburgh 1904; repr. 1906), pp. 236–71.

Lutton, Robert. *Lollardy and Orthodox Religion in Pre-Reformation England: Reconstruction Piety* (Woodbridge 2006).

Luxton, Imogen. "The Lichfield Court Book: A Postscript," *Bulletin of the Institute of Historical Research* 44 (1971) 120–25.

Lyndwood, William. *Provinciale; seu, Constitutiones Angliae* (Oxford 1679; repr. Farnborough 1968).

MacCulloch, Diarmaid. *A History of Christianity: The First Three Thousand Years* (London 2009; I follow the pagination of the Penguin reprint, London 2010).

Magrath, John Richard, ed. *The Obituary Book of Queen's College, Oxford* (Oxford 1910).

Mallett, Charles Edward. *A History of the University of Oxford*, 3 vols. (London 1924–27).

Mansi, J. D. *Sacra concilia*, 54 vols. (Paris 1901–27).

"Mars Revealed: A New Look at Forces That Shape the Desert Planet," map supplement, *National Geographic*, February 2001.

Marsden, Richard. "The Bible in English in the Middle Ages," in *The Practice of the Bible in the Middle Ages*, ed. Susan Boynton and Diana J. Reilly (New York 2011), pp. 272–95.

Marsden, Richard, and E. Ann Matter, eds. *The New Cambridge History of the Bible*, vol. 2, *From 600 to 1450* (Cambridge 2012).

Marsh, Adam. *Epistolae fratris Adae de Marisco de ordine Minorum*, ed. J. S. Brewer, *Monumenta franciscana*, vol. 2, Rolls Series 4.1 (London 1858), pp. 77–489.

Marshall, Peter. "Lollards and Protestants Revisited," in *Wycliffite Controversies*, ed. Mishtooni Bose and J. Patrick Hornbeck II (Turnhout 2011), pp. 295–318.

Martin, Gregory. *Roma sancta (1581)*, ed. George Bruner Parks (Rome 1969).

Mascall, Robert. *Registrum Roberti Mascall, Episcopi Herefordensis, A.D. MCCCCIV–MCCCCXVI*, ed. Joseph H. Parry (London 1917).

Matthew, F. D. "The Authorship of the Wycliffite Bible," *English Historical Review* 10 (1895) 91–99.

———, ed. *The English Works of Wyclif, Hitherto Unpublished*, EETS o.s. 74 (London 1880; rev. ed. 1902).

McCoog, Thomas M. "Martin, Gregory (1542?–1582), Roman Catholic Priest and Biblical Translator," in *OxDNB*.

McCormack, Frances. *Chaucer and the Culture of Dissent: The Lollard Context and Subtext of the Parson's Tale* (Dublin 2007).

McFarlane, K. B. *John Wycliffe and the Beginnings of English Nonconformity* (London 1952).

McIntosh, Angus, M. L. Samuels, and Michael Benskin, with Margaret Laing and Keith Williamson. *A Linguistic Atlas of Late Mediaeval English* (*LALME*), 4 vols. (Aberdeen 1986).

McSheffrey, Shannon. *Gender and Heresy: Women and Men in Lollard Communities, 1420–1530* (Philadelphia 1995).

———. "Heresy, Orthodoxy and English Vernacular Religion, 1480–1525," *Past and Present* 186 (February 2005) 47–80.

McSheffrey, Shannon, and Norman Tanner, eds. *Lollards of Coventry, 1486–1522* (Cambridge 2003).

Middle English Dictionary (*MED*), 17 vols. (Ann Arbor 1952–2001).

Minnis, Alastair. *Translations of Authority in Medieval English Literature: Valuing the Vernacular* (Cambridge 2009).

Moessner, Lilo. "Translation Strategies in Middle English: The Case of the Wycliffite Bible," *Poetica* (Tokyo) 55 (2001) 123–54.

Moorman, John R. H. *Church Life in the Thirteenth Century* (Cambridge 1945; corr. repr. 1955).

More, Thomas. *A Dialogue Concerning Heresies*, vol. 6, in 2 parts, of *The Complete Works of St. Thomas More*, ed. Thomas M. C. Lawler, Germain Marc'hadour, and Richard C. Marius (New Haven CT 1981).

Morey, James. *Book and Verse: A Guide to Middle English Biblical Literature* (Urbana IL 2000).

Morrison, Stephen. *A Late-Fifteenth-Century Dominical Cycle*, EETS o.s. 337–38 (London 2012).

Mustanoja, Tauno F. *A Middle English Syntax* (Helsinki 1960).

The Myroure of Oure Ladye. Ed. John Henry Blunt, EETS e.s. 19 (London 1873).

Netter, Thomas, of Walden. *Doctrinale antiquitatum fidei catholicae ecclesiae*, ed. Bonaventura Blanciotti, 3 vols. (Venice 1758–59; repr. Farnborough 1967).

The New Testament of Jesus Christ, Translated Faithfully into English out of the Authentical Latin . . . in the English College of Rheims (Rheims 1582; *BIE*).

Nichols, Ann Eljenholm. "The Illustrations of Corpus Christi College MS 32: 'Þe Glose in Englissche Tunge,'" in *Image, Text, and Church, 1380–1600: Essays for Margaret Aston*, ed. Linda Clark, Maureen Jurkowski, and Colin Richmond (Toronto 2009), pp. 37–67.

Norton, David. *A History of the Bible as Literature*, 2 vols. (Cambridge 1993).

———. *A History of the English Bible as Literature* (Cambridge 2000).

Novum Testamentum Latine, ed. Kurt Aland and Barbara Aland, ed. 2 (Nördlingen 1992).

Ocker, Christopher. "The Bible in the Fifteenth Century," in *Christianity in Western Europe, c. 1100–c. 1500*, ed. Miri Rubin and Walter Simons, vol. 4 of *Cambridge History of Christianity* (Cambridge 2009), pp. 472–93.

Ogle, Arthur. *The Canon Law in Mediaeval England: An Examination of William Lyndwood's "Provinciale," in Reply to the Late Professor F. W. Maitland* (London 1912).

[———]. "Dr. Gasquet and the Old English Bible," *Church Quarterly Review* 51 (1900–1901) 138–46, 265–98.

———. *The Marquis d'Argenson: A Study in Criticism, Being the Stanhope Essay* (Oxford 1893).

———. *The Tragedy of the Lollards' Tower: The Case of Richard Hunne, with Its Aftermath in the Reformation Parliament, 1529–33; A Review of Events from the Downfall of Wolsey to the Birth of Elizabeth* (Oxford 1949).

Oxford Dictionary of National Biography (*OxDNB*), 60 vols. (Oxford 2004).

Oxford English Dictionary (*OED*), 2nd ed., 20 vols. (Oxford 1989).

Parks, George Bruner. "The Life and Works of Gregory Martin," in Parks's edition of Martin's *Roma sancta (1581)* (Rome 1969).

Paues, Anna C. *A Fourteenth Century English Biblical Version* (Cambridge 1904).

Pecock, Reginald. *The Repressor of Over Much Blaming of the Clergy*, ed. Churchill Babington, 2 vols., Rolls Series no. 19 (London 1860).

———. *The Reule of Crysten Religioun*, ed. William Cabell Greet, EETS o.s. 171 (London 1927).

Peikola, Matti. *Congregation of the Elect: Patterns of Self-Fashioning in English Lollard Writings* (Turku 2000).

———. "The Sanctorale, Thomas of Woodstock's English Bible, and the Orthodox Appropriation of Wycliffite Tables of Lessons," in *Wycliffite Controversies*, ed. Mishtooni Bose and J. Patrick Hornbeck II (Turnhout 2011), pp. 153–74.

———. "The Wycliffite Bible and 'Central Midland Standard': Assessing the Manuscript Evidence," *Nordic Journal of English Studies* 2 (2003) 29–51.

Pintzuk, Susan, and Ann Taylor, "The Loss of OV Order in the History of English," in *The Handbook of the History of English*, ed. Ans van Kemenade and Bettelou Los (Malden MA 2006) 249–78.

Pollard, Alfred W. Review of *The Lollard Bible*, by Margaret Deanesly, in *History* 5 (1920–21) 223–26.

Poole, Reginald Lane, ed. *Tractatus de civili dominio*, by John Wyclif, 3 vols. (London 1895; Wyclif, *Latin Works* [1966], 18:1–3).

Pope, Hugh. *English Versions of the Bible*, rev. Sebastian Bullough (St. Louis MO 1952).

Random House Dictionary of the English Language, 2nd ed. unabridged (New York 1987).

Reddan, M. "Domus Conversorum," in *The Victoria History of London*, ed. William Page, vol. 1 (London 1909), pp. 551–54.

Rede, Robert. *The Episcopal Register of Robert Rede, Ordinis Predicatorum, Lord Bishop of Chichester, 1397–1415*, ed. Cecil Deedes, 2 vols., Sussex Record Society, vols. 8, 11 (Lewes 1908–10).

Repingdon, Philip. *The Register of Philip Repingdon, 1405–1419*, ed. Margaret Archer, 3 vols. (Hereford 1963–82).

Rex, Richard. *Henry VIII and the English Reformation*, 2nd ed. (Houndmills 2006).

———. *The Lollards* (Basingstoke 2002).

"Rheims Annual Report, 1579–80," ed. Burton and Williams, *The Douay College Diaries* (q.v.), pp. 553–59 (trans., pp. 559–66).

Richardson, H. G. "Heresy and the Lay Power Under Richard II," *English Historical Review* 51 (1936) 1–28.

Robson, J. A. *Wyclif and the Oxford Schools: The Relation of the "Summa de ente" to Scholastic Debates at Oxford in the Later Fourteenth Century* (Cambridge 1961).

Ross, Charles Hunter. "The Absolute Participle in Middle English and Modern English," *Publications of the Modern Language Association* 8 (1893) 245–302.

Rotuli Parliamentorum, 6 vols. (London 1767–77); new edition, *The Parliament Rolls of Medieval England, 1275–1504*, ed. Chris Given-Wilson, 16 vols. (Woodbridge 2005).

Salter, H. E. "Documents from Faustina C.vii and Other Sources, Dealing in Particular with the Years 1409 and 1411," in *Snappe's Formulary and*

Other Records, Oxford Historical Society, vol. 80 (Oxford 1924), pp. 90–193.

Sargent, Michael. "Censorship or Cultural Change? Reformation and Renaissance in the Spirituality of Late Medieval England," in *After Arundel: Religious Writing in Fifteenth-Century England*, ed. Vincent Gillespie and Kantik Ghosh (Turnhout 2011), pp. 55–72.

Saul, Nigel. "Anne [Anne of Bohemia]," in *OxDNB*.

———. *Richard II* (New Haven CT 1997).

Scase, Wendy. "Pecock, Reginald," in *OxDNB*.

———. "Re-inventing the Vernacular: Middle English Language and Its Literature," in *The Cambridge Companion to Medieval English Literature, 1100–1500*, ed. Larry Scanlon (Cambridge 2009), pp. 11–23.

———. "St. Anne and the Education of the Virgin: Literary and Artistic Traditions and Their Implications," in *England in the Fourteenth Century: Proceedings of the 1991 Harlaxton Symposium*, ed. Nicholas Rogers (Stamford CT 1993), pp. 81–96.

Scattergood, V. J., and J. W. Sherborne, eds. *English Court Culture in the Later Middle Ages* (London 1983).

Schirmer, Elizabeth. "Canon Wars and Outlier Manuscripts: Gospel Harmony in the Lollard Controversy," *Huntington Library Quarterly* 73 (2010) 1–36.

Sherborne, J. W. "Aspects of English Court Culture in the Later Fourteenth Century," in *English Court Culture in the Later Middle Ages*, ed. V. J. Scattergood and J. W. Sherborne (London 1983), pp. 1–27.

Smalley, Beryl. "The Biblical Scholar," in *Robert Grosseteste, Scholar and Bishop: Essays in Commemoration of the Seventh Centenary of His Death*, ed. D. A. Callus (Oxford 1955), pp. 70–97.

———. "Jean de Hesdin O.Hosp.S.Ioh.," *Recherches de théologie ancienne et médiévale* 28 (1961) 283–330.

———. "John Wyclif's *Postilla super totam Bibliam*," *Bodleian Library Record* 4 (1953) 186–205.

———. "Problems of Exegesis in the Fourteenth Century," in *Antike und Orient im Mittelalter*, ed. Paul Wilpert (Berlin 1962), pp. 266–74.

Smith, David M. *Guide to Bishops' Registers of England and Wales* (London 1981).

[Smith, Miles.] "The Translators to the Readers," preface of the King James Version (q.v.).

Smith, Paul. "Could the Gospel Harmony *Oon in Foure* Represent an Intermediate Version of the Wycliffite Bible?" *Studia Neophilogica* 80 (2008) 160–76.

Solopova, Elizabeth. "Manuscript Evidence for the Patronage, Ownership, and Use of the Wycliffite Bible," in *Form and Function in the Late Medieval Bible*, ed. Eyal Poleg and Laura Light (Leiden 2013).

Somerset, Fiona. "Censorship," in *The Production of Books in England, 1350–1500*, ed. Alexandra Gillespie and Daniel Wakelin (Cambridge 2011), pp. 239–58.

———. *Feeling Like Saints: Lollard Writings After Wyclif* (Ithaca NY 2014).

———, ed. *Four Wycliffite Dialogues*, EETS o.s. 333 (Oxford 2009).

———. "Professionalizing Translation at the Turn of the Fifteenth Century: Ullerston's *Determinacio*, Arundel's *Constitutiones*," in *The Vulgar Tongue: Medieval and Postmedieval Vernacularity*, ed. Somerset and Nicholas Watson (University Park PA 2003), pp. 145–57.

Southern, A. C., ed. *Elizabethan Recusant Prose, 1559–1582* (London [1950]).

Spencer, H. Leith. *English Preaching in the Late Middle Ages* (Oxford 1993).

Stafford, John. *The Register of John Stafford, Bishop of Bath and Wells, 1425–1443*, ed. Thomas Scott Holmes, 2 vols. (London 1915–16).

Statuta antiqua Universitatis Oxoniensis, ed. Strickland Gibson (Oxford 1931).

Statutes of the Realm, 12 vols. (London 1810–28; repr. 1963, 1993).

Stavsky, Jonathan. "As the Lily Among Thorns: Daniel 13 in the Writings of John Wyclif and His Followers," *Viator* 46:1 (Spring 2015) 249–76.

Stow, George B., Jr., ed. *Historia vitae et regni Ricardi secundi* (Philadelphia 1977).

Strype, John. *Memorials of Cranmer* (London 1694; repr. 1812).

Summerson, Henry. "Boughton, Joan (c.1414–1494)," in *OxDNB*.

———. "An English Bible and Other Books Belonging to Henry IV," *Bulletin of the John Rylands Library* 79 (1997) 109–15.

Swanson, R. N. *Church and Society in Late Medieval England* (Oxford 1989).

———. "Hallum, Robert," in *OxDNB*.

———. "Learning and Livings: University Study and Clerical Careers in Later Medieval England," *History of Universities* 6 (1986–87) 81–103.

Tanner, Norman P., ed. *Heresy Trials in the Diocese of Norwich, 1428–31*, Camden Society, 4th ser., no. 20 (London 1977).

———, ed. *Kent Heresy Proceedings*. Kent Archaeological Society, Kent Records, 26 (Gloucester 1997).

Taylor, Andrew. "Anne of Bohemia and the Making of Chaucer," *Studies in the Age of Chaucer* 19 (1997) 95–119.

Taylor, Henry Osborn. *Thought and Expression in the Sixteenth Century*, 2nd ed., 2 vols. (New York 1930).

Thirty-Seven Conclusions, ed. Josiah Forshall under title of *Remonstrance Against Romish Corruptions in the Church, Addressed to the People and Parliament of England in 1395, 18 Ric. II* (London 1851).

Thomas, A. H., and I. D. Thornley, eds. *The Great Chronicle of London* (London 1938).

Thomson, John A. F. *The Later Lollards, 1414–1520* (London 1965).

Thomson, Williell R. *The Latin Writings of John Wyclyf: An Annotated Catalog* (Toronto 1983).

Thurston, Herbert. "Dr. G. G. Coulton and Cardinal Gasquet," *Month* 172 (July–December 1938) 493–503.

———. *Some Inexactitudes of Mr. G. G. Coulton: A Sheaf of Criticisms and Rejoinders Arising Mainly Out of Mr. Coulton's Volume "The Medieval Village"* (London 1927).

Tombs, Robert. *The English and Their History* (London 2014).

Trefnant, John. *Registrum Johannis Trefnant, Episcopi Herefordensis [1389–1404]*, ed. W. W. Capes (London 1916).

Trevisa, John. *Dialogus inter dominum et clericum* [1387], ed. Roger Waldron, "Trevisa's Original Prefaces on Translation: A Critical Edition," in *Medieval English Studies Presented to George Kane*, ed. Edward Donald Kennedy, Ronald Waldron, and Joseph S. Wittig (Woodbridge 1988), pp. 285–99. Also edited from Caxton's edition of Trevisa's *Polychronicon*: *Dialogue Between a Lord and a Clerk upon Translation*, ed. Alfred W. Pollard, *Fifteenth Century Prose and Verse* (Westminster 1903), pp. 203–10.

Tyndale, William. *The New Testament: The Text of the Worms Edition of 1526 in Original Spelling*, ed. W. R. Cooper (London 2000).

Ullerston, Richard. *Tractatus de translacione Sacre Scripture in vulgare*, Vienna, Österreichische Nationalbibliothek, MS 4133, fols. 195–207v; conclusion also in Cambridge, Gonville and Caius College MS 803/807 frag. 36.

Ussher, James. *Historia dogmatica de Scripturis et sacris vernaculis*, ed. Henry Wharton (London 1690).

van Liere, Frans. *An Introduction to the Medieval Bible* (Cambridge 2014).

von Nolcken, Christina. "Another 'Lollere in the Wynd'? The Miller, the Bible, and the Destruction of Doors," in *Through a Classical Eye: Transcultural and Transhistorical Visions in Medieval English, Italian, and Latin Literature in Honour of Winthrop Wetherbee*, ed. Andrew Galloway and R. F. Yeager (Toronto 2009), pp. 238–66.

———. "A 'Certain Sameness' and Our Response to It in English Wycliffite Texts," in *Literature and Religion in the Later Middle Ages: Philological Studies in Honor of Siegfried Wenzel*, ed. Richard G. Newhauser and John A. Alford (Binghamton 1995), pp. 191–208.

———. "Lay Literacy, the Democratization of God's Law, and the Lollards," in *The Bible as Book: The Manuscript Tradition*, ed. John L. Sharpe III and Kimberly van Kampen (London 1998), pp. 177–95.

Walden, Thomas. *See* Netter, Thomas, of Walden.

Walsh, Katherine. "Wyclif's Legacy in Central Europe in the Late Fourteenth and Early Fifteenth Centuries," in *From Ockham to Wyclif*, ed. Anne Hudson and Michael Wilks (Oxford 1987), pp. 397–417.

Walsingham, Thomas. *The St. Albans Chronicle: The Chronica Maiora of Thomas Walsingham*, ed. and trans. John Taylor, Wendy R. Childs, and Leslie Watkiss, 2 vols. (New York 2003–11).

[Wanley, Humfrey, et al.] *A Catalogue of the Harleian Collection of Manuscripts*, 2 vols. (London 1759[–63]).

Watson, Andrew. *Catalogue of Dated and Datable Manuscripts c. 435–1600 in Oxford Libraries*, 2 vols. (Oxford 1984).

Watson, Nicholas. "Censorship and Cultural Change in Late-Medieval England: Vernacular Theology, the Oxford Translation Debate, and Arundel's Constitutions of 1409," *Speculum* 70 (1995) 822–64.

———. "Theories of Translation," in *The Oxford History of Literary Translation in English*, vol. 1, *To 1500*, ed. Roger Ellis (Oxford 2008), pp. 73–91.

Weigle, Luther A., ed. *The New Testament Octapla* (New York [1962]).

Weisheipl, James A. J. "Curriculum of the Faculty of Arts at Oxford in the Early Fourteenth Century," *Mediaeval Studies* 26 (1964) 143–85.

———. "Ockham and the Mertonians," in *HUO* 1:607–58.

Wenzel, Siegfried. *Latin Sermon Collections from Later Medieval England: Orthodox Preaching in the Age of Wyclif* (Cambridge 2005).

The Westminster Chronicle, 1381–1394, ed. and trans. L. C. Hector and Barbara F. Harvey (Oxford 1982).

Why Poor Priests Have No Benefice. In Matthew, *English Works*, pp. 244–53.

Wharton, Henry. *Auctarium* (Supplement) to his edition of James Ussher's *Historia dogmatica* (q.v.), pp. 307–468.

Wilkins, David. *Concilia Magnae Britanniae et Hiberniae*, 4 vols. (London 1737).

Wilks, Michael "Misleading Manuscripts: Wyclif and the Non-Wycliffite Bible," *Studies in Church History* 11 (1975) 147–61.

Wood, Anthony. *Historia et antiquitates Universitatis Oxoniensis*, 2 vols. (Oxford 1674; ECCO); English translation, *The History and Antiquities of the University of Oxford*, trans. John Gutch, 2 vols. (Oxford 1792; ECCO).

Woodford, William, O.F.M. *Responsum contra Wiclevum et Lollardos*, in Eric Doyle, "William Woodford," pp. 120–87.

Workman, Herbert B. *John Wyclif: A Study of the English Medieval Church*, 2 vols. (Oxford 1926).

Wyclif, John. *Latin Works*, 22 vols. in 35 (London 1883–1922; repr. New York, 1966 [variously listed]).

———. *On the Truth of Holy Scripture*. Abridged trans. by Ian Chrostopher Levy (TEAMS: Kalamazoo 2001).

———. *Tractatus de veritate sacre Scripture*. See Buddensieg.

Wyclif's Wicket: *Wyclyffes Wycket* (Norenburch [London] 1546; EEBO, STC 25590).

Yonekura, Hiroshi. "John Purvey's Version of the Wycliffite Bible: A Reconsideration of His Translation Method," *Studies in Medieval English Language and Literature* 1 (1986) 67–91.

———. *The Language of the Wycliffite Bible: The Syntactic Differences Between the Two Versions* (Tokyo 1985).

———. "The Wycliffite Bible: John Purvey's Translation Method," *Linguistics and Philology* 5 (1984) 1–25.

Index